AF348625

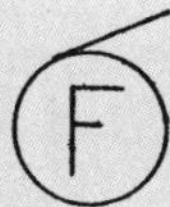

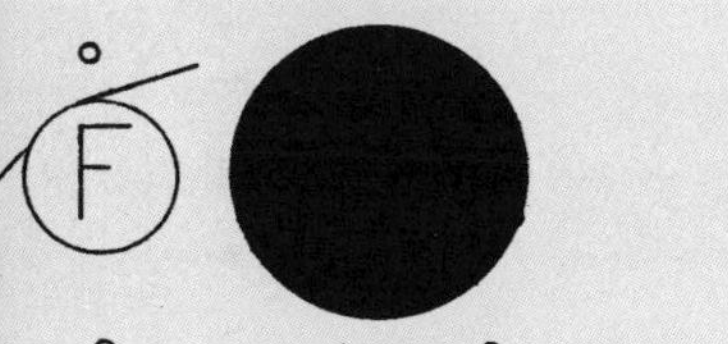

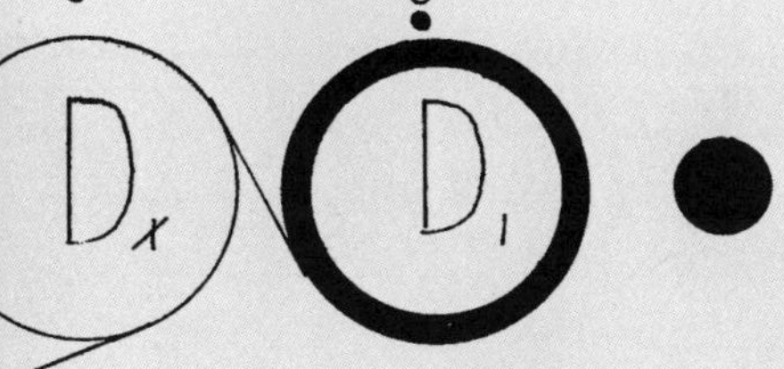

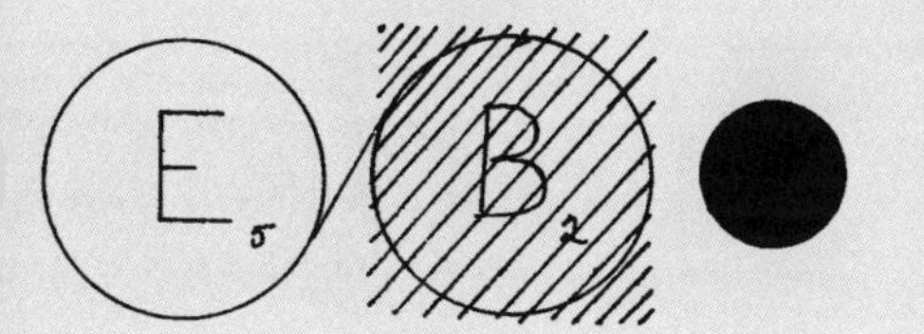

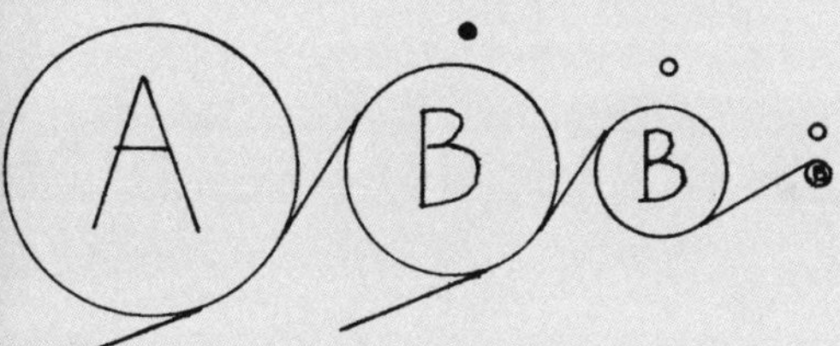

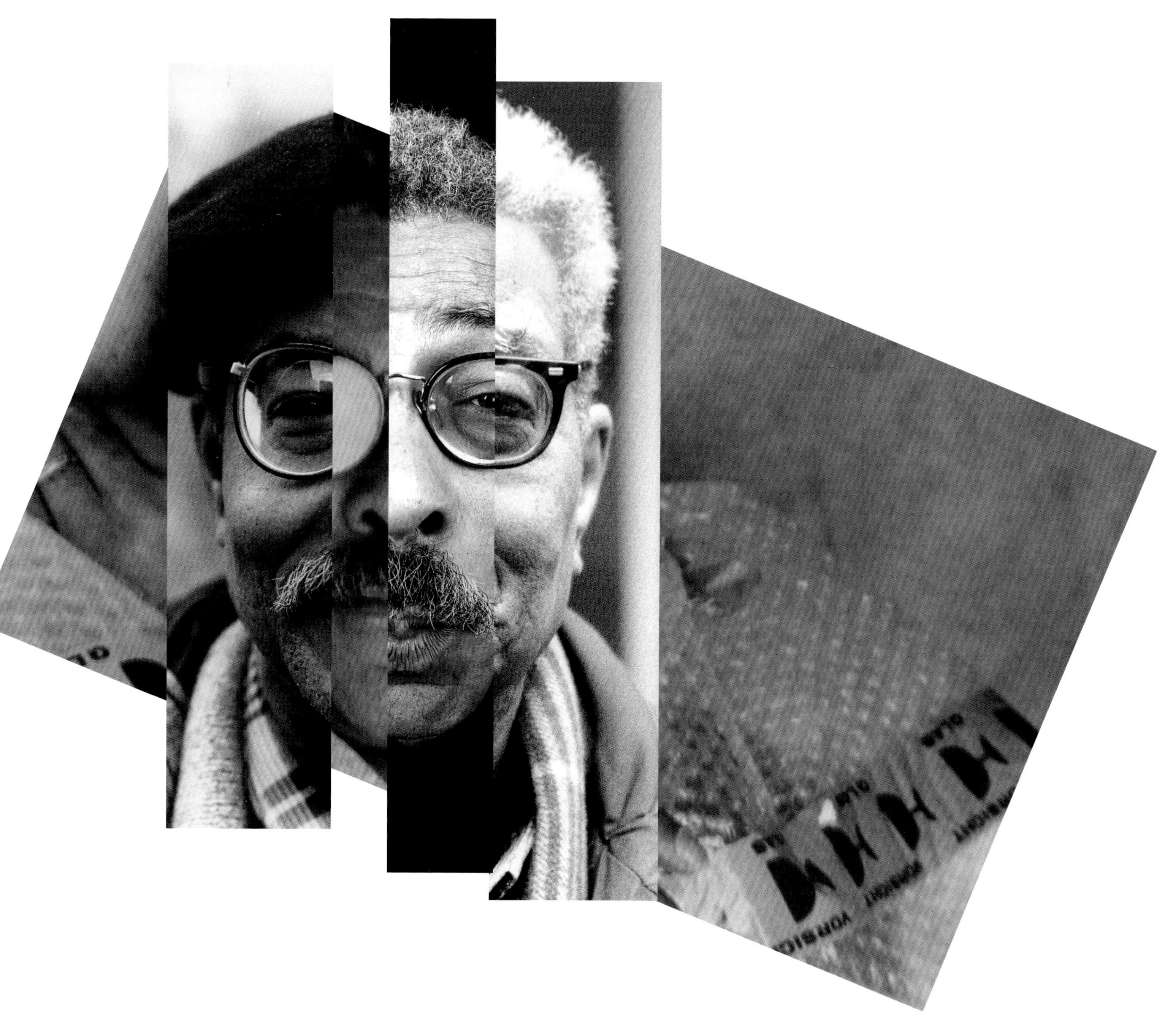

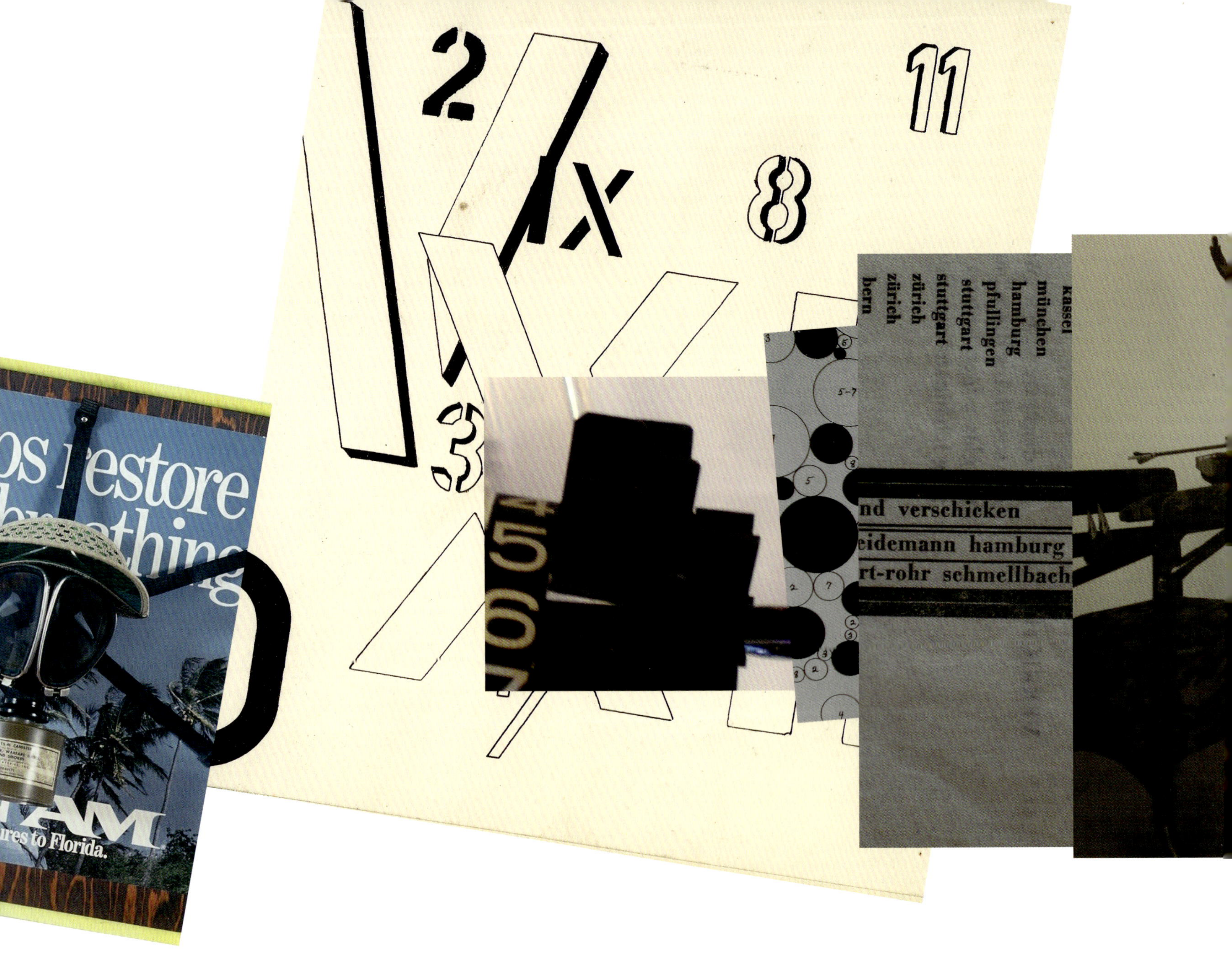
2
11
x
8
3
os restore
mathing
AM
res to Florida.
kassel
münchen
hamburg
pfullingen
stuttgart
stuttgart
zürich
zürich
bern
nd verschicken
eidemann hamburg
rt-rohr schmellbach

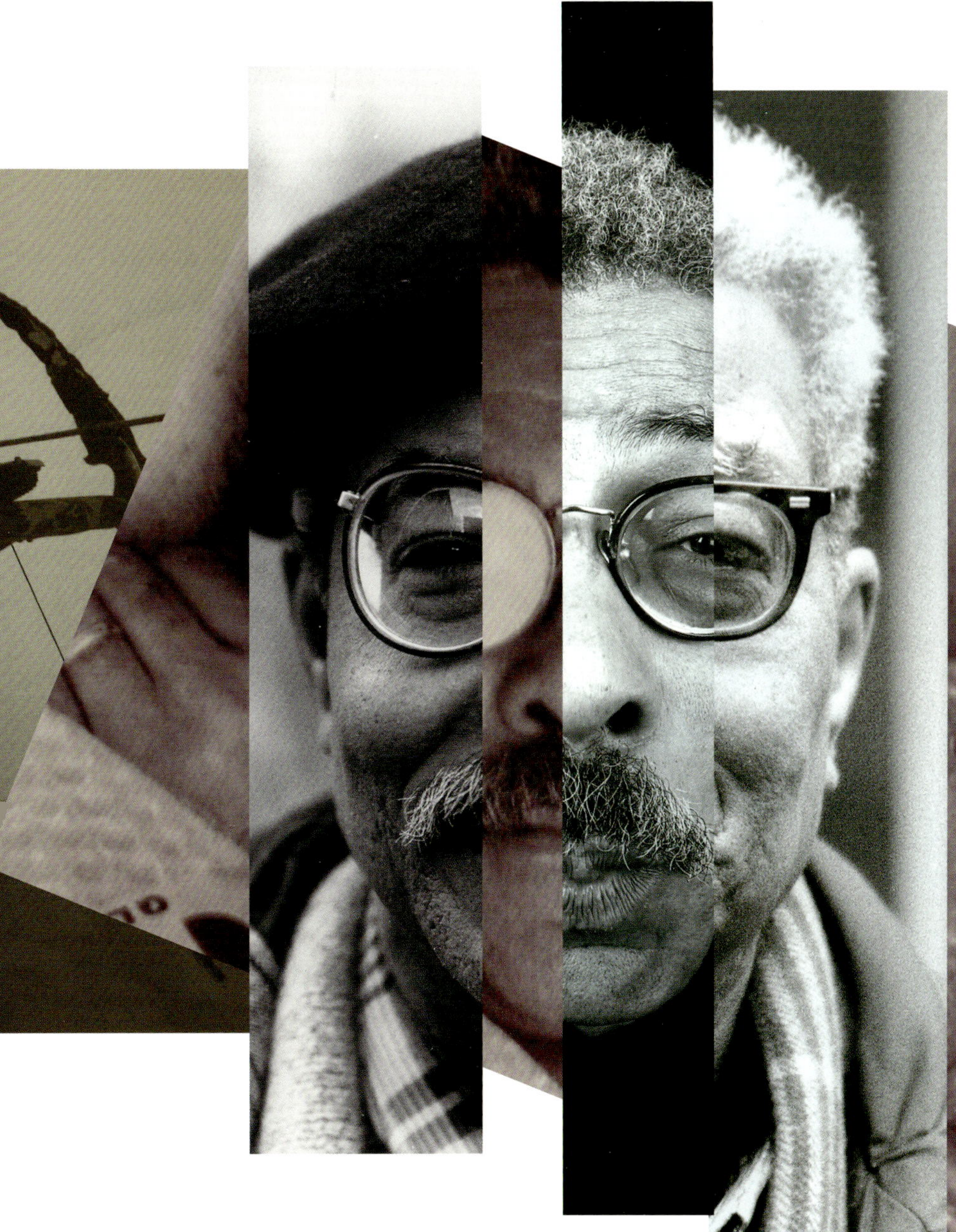

Benjamin Patterson

Born in the State of FLUX/us

VALERIE CASSEL OLIVER

With essays by
BERTRAND CLAVEZ
CHARLES GAINES
JON HENDRICKS
GEORGE E. LEWIS
FRED MOTEN
BENJAMIN PATTERSON
MARCIA REED

CONTEMPORARY ARTS MUSEUM HOUSTON

Published in conjunction with the exhibition *Benjamin Patterson: Born in the State of FLUX/us*, organized by Valerie Cassel Oliver, Senior Curator, for the Contemporary Arts Museum Houston.

Exhibition itinerary:

Contemporary Arts Museum Houston
November 6, 2010–January 23, 2011

The Studio Museum in Harlem
March 31–June 26, 2011

Nassauischer Kunstverein Wiesbaden
June 2–September 30, 2012

Benjamin Patterson: Born in the State of FLUX/us is supported by generous grants from The Andy Warhol Foundation for the Visual Arts and the National Endowment for the Arts. Additional support is provided by the Houston Museum of African American Culture.

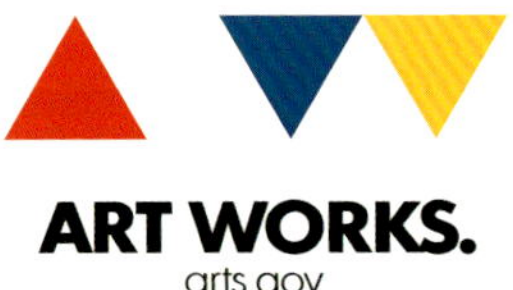

Support for shipping was generously provided by Luigi Bonotto, Christo/CVJ Corporation, Jean Dupuy, Letty Lou Eisenhauer, Henry Flynt, Olivenza, Mercedes Guardado, Geoffrey Hendricks, Jon Hendricks, Milan Knizak, Kunstbibliothek, Yoko Ono Lennon, Phoebe Neville and Philip Corner, The Oldenburg van Bruggen Foundation, Jeffery Perkins, Lila and Gilbert Silverman, Miyuki Sugaya and Toshiyuki Nemoto, Jean Toche, and Yoshimasa Wada.

This exhibition has been made possible by the patrons, benefactors and donors to the Museum's Major Exhibition Fund:

Major Patron
Chinhui Juhn and Eddie Allen
Fayez Sarofim
Michael Zilkha

Patrons
Louise D. Jamail
Mr. and Mrs. I. H. Kempner III
Ms. Louisa Stude Sarofim
Leigh and Reggie Smith

Benefactors
City Kitchen Catering
George and Mary Josephine Hamman Foundation
Jackson Hicks / Jackson and Company
Marley Lott
Poppi Massey
Beverly and Howard Robinson
Andrew Schirrmeister III
Susan Vaughan Foundation, Inc.
Mr. and Mrs. Wallace Wilson

Donors
A Fare Extraordinaire
Anonymous
Baker Botts, L.L.P
Bergner and Johnson Design
The Brown Foundation, Inc.
Jereann Chaney
Susie and Sanford Criner
Elizabeth Howard Crowell
Ruth Dreessen and Thomas Van Laan
Marita and J. B. Fairbanks
Jo and Jim Furr
Barbara and Michael Gamson
Mr. and Mrs. William Goldberg / Bernstein Global Wealth
    Management
King & Spalding L.L.P.
KPMG, LLP
Judy and Scott Nyquist
David I. Saperstein
Scurlock Foundation
Karen and Harry Susman
Martha Claire Tompkins

The catalogue accompanying the exhibition is made possible by a grant from The Brown Foundation, Inc.

The Museum's operations and programs are made possible through the generosity of the Museum's trustees, patrons, members, and donors. The Contemporary Arts Museum Houston receives partial operating support from the Houston Endowment, the City of Houston through the Houston Museum District Association, the National Endowment for the Arts, the Texas Commission on the Arts, and The Wortham Foundation, Inc.

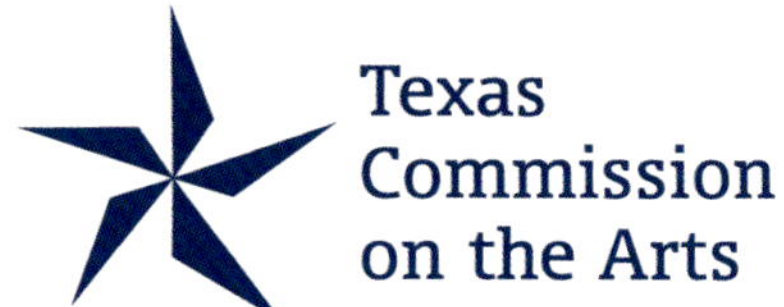

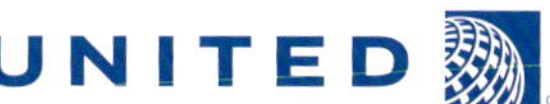

Official airline of the Contemporary Arts Museum Houston.

The Wiesbaden showing of the exhibition is supported by the German Federal Cultural Foundation, the Hessische Kulturstiftung, the Consulate General of the United States in Frankfurt, the Wiesbaden Kulturamt, and the Fluxus50 Festival.

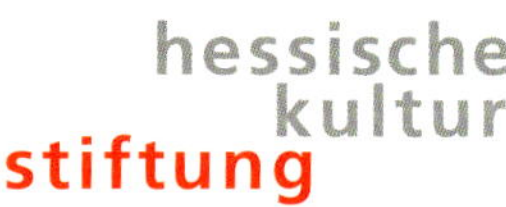
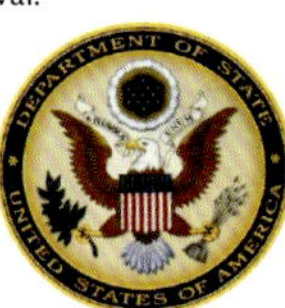

Published by
Contemporary Arts Museum Houston
5216 Montrose Blvd., Houston, TX 77006
Tel: (713) 284-8250
www.camh.org

Produced by Marquand Books, Inc., Seattle
www.marquand.com

Available through D.A.P./Distributed Art Publishers
155 Sixth Avenue, 2nd floor, New York, NY 10013
Tel: (212) 627-1999   Fax: (212) 627-9484
www.artbook.com

Copyright © 2012 Contemporary Arts Museum Houston
All rights reserved. No part of this publication may be reproduced or transmitted in any form or by any means, electronic or mechanical, including photocopying, recording, or any information storage or retrieval system, without permission in writing from the publisher.

Library of Congress Control Number: 2010932361
ISBN: 978-1-933619-29-3

Front cover: Benjamin Patterson, *Variations for Double Bass (Version for Prague—May 21, 1991)*, 1991
Back cover: Benjamin Patterson, *Décollage Solo for Wolf Vostell*, 1961 (detail)
Endsheets: *String Music*, 1960 (detail)
Title page: composite portrait of Benjamin Patterson; courtesy the artist
Frontispiece: left to right, courtesy Galerie Schüppenhauer, Cologne; Getty Research Institute, Los Angeles; Museum of Modern Art, New York; the artist

Edited by Karen Jacobson
Designed by Zach Hooker, iamabookdesigner.com
Typeset in Cronos Pro
Color management by iocolor, Seattle
Printed and bound in China by C&C Offset Printing Co., Ltd.

Contents

Foreword

There was a time when the artists associated with Fluxus did not garner due respect from many museum professionals. Fluxus was neither a movement nor a period in the sense that art historians usually define those terms. Perhaps it is best understood as a philosophy or a radical ideology, a stance equal parts Zen and revolution that sprung to life in the 1960s but is still in active play today. Even ten years ago it was considered too incorporeal to collect, its most accomplished practitioners rarely using fine art materials and giving away their objects as often as selling them. As such its output was also too aggressively uncommodifiable to be preserved as rare luxury museum objects. It was understood as anti-art, resistant to being collected, studied, analyzed, and respected because its makers obeyed few of the standard art rules.

In recent years a generational shift has occurred in the seats of cultural power. In that changing of the guard, Fluxus has stealthily infiltrated the establishment, one poetic whisper at a time. Great private collections of Flux work have been acquired by leading institutions such as the Museum of Modern Art in New York; the Staatsgalerie in Stuttgart, Germany; and the Getty Research Institute in Los Angeles. And museums such as the Tate Modern, London; the Walker Art Center, Minneapolis; the Centre Pompidou, Paris; and the Moderna Museet, Stockholm, have developed important holdings. Sometimes museum registrars discovered that key Fluxus objects were already sitting in flat files in their institutions, having been gathered by visionary museum librarians and archivists when they arrived in the morning mail but not actually accessioned until decades later. (A thesis needs to be written about the value of the loose tribe of museum librarians who successfully circumvented the power of collections committees and allowed radical artworks to be under the same roof as Jasper Johns well before the curatoriat was ready.)

Because of chance anomalies in my intellectual biography, I was reared in a climate in which the provocations of Fluxus artists were widely seen as beautiful and worthy. As a child I went to Friends Seminary, a Quaker school in New York City, where John Cage was a god and avant-garde poets and visual artists were on the faculty. The father of my best friend in junior high was a leading critic who had works by Fluxus-associated video pioneer Nam June Paik around the house. And finally, my first full-time job in the art world was in the same building as Re-Flux Editions, so I would wander upstairs during lunch and play with and often buy for myself the amazing and affordable Flux multiples. It was not uncommon to leave there with a great work of art that cost less than my lunch.

As I write this foreword, I have Larry Miller's *Orifice Flux Plugs* and a Yoko Ono *Box of Smile* near my desk. The Miller is a plastic box of objects, from pacifiers to bullets, that could in theory plug bodily orifices, and the *Box of Smile*, without revealing its secret, is meant to be given to someone to make them smile, and it is highly effective. These interactive editions have kept me sane in the face of many writing deadlines, and I have kept them within reach for nearly thirty years. In that time their status has changed . . . slowly. For while they are today firmly part of the canon of postwar art, their cheap materials and the fact that they need to be handled to function make them unlikely masterpieces.

When I assumed the directorship of the Contemporary Arts Museum Houston in the spring of 2009, I was startled to see a survey of Ben Patterson on the schedule of future exhibitions. I had never seen a show in a U.S. museum devoted to a single Flux-associated artist, with the exceptions of Yoko Ono and Nam June Paik. Even Fluxus leader George Maciunas had not been thoroughly examined in this country. As for Patterson himself, I had known his name as an early Flux artist but had, like most U.S.-based art lovers, seen and experienced little in person.

Monographic museum shows are the single best way of getting to know an artist's trajectory and thought processes, and for an antimovement like Fluxus, this treatment seems ideal. I, for one, cherished the opportunity to really get to understand Patterson's achievement. So many of his signature gestures—such as musically employing the sounds that result from ripping, tearing, and crumpling different types of paper—are now somewhat mainstream, used by celebrated composers like Academy Award winner Tan Dun. The general public today is open to hearing the musicality in such sounds. Yet Patterson's most radical gestures were always tempered by the fact that he involved nonprofessionals in making the sounds that they were enjoying—who can resist the sound of paper ripping when one is actually doing the ripping!

Patterson was closely tied in with the musical activities of the period, and the narrative of his art production begins with his musical activities. Yet as this show makes clear, it is almost impossible to mark a clear division between sound and sculpture, between action and object, and in earlier periods before the (over)professionalization of the art world, the avant-gardes in music, art, film, and literature tended to be very closely linked, and artists were less prone to defining themselves through specific mediums. That sort of deliberate confusion of genres and categories is the spirit of Fluxus.

Valerie Cassel Oliver has been working on this exhibition for several years. In many ways that was required because Fluxus (like Dada, the earlier art movement to which it is most closely allied) thrives on far-flung networks and itinerant practices. This is an intimate art requiring a meditative, attentive state, and her expertise in its nuances has been earned over time. As such, this has been a labor of love, and her passion for Patterson's work is infectious. As a curator Valerie is known for projects that rewrite the standard histories. Having read the drafts of this book's essays, I am sure that I will see these texts cited by art historians for decades to come. That is a tremendous accomplishment and what one hopes for when a contemporary art museum considers a figure with such a long history.

We could not have made this exhibition a reality without the generous support of the Andy Warhol Foundation for the Visual Arts and the National Endowment for the Arts. Their acknowledgment of the importance of this project means so much to a museum like CAMH. I extend to them our sincere thanks for supporting Valerie's conviction that Patterson is an artist whose time is now.

All the many supporters of the museum have helped make this exhibition a reality, but it is truly the work of our Major Exhibition Fund donors that allows CAMH to pursue curatorial excellence unencumbered. Their vision and generosity year after year allow our great curators to do their important scholarly work, and being able to count on them is the lifeblood of our museum.

Curator, writer, archivist, sage, and guru of all things Fluxus Jon Hendricks has been crucial from the beginning of this project, and when we faced a crisis late in the process due to some unexpectedly swollen expenses, a letter from him rallied a considerable amount of support. For that, along with the many types of support and wisdom that he so willingly shares, we are eternally grateful. And to all of those who responded to Jon's appeal, thank you one thousand times!

This catalogue is made possible by a grant from the Brown Foundation, Inc. Its support is pivotal in allowing the research and scholarship so carefully developed by

Valerie Cassel Oliver to illuminate this wonderful art for thousands of people, particularly future art and music students who might now be inspired by Patterson's achievements. Essayists Bertrand Clavez, Charles Gaines, Jon Hendricks, George Lewis, Fred Moten, and Marcia Reed have added much to my education on Patterson and his times, and I thank them for the clarity that they bring to his achievements.

The CAMH staff has once again dedicated its considerable expertise to making this an exhibition to be engaged. Special thanks go to former curatorial manager Justine Waitkus and registrar Tim Barkley for dealing with the complicated logistics of a show with many small, fragile artworks traveling from many locations on the planet. I would also like to thank former director Marti Mayo and interim director Linda Shearer for their earlier support of the project. Without their vision this exhibition would not be a reality today.

My final thanks go in advance to you, the museum public, as this art requires a fair degree of engagement to be fully enjoyed. While I can guarantee that the openness and spirit of Fluxian play you bring through our doors will be repaid in joy and intellectual stimulation, it is really up to you to be willing to bring the artworks of Benjamin Patterson to life. And for that we at CAMH thank you in advance.

BILL ARNING
Director

Acknowledgments

Benjamin Patterson: Born in the State of FLUX/us is the manifestation of several years of research and involved the efforts of many people. The initial impetus for the project, however, came from Jon Hendricks, former curator of the Gilbert and Lila Silverman Fluxus Collection and currently Fluxus consulting curator at the Museum of Modern Art, New York, which now houses the Silverman collection. In 2001 Jon traveled to Houston to oversee the installation of the exhibition *Yes: Yoko Ono* at the Contemporary Arts Museum Houston. During the installation Jon and I talked constantly. Our easy conversations about Fluxus and the constellation of artists at its core meandered, but there was one name that Jon brought up repeatedly: Benjamin Patterson. It was not until later—when I was looking at a photograph of Philip Corner's *Piano Activities* and asking, "Who is the black man in this picture?"—that I understood Jon's reference. That man *was* Ben Patterson, a radical presence in the midst of a radical avant-garde. It would take an additional five years and a Getty Curatorial Research Fellowship before I would begin in earnest to research his work. What I found was little written documentation but a groundswell of encouragement to continue my research. Along the way I have been assisted by numerous individuals, and to all those who have touched this project in large and minute ways, thank you!

For support in the early stages of the project, I am indebted not only to Jon Hendricks but also to Carl Solway, who provided me with a means of contacting Patterson, who has long lived in Germany. Michael Solway and Angela Jones of SolwayJones Gallery in Los Angeles were instrumental in coordinating my first meeting with Patterson. Marcia Reed, chief curator at the Getty Research Institute in Los Angeles, deserves special recognition for her unwavering enthusiasm and for encouraging me to rummage through the Jean Brown Papers, an extraordinary repository of Fluxus materials that is now part of the Getty's holdings. I must also acknowledge Elfi Kreiter for her immense generosity in housing me during my many visits to Wiesbaden.

Organizing an exhibition such as this—a retrospective that represents more than fifty years of an artist's work—is a considerable endeavor, and I am tremendously grateful to my personal and professional families for supporting me through the journey. The Contemporary Arts Museum Houston allowed me to take a sabbatical to conduct the initial research for the project. It is rare to have not only the financial support of an institution but also the resource of time to develop an exhibition from primary research. I am grateful to Marti Mayo, former director, who initially granted me the gift of focused time; Linda Shearer, who continued the commitment of institutional support; and Bill Arning, under whose directorship this project has come to fruition.

Invaluable support during the early phases of my research was provided by interns in both Houston and Wiesbaden. I am grateful to Jean Duffet, Sarah Levitt, Cheyanne Ramos, and Lisa Solomine for their foundational efforts.

I also owe a debt of gratitude to the many private and public supporters and collectors of Patterson's work. They not only opened their galleries, archives, and homes for research but also generously lent works to this exhibition. They include Paul Anczykowski, Kleiner Raum Clasing & Galerie Etage, Münster, Germany; Luigi Bonotto, Molvena, Italy; Carola Bodenmuller, Frank Kleinbach, and Manfred Prinziky, Institut für Auslandsbeziehungen, Stuttgart, Germany; Enzo Cattelani and Tiberio Cattelani,

Modena, Italy; Emanuele Carcano, Milan; Bertrand Clavez, Paris; the late Francesco Conz, Cristina Conz, Gian Luca Conz, and Esther Widmar, Archivo Conz, Verona, Italy; Dr. Sabrina and Klaus Fehlemann; Rosa Fioretto, Fioretto Arte Contemporanea, Padua, Italy; Marcel Fleiss, David Fleiss, Sylvain Rouillon, Julie Richard, and Rodica Sibley-ras, Galerie 1900–2000, Paris; Peter Frei and Ilona Lütken, Staatsgalerie Stuttgart, Germany; Rosalee Goldberg, Per-forma, New York; Elke Gruhn, Nassauischer Kunstverein Wiesbaden; Catarina Gualco, Genoa, Italy; Jon Hendricks, Fluxus consulting curator, Museum of Modern Art, New York; Elfi Kreiter, Wiesbaden; Marcia Reed, Jeanette Cologne, Natilee Harren, and Irene Lotspeich-Phillips, Getty Research Institute, Los Angeles; Harry Ruhé, A Gallery, Amsterdam; Heinrich W. Risken, Bad Rothen-felde, Germany; Christel Schüppenhauer, Cologne; Marc Schultz, Hannover, Germany; Michael Solway and Angela Jones, SolwayJones Gallery, Los Angeles; Sandra Solimano and Francesca Serratie, Museo d'Arte Contemporanea di Villa Croce, Genoa, Italy; Gretchen Wagner, Museum of Modern Art, New York; Donna Wingate, New York; and Christian Xatrec, Emily Harvey Foundation, New York. For negotiating crucial loans, I want to especially acknowl-edge Paul Anczykowski, Caterina Gualco, and Christel Schüppenhauer.

Also crucial in shaping this exhibition were my con-versations throughout the process with Charles Gaines, Rosalee Goldberg, Jürgen Heinrich, Jon Hendricks, Han-nah Higgins, Alison Knowles, Clifford Owens, Xaviera Simmons, and Carl Solway. Other conversations over the course of time were invaluable in helping me to understand the totality of Patterson's influence, includ-ing encounters with Geoffrey Hendricks, Elaine Summers, Sur Rodney Sur, and Christian Xatrec.

No project of this magnitude can be undertaken without the full support and encouragement of the staff of the organizing museum, and I want to thank each of my colleagues for their work on this project during its development and presentation. In the museum's edu-cation department, special thanks go to Paula Newton, director of education and public programs, and Peter Lucas, education associate, who created wonderful didactic materials. They organized a substantive series of lectures and performances, inviting some great minds to ruminate on the work of Ben Patterson. They have also continued the museum's efforts toward significant col-laborations with local arts organizations. For this project, CAMH continued its collaboration with Musiqa, which featured Patterson in an evening concert; the Houston Museum of African American Culture, which cospon-sored a performance by Pamela Z; and the University of Houston and Rice University, which brought Pat-terson into the classroom to work with students. For ably coordinating various aspects of this project and the publication as well as keeping it all on track, I am indebted to former curatorial manager Justine Waitkus and interim curatorial manager Jennie King. Tim Barkley, registrar, deserves special thanks for his Herculean abil-ity to oversee complicated national and international shipping and loan agreements, as does head preparator Jeff Shore, for his amazing exhibition design. The instal-lation would not have been possible, nor would it have looked so good, without the talent and dedication of the museum's installation crew. I am also appreciative of the museum's director for external affairs, Connie McAllister, for her diligence in ensuring this project's visibility locally, regionally, nationally, and internationally. Cheryl Blissitte, assistant to the director, deserves recognition for read-ing through multiple incarnations of this catalogue from draft to final copy with astonishing thoroughness. And last but not least, Amber Winsor, director of develop-ment and administration, and her team deserve special thanks for their enormous efforts in securing funding for this project.

Initial work on the exhibition was supported by the Getty Foundation, which generously provided me with a Curatorial Research Fellowship. The importance of this project was validated by grants from the Andy Warhol Foundation for the Visual Arts, which stepped in at the very beginning with crucial support, and the National Endowment for the Arts, whose generosity infused this project with new dynamism. When we were faced with last-minute expenses, Jon Hendricks spearheaded an initiative to raise much-needed funds among the Fluxus family and friends. We were very fortunate to have financial support from Christo/CVJ Corporation, Jean Dupuy, Letty Lou Eisenhauer, Henry Flynt, Geoffrey Hendricks, Jon Hendricks, Yoko Ono Lennon, Phoebe Neville and Philip Corner, the Oldenburg van Bruggen Foundation, Jeffery Perkins, Lila and Gilbert Silverman, Miyuki Sugaya and Toshiyuki Nemoto, Jean Toche, and Yoshimasa Wada. Thank you, thank you, thank you!

For this extraordinary publication, I want to thank all at Marquand Books: Ed Marquand, Sara Billups, Zach Hooker, Adrian Lucia, and Brynn Warriner among many others. They showed immense acumen in organizing the various components of this important document. The book also benefited from the considerable expertise of Bertrand Clavez, Charles Gaines, Jon Hendricks, George E. Lewis, Fred Moten, and Marcia Reed, who contributed essays, as well as Emanuele Carcano, who compiled the musical documentation for the double compact disc featured in the publication. Additionally, Meredith Goldsmith, former curatorial associate at the museum, was instrumental in compiling the substantial chronology of Patterson's life and work. She deserves a special note of appreciation not only for tackling such an immense task but also for securing copyright waivers and permissions for many of the photographs featured throughout this publication. I am grateful for the exceptional talents of Karen Jacobson, editor of this publication, who painstakingly pored over the texts to create a seamless and unified narrative. My hope is that this catalogue will become essential reading for anyone interested in the life and practice of this important artist.

For their contributions in providing or securing images for this book, I am grateful to Cristin O'Keefe Aptowicz, Wolf Vostell Estate; Jennifer Belt, Art Resource, New York; Lourdes Castro, Lisbon; Bertrand and Claudia Clavez, Paris; Maro Cuman and Paula Lahad-Bozzotto, Archivo Bonotto, Modena, Italy; Jon Hendricks, New York; Frank Kleinbach, IFA, Stuttgart; Irene Lotspeich-Phillips, Getty Research Institute, Los Angeles; Barbara Moore, VAGA, New York; Anna Noel, Düsseldorf; Christel Schüppenhauer, Galerie Schüppenhauer, Cologne; Jacqueline Tarquinio, Susanne Vielmetter Los Angeles Projects; Wolfgang Träger, Wiesbaden, Germany; Donna Wingate, New York; and Lydia Yee, Barbican Art Centre, London.

Sarah Levitt helped to organize much of the information that would later become essential in mounting this exhibition and also produced a wonderful short documentary on Patterson featured in the museum's resource room. A project of this magnitude also necessitated the assistance of many to produce or digitize images and video and sound works. I am deeply indebted to Wolfgang Träger, who was always willing to document existing and new work; Don Quaintance, who not only scanned numerous documents for this catalogue but also generated the first iteration of the publication; and Rick Gardner, who contributed significantly to ensuring that a batch of last-minute performance documents were digitized for this publication. In addition to works reproduced in the catalogue, the exhibition included video documentation of performances. I am appreciative of Espace multimédia Gantner, Bourogne, France, whose funding allowed the artist to transfer film and video documentation into digital files. The transfer of these files for the museum's presentation was made possible by

Michael Eibes Studio, Wiesbaden. I am grateful to Kenya Evans for transferring original sound works presented in the exhibition from audiotapes into digital files.

For their willingness to ensure that this exhibition is seen by a larger audience, I am grateful to Thelma Golden, Naomi Beckwith, Thomas Lax, and Lauren Hayes at the Studio Museum in Harlem, New York, and Elke Gruhn at Nassauischer Kunstverein, Wiesbaden.

Finally, I would like to thank Benjamin Patterson for entrusting me with contextualizing his enormous contributions not only to the avant-garde but also to the field of contemporary art. My first encounter with him came in the form of a recorded message left at my office. He was calling in response to a letter that I had faxed to him only days earlier, telling him of my interest in researching not only his role in Fluxus but also his contributions in its aftermath. Patterson, always measured in his speech, asked, "Are you sure you have the right person?" That response, humorous and self-deprecating, marks his true genius. It has been an extraordinary honor to become familiar not only with this artist's practice but also with the artist himself. This project is a testament to his tremendous generosity in opening his life to me. It is but a very small measure of his immense contributions, which simply cannot be contained in a finite space or seen in a finite period of time. This catalogue is nevertheless an invaluable document, and neither it nor the exhibition would have been possible without his persistence, extraordinary talent, and radical presence.

VALERIE CASSEL OLIVER
Senior Curator

Lenders to the Exhibition

Archivo Bonotto, Molvena, Italy

Carlo Cattelani, Modena, Italy

Enzo Cattelani, Modena, Italy

Tiberio Cattelani, Modena, Italy

Bertrand Clavez, Paris

Klaus Fehlemann, Dortmund, Germany

Marcel Fleiss and David Fleiss, Galerie 1900–2000, Paris

Enzo Gazzerro, Genoa, Italy

The Getty Research Institute, Los Angeles

Jean-Louis Grobel, Paris

Catarina Gualco, Genoa, Italy

The Emily Harvey Foundation, New York

Institut für Auslandsbeziehungen, Stuttgart, Germany

Elfi Kreiter, Wiesbaden, Germany

Museo d'Arte Contemporanea di Ville Croce, Genoa, Italy

The Museum of Modern Art, New York

Benjamin Patterson, Wiesbaden, Germany

Heinrich W. Risken, Bad Rothenfelde, Germany

Marc Schultz, Hannover, Germany

Christel Schüppenhauer, Galerie Schüppenhauer, Cologne

Staatsgalerie Stuttgart, Stuttgart, Germany

The Curious Case of Benjamin Patterson

VALERIE CASSEL OLIVER

Such developments as conceptual art, text art, video art, performance art, minimalism, simulation and even the social engineering arts or the political art of people such as Joseph Beuys are being re-examined, and the roots are being found, perhaps in Fluxus. What exactly was my role in all of this? Quite simply I was there at the instant of birth, so to speak.

—BENJAMIN PATTERSON[1]

In a bit of irony, Benjamin Patterson stepped onto the stage of art history at the dawn of the 1960s, amid a groundswell of political, social, and cultural upheaval. His emergence is owed in part to political and social conventions that sought to render his own presence invisible. And so, at the beginning of the 1960s and in a land foreign from that of his birth, Patterson, a classically trained African American musician, joined the avant-garde. His was a radical presence, not simply because of his blackness but also because of his participation in the birth of Fluxus, a practice and ideology determined by a loose constellation of artists, which would arguably become the most influential experiment in the history of art, changing the course of art history and laying the foundation for contemporary art practice.

The fact that Patterson, a celebrated cultural icon in Europe, is underrecognized in cultural and academic circles in the United States speaks to myriad issues with regard to how the history of art is recorded, selectively reproduced, and perpetuated as fragmented narrative. In contextualizing Patterson's early contributions and his more recent practice as being anything but integral to Fluxus, one is immediately faced with the inherent limitations of avant-garde criticism. One could argue that Patterson himself was born in a state of flux, never truly embraced by historians of the avant-garde and virtually erased in many assessments of Fluxus while being celebrated in his adopted country of Germany.

To be generous, the artist's apparent status as a minor player in the annals of the avant-garde may have been predetermined by his early "retirement" from Fluxus in the mid-1960s.[2] Moreover, his continued absence until the 1980s, some twenty years, could also account for his frequent omission from the pantheon of artists associated with the movement—including George Maciunas, George Brecht, John Cage, Nam June Paik, Joseph Beuys, and Yoko Ono—whose works produced seismic shifts in how we now understand artistic practices of the later twentieth century. Patterson's imprint could never fully be erased, however, not only because his compositions have been presented as standard fare in Fluxus concerts but also because we find iterations of his "compositions for actions," or action scores, now being performed, discussed, and examined by a new generation of artists. So while his contributions may have been overlooked in recent scholarly presentations examining the phenomenon of Fluxus, a fuller examination of Patterson's development as an artist—in particular, his innovative practice of the "action as composition" in experimental music—points to his presence at the very formation of the movement and his invaluable contributions to it. Moreover, as one of the last surviving artists from its core group, Patterson represents the continuation of Fluxus.

Born in Pittsburgh between the World Wars, Patterson exhibited a voracious appetite for learning at an early age. In his teens, he was already well versed in classical music and the sciences (both parents had advanced degrees, in engineering and chemistry), and he excelled in sports. His life typified a black America rarely recounted. His family defied the prevailing African American stereotype of the era in that it was not only middle class but also highly functional. Throughout high school and from the outset of his studies at the University of Michigan—where he majored in music, focusing on composition, conducting, and double bass—Patterson was on a crusade to be "the first black to 'break the color-barrier' in an American symphony orchestra."[3]

Patterson's crusade was, however, short-lived. Upon graduation he was unable to secure a position in an American orchestra. Instead, he found employment in Canada, where he served as principal bassist and an assistant conductor for the Halifax Symphony Orchestra. While he played classical music by day, he was conducting experiments in new music formats by night. Most likely, the seeds of his interest in new music were planted during his days at the University of Michigan, where he studied under composer Leslie Bassett and knew of the work of Gordon Mumma.

In 1957, a year after Patterson's graduation and departure from Michigan, Mumma, along with Robert Ashley and three other composition students from the University of Michigan (Roger Reynolds, George Cacioppo, and Donald Scavarda), would establish Once Group, a platform for experimental music in Ann Arbor. Patterson would also have known Space Theater, the venue founded by the painter-turned-multimedia-artist Milton Cohen, who insisted on the radical concept of "stretching imagery into a format or presentation in real time, real motion, real space."[4] Cohen also insisted on several principles on which Space Theater would be established, including to "shrink distance between artist and spectator, spectator and spectacle; to score music, light, poetry,

dance with a single notational system, pressing unity vision; suggest the museum as a creative presence of living performance, of spontaneous action; and to exploit contemporary technology as a means to broaden mystery and subvert the machine."[5] While Patterson was well on his way to articulating his own practice, his time in Canada would be interrupted. In an absurd twist, the young musician (who had to leave the United States because institutionalized segregation in the South and de facto segregation in the North prevented him from getting a job with an American orchestra) would be conscripted into the United States Army.

For two years Patterson served in the Seventh Army Symphony Orchestra, based in Stuttgart. While the orchestra toured extensively to major and minor concert halls throughout Europe, Patterson took advantage of its home base in Germany. In Stuttgart as well as in Cologne, he found a burgeoning scene for experimental music practices. The social, political, and cultural arenas in the aftermath of World War II not only reflected the tensions between traditional convention and "new practices" already being felt in the United States but also offered fertile ground to invent and reinvent cultural practices. After being discharged, Patterson returned to Canada, this time working at the Philharmonic Orchestra of Ottawa. He also resumed his experiments with new music, working in an electronic music studio at the National Research Center. The prevailing binaries of new music surrounded concepts of serialism and "free choice in predetermined sectors of a score" versus that of indeterminate actions. At the time Patterson's compositions leaned heavily toward serialism, a method of composing that subjected notes to either systematic recurrence or assigned them equal numerical proportions without regard for traditional tonality.[6] At the time serialism was championed principally by composers Karlheinz Stockhausen and Pierre Boulez. Once Patterson returned to Europe, however, his predisposition would abruptly be reversed within a twenty-four-hour period, after a planned meeting with Stockhausen and an unplanned meeting with John Cage. In addition, Patterson would later set aside his interest in electronic music in favor of simplified actions and humble materials.

The Immutable Convergence of Experimentation

Living and working in Ottawa, Patterson was eager to get back to Europe. The experimental music scene was rapidly evolving, and its vital centers sat squarely in Germany. He decided to attend the Internationale Gesellschaft für Zeitgenössische Musik (International Society for Contemporary Music), or IGZM, festival in Cologne, which would feature Stockhausen and Boulez. It was 1960, and Patterson, armed with a letter of introduction, had the opportunity to meet Stockhausen, arguably the most prolific and visible of the serial music composers of his generation. The meeting, which Patterson has often described as a disaster, would forever alter his future as a musician and, subsequently, an artist. Rather than attending the remainder of the IGZM conference/festival, Patterson soon found his way to Mary Bauermeister's studio, which was hosting the counterfestival of new, new music. At the festival, designed to showcase the most "radical" experimentation in music, he found himself in the company of young composers from around the world who wanted a solid break with the traditions of the past. Among these composers were John Cage, Nam June Paik, David Tudor, Cornelius Cardew, François Biel, and Sylvano Bussotti. Patterson spoke with Cage after the performance and was invited to join the following evening's performances. That event would prove to be a turning point in his life and work.

On the following evening Patterson did join Cage, Tudor, Cardew, and others to perform seminal works by such composers as La Monte Young, Toshi Ichiyanagi, George Brecht, and Cage himself. The ease with which he found himself immersed in the scene was astounding, so much so that Patterson extended his scheduled one-week stay into weeks. A strike by the Ottawa orchestra, which resulted in the cancellation of its season, all but solidified his presence in Europe for the remainder of 1960 and the years to follow. His time in Germany would prove fruitful not only in the extension of his new network of friendships and collaborations but also in the development of his own distinct musical style, which moved further away from serialism and toward the indeterminate practices of composers like Cage and Young. For Patterson, the indeterminate practice not only offered a chance to extend conversations around improvisation that he had already begun investigating within the classical music sphere but also raised questions regarding the incorporation of action into the creation of musical composition. This was the very concept behind *Paper Piece* (1960), a work that he had composed in direct reaction to Stockhausen's composition *Kontakte* (1958–60), which integrated electronic and instrumental music.[7] Unable to travel to Pittsburgh for the holidays, Patterson sent his family a composed "action" to be performed for their amusement. He provided instructions for the performance of the work: number of participants, materials to be used, and actions to be taken, such as the tearing, crumpling, twisting, and rubbing together of discarded wrapping paper. The letter would serve as the first iteration of *Paper Piece.*

Patterson would continue to develop *Paper Piece*, publishing the work later that year in an issue of the Hamburg art paper *Ich bin schön*. He would also publish the essay "An Experiment in Extended Rhythms" in the Hamburg independent arts journal *Die Villa ist verstaubt.*[8] The essay was important for two reasons. First, it provided a platform for Patterson to discuss critical issues in music production, showing how alternating and

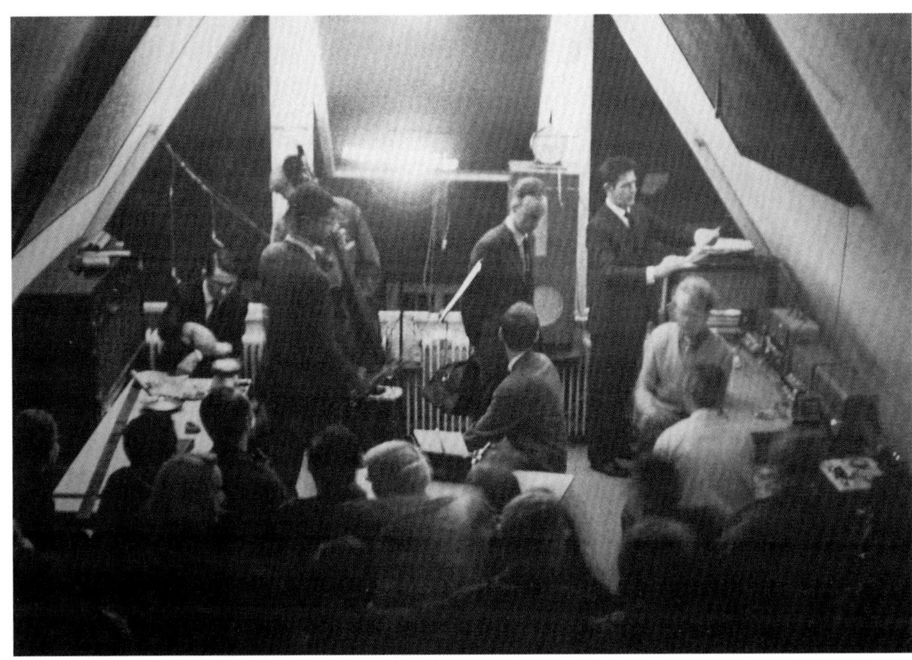

Contre Festival at Bauermeister studio, 1961

performing at exhibition openings. For Wolf Vostell's exhibition, Patterson performed *Paper Piece, Décollage for Wolf Vostell* (1961), *Situations for Three Pianos* (1960), and *Duo for Voice and a String Instrument* (1961; with William Pearson, a noted African American bass-baritone who taught at the Robert Schumann Conservatorium in Düsseldorf). Later he would present *Variations for Double Bass* (1961) for the opening of an exhibition of work by Mimmo Rotella and a short program of action compositions in conjunction with an exhibition of works by Daniel Spoerri, also at Galerie Haro Lauhus. Patterson's use of the annotated score format became more prevalent during this period, in part because it helped him to render notations of action visually as well as to emphasize the concept of chance and indetermination in the presentation of action as performance.

It would not be until the creation of *Lemons* (1961), however, Patterson's first opera, that he would successfully bridge sound with visual and kinetic material. His presentation at Studio Vostell in Cologne marked his first interdisciplinary project, integrating music provided by Patterson and Pearson; dance performed by Gisela Olroth; and deconstructed paintings by Vostell. The success of *Lemons* propelled Patterson to extend his thinking beyond the confines of music and into areas of poetry, theater of spectacle, and the visual arts. To fully realize this interdisciplinary approach in his work, in 1961 he decided to leave Cologne for Paris, where he felt that he could extricate himself and his practices from the narrow framework of experimental music.

Radical Presence: The Birth of Fluxus

Commuting between Paris and West Germany, Patterson began working with George Maciunas to help organize and perform in a series of concerts and events in Germany and beyond. Maciunas, Lithuanian by birth and living in New York, already knew many of the artists who

extending the modality of notes could affect a listener's perception, particularly in his early experiments in looped electronic music. The text also became foundational in that he began to develop further his ideas regarding action as music, a concept that sat at the intersection of sound materiality and signification. He found that music actions could accomplish different kinds of representations culturally and psychologically. For instance, Patterson noted that by defying the expected action of playing the double bass with his fingers or the bow, as dictated in classical music, and by playing the instrument with various nontraditional objects, he shifted the action into an area of sound materiality.[9] Secondly, the article provided evidence of what would become Patterson's sustained interest in psychology, as seen in his later writings and works.

Patterson would become a prolific composer during this time, creating a substantial body of scores for music and actions. He would debut many of his seminal early works in 1961 at Galerie Haro Lauhus in Cologne, initially

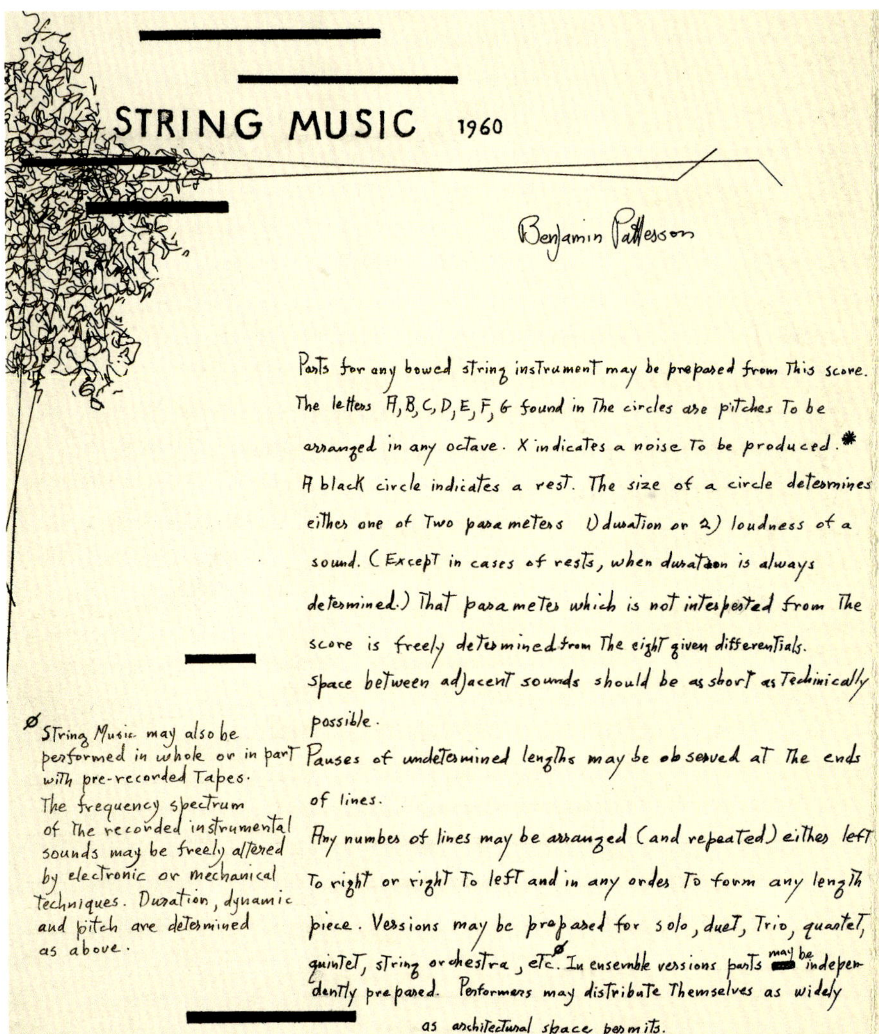

String Music, 1960

participated in the performances at Mary Bauermeister's studio. The idea of staging concerts featuring experimental music and events was a direct response to the success of the counterfestival. They would help capitalize on the moment and momentum as well as providing additional outlets for the groundswell of experimentation. Many artists who had participated in the events at Bauermeister's studio were still living in Germany, concentrated in pockets around Cologne, including the cities of Düsseldorf, Wuppertal, Hamburg, and Wiesbaden.

The first of these concerts was Kleines Sommerfest: Après John Cage, organized by Maciunas and featuring performances by Patterson. The event was held at Galerie Parnass in Wuppertal. At the event, Maciunas gave the lecture "Neo-Dada in Music, Theater, Poetry and Art," a kind of manifesto for new practices, as a prelude to the evening's performances. In truth, the event, in Patterson's words, served as the "unofficial birth" of Fluxus.[10] Patterson also performed at the Neo-Dada Music Concert at the Kammerspiele in Düsseldorf. The concert, organized by Paik, featured Patterson and Tomas Schmit performing their own works as well as works by George Maciunas, George Brecht, Dick Higgins, Toshi Ichiyanagi, Jackson Mac Low, and La Monte Young. Drawing upon the constellation of artists whose works were featured at the events in Wuppertal and Düsseldorf as well as the counterfestival in 1960, Maciunas would begin work on a much larger festival to be held in September. He enlisted the help of Patterson, Emmett Williams, and Wolf Vostell to construct the foundation for what would become the historic Internationale Festspiele neuester Musik, held at the Städtisches Museum in Wiesbaden in 1962.

The presentation of an event at the municipal museum not only served to validate the ideas and practices of Fluxus but also shifted its ideology from the margins of a "subculture" to the center of high art. Keenly aware of this opportunity, Maciunas sought to extend the presence of this radical group. He worked with Patterson, Williams, and Vostell to organize a festival to be held over two weeks. To promote the festival, Williams, then editor of the travel section of the U.S. Army's daily newspaper, *Stars and Stripes,* interviewed Patterson about the scheduled events. This interview would become the first article about Fluxus to be published. Similarly, the first film documentation of Fluxus, news coverage by a local German television station, featured Patterson's performance of his composition *Variations for Double Bass*. *Variations* and Philip Corner's *Piano Activities* (1962) were provocative in that they directly challenged the traditions of classical music in their seemingly reckless abandon and their attacks upon the instruments themselves. The presentation of Patterson's composition *Paper Piece* would also prove significant in that, for the first time since Cabaret Voltaire (founded in Zurich in 1916), the great divide between audience and performer would be challenged.[11] The work, once initiated by the five performers onstage, spread outward into the audience, who were no longer passive spectators but active participants—crumpling, tearing, folding, and waving paper. Patterson recalls: "It was by accident but was incorporated into the composition and subsequent events—a happy happenstance. The event, which began onstage, suddenly worked its way into the audience. And, so this is how it would be from that point forward."[12]

Also happenstance was the use of printed copies of the now iconic manifesto written by Maciunas. The text was read by Giuseppe Chiari at the beginning of the concert, and copies were then thrown into the audience, which subsequently used these sheets of paper to participate in *Paper Piece*. While Fluxus concerts continued throughout 1962 and into the following year, Patterson left Paris, returning to New York. Several of his compositions, however, continued to be performed in absentia, including *Paper Piece*, along with *Septet from Lemons* (1961), among others. In fact, in correspondence with Patterson from 1963, Maciunas reported the success of finding the requisite teakettles and hot plates for presenting *Septet from Lemons* for the Fluxus concert in Stockholm. While many of the artists working in Europe would also decide to return to the United States, specifically New York, for Patterson the sense of solidarity and shared purpose of his early years in Europe would never fully be reconstructed.

I feel most colored when I am thrown against a sharp white background.

—ZORA NEALE HURSTON[13]

Patterson returned to New York amid the backdrop of complex social, cultural, and political events both in Europe and at home. Germany had been divided by the Berlin Wall. The war in Vietnam, which began in 1959, was escalating. And European colonies in Africa were fighting, successfully so, for their independence. In the United States the civil rights movement was gaining momentum despite political setbacks. The violent responses to student sit-ins and voter registration events in the South had all but solidified the necessary political resolve to sign civil rights measures into law.

Patterson did not see his artistic engagement with Fluxus as antithetical to the social and political issues at home. After all, Maciunas's early manifesto was predicated upon an ideology of revolution—social, cultural, and political. Breaking with the conventions of society was part and parcel of what this "radical" band of artists had set out to do, and their actions, while rooted in art, took aim at the greater sociopolitical and cultural hierarchies of the day. Although there was consensus and solidarity around opposition to the Vietnam War and other political causes of the time, that solidarity seemed to wane in the year of his return, especially in regard to civil rights.

The year 1963 was a major turning point in the civil rights movement. And while Patterson's decision to return to New York was not prompted by this critical moment in history, it became paramount for him to participate. This impetus, however, was not shared by those of his Fluxus colleagues who were living in the United States.[14] This sorely disappointed Patterson, who for the first time felt the corporeal reality of his blackness among his liberal friends. Though he cited his sometime discomfort as an "other" living in Germany in the early 1960s, he had always felt an unfettered comfort among this diverse and international constellation of artists with whom he shared a radical practice.

In the book *Postface*, Dick Higgins marvels at Patterson's ability not to be tethered to the preconceptions of race:

> And so Patterson married and went to France, as he had gone from the U.S. before, where he did not want to be a "negro artist" but just one Hell of a good one and, among other things, a negro. Only James Baldwin and Benjamin Patterson have ever attained that proportion. Actually Patterson's way of using periodic repeats and the blues feeling that this produced being so ingrained and natural struck me so much that when he first sent me a copy of methods and processes, I wrote to him and guessed he was a negro. But considering this does not get one very far with what he does. The main thing is that his work acquires a remarkable unity with our lives as we absorb and forget it. It seems oddly ethical, oddly concrete.[15]

Although Patterson was not bound by race, he was neither indifferent to it nor insulated from the racial upheaval at hand. He participated in the March on Washington for Jobs and Freedom in 1963. He understood the ideology behind Fluxus to be about revolution, and since the March on Washington was about revolution, he was unclear as to why he stood alone. Ultimately issues of race forced a particular reality upon the artist, not unlike the feeling of being a "stranger in the village" described by James Baldwin.[16] In "I'm Glad You Asked Me That Question," his self-interview published in the present volume, Patterson recounted the incident, adding, "But now I recognize that we simply did not share the deep-rooted (albeit hidden) alienation that I lived with as the only black in this crowd."

As Higgins noted, Patterson did marry in Europe and moved back to New York, and this forced another reality upon him, one of economics. Now a father, he determined that gainful employment was more of an imperative than taking down the status quo through the antics and actions of Fluxus. Although he would continue to participate in numerous events presented in New York under the banner of Fluxus (including meeting with George Brecht and Robert Watts to plan the Yam events), Patterson soon withdrew from the group in search of an "ordinary life." Enrolled in Columbia University, he earned a master's degree in library science and worked as a reference librarian for the emerging performing-arts division of the New York Public Library at Lincoln Center. There he began organizing "new music" concerts. The experimental nature of the music proved problematic, however, and the quiet life of a librarian that he envisioned was short-lived. Patterson's passion for new music and his ability to provide composers and musicians with opportunities to present their work resulted in his development of his own music management company, Ben Patterson Limited.

Patterson's passion and administrative acumen virtually ensured that the ordinariness that he sought in his professional career would be elusive, and he went on to develop an extensive professional resume as an arts administrator. He was author of a program for the New York State Council on the Arts to sponsor performances for "new music" composers; deputy director of the Department of Cultural Affairs, City of New York; director of several music organizations; director of development for the Negro Ensemble; professor and chairman of the Department of Performing and Creative Arts at Staten Island Community College; and arts consultant par excellence. Patterson was even principal fund-raiser for the historic meeting of the South African political arms of the African National Congress and the South West Africa People's Organization at Riverside Church in New York prior to the release of Nelson Mandela and the advent of the all-race elections in that country.

Despite the passing of twenty years and impressive professional achievements, Patterson's self-imposed "retirement" from Fluxus was nearing an end. Although he reemerged for the perfunctory anniversary events, it would not be until 1988, with his solo exhibition at the Emily Harvey Gallery in New York, that Patterson would resume his artistic career. The exhibition, simply titled *Ordinary Life,* was a mature articulation, drawing equally on the tongue-in-cheek Fluxus humor of the 1960s and a more astute awareness of the political and social dynamics of contemporary times. The *intermedia* nature of the exhibition—which included painting, sculpture, and installation work—also denoted a profound evolution beyond the artist's earlier forays into interdisciplinary practices.[17] Early antecedents included not only the artist's extensive performance work, which would become the bedrock of his practice, but also annotated scores, the opera *Lemons,* and seminal work initiated in Paris in 1962.[18] Patterson's brief time in France would prove formative in that it allowed him the opportunity to fully explore conceptual practices that would integrate music and performance with literature and the visual arts. While the limited scholarship on Patterson's work has focused on his early compositions for action, which I will revisit here, it is equally essential to look at the artist's early and subsequent visual art practice.

Constructed Operations: Action Poems and Instructions

The opera *Lemons* broadened Patterson's conception of his work beyond the framework of music, although music would remain central to his practice. While the use of the libretto or operatic narrative would prove a natural extension of his work as a classical musician, it would also open the door for the artist to embrace literature, and more specifically poetry, as a vehicle of action or performance. Conflating the device of compositional scoring with concrete poetry, Patterson would also incorporate imagery to further reinforce instructions for movement or to psychologically interrogate the disconnect between image, idea, and ideology.[19] In 1962, with the assistance of Daniel Spoerri, he would self-publish his first and most significant book of poetry, *Methods and Processes.*

Patterson's first poem appears on the cover of the book: the phrase "grasp here" is positioned in the lower right-hand corner, accompanied by a bold black line originating from the lowest point of the corner and arcing to the left with an arrow at its tip, denoting the action of turning the page grasped between one's fingers to the left. This device is subtle in that it makes visible an action rarely dissected: the simple act of turning a page while reading a book. Within the book, short poems—some no more than a few words or lines long—ask the viewer to perform actions:

> discover interesting sound
> capture it
> preserve it
> perform it

In *Methods and Processes,* Patterson transforms the act of reading from one of passive engagement in imagining to one of active engagement and performance.[20]

As with his scores for actions, Patterson grew prolific in creating "action poems." In addition to *Methods and Processes,* he would produce several artist's books, including *Untitled (A Case for Bombing Pause)* (c. 1962; p. 44) and *ABC's* (c. 1961; p. 43). The artist would also begin a collaboration with the artist Lourdes Castro, the founder of the alternative arts magazine *KWY.* Together they would produce two publications: a volume of the magazine featuring several poems from *Methods and Processes* and a special edition called *Prints and Comments* (1962; p. 44), which featured new poems by Patterson in response to images created by Castro.

Patterson would also collaborate with Robert Filliou, a fellow artist within the constellation of Fluxus, in the presentation of his puzzle-poems. As the name suggests, puzzle-poems were at the simplest level puzzles. The viewer had to literally put the pieces of the poems together to read the work. These stand-alone pieces were made of cardboard, onto which words and images were collaged recto and verso. The collages were then cut into pieces like actual puzzles and were often placed in ready-made containers such as discarded food or other product packaging. The imagery—drawn from fashion magazines, newspapers, and printed advertisements—threw into sharp relief the burgeoning generational, social, and political divides of the 1960s. The works showed images of famine in Africa, shocking scenes from the Algerian War, fashion, disaffected youth, and political and religious leaders. Juxtaposed with collaged words and phrases drawn from similar sources, these images provide oblique commentary on the cultural, social, and political tensions of the day.

The puzzle-poems demanded not only a performative dimension but also engagement. Patterson's collaboration with Filliou in presenting the works paralleled the participatory constructs of his earliest work, *Paper Piece*, in that the work was put out into the public realm, where the spectator became a participant. In his self-interview, Patterson recalls: "It was only toward the end of 1962, when I was living in Paris, that I began to make visual objects, works that I called 'puzzle-poems.' Robert Filliou liked these works very much and offered me an exhibition of miniature 'puzzle-poems' in his *Galerie Légitime*, which was located on top of his head under his hat. Since such a gallery obviously had great mobility, we decided that for the 'opening' we should go to the public rather than asking them to come to the gallery." Patterson and Filliou traveled Paris over a twenty-four-hour period by foot, metro, and bus, encountering thousands and selling puzzle-poems from Filliou's beret-cum-gallery. Conceived as prelude to the upcoming Fluxus concert, the event would become Patterson's first exhibition in France. It also became a means of widely distributing his poems across the city to people of diverse backgrounds and experiences.

After his return to the United States, Patterson made only a few more puzzle-poems but continued to create artist's books and a limited number of mail art pieces. His mail art, created by collaging printed matter, echoed the politics of the moment as well as the pulse of New York in the early 1960s. His artist's books, in contrast—initially created using repurposed cast-offs, detritus, and discarded consumer items—served the duality of challenging the hierarchy of art through the use of everyday materials and allowed the artist (who had been trained as a musician) to create a significant body of visual art.

Necessary Objects: Into and Out of Actions

From the beginning of his artistic career, Patterson's work has existed primarily in the intangible realm of performance. Much of the focus of his artistic production has been his scores for actions or documentation of these actions. As works such as the puzzle-poems and the artist's books indicate, however, his practice has also embraced the creation and use of the object. Drawing upon early twentieth-century concepts of the readymade, as popularized by Marcel Duchamp and Kurt Schwitters, Patterson has developed a substantial body of works, some designed in the service of and as relics of performative actions; others, as stand-alone objects.[21]

Early evidence of Patterson's interest in the object as residual or evidence of performance can be seen in several of his earliest action scores, including *Septet from Lemons*

(1961), in which teakettles filled with water are heated to inflate balloons attached to the spouts. The inflated balloons are then targeted by a series of participants using darts. *Solo for Dancer* (1961) required a pulley, with which a dancer would try to hoist herself up until exhausted, and *Pond* (1962; p. 155) employed mechanical toys on a grid drawn in chalk on a floor, to determine a sound, its duration, and its volume.

While there are precedents within the Fluxus movement for the creation of works as residuals of actions, it is also productive to think of Patterson's work within the framework of Nouveau Réalisme. In Paris, Patterson formed a close relationship with Daniel Spoerri, who is associated with both Fluxus and Nouveau Réalisme. Spoerri was formally trained as a ballet dancer but soon turned to the avant-garde practices of the day. The two met almost daily over coffee or wine during Patterson's yearlong residence in France. It was Spoerri who encouraged him to publish *Methods and Processes* and who introduced him to Robert Filliou. The concept of distributing his puzzle-poems in a "happening," under the aegis of Filliou's *Galerie Légitime*, appropriately places Patterson's use of the readymade within the concentric spheres of these complementary practices. Many of the artists affiliated with Nouveau Réalisme rejected painting in favor of making assemblages from everyday objects, but above all their work is characterized by "the primacy . . . placed on the act, both in the production of objects for exhibition and the execution of performative actions."[22]

After his return from retirement, Patterson would continue to create objects both as props in the service of performances or actions and, conversely, "out of actions," as residuals of performances. The present exhibition includes several striking examples of works created out of actions. *Smoker's Rights* (1988; p. 78), for instance, is an object that was transformed into an artwork after the artist had completed a series of actions, such as removing

a cigarette from its package, lighting it, drawing upon it, and then affixing it onto a bottle rack. In this work, action and duration figure prominently, as does the transformative impact of performance upon the object. Likewise, *Flying Bass* (1989–2002) was created after the artist performed upon the double bass over a period of five years. After each performance, Patterson would document the experience with a short narrative written directly onto the bass, creating an accumulated history of experiences. After the written narrative had consumed the surface of the instrument, he added wooden wings accessorized with small torches to simulate the double bass's transformation into a turbojet. In its present form, the piece is suspended from the ceiling to create the illusion of the instrument in flight (p. 105).

Another work created out of an action is *Two for Violin after Nam June Paik's One for Violin* (1991; p. 87), in which Patterson performed Paik's 1962 action score *One for Violin Solo*. The violin is lifted slowly overhead and then smashed upon a table or another solid fixture. Patterson, however, extends the life cycle of the object by assembling its fragments as still life. Closer to his own origins as a classical musician, Patterson has created a number of functioning musical instruments that he has used in performance. The sculptures *Cello (Yellow), Cello (Red),* and *Cello (Blue)* (2003; p. 99) were composed by assembling birdhouses to push brooms, then adding steel wires and frets. While limited in their range of notes, the cellos are functional instruments, and Patterson used them in his performance of the compositional work *A Clean Slate* (2001; p. 201). In 2004 Patterson embarked upon a trans-Siberian journey to celebrate his seventieth birthday on top of Mount Fuji. The journey itself became a performance work, and the chronicled events, an object. Writing on time cards, he chronicled his monthlong journey in dated entries. The cards were set into a rack and left to exist as a residual of the event (p. 101).

In his early practice Patterson also exhibited leanings toward creating objects to be used either as props for performances or as devices to engage the public in an action. Early precursors of his use of objects as devices for action and audience participation include his puzzle-poems as well as a series of objects that he would create prior to and in the aftermath of his "retirement." Beyond the puzzle-poems Patterson created a body of work in the early 1960s under the rubric of Instructions. *Instruction No. 2* (1964; p. 60), probably created for one of Maciunas's Fluxkits, provides a paper washcloth and novelty soap within a box. Upon the washcloth is stenciled, "Please wash your face." Patterson also created other instruction works, including a series of instructions in the form of dance diagrams. *Instruction No. 1* (1964; p. 58) is a dance diagram composed of several large sheets of paper with the outline of shoes with stenciled numbers arranged across each sheet. Patterson and audience members performed this work at Maciunas's Flux Concert held at his Canal Street loft. Also included in this early body of work were a number of "examinations" that Patterson would ask his audiences to take.[23] Audience members were asked to "define and elaborate [on]" their attitudes toward death and dying, as well as art making as a durational, ephemeral, and elusive concept. Patterson would keep completed exams as documents of his performances, and several are presented in this exhibition. While his "examination" works were accumulated and presented as objects, Patterson employed other sculptural objects designed to engage the viewer. One such work is *Uncle Ben's Art Shoppe* (1992; p. 88), an old-fashioned toy dispenser that he repurposed as a mechanism to "sell" his art. Viewers were invited to insert a coin and turn the knob, and the machine would dispense an original work of art.

Patterson also created several large-scale installations that mimicked ordinary social contexts, an aspect of his practice that presages the artistic tendencies of the 1990s that Nicolas Bourriaud discussed under the rubric of "relational aesthetics."[24] The first of these works was *Ben's Bar,* initially created at the Salvatore Ala Gallery in New York in 1990. The installation, a functioning bar, featured a wooden bar, padded wall panels, tables, chairs, and a three-panel mirror with one of the following phrases— "to be heard," "to be seen," "to be there"—written in vinyl across each panel. Patterson also designed a drink menu and served as the bartender, engaging the public as they ordered their drinks. The bar was reinstalled at the Ala Gallery in 1994, before being shipped to Germany, where it was first installed at the Friends of Fluxus Society in Wiesbaden. After the society closed its doors, the work was relocated on permanent loan to the Nassauischer Kunstverein in Wiesbaden, where it continues to function as a bar. *Ben's Bar* typifies later performance works in the artist's repertoire, which are discussed later in this essay.

Another large-scale installation that typifies Patterson's eye toward participatory engagement is *Blame It on Pittsburgh; or, Why I Became an Artist* (1997; p. 95), which has been reconstituted for the present exhibition. To create this work, Patterson sat for nearly twenty-six sessions with a psychotherapist, who analyzed the artist's life for clues as to why he became an artist. Patterson tape-recorded the sessions and reconstituted the fragmented narratives, combining them with photographs from his life as a child, youth, and adult. Text and images were then silk-screened onto large Plexiglas panels and hung in a darkened room. Viewers are asked to take a flashlight and essentially walk through the mind of the artist.

Stand Alone: Readymades

In addition to objects created for and out of actions, Patterson has also produced a substantial body of stand-alone assemblages and readymades. Early examples of readymades can be seen in a series of books that he created in the late 1960s, such as *Speed of Light* (1965),

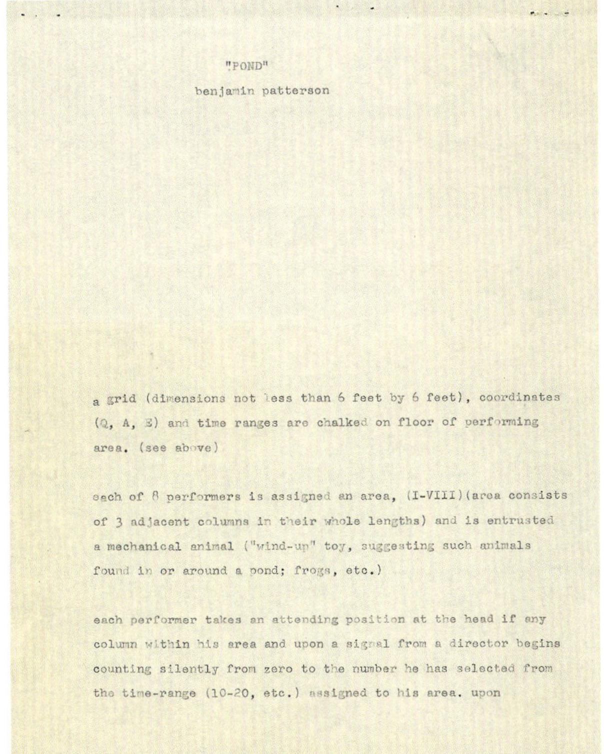

"POND"

benjamin patterson

a grid (dimensions not less than 6 feet by 6 feet), coordinates
(Q, A, E) and time ranges are chalked on floor of performing
area. (see above)

each of 8 performers is assigned an area, (I-VIII)(area consists
of 3 adjacent columns in their whole lengths) and is entrusted
a mechanical animal ("wind-up" toy, suggesting such animals
found in or around a pond; frogs, etc.)

each performer takes an attending position at the head if any
column within his area and upon a signal from a director begins
counting silently from zero to the number he has selected from
the time-range (10-20, etc.) assigned to his area. upon

Pond, 1962

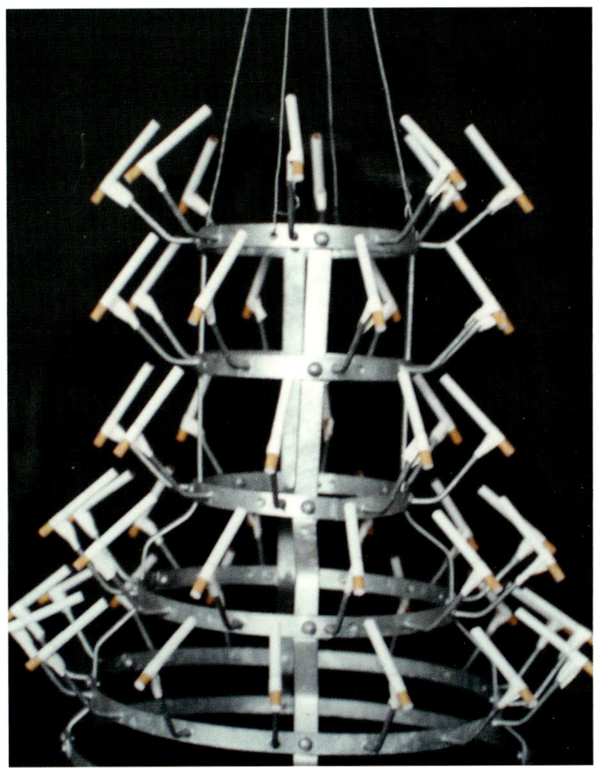

Smokers Rights, 1988

Valigetta (1966), and *The Book of Genesis* (1969; p. 64). Combing through junk shops and often simply walking through the streets of New York, Patterson found objects that he would later use in the creation of works. He would minimally alter the found objects through the use of text or by juxtaposing the piece with another object to create an illusion around it, an alternate narrative of its origins and purpose. This would be true of other books that the artist would create in the late 1980s, such as *Joyce and Eugene* (1989; p. 66), in which he combined two found diaries of young girls, placing them side by side to create the illusion that the girls knew each other and shared experiences; *Nearly-Ninety* (1989), consisting of jewelry placed in velvet bags and then placed in a tin reminiscent of a safe deposit box in a bank vault to give

the illusion of wealth and preciousness; and *Aphrodisiacs* (1990; p. 67), a small valise filled with vials of love "potions."

Perhaps the most visually arresting of the stand-alone sculptures that Patterson created utilizing the conceptual framework of the readymade are the "tackle boxes" that he made between 1980 and 1981. An avid fisherman, he ties his own fishing lures, and he began producing them as artworks, meticulously crafting each lure to communicate with, critique, and engage the viewer. In *Hooked* (1980), he used a tackle box as the container for a succession of lures made from materials as disparate as a hotel key ring or one of his own neckties, so that the work becomes a self-portrait. Less autobiographical, *Trout Bag* (1981; p. 74) contains ten lures that Patterson handcrafted using found materials. The lures, each

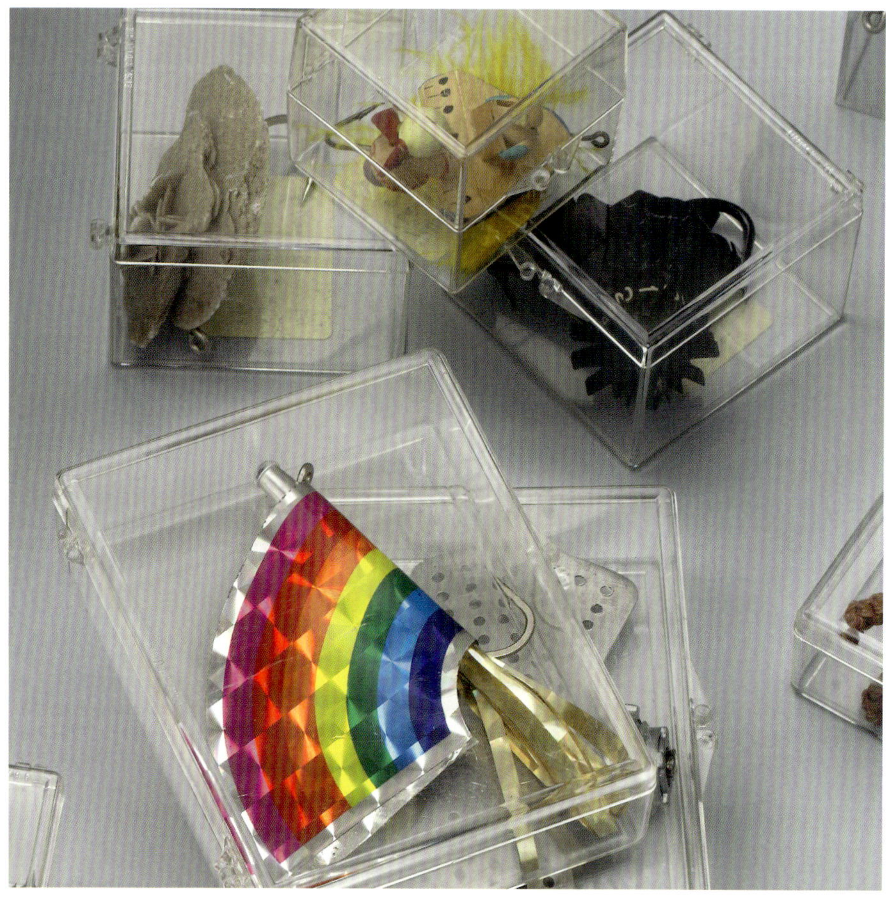

were altered by adding found objects within and outside the frame of the text and images. The issues confronted within this body of work include immigration, unplanned pregnancies and women's reproductive rights, education, imperialism, and class structures. Among his most powerful works from this period is *Hell on Wheels* (1988), a child's desk covered in padded camouflage cloth. The work is poignant in its support of education as a means to empower the masses.

Patterson pays homage to the avant-garde in *A Short History of Twentieth-Century Art* (1993; pp. 89–92), whose four panels with assembled objects and plastic lettering acknowledge the seismic shifts in art practice and the seminal artists who forever altered the various disciplines. It reads in part: "Since John Cage, this is music. . . . Since Merce Cunningham, this is dance." More recently, Patterson has created other works that pay homage to his colleagues in the art world. *Fluxus Constellation* (2003; p. 100) celebrates the international artists who were part of the vast network of Fluxus. The artists are profiled by their astrological signs, which are silk-screened and stretched over domed lights. As with a constellation of stars, the lights alternate as if mimicking the pulsing patterns of stars in the heavens. In *Fluxus Constellation*, Patterson provides insight into his ability to use the ready-made or found object and transform it into something through subtle manipulation and by shifting its context through assemblage. In extending his practice, however, he also transformed an ordinary object into something extraordinary.

Transference: The Ordinary as Extraordinary

Patterson has not often been afforded the opportunity to work with precious materials, but when he has, the results have been nothing short of visually arresting. In the past decade he has worked in factories and in collaboration with artisans, particularly in Italy, to realize a number of

contained in a separate plastic box, are meant to evoke the idea of a customized store-bought lure. With names like *Darthvader*, they provide a snapshot not only of Patterson's life and interests but also of popular culture. There is an origami swan lure as well as a reindeer lure created using woven bits of plastic string (a popular craft activity in the late 1970s).

While much of Patterson's work employs humor, some works also train a critical eye on social and political issues. This is true of the assemblage works that the artist produced in the late 1980s, after a decade of conservative political policies. The Subway Paintings (1990) were created using advertising cards that Patterson would collect on his evening subway rides. The advertisements

projects. The first of these works was commissioned by Francesco Conz of Archivo Conz. *Marble Hat* (1991) is a panama hat that was meticulously crafted from the famed Carrara marble from the region of Verona, where Conz resided. Upon first glance the piece seems artificial, but the pristine quality of the white marble proves otherwise. The weighty marble stands in marked counterbalance to the virtual weightlessness of the straw ordinarily used to make such hats. In using marble mined from the same quarries that produced the material used by Michelangelo some five centuries earlier, Patterson transforms our perception of an ordinary object.

Over a period of years, Patterson has also collaborated with Massimo Lardiano. Working in glass, the two have created numerous works, two of which appear in this exhibition: *Il primo segreto della grappa* (1994; p. 93) and *A Nose for Wine* (2008; p. 103). Patterson engaged twelve close friends in the creation of the latter work. Carefully casting their noses with modeling clay, he then worked

with his collaborator to create "portraits" in glass by incorporating the molds taken from each into wine bottles.

Recently Patterson was again commissioned by Francesco Conz/Archivo Conz to create an edition. Using plastic toy tools as ready-made molds, he cast them in silver. The transformation of a child's toy into a precious object placed in a jewel box underscores the artist's astute insight into society and its values. Tongue-in-cheek humor, dry wit, and haiku-style commentary on the social and political landscape characterize Patterson's work in all media, whether objects crafted in precious materials or ephemeral performances.

Performance Revisited

While a more thorough examination of Patterson's performance work and its legacy is presented by Charles Gaines in his essay for this catalogue, I would be remiss in not discussing performance within the larger context of Patterson's work. Throughout Patterson's career his performance work has been predicated on "scores," or "instructions," for action. While there are a few exceptions, it is important to note that at the outset of his career, terms like *performance artist* simply did not exist. What scholars and curators who focus on contemporary art have come to accept as a given was established in part because of Patterson's practice and the endeavors of those around him. His collection of scores—*Benjamin Patterson: "The Black and White File": A Primary Collection of Scores and Instructions for His Music, Events, Operas, Performances, and Other Projects: 1958–1998*, which he self-published in 1999 (p. 165)—provides a succinct overview of the artist's practice over a forty-year period. Upon review of this collection and in the context of subsequent work, several observations surface, the first of which is that one can easily trace Patterson's evolution as an artist, his interests and preoccupations, through the scores presented in the volume. This is markedly true in

Marble Hat, 1991

reviewing works from the early 1960s in which he fluctuates between graphic scores and scores for actions as a means to create indeterminacy; from the mid- to late 1960s, when his investigations into psychoanalysis figure prominently; from the late 1980s, when scores were designed as an elaborate staging for public interventions or as devices to engage unsuspecting audiences, as in *The Clinic of Dr. Ben (BM, MS)* (1992; p. 200) and his travel agency, *Reisebüro Fluxus* (1994); and from the late 1990s, which saw a return to iconic classical works. In the aforementioned works, Patterson uses commonplace venues to stage his artistic interventions. For *The Clinic of Dr. Ben*, the artist used a former doctor's office in downtown Wiesbaden to set up a makeshift practice. The public, some knowingly and others inadvertently, found themselves engaged in an artwork that included a brief examination and a very lengthy diagnosis that bordered upon the absurd. In *Fluxus Reisebüro*, Patterson set up a tourist office in the window of PrivArt Gallery, near the train station in Wiesbaden. Visitors to the gallery and those passing by could book travel to see Fluxus sites in France, Germany, or Italy. The price points varied for each location, but the engagement was real, and those who booked travel were not merely treated to a tour but also given the opportunity to participate in various Flux games and performances, such as the artist's action score *First Symphony* (1964), in which, for a short period, guests were led blindfolded through the streets of Verona.

A second observation is that Patterson has continued to experiment with modes and formats for presentation that determine not only duration, volume, and tempo, as in his earlier works, but also "place." Site-specificity becomes important as a political, social, and cultural device for framing the work. *Kohler Koffer* (1999; p. 98), a performance work, is predicated upon both place and time. The work was prompted by the political scandal involving illegal campaign contributions that snared

former German chancellor Helmut Kohl and his conservative Christian Democratic Union. The work was conceived as a public intervention in which the artist walks the streets wearing a black fedora and overcoat and carrying a briefcase, advertising his "cleaning business" to those he encounters. Another work about place as figurative and literal site of engagement is *The Museum of the Subconscious* (1996). This work, in which Patterson performs in the role of curator, offers members of the public the opportunity to donate their subconscious upon their deaths. With more than two hundred pledged to date, Patterson has dedicated not only a site in Namibia but also a second site in Tel Aviv and, most recently, a third, at the site of a condor's nest near the banks of Rio Candelaria in the Salta Province of Argentina. In conjunction with this exhibition, Patterson will create a fourth site in Texas and, during the period of the exhibition, accept applications from visitors who wish to make a donation. Part performance and part haiku to mortality and spirituality, *The Museum of the Subconscious* interrogates site as poetic and polydimensional but ultimately unknowing.

A final observation regarding Patterson's performance work is his return to his classical foundations as an act of reclamation. Notable in this respect is his reconfiguration and distillation of operas, beginning in 1994 with Maurice Ravel's *Boléro*, followed in 1997 by Giacomo Puccini's *Madama Butterfly*, Georges Bizet's *Carmen*, and Richard Wagner's *Tristan und Isolde*. In distilling these iconic works, Patterson transforms their respective librettos into Cliffs Notes for performance. Each work, which portrays the dynamics of love and longing, is reduced to a duration between eight and twenty minutes, with Patterson, actors, and the audience participating in the performance. With these performances, Patterson continues the deconstruction of classical tradition that he began in the early 1960s in an effort to make these works accessible, even relevant to new generations. Ironically the artist is also reframing these narratives to highlight their humble origins, which include short stories, folkloric myths, and vaudeville. In a very poignant way, Patterson's desire to deconstruct and dematerialize what could be deemed elite structures reaffirms his practice as one still very deeply rooted in Fluxus.

> Within the strictures of an ethics of dematerialization, Patterson disappears. He reemerges in republication, in enactment, in repertory, by way of the recording and its digital and cybernetic reproduction—the para-ontological remains of Patterson's performances, which take the form of a sifting of and through remains, a continual serving of leftovers, of fucked-up, funny, generatively unfunky licks and pieces of licks. Matter is art's embarrassment; enjoyment is its shame. This double illegitimacy betrays so much of what is valorized under the rubric of Fluxus, which moves within a disingenuous forgetting of this fact, which is, in turn, disingenuously and sometimes profitably forgotten.
>
> —FRED MOTEN[25]

Benjamin Patterson is one of the great visionaries of our time. In the early 1960s, when he first emerged as a member of the avant-garde, his presence was radical not only because of his identity as an African American but also because of his innovations in music, action, and spectacle. Although Patterson was a participant in the inception and birth of Fluxus and a contributor to its development, he rarely figures prominently in books and articles on the movement published outside Germany. Nevertheless, his notion of "action as composition" was seminal in helping to define and shape our understanding of Fluxus, arguably the most groundbreaking experiment in the history of art. Fluxus gave rise to many of today's contemporary art practices—from Conceptualism to Minimalism to performance art to interdisciplinary and multimedia forms of art and beyond. Patterson's prolific work in the 1960s provided a blueprint for contemporary practices, particularly in the arenas of performance and engagement within social contexts. His influence has also helped to shape a generation of younger artists, among them Clifford Owens, Rodney McMillian, and Xaviera Simmons. Moreover, Patterson's work as a music manager and administrator, particularly for the Department of Cultural Affairs in New York City, provided both advocacy and financial support for the burgeoning yet still underappreciated genres of experimental and new music in the early 1970s. His influence on experimental music and performance alone justifies his inclusion in the art historical canon.

Patterson's legacy, although still underappreciated, has been building gradually over the decades. The recognition that he has received is due in no small part to the exemplary efforts of scholars like fellow Fluxus artist Geoffrey Hendricks, who until his retirement persisted in teaching the totality of Fluxus. Patterson himself has also played a significant role in ensuring his growing recognition. As one of the last surviving members of its core group, he has been an ambassador not only for his own work but also that of others who embraced the practices of Fluxus. His relevance to and imprint upon contemporary art practice—particularly performance art, experimental music/sound art, and visual art—is unquestionable. And so, in an ironic twist, it is fitting that a retrospective of the artist's work should be mounted in Houston, a city that in 1956 refused to include him in its orchestra because of the transgressive nature of his presence as a lone black figure upon the stage.[26] While Patterson did not succeed in breaking the race barrier in U.S. symphonies in the late 1950s, he did help to usher in one of the most enduring, inventive, and influential movements in twentieth-century art. And that changed everything.

NOTES

1. Catherine Lord and Charles Gaines, *The Theater of Refusal: Black Art and Mainstream Criticism* (Irvine: Fine Arts Gallery, University of California, 1993), 61.

2. See Patterson's self-interview, "I'm Glad You Asked Me That Question," in this volume.

3. Ibid.

4. Milton Cohen, "Space Theater," *Dimension*, no. 14 (1963), University of Michigan Bentley Historical Library.

5. Ibid.

6. Robert Morgan, "Stockhausen's Writings on Music," *Musical Quarterly* 61 (January 1975): 1–16; reprinted in *Musical Quarterly* 75 (Winter 1991): 194–206.

7. Patterson recalled that it took approximately two hundred hours of rehearsal time for the instrumentalists to master Stockhausen's *Kontakte* (conversation with the author, March 5, 2010). *Paper Piece,* which made use of everyday materials, was second nature for anyone to master.

8. Both publications were created by Ivar Rakowitz.

9. Hannah Higgins, *Fluxus Experience* (Berkeley and Los Angeles: University of California Press, 2002), 55. While Higgins mentions *Paper Piece,* the work is not analyzed in light of Philip Corner's *Piano Activities.* The analysis, which focuses on the idea of creating a visual gestalt of action and the subject-object relationship, is, however, also apropos. Higgins also introduces David Michael Levin's concept of "metaphysics of presence." I would like to extend this concept to encompass Patterson's presence on the stage as both metaphysical and, in his blackness, radical.

10. See *Ben Patterson Tells Fluxus Stories (from 1962 to 2002),* ? Records/Hundertmark, 2002 (compact disc). Patterson recounts his involvement with Maciunas and their work together leading up to and during the mounting of the Internazionale Festspiele neuester Musik in Wiesbaden.

11. For information on Zurich and Dada and the precursors of participation art before Fluxus, see Rudolf Frieling, *The Art of Participation: 1950 to Now* (San Francisco: San Francisco Museum of Modern Art, 2008), 25.

12. Benjamin Patterson, conversation with the author, August 1, 2010.

13. Zora Neale Hurston, "How It Feels to Be Colored Me," in *The Best American Essays of the Century,* ed. Joyce Carol Oates and Robert Atwan (Boston: Houghton Mifflin, 2000), 116.

14. See Patterson, "I'm Glad You Asked." Subsequent conversations with the artist reinforced his surprise and disappointment at the lack of involvement of Fluxus in the issue of equal rights for blacks living in the United States.

15. Dick Higgins, *Postface* (New York: Something Else Press, 1964), 59–60.

16. See James Baldwin, *Notes of a Native Son* (Boston: Beacon, 1955), especially the essay "Stranger in the Village," in which Baldwin recounts his experience of being the only black living in a rural European village. The psychological portrait is poetic. While Patterson was not living among strangers in the rural towns of the Alps, he does understand that his colleagues could not embrace the issues despite their liberal leanings.

17. *Intermedia*, a term coined and popularized by Dick Higgins, refers to works that combine two or more disciplines.

18. Patterson recalled that while he had created several scores that incorporated the graphic technique, he never embraced these as anything other than musical in scope (conversation with the author, February 17, 2010).

19. In writing about Patterson's poetry, I am focusing on the work that predominated during this period. Three were exceptions and other hybrid forms, including the poem-score titled *B. A. P. Regimental History (Fragments) for Jackson Mac Low* in 1962–63. The "human voice" completed the work, which was conceived to be spoken.

20. Benjamin Patterson, conversation with the author, August 2, 2010. Patterson would later liken these action poems to his compositions for action.

21. Patterson's objects produced as residuals of performances find parallels in the "relics" that artist Chris Burden created in conjunction with his performance works of the early 1970s. Burden was considered primarily a performance artist, but his performance events yielded quite a number of objects, including the rifle from *Shoot* (1971), the bed from *Bed Piece* (1972), and the nails from *Transfixed* (1974). For a more in-depth discussion of Burden's practice, see Paul Schimmel, "Leap into the Void: Performance and the Object," in *Out of Actions: Between Performance and the Object, 1949–1979* (Los Angeles: Museum of Contemporary Art; New York: Thames & Hudson, 1998), 94–99.

22. Ibid., 31.

23. In a number of conversations Patterson referred to his examinations as "event scores." I have, however, framed the actual exam and the completed responses of the participants as "objects," or residuals from the event.

24. See Nicolas Bourriaud, *Relational Aesthetics,* trans. Simon Pleasance and Fronza Woods (Dijon: Presses du Réel, 2002).

25. This quotation was taken from initial notes for the essay written by Fred Moten for this catalogue. It has been used with the permission of the author.

26. Patterson wrote in regard to his exhibition in Houston: "Recently, I remember that of all the twenty or so conductors of American orchestras for whom I auditioned in the Spring of 1956, only Leopold Stokowski—then conductor of the Houston Symphony Orchestra—really tried to make a difference. After asking me to play for nearly 2 hours (a normal audition is finished within fifteen minutes) in his 5th Ave., New York apartment, Stokowski said: 'I really like your playing and want you to come to Houston. But, you know we have a problem. However, I am going back to Houston to fight with the Board of Directors and see if we can't solve this problem.' Thus, over the next months I received several telegrams, saying 'We have another Board member on our side' . . . until a telegram in late May, reading 'Very sorry. Last night the Board voted "No."' This however, was not the last telegram I received from the Maestro. In late July I received another telegram, asking ME to "reconsider MY decision not to join the Houston orchestra" and that he was still looking for a double-bassist! It seems that the Maestro had a fantastic ear for orchestral sound and color, but was visually/mentally 'color-blind'! He had truly forgotten the 'problem,' about which I had to remind him in a return telegram. The 'irony,' of course, is this retrospective in Houston a half-century later!"

Sophisticated Refuse: *Benjamin Patterson's Cool Works on Paper*

MARCIA REED

Unpresuming and eminently disposable, paper is an unlikely material to select as a signature medium. Yet twentieth-century artists have embraced paper for books and prints, installations and performance. Compared with major works collected by museums, sold at auction, and shown in galleries, paper makes a direct, unmonumental statement that is emblematic of the new. Among artists associated with Fluxus in the early 1960s, Benjamin Patterson was an early adopter of paper. He used it in performances and as a performative medium for instruction sequences and events. The works employing paper parallel his musical compositions; often these came together in the same piece.

Defining Words

The two heteronymic words *sophisticated* and *refuse* work well to describe Patterson's mindful selections of materials.[1] They acknowledge the ambivalent content he presents and the overarching importance of methods and processes.[2] Sophistication, not a pure or original state, conveys seasoned knowledge with some extra wrinkles that imply fixing or adulteration. Particularly in the book trade, *to sophisticate*—the last syllable is pronounced "Kate"—means to alter, doctor, or make up copies, which then lose their authenticity as historical objects. In terms of Patterson's work, it points to his subtle layers of meaning beyond a facade of simple materials and basic presentations.

Refuse is both a noun and a verb. The noun refers to something that is left over or discarded. As a verb, to refuse is to deny or be unwilling to comply. It positions Patterson's negating response to traditional art, music, literature, and performance. Unlike *sophisticated*, neither use of *refuse* conjures images of the pleasant or the polite. Patterson's material could easily come from the wastebasket or go into it. But his selection of refuse is purposeful, a refusal to engage with major media. It is both a challenge and a discipline to make something from whatever is on hand. Notably mongrel, his works on paper could appear to be superficial and spontaneous. Privileging process, the activity of art itself is transformative. Works are frequently on paper that was formerly something else: a magazine, a newspaper, a postcard. There is an implicit change of identity, but it is hardly ever like a butterfly emerging from a cocoon or the male peacock flourishing his magnificent tail. Rather Patterson's cutouts from popular magazines are quietly provocative; occasional suggestive snips are meant to disturb the decorum. As with Patterson's instruction pieces, made to be performed or just to be pondered, simply viewing his works sets the mind on a path. These works are sophisticated because they are composed, never just thrown together. They seem so cool and casual that they fake you out in a positive way.

ABCs

As a serviceman stationed in Germany, Patterson used a French-language children's ABC coloring book as a scrapbook in which he filed and pasted pictures and ephemera alphabetically. Collecting material for the book, Patterson engaged in an "old-lady" pastime, clipping articles or columns from magazines and newspapers.

If you know your ABCs, it means that you know what you're doing. Inside the cover of the coloring book is a printed sheet on which the following phrase is repeated in lines of type that get progressively smaller: "Der Erfolg der Anzeige hängt von der Gestaltung ab" (The success of the endeavor depends upon design). Each opening presents its own picture cutouts, with collaged comments or a small composition pasted in. Illustrating the range of Patterson's influences in his late twenties, *ABC's* (c. 1961; p. 43) portends the array of media that feed into his work. He used old postcards: "Bonne Fête" (Happy Birthday) shows a boy holding a large pink bouquet pasted on a foldout of the Alps from *Paris Match* paired with a poem in German titled "für Benjamin," dated July 1961. On the verso of *B* is pasted another postcard: "Bébé à vendre" (Baby for sale). The page for the letter *J* holds a small collage book with photos of Johnny Hallyday, the French popular singer. On *V* is pasted a handwritten text for Patterson's project *Roden's Ants* (1960–62) on the back of one of the images of ants from the project. This, "A six minute activity of a number of ants in a park in Düsseldorf, Germany on an August afternoon is represented through graphic reduction of a series of photographs recording this event." Reuse and revision are ongoing compositional strategies.

Patterson evades fantasy or silliness by frequently making reference to current events, stressing the disconnects. He pairs a photo of Nikita Khrushchev on *K* with an enigmatic poem, perhaps notes by a soldier, next to it:

> Killed cow.
> Wrecked plane.
> Scared me.
> Smith.

The scrapbook holds popular culture, news, and favorite subjects. *L* has funny French cartoons about kisses, "Le langage des baisers en dix-huit dessins" (The language of kisses in eighteen drawings), and a photograph of Elizabeth Taylor wearing very little, labeled "Liz" in red crayon. Opposite, on the *M* page, is a large portrait of Miles Davis, with Mao on the verso. From jazz to China, in essence this is Ben Patterson's world.

P Is for Patterson

The page for *P* has printed phonetic pronunciations: *pli— pro—piv—pom—pur*. Perfect for Ben's acoustic propensities, sounds are seen on paper. Pictures from magazines show a father, labeled in red crayon "Papa," and "Pablo" (Picasso). Clipped texts include: "pour rester jeune" (to stay young), "pour garder la ligne" (to hold the line), "Pour avoir des mains irrésistibles" (To have irresistible hands). "Post-Office Department" is pasted in the center of the page:

> Postal officials are working on a plan to help survivors of a nuclear attack locate family and friends. Survivors would register by past and present address. A central office would collate the data, be able to answer individual queries about the whereabouts of all registered survivors.

En français, *P* is for *palette* and *papillon*. Paste-ins include a collage of a parking lot with miniature car shapes cut out so that only silhouettes of autos remain and an excerpt from Patterson's *Project 457b*, an 8½-by-11 sheet with typed text:

> an anti-"passive-consumptive" action
> a restatement of cause and effect as amended
> by probability

The image at center left shows three collaged soldiers holding swords on a seesaw, with notations in pen and ink. The caption for the central soldier reads: "To the left: for all other colors <-----; to the right: for blue eyes only ------>."

The *ABC's* scrapbook illustrates Patterson's connections: simultaneously simple and arcane, personal and political. Unlike many of his Fluxus colleagues, he has always lived and worked day jobs in the nine-to-five world, doing library work, administration, and fund-raising, activities that have supplied subject matter and media. The

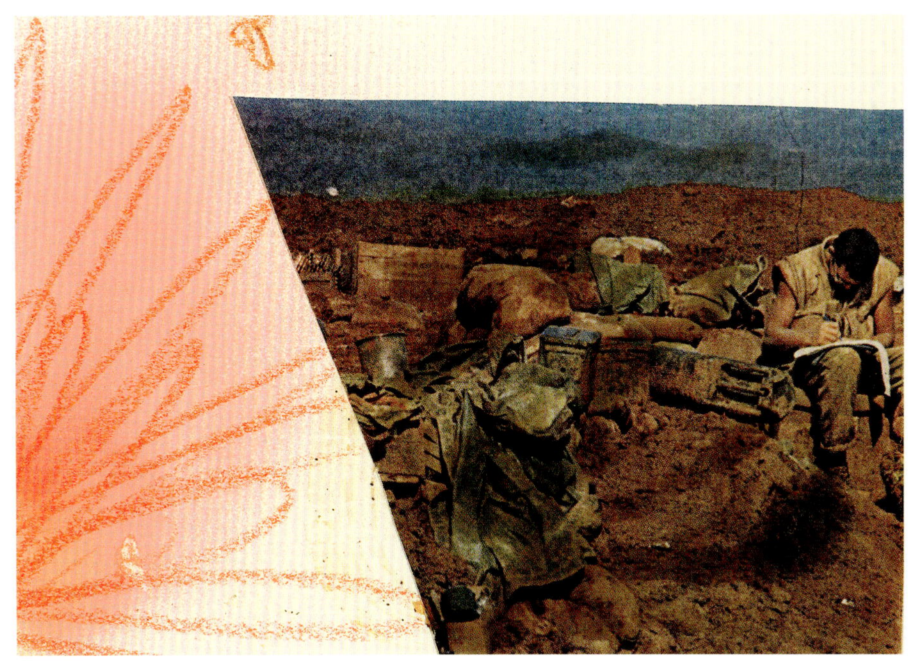

Untitled (A Case for Bombing Pause), c. 1962

compilation of *ABC's* forecasts the paper formats that he would use in later publications and performances. Coincidentally, *ABC's* now shares the same archival box in the Getty collections with a sketchpad titled *Untitled (A Case for Bombing Pause)* (c. 1962; p. 44). Combining brief observations with *Life*-like photojournalistic images, Patterson's seven-page text points out beneficial effects of suspending military activities for victims, soldiers, and their families. At the end of the sketchbook is a score with a photocopied one-page explanation, "Six transparent sheets having single straight lines, five having points,"[3] and a six-page handwritten score for amplifier, sarangi, and tape recorder.

Acoustics and Surprising Sounds

Words, images, and music flow together. All Patterson's work is informed by his natural talent for music and his engagement with sound. He plays the double bass, and he is deeply absorbed in composition. In an interview recorded in 2002 in Wiesbaden, Germany, he reflects on

early Fluxus performances, stressing that many of the artists involved were trained musicians, and emphasizes the place of music in his own work. On the CD he has a bad cold, so there is an additional chance element of sound— throat clearing, coughing. The conversation proceeds in competition with a recording of Richard Strauss's *Ein Heldenleben* (A Hero's Life). In the liner notes Patterson mentions that the classical piece was his selection. At a particularly loud moment of Strauss, Patterson speaks to the question of whether his works are provocative, referring to *Paper Piece:* "If you announce that this is a quintet for paper and start tearing up paper or throwing it at the audience, you will be surprised. My initial interest in making this piece was the sound of paper which was an extraordinarily variable element." He crumples a piece of paper loudly into the microphone, producing crackling sounds that drown out Strauss.[4]

Normally the bass player provides rhythm and color in the background. For Fluxus performances and other events, Patterson foregrounds his role as a composer and musician, often playing solo. Sound contributes an essential element, often paired with words. Patterson's compositions are not electronic or symphonic but rather emphatically acoustic, whether they employ the sounds of the double bass, crumpled paper, or dripping water. Describing the goals of Fluxus in the same interview, Patterson stresses protest against materialism in art. It is not about buying and selling but about ideas or changing people's ideas. Thus manifestations of Fluxus are ideally immaterial. The model is a performance or event that could be experienced by a live audience with whom the performers could engage spontaneously.

P Is for Paper

Patterson's *Paper Piece* has become a canonical example of a paper performance. His handwritten score, penned in Cologne and dated August 1960, details the elements of the paper-based work for five performers and varied kinds of paper, including newspaper, tissue, heavy drawing paper, cardboard, and three paper bags. Sounds of paper are organized by timings, designated by quantities of paper sheets, with onomatopoetic names:

7 sheets . . . "Shake, Break, Tear"

5 sheets . . . "Crumple, Rumple, Bumple"

3 sheets . . . "Rub, Scrub, Twist"

3 bags . . . inflated by mouth "Poof, Pop"

Patterson notes that performers can select their materials and arrange the sequence of events. "Dynamics" should be carefully improvised within the material boundaries of the approximate "fff" (an air sound) of the "Pop" and the "ppp" of "The Twist."[5] Similar alphabetical figures for the sounds appear again in the 1960 visual score for *String Music*.

The title of *Paper Piece*—especially its German title, *Papierstück für fünf Spieler* (Paper Piece for Five Players)—echoes those of earlier classical musical compositions as well as works by Fluxus colleagues: Philip Corner's *Piano Activities* (1962) and Tomas Schmit's *Piano Piece No. 1* (1962), as well as Robert Watts's *Piece with Balloon* (c. 1962). As with George Brecht's *Drip Music* (1962), its focus is elements of sound, both previously designated and performance-specific. *Paper Piece* is a short concert of tearing, crumpling, and throwing paper. The artwork, paper, is both the instrument and the source of sound, and is eventually obliterated as it is thrown out to the audience. Carefully timed, *Paper Piece* is a transactional event; its sounds cease when the allocation of paper has been expended. This early performance points to one of the principal ways Patterson composes for paper, using it as a medium of exchange with the audience. Unlike parallel performances in which the audience watches occasionally sophomoric activities of the Fluxus artists on stage, such as pissing into a pail, Patterson's events

Papierstück, 1960

engage the audience. The pieces enlist whoever wishes to participate and generously share the activity, in both substance and content.

Patterson's compositions did appear in polemical circumstances. At the 1962 Festvs Flvxorvm Fluxus at the Kunstakademie Düsseldorf, *Paper Piece* was part of a performance, dramatically introduced by the gallery director and art critic Jean-Pierre Wilhelm: "Should a manifesto be launched today? It would be too beautiful, too easy. The heroic epoch of manifestoes—Dada, Surrealists . . . is well past . . . no longer a matter of yelling, it's a matter of mattering."[6] The concert began with *Paper Piece*. Two performers came on stage carrying large sheets of paper; sounds of paper crumpling and tearing were heard, coming from behind a screen. The large sheets dropped down at the same time as shreds and balls were thrown out at the audience from behind the screen. Printed sheets with a text, taken from George Maciunas, a kind of manifesto, were dumped on the audience: "PURGE the world of bourgeois sickness, 'intellectual', professional & commercialized culture. PURGE the world of dead art, imitation, artificial art, abstract art, illusionistic art, mathematical art. PURGE the world of 'EUROPEAN-ISM'! . . . PROMOTE A REVOLUTIONARY FLOOD AND TIDE IN ART. Promote living art, anti-art, promote NON-ART REALITY to be grasped by all peoples, not only critics, dilettantes and professionals . . . FUSE the cadres of cultural, social & political revolutionaries in united front & action." Printed matter was the signature material. Following Patterson's piece, Wolf Vostell presented *Decollage Kleenex*, and Maciunas and others performed *In Memoriam to Adriano Olivetti*, reading scrolls of typed paper in performers' hands.

Not infrequently Patterson introduces a common format in a unique presentation. A world map shows up in *Variations for Double Bass* (1961), serving as a location device for this iconic musical performance. Patterson's typescript score presents an array of ways to use paper acoustically:

I. Unfold a world map on floor. Circle with pen, pencil, etc. city in which performance is being given. Locate end pin of the bass in circle. . . .

V. weave strips of gold papers through the strings . . .

XI. agitate strings with . . . 2. corrugated cardboard, 3. a newspaper holder (wooden sticks used by libraries) filled with tissue paper, newspaper . . . toilet paper, etc. . . .

XIII. lay bass on side . . . 1. fan with japanese or spanish hand fan . . .

XV. peg-box previously prepared with . . . colored paper . . . [and] 3. Choose texts or pictures from newspaper, magazine, etc., crumple and place in peg box.

In the final section (XVII), "the performer should address, write message (reading aloud) and stamp picture postcard. Post in f-hole."[7]

Paper works and musical compositions fall into two types. *Paper Piece, String Music,* and *Variations for Double Bass,* among others, are performances intended for an audience. Patterson's scores and instructions for these works are composed graphically, as visual works on paper. Other works, like *ABC's,* are made for single viewers, possibly only Ben Patterson. Scores, poems, and collages are texts to be read; meditative words or visual poems in boxes and games in envelopes stimulate participation and encourage reflection. Even the compilation title—*Benjamin Patterson: "The Black and White File": A Primary Collection of Scores and Instructions for His Music, Events, Operas, Performances, and Other Projects: 1958–1998* (p. 165)—is a graphic reference to the colors of printed matter as well as a double entendre concerning race. *String Music* has elaborations in pen and ink, and *Duo for Voice and a String Instrument* (1961) is embellished with abstract notations. Photographs are not a frequently used medium, but for *Ants, a 1960 composition of benjamin patterson to be used in conjunction with 1962 compositions of george maciunas,* Patterson provides visuals in the form of nine-by-twelve photographs, each with twenty to thirty tiny ants. Patterson rarely forgoes an opportunity for humor, and his life-size insect portraits might also be seen as performance documentation.

P Is for Puzzle

Putting together the assembled collages of a two-sided jigsaw puzzle, a puzzle-poem (1964),[8] reveals a prurient undercurrent. On one side, text borrowed from an advertisement is paired with an image of a diver circled by a shark: "That feel-better feeling is just a swallow away." On the reverse, scenes of rockers and a stripper kneeling in front of a man are punctuated by a printed clipping on

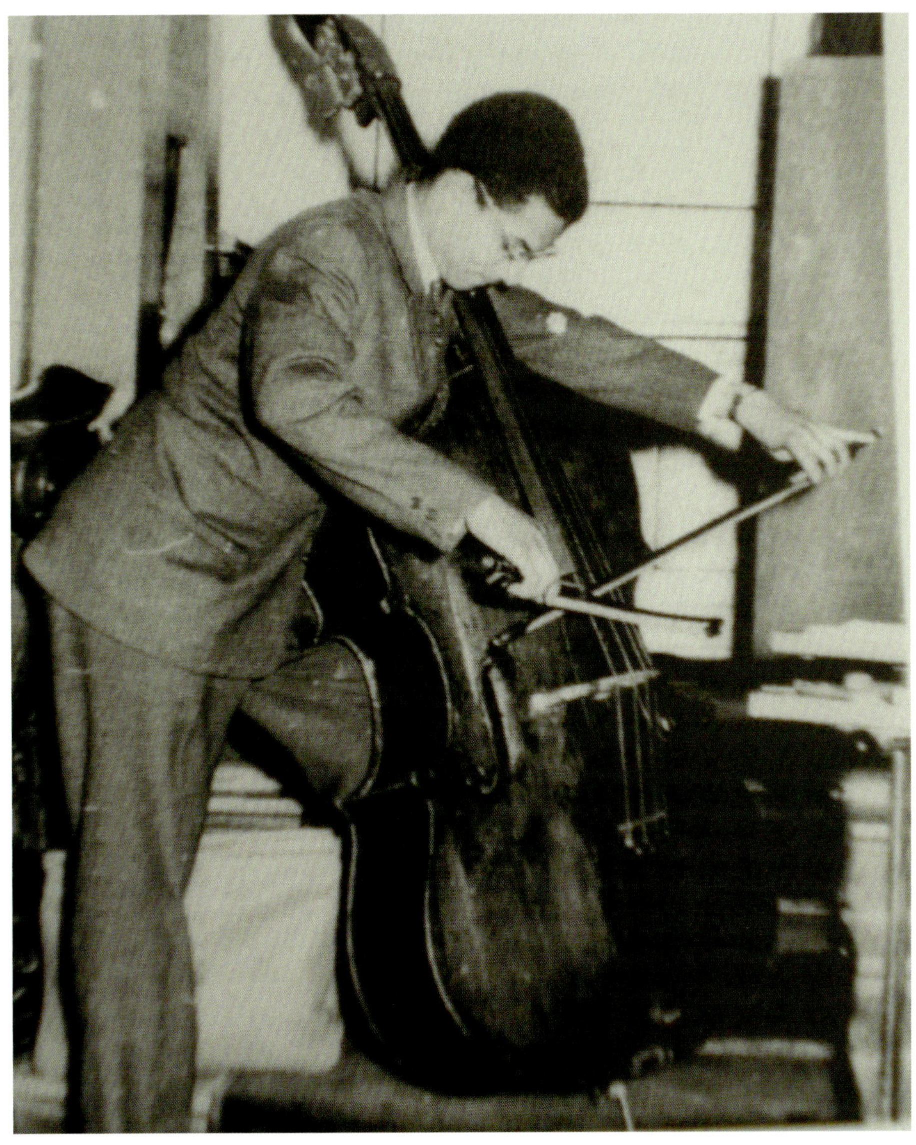

Patterson performing *Duo for Voice and a String Instrument*, 1961

the Christian symbolism of a German abbey altar. The activity of fitting together the pieces of the puzzle-poem until it is legible ends in an epiphany that the subject could be sex.

Patterson in the Archive

The range of Patterson's paper works is seen in the archive that the collector Jean Brown acquired from him in 1978.[9]

Living in western Massachusetts, Brown filled her Shaker Seed House with Fluxus archives, multiples, and objects, spiking the atmosphere with working visits from her favorite artists, principal among them George Maciunas, who advised her on what to collect. An independent-minded patron, Brown carved out a unique, participatory role as a collector of these new media. She had a particular sensibility for books and a developed appreciation for works on paper. She saw her archive not as a museum but rather as a lively place for the exchange of ideas. With Shaker-style drawers to store multiples and a large trestle table for work, the archive was for display and hands-on experience of new kinds of art.

Brown had been in touch with Patterson since 1972 about acquiring his archive, but this took place only in 1978, the year Maciunas died. Patterson wrote to Brown about how much the news affected him. Possibly it made him think of taking care of his own work for posterity. Fortunately, he rarely threw away his notebooks, letters, instructions, and the resulting drafts and works. (It seems that *P* could also stand for pack rat.) Files hold correspondence, event scores, drafts, numerous versions of musical scores, publications such as the 1962 collage photochoreography of *Methods and Processes*, concrete poetry,[10] works created from library catalog cards, researchers' note cards,[11] and processing streamers.[12] Given his emphasis on the immateriality of art and the importance of its shared experience by the performer and the audience, reading through the archive provides a kaleidoscopic view of Patterson's art. The paper works are highly personal, mostly accessible, not wholly self-referential, witty, and, occasionally, appropriately unsettling. Although he repeats performances of notable pieces, he rarely does anything twice. Dual constants are his radical approach to acoustics and instrumentation, often paired with paper as a medium. A rubber-stamped, strangely stained instruction card offers his viewers a simple dare: "WATCH ME."

NOTES

I would like to thank my former research assistant Natilee Harren for her research, corrections, suggestions, and assistance with obtaining photographs.

1. A heteronym is one of two or more words that have the same spelling but differ in pronunciation and meaning.

2. Emphasizing their importance, Patterson gave the title *Methods and Processes* to his 1962 booklet.

3. This seems to be a direct borrowing from John Cage's *Variations I and II.*

4. *Ben Patterson Tells Fluxus Stories (from 1962 to 2002),* ? Records/ Hundertmark, 2002 (compact disc).

5. Jean Brown Papers 890164, box 39, folder 32, Getty Research Institute, Los Angeles, includes the handwritten score and printed ephemera for the event performed in Cologne, September 1960.

6. George Maciunas's manifesto, quoted by Owen Smith, "Developing a Fluxable Forum: Early Performance and Publishing," in *The Fluxus Reader,* ed. Ken Friedman (Chichester, England, and New York: Academy Editions, 1998), 3–4, 2011.

7. "VARIATIONS FOR DOUBLE BASS," Jean Brown Papers 890164, box 39, folder 32, Getty Research Institute, Los Angeles.

8. This multiple exists in at least two copies at the Getty Research Institute and the Silverman Fluxus Collection at the Museum of Modern Art, New York.

9. Jean Brown to Benjamin Patterson, October 13, 1972. Ever the enthusiastic collector, she writes: "I do, of course, want everything you can send to me. My Fluxus archive is growing very rapidly. I saw George Maciunas twice last week and he is helping me enormously." See also letters from Patterson dated October 13, 1977, and June 7, 1978, and on December 13, 1978, a letter from Jean Brown concerning her "going through" his papers. This collection is now at the Getty Research Institute.

10. *Regimental History: Fragments (for Jackson Mac Low)* (c. 1962–63; p. 51), with words for servicemen's status (such as *deceased* and *discharged*) organized in blocks of eight.

11. Such as *American Studies,* with its difficult questions typed on five-by-eight-inch note cards in a dark brown file envelope.

12. *It's Vital,* Jean Brown Papers 890164, box 39, folder 33, Getty Research Institute.

Chance Operations:
Instructions, Poems, and Books

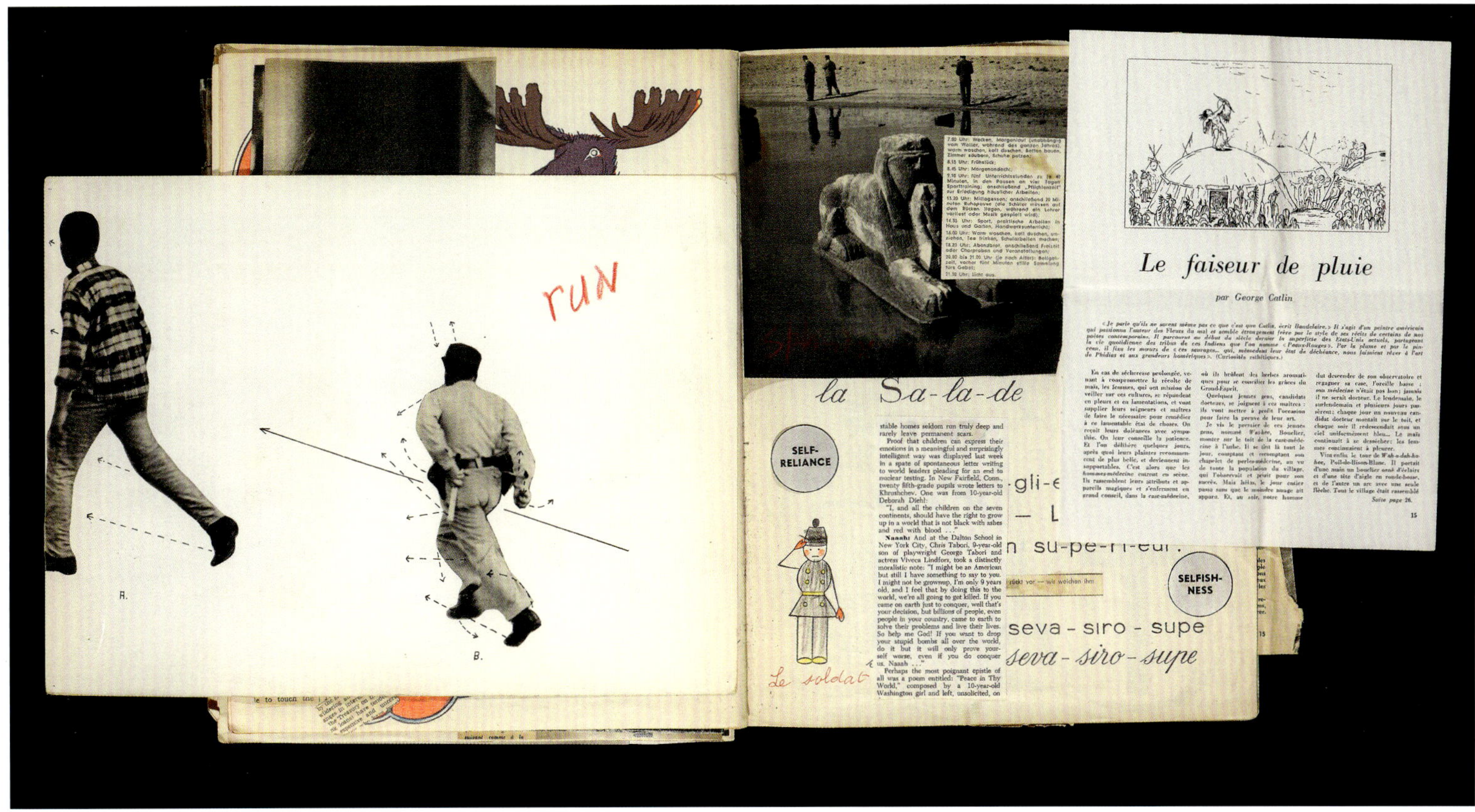

ABC's, c. 1961

Children's coloring book, ink, crayon, collage
13 × 10¼ × 13/16 inches
Getty Research Institute, Los Angeles

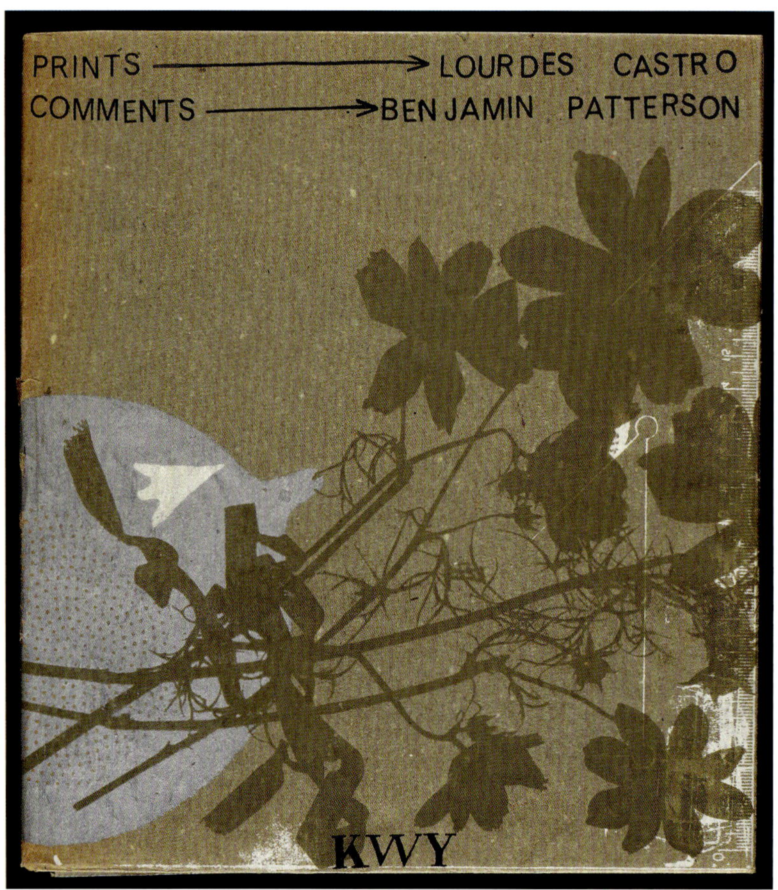

Prints and Comments (Prints, Lourdes Castro;
Comments, Benjamin Patterson), 1962
Handmade paper, vellum, ink
10¹⁄₁₆ × 8⅞ × ⁹⁄₁₆ inches
10⅝ × 9 × ¹³⁄₁₆ inches
Getty Research Institute, Los Angeles

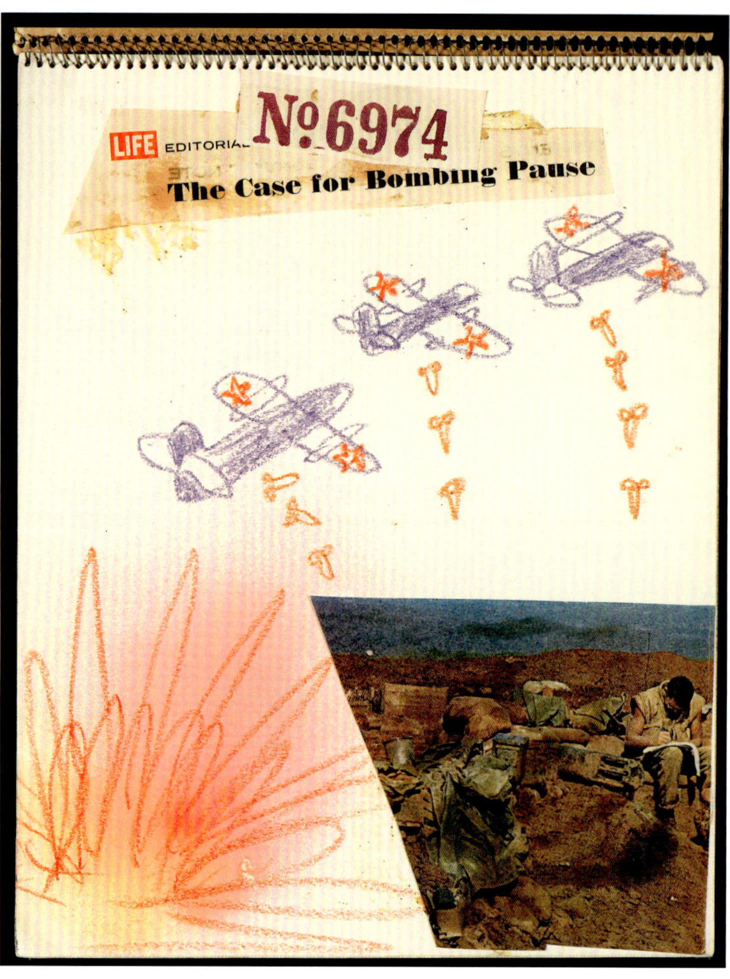

Untitled (A Case for Bombing Pause), c. 1962
Spiral-bound notebook, ink, crayon, collage
11½ × 8½ inches
Getty Research Institute, Los Angeles

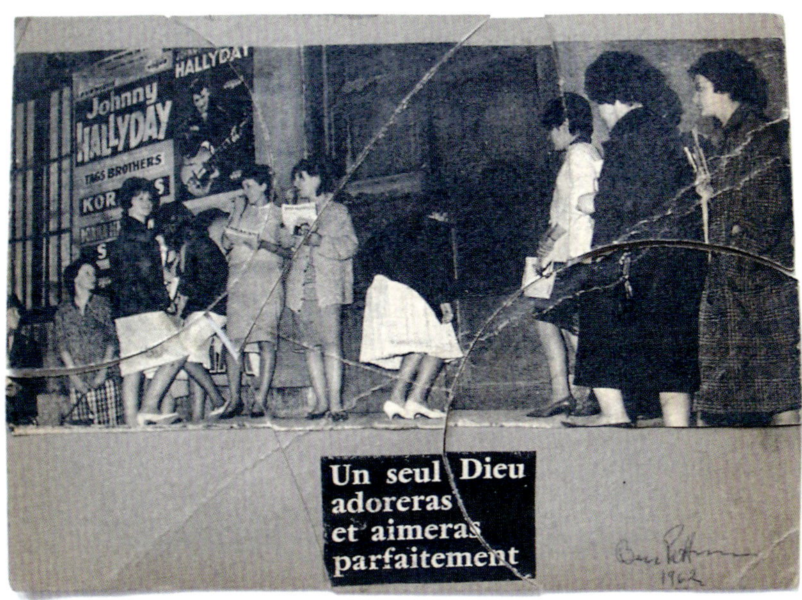

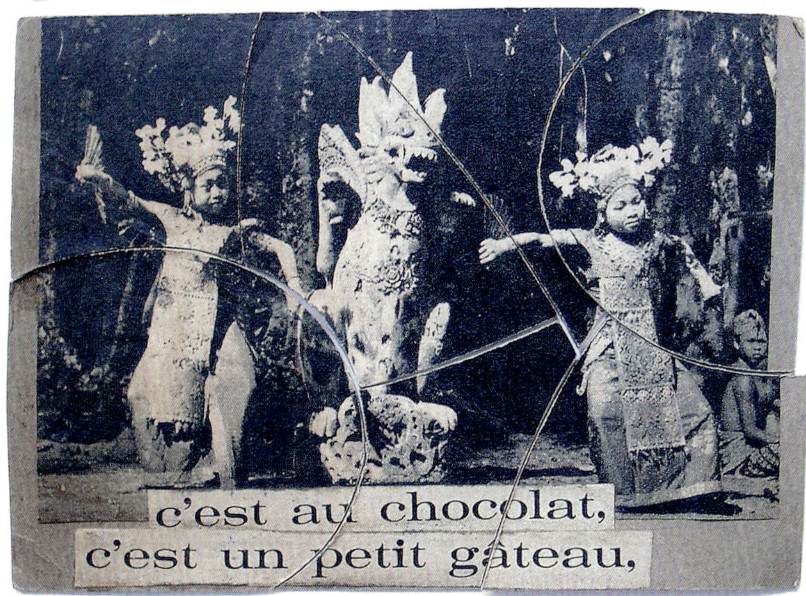

Puzzle-Poems, 1962
Collage on card, metal box
Box: 9/16 × 3 7/16 × 3 5/16 inches
Puzzle-poem: 5 9/16 × 4 15/16 inches
The Museum of Modern Art, New York;
The Gilbert and Lila Silverman Fluxus Collection Gift

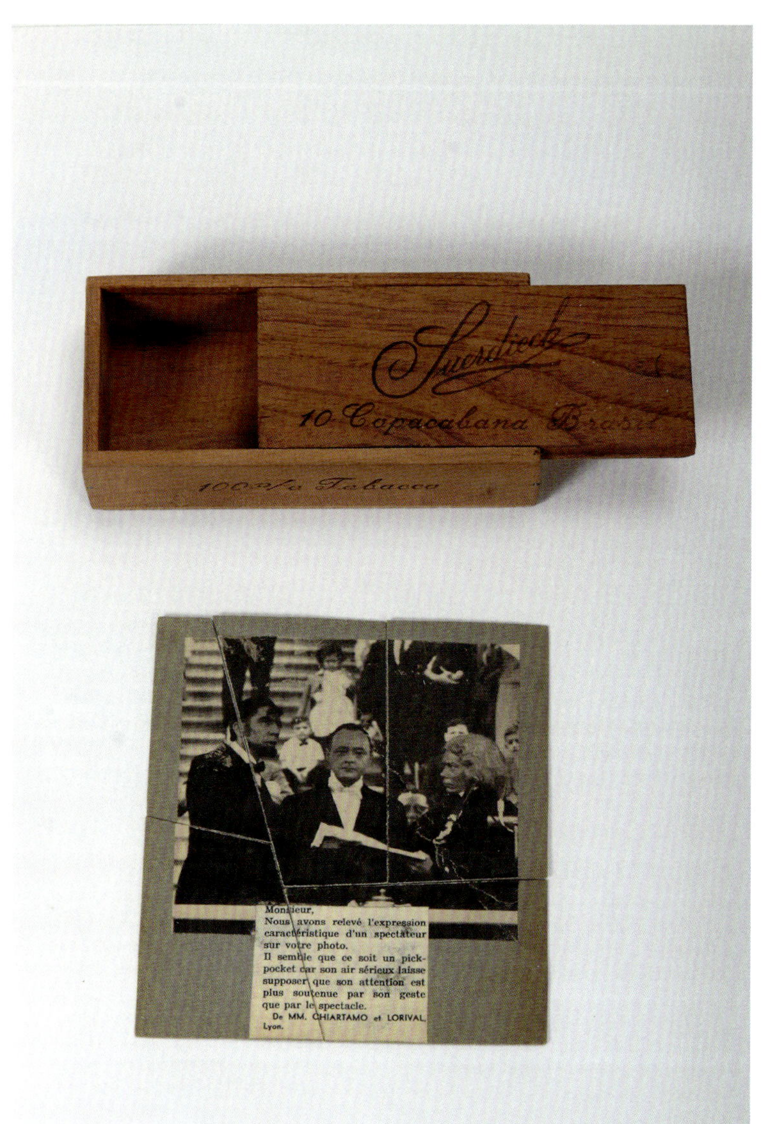
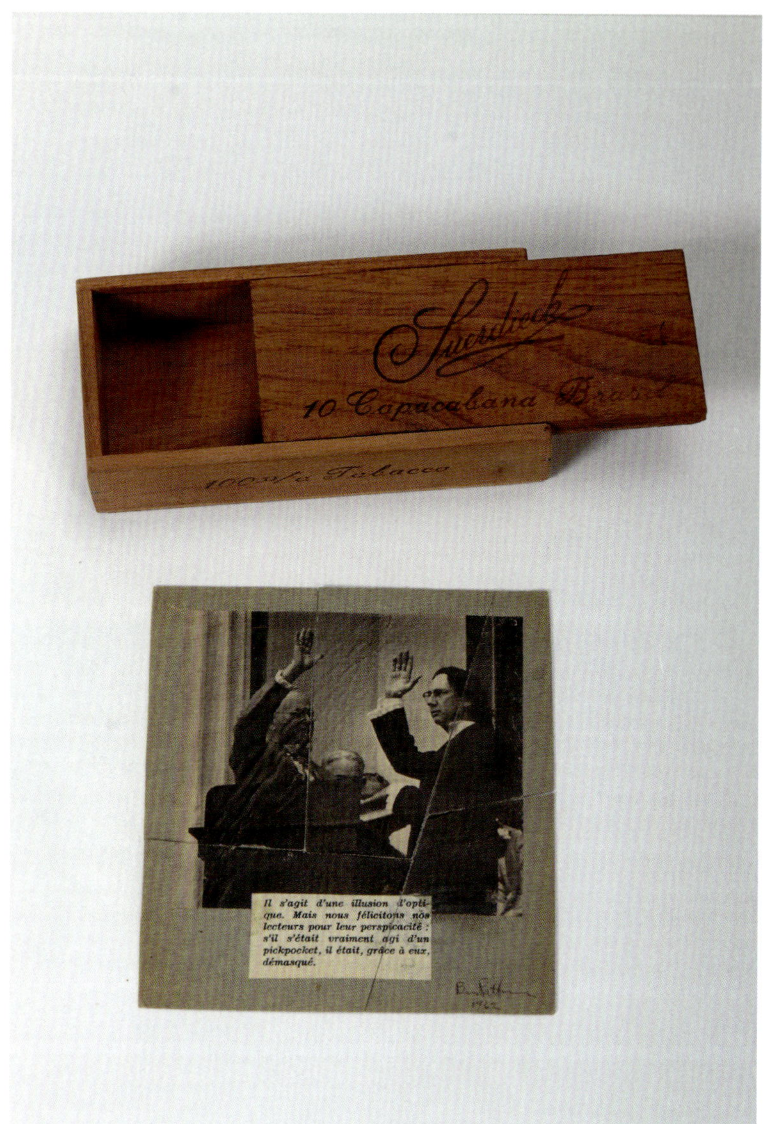

Puzzle-Poems, 1962
Collage on card, wooden box (recto/verso)
Wooden box: 5¾ × 2¾ × 1½ inches
5-piece puzzle poem: 6 × 5 inches
Courtesy the artist

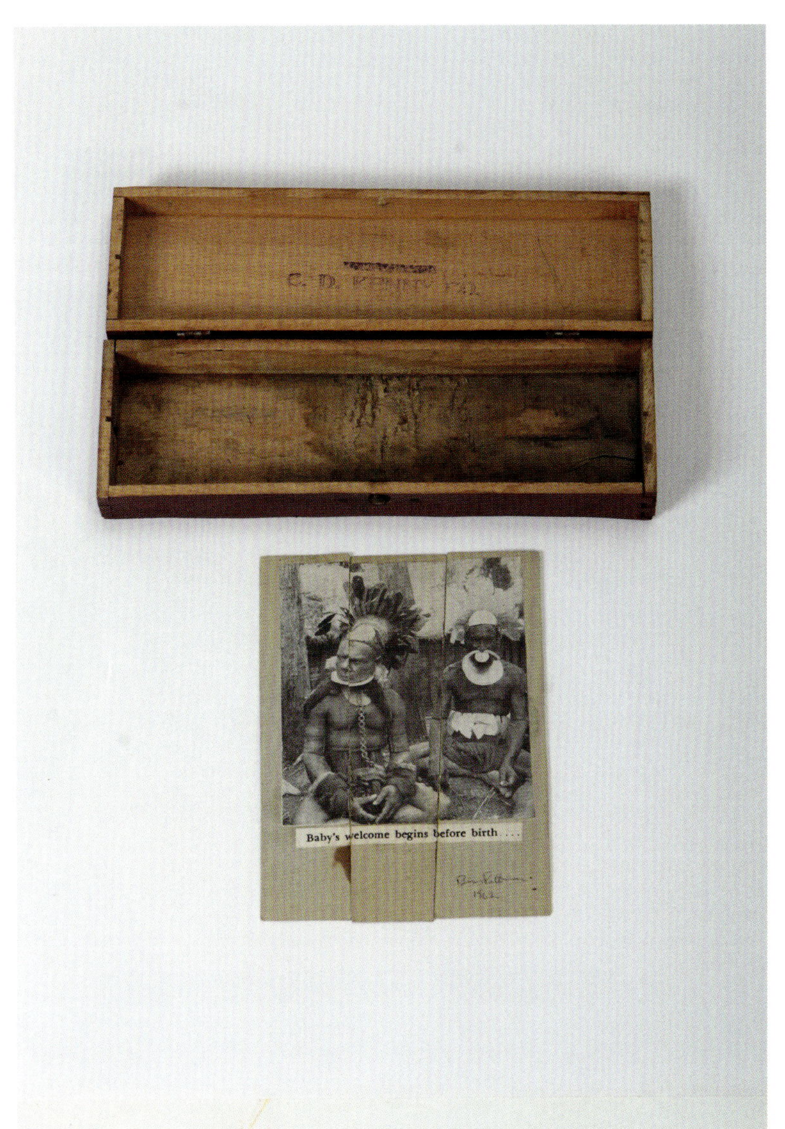

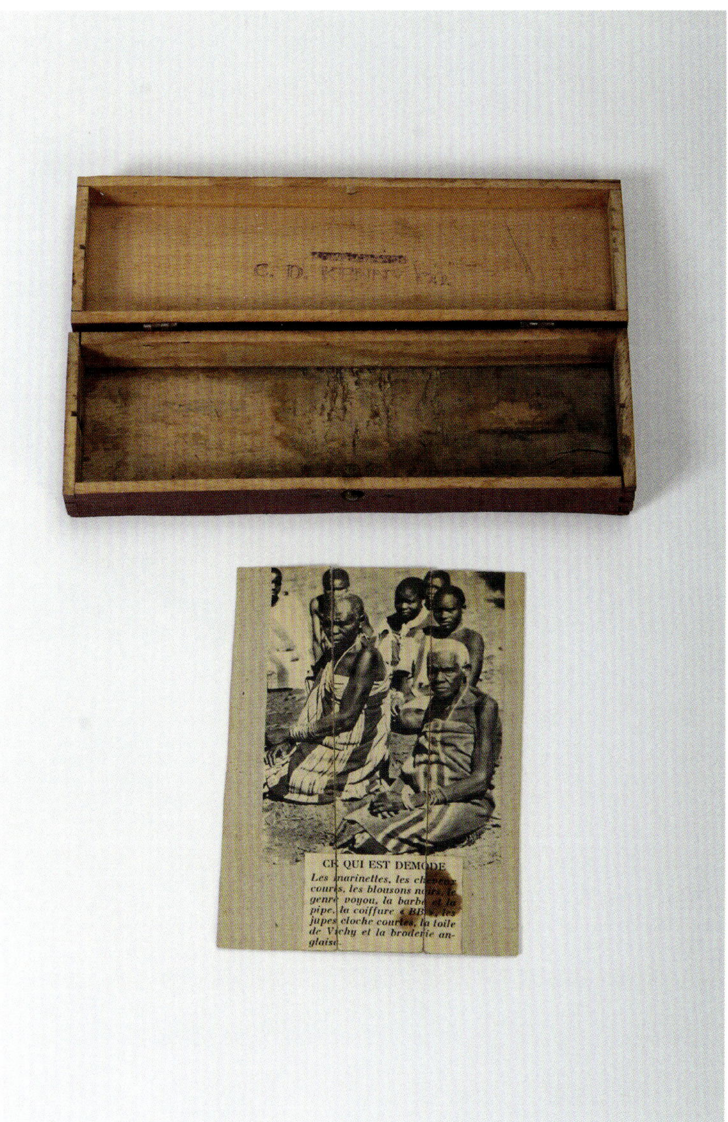

Puzzle-Poems, 1962
Collage on card, wooden box (recto/verso)
Wooden box: 8 × 2½ × 1¾ inches
3-piece puzzle-poem: 5½ × 4 inches
Courtesy the artist

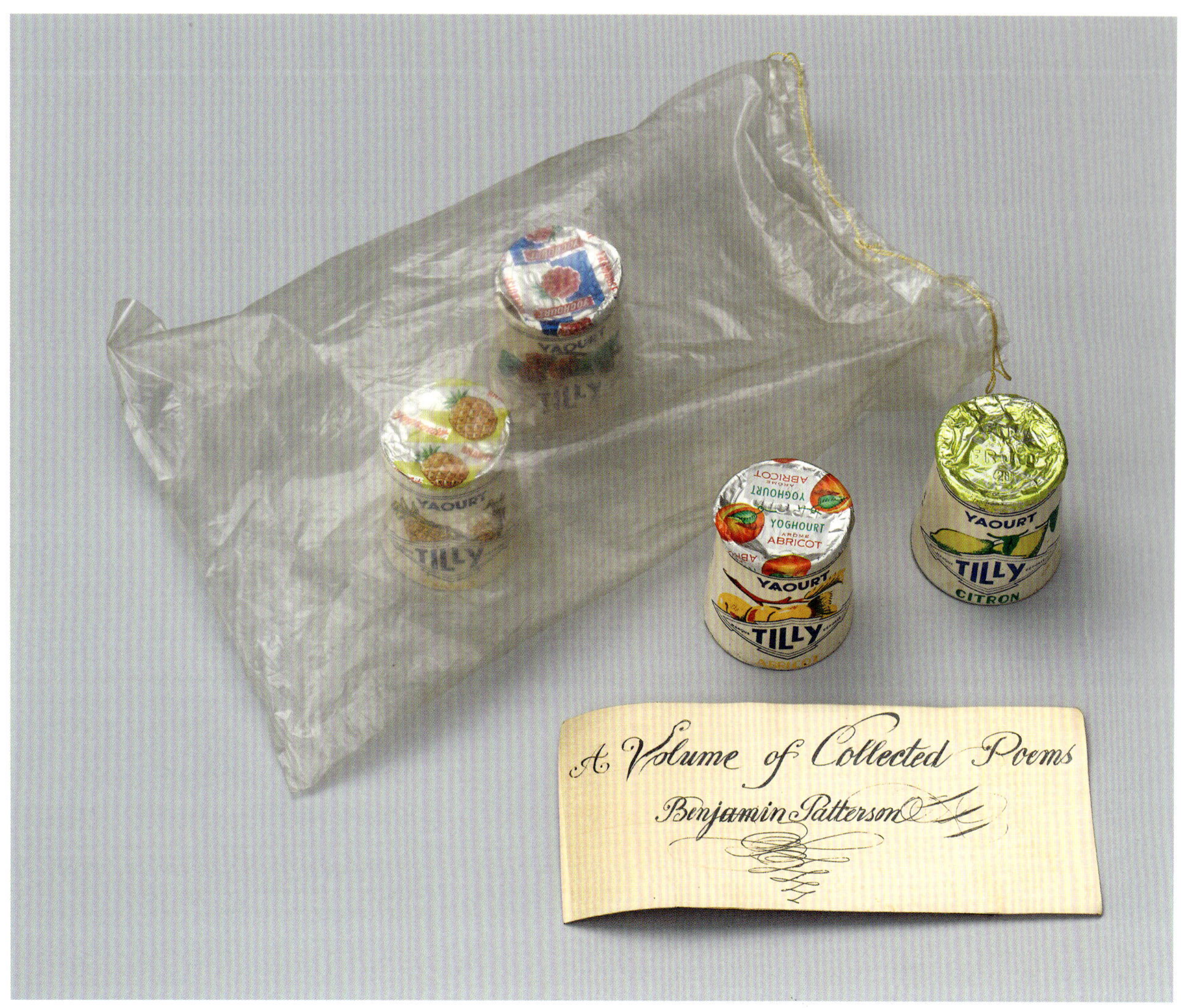

A Volume of Collected Poems, Volume 1, Poem 2,
1962
Collage on card, yogurt cups, plastic bag
Plastic bag: 14⅝ × 9⅞ inches
Card: 3¾ × 8⅝ inches
Apricot: 3¹⁄₁₆ × 2⁷⁄₁₆ inches
Bananas: 3¹⁄₁₆ × 2⁷⁄₁₆ inches
Citron: 3¹⁄₁₆ × 2⁷⁄₁₆ inches
Framboise: 3¹⁄₁₆ × 2⁷⁄₁₆ inches
The Museum of Modern Art, New York;
The Gilbert and Lila Silverman Fluxus Collection Gift

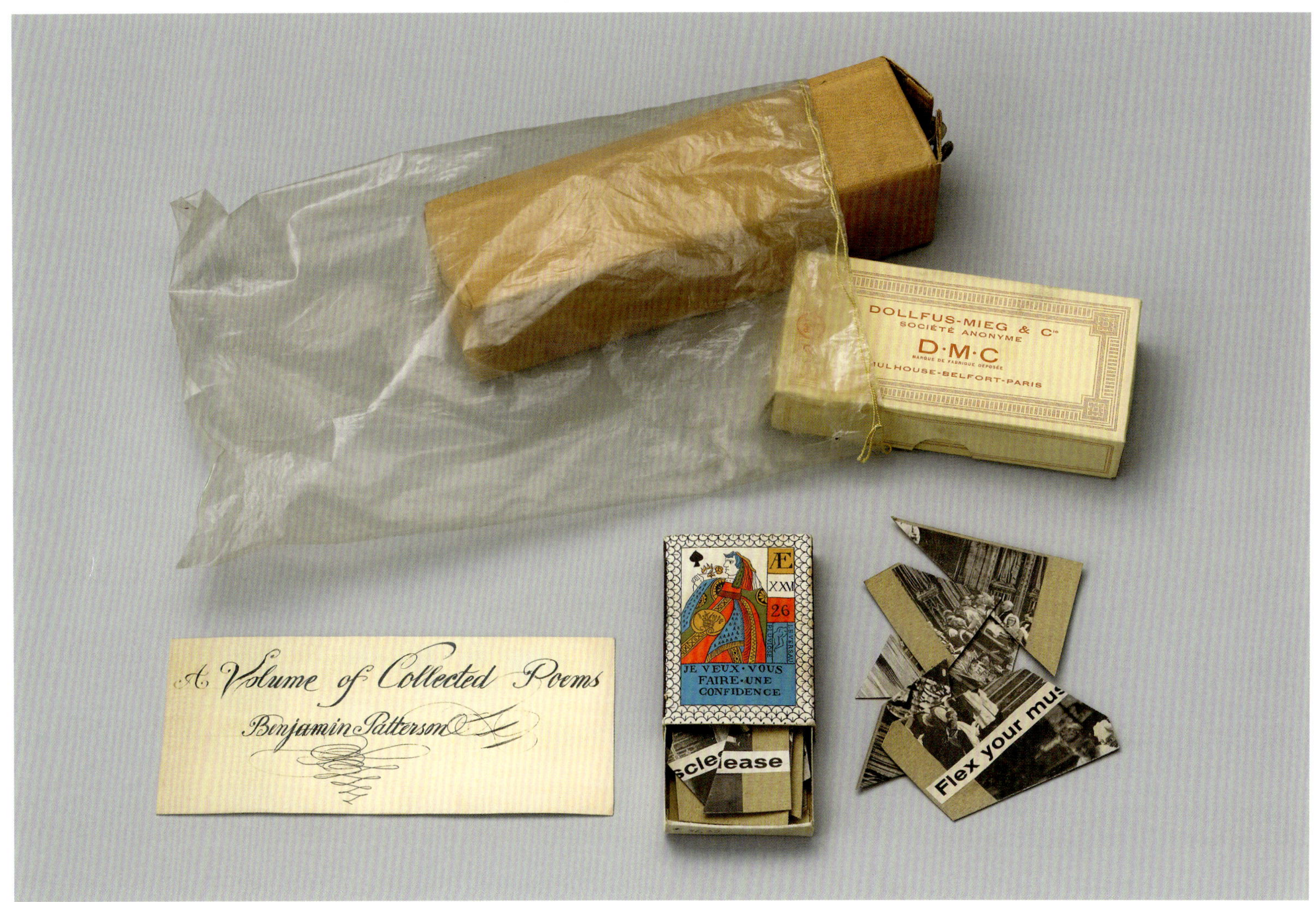

*A Volume of Collected Poems, Volume 5, Poems
20, 21, 22, 23 and 24, 25,* 1962
Collage on card, paper and linen boxes, plastic bag
Plastic bag: 14½ × 9⅞ inches
Card: 3¾ × 8⁹⁄₁₆ inches
Linen box: 2¹³⁄₁₆ × 11⅛ × 2⅞ inches
8-piece puzzle-poem: 17¹⁵⁄₁₆ × 8⁹⁄₁₆ inches
Matchbox: 16 × 2¹⁵⁄₁₆ × 4⁵⁄₁₆ inches
15-piece puzzle-poem: 12⅜ × 6⁹⁄₁₆ inches
The Museum of Modern Art, New York;
The Gilbert and Lila Silverman Fluxus Collection Gift

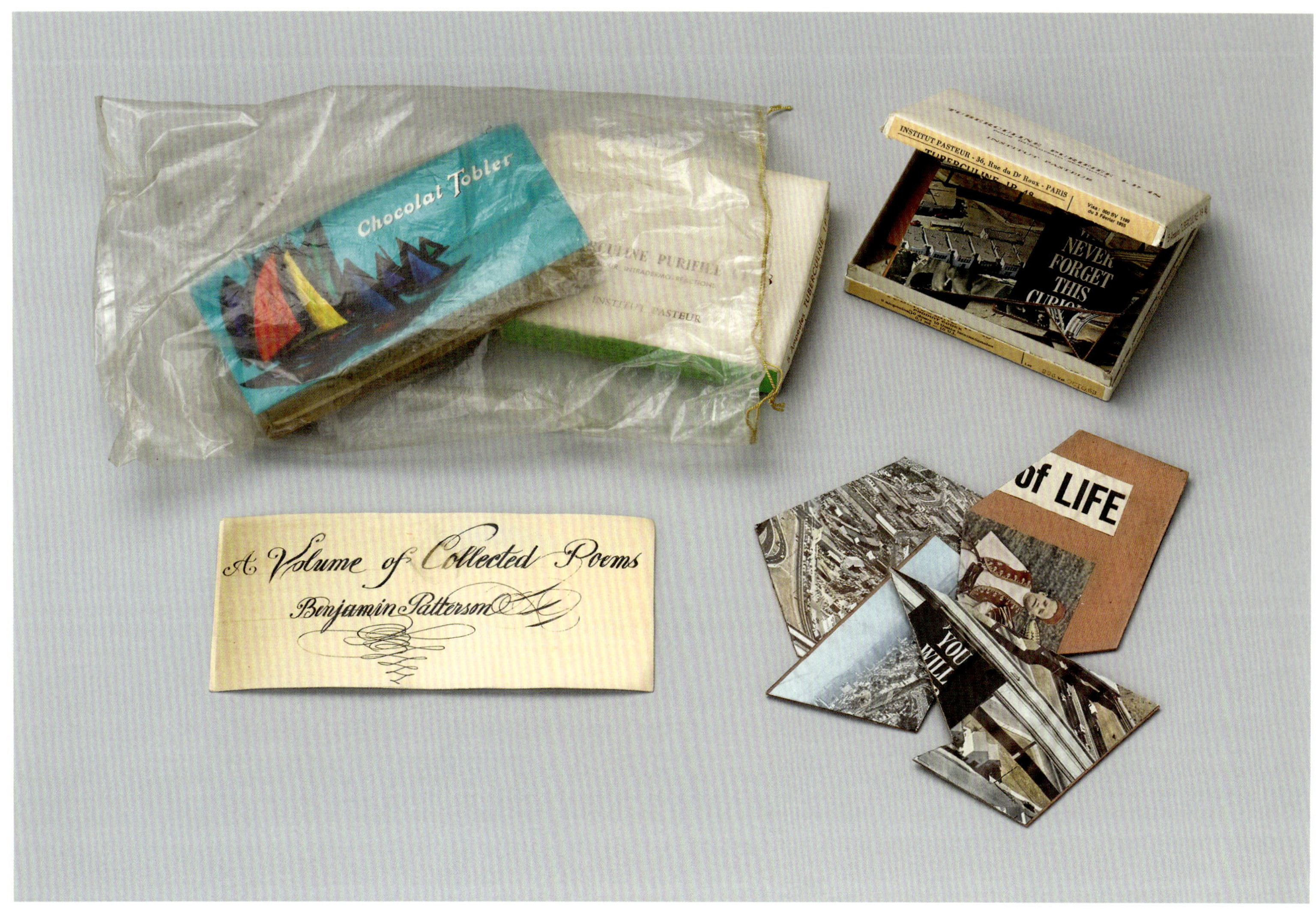

*A Volume of Collected Poems, Volume 7, Poems
32, 33, 34, 44 and 36, 37,* 1962
Collage on card, paper boxes, plastic bag
Plastic bag: 14¹¹⁄₁₆ × 9⅞ inches
Card: 3¾ × 8⁹⁄₁₆ inches
Tobler chocolate box: 1⅛ × 7½ × 3¹¹⁄₁₆ inches
9-piece puzzle-poem: 20¹³⁄₁₆ × 6⁹⁄₁₆ inches
Tuberculine Purifiée box: 1 × 6³⁄₁₆ × 4¾ inches
12-piece puzzle-poem: 21³⁄₁₆ × 7³⁄₁₆ inches
The Museum of Modern Art, New York;
The Gilbert and Lila Silverman Fluxus Collection Gift

B.A.P.

REGIMENTAL HISTORY
(fragments)
for Jackson MacLow

Discharged   Died   Discharged
Discharged   Discharged   Rejected
Discharged   Discharged   Discharged
Discharged   Discharged   Discharged
Discharged   Deserted   Died
Deserted   Deserted   Killed in action
Discharged   Deserted   Discharged
Claimed apprentice Discharged   To Royal Navy

Discharged   Discharged   Discharged
Discharged   Discharged   Discharged
Discharged   To 10th R.V. Bn.   Died
Deserted   Deserted   Discharged
Discharged   Discharged   Discharged
Deserted   P.W.   Discharged
Died   Deserted   Deserted
Discharged   Deserted   Discharged

Discharged   Discharged   Died
Discharged   Died   Rejected
Died   Discharged   Discharged
Discharged   Discharged   Discharged
Died   Died   Discharged
Died   Died   Discharged
Discharged   Discharged   Died
Discharged   ——————————   Died

Discharged   Discharged   Discharged
Discharged   Discharged   Discharged
Discharged   Died   Deserted
Discharged   Deserted   Shot for dersertion
Transported for life P.W.   Deserted
Died   Discharged   Discharged, wounds
Deserted   Discharged   Died
Discharged   Killed in action   Discharged

*Regimental History: Fragments
(for Jackson Mac Low)*, c. 1962–63
Ink on paper
11 × 8 1/16 inches
Getty Research Institute, Los Angeles

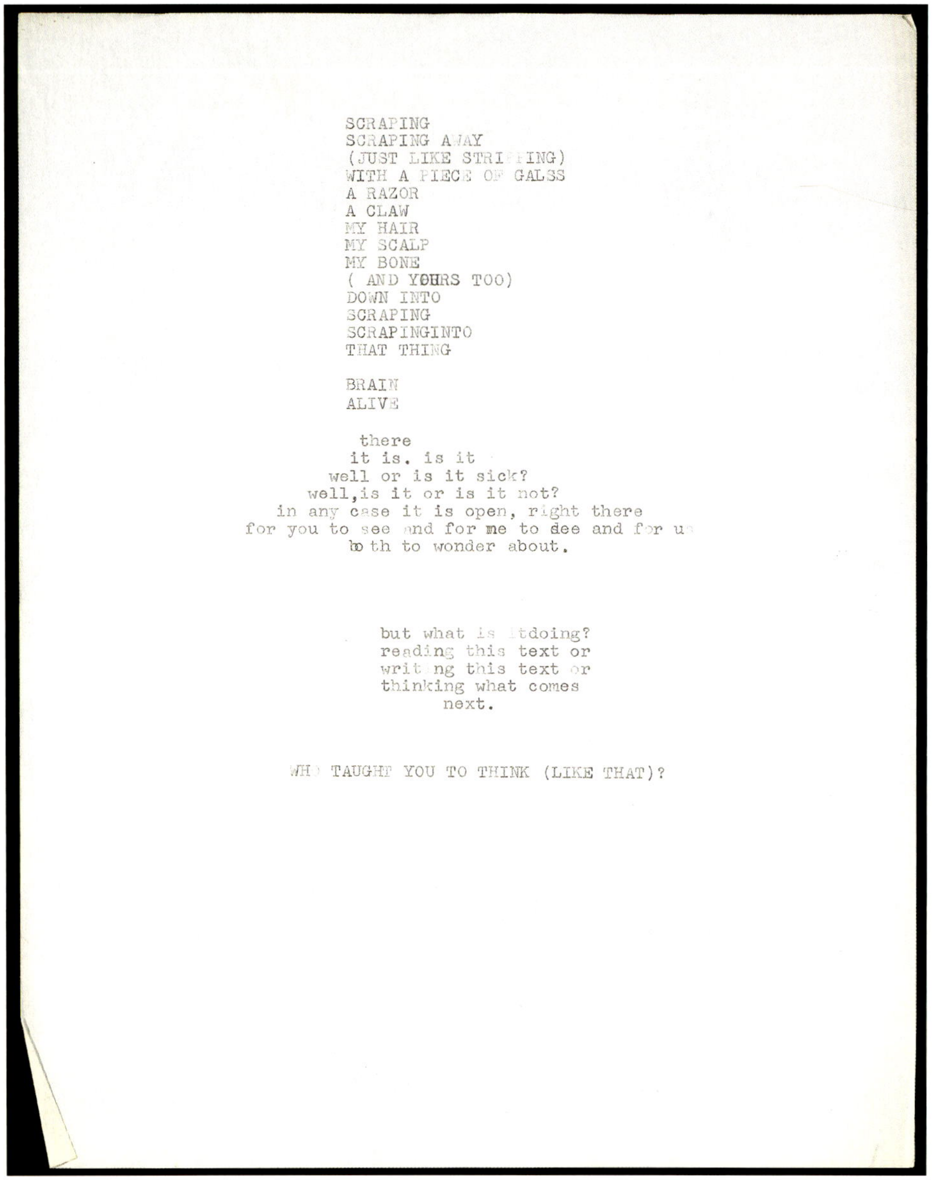

```
SCRAPING
SCRAPING AWAY
(JUST LIKE STRIPPING)
WITH A PIECE OF GALSS
A RAZOR
A CLAW
MY HAIR
MY SCALP
MY BONE
( AND YOURS TOO)
DOWN INTO
SCRAPING
SCRAPINGINTO
THAT THING

BRAIN
ALIVE

  there
   it is. is it
 well or is it sick?
well,is it or is it not?
in any case it is open, right there
for you to see and for me to dee and for us
    both to wonder about.



     but what is itdoing?
     reading this text or
     writing this text or
     thinking what comes
          next.


WHO TAUGHT YOU TO THINK (LIKE THAT)?
```

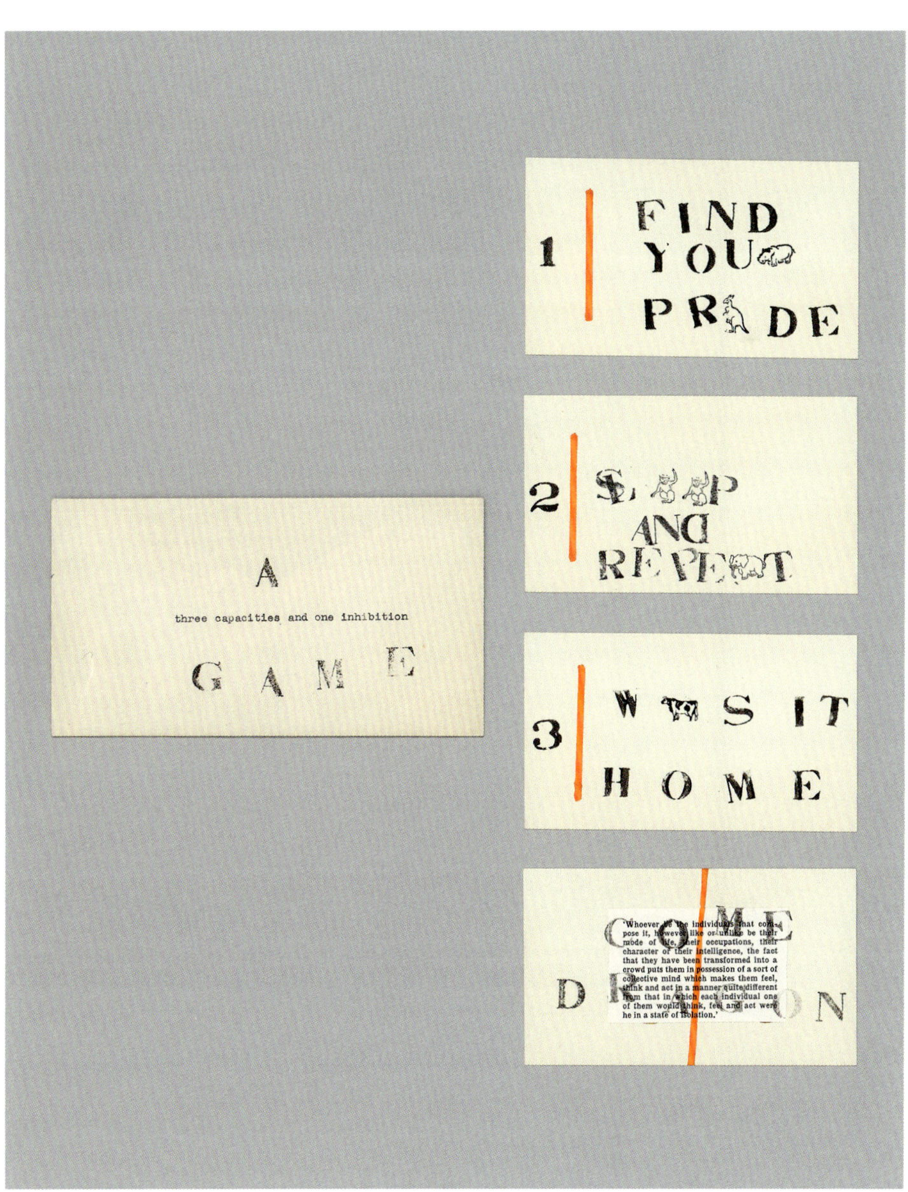

A Game: Three Capacities and One Inhibition, c. 1963
Index cards, collage, stamped ink, marker
4 index cards, 3 × 5 inches each
Envelope: 3⅝ × 6⁷⁄₁₆ inches
The Museum of Modern Art, New York;
The Gilbert and Lila Silverman Fluxus
Collection Gift

A STUDY *
by
Benjamin Patterson

Some results based on a questionnaire completed by 23
members of an audience of approximately 250.

age profile: range 19-50; 6 females, 9 males 25 or
    under; 2 females, 6 males 26 or over

13 reported self as "artists" or "art student", 8 as
    "non-artists" and 2 pointed out that they were
    concerned with philosophy.

To the question, "Do you feel that what has been
    presented here is ART?" 11 answered YES or YES-
    qualified, 9 NO or NO-qualified and 3 were in-
    different or undecided. 8 answering YES and 5
    answering NO were 25 or under, indifference
    appearing in the 46 or over bracket. 6 YES to
    2 NO count amonggfemales with a 6-6 deadlock
    among males.

To the question "Would you have liked to have partici-
    pated?" 5 females and 4 males answered YES, 1
    female and 4 males answered NO, 2 females and
    6 males reported that they had participated and
    1 male was indifferent. 11 of those answering
    YES or "did participate" were 25 or under.

Of the 18 persons who felt that they would tell their
    mother about these events only 4 were female.

The third part of this questionnaire involved the
    performance of the following non-performance
    piece by Dick Higgins.

Of the first set to be checked 13 kisses were regist-
    ered, 5 cigarettes and 3 monkeys. One philoso-
    pher choose to answer by drawing-in and check-
    ing a blank blank; and an artist checked all
    (repeating same in second set).

Qualities (second set) assigned to these subjects
    were as follows:
                    kiss
    (female)   (male)
silly   aware
green   deep
laxative   laxative
sexy   musical
                        green
                        fluffypinkish
                        metaphysical
            monkey
(no response)   mercenary
                        metaphysical
                        vaguely yes

A Study, 1963
Carbon copy on onionskin paper
2 pages, 11 × 8 9/16 inches each
Getty Research Institute, Los Angeles

---

notes

"instructions for the use of a new musical instrument"

remove from protective case

place one each of the two matching (from the three) extremeties
of this instrument in each ear. place or rub the third extremety
over any of the following materials, etc. to hear these compositions.

1. place over left breast of any mammal or against a locomotive,
    or a pump, or an air hammer, or a watch to hear music with a
    "beat".

2. rub it over page 77. hindemith's "musical craftmanship" to
    hear harmony.

3. rub it over the first six measures of the shubert "unfinished
    Symphony" to hear melody.

4. have a musican play a composition for another musician, place
    instrument against first musician to hear "music for a musican"

5. (dip)it in)honey to hear "dolce". (quickly "dolce vivace")

6. (rub it in) oil to hear "glissando"

7. place it against a stick of dynamite to hear "fireworks music".

8. hold it under water to hear "water music".

9. place it inside a beehive to hear the "flight of a bumble bee".

10. rub it over the bible to hear religious music.

11. place it in a turkey and cover it with straw to hear *american
    folk music.

12. (tie it to)a monkey's tail and hold a tin cup to hear italian
    folk music.

13. (tie it to) a beer can and thrown off a mountain top to
    hear barvarian folk music.

14. (give it to) some natives in exchange for land and hear english
    folk music.

15. (cut it in)two parts to hear two part conterpoint.

16. (cut it in)three parts and hear a trio.

17. (cut it in)four parts)and tie together with a string to hear
    a string quartet.

Notes: Instructions for the use of a new musical
instrument, c. 1963
Typed ink on paper
2 pages, 10 9/16 × 8 1/4 inches each
Getty Research Institute, Los Angeles

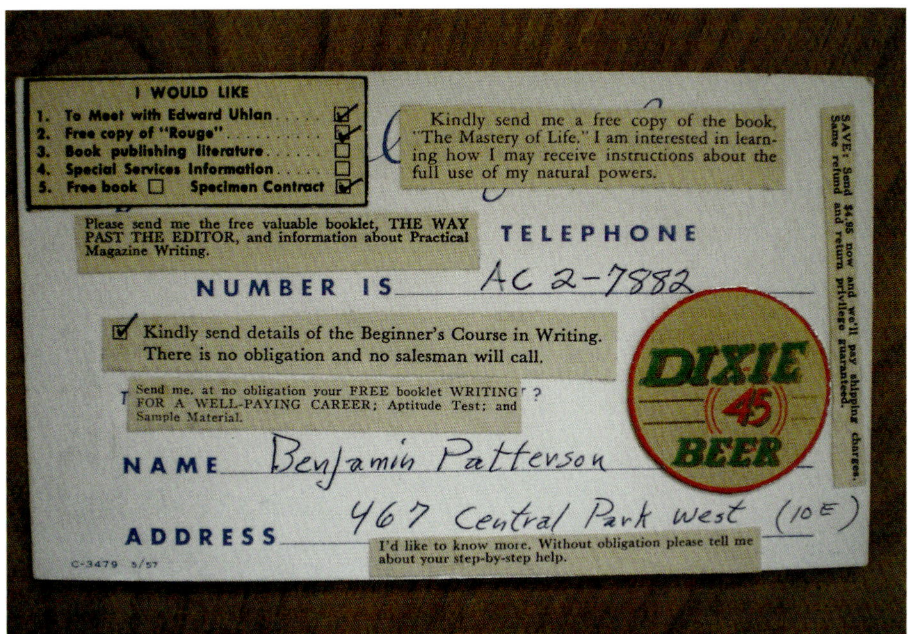

Untitled (Dixie Beer), 1963
Typed ink and collage on index card
3 × 5 inches
Staatsgalerie Stuttgart, Hanns Sohm Archive

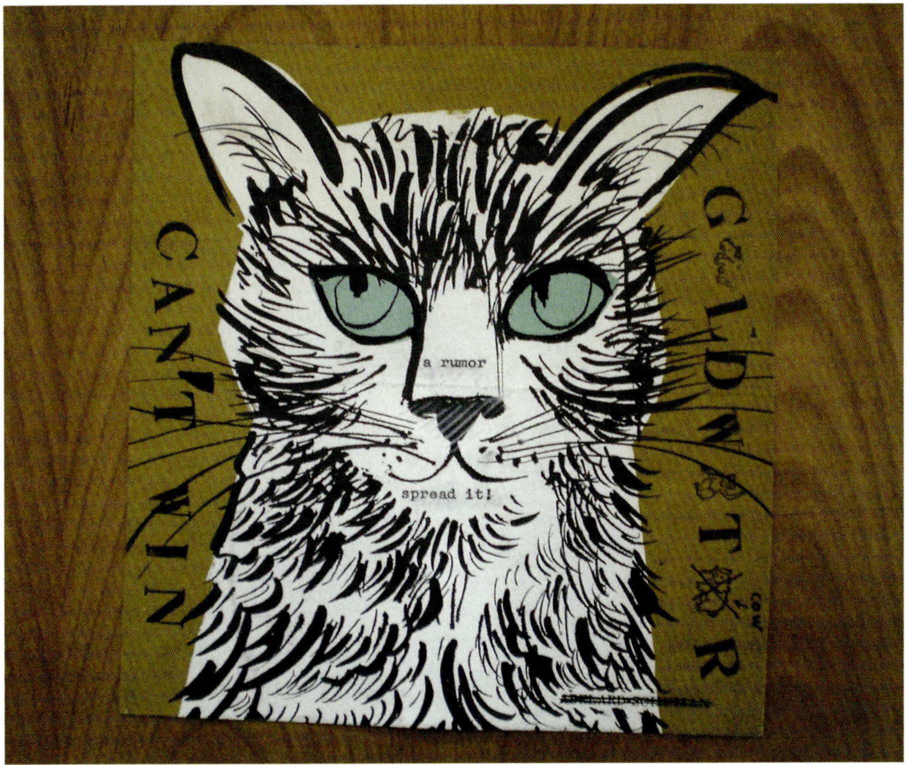

Untitled (Goldwater Can't Win), c. 1963
Typed ink and collage on card stock
7 × 7 inches
Staatsgalerie Stuttgart, Hanns Sohm Archive

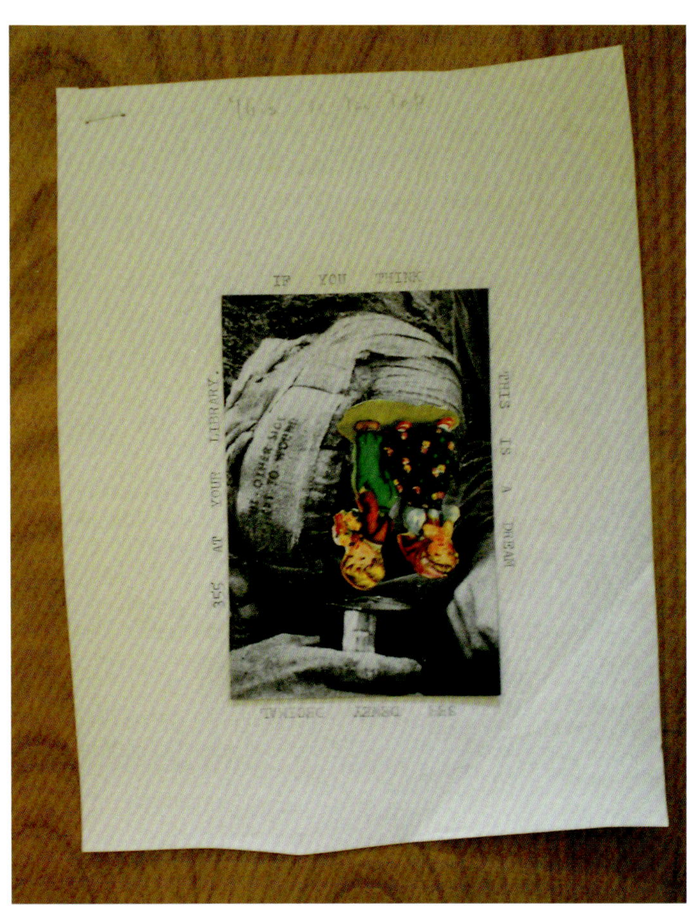

Untitled (If You Think This Is a Dream), c. 1963
Typed ink and collage on paper
7½ × 6 inches
Staatsgalerie Stuttgart, Hanns Sohm Archive

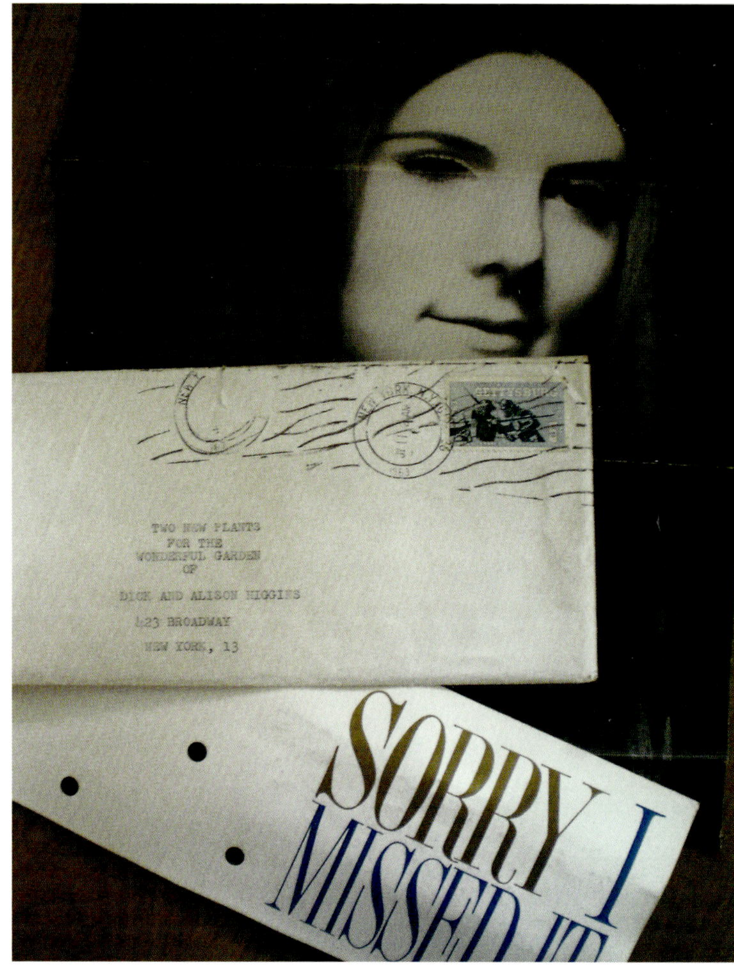

Untitled (Sorry I Missed It), 1963
Paper collage, ink, envelope
2 pages, 11½ × 9 inches each
Envelope: 4⅛ × 9½ inches
Staatsgalerie Stuttgart, Hanns Sohm Archive

Watch Me, c. 1963
Stencil and marker on index card
3 cards, 2¹⁵⁄₁₆ × 4¹⁵⁄₁₆ inches each
Getty Research Institute, Los Angeles

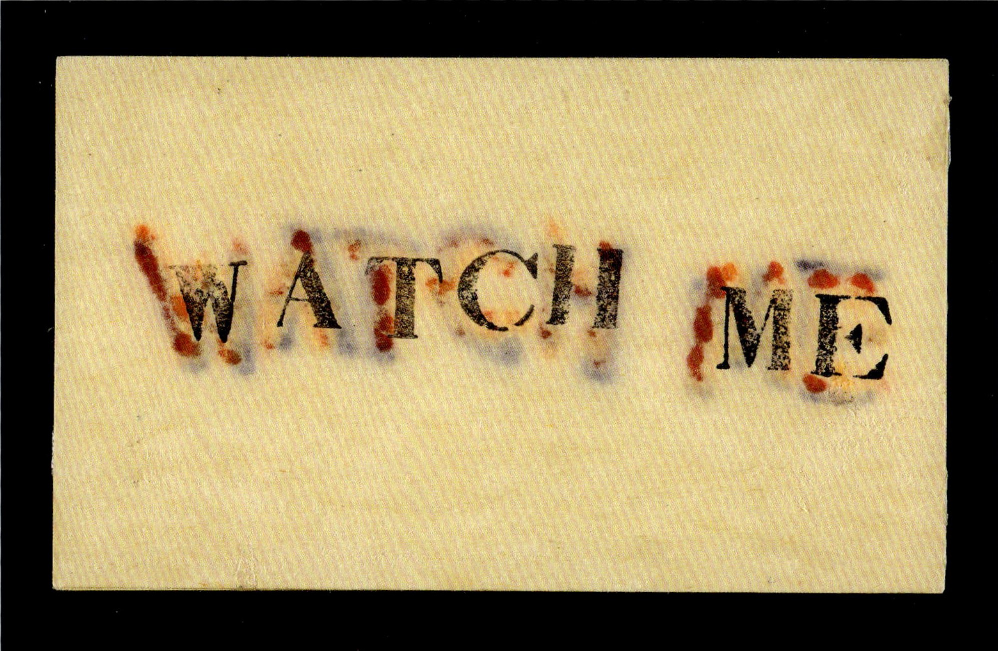

What else is necessary?, 1963–64
Ink on index card, envelope
5 cards, 3 × 4¹⁵⁄₁₆ inches each
Envelope: 3⅝ × 6⁹⁄₁₆ inches
Getty Research Institute, Los Angeles

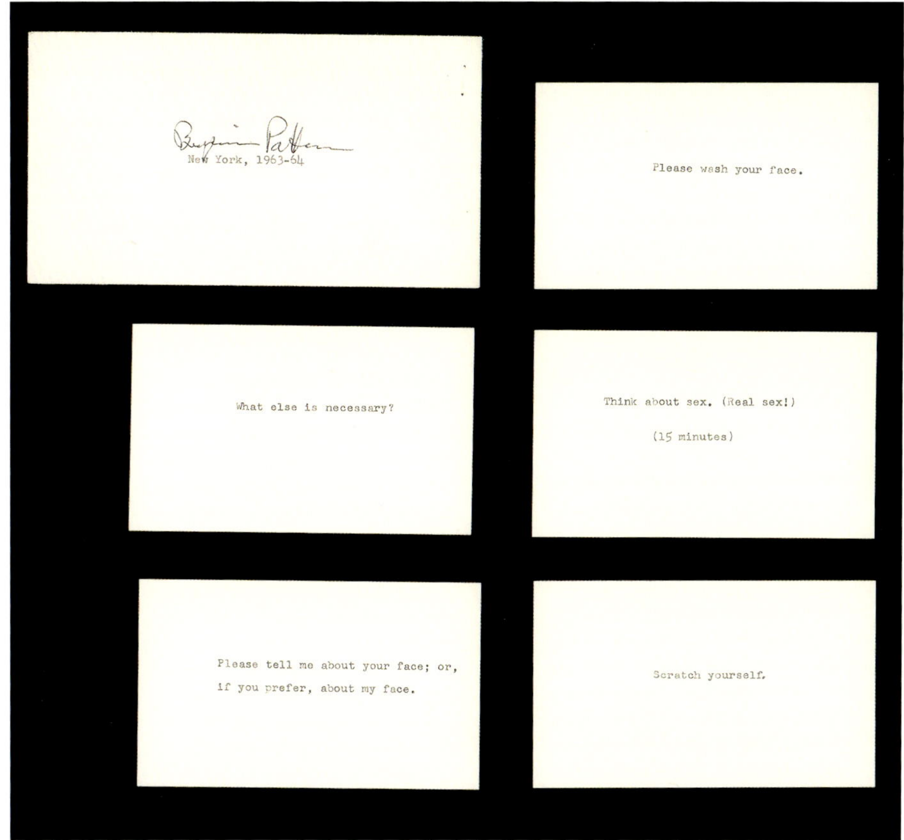

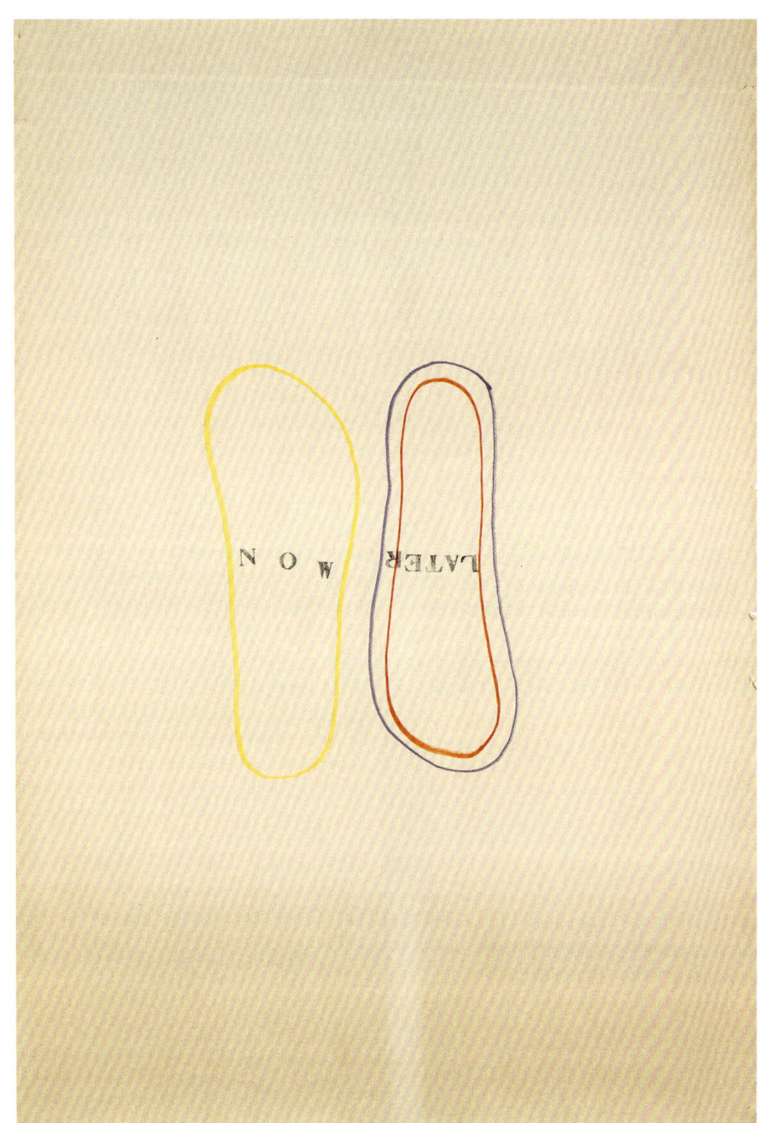

Instruction No. 1 (Now, Later), 1964
Ink and rubber stamp on construction paper
37⅝ × 26¾ inches (frame)
30¹¹⁄₁₆ × 20¼ inches (sheet)
The Museum of Modern Art, New York;
The Gilbert and Lila Silverman Fluxus Collection Gift

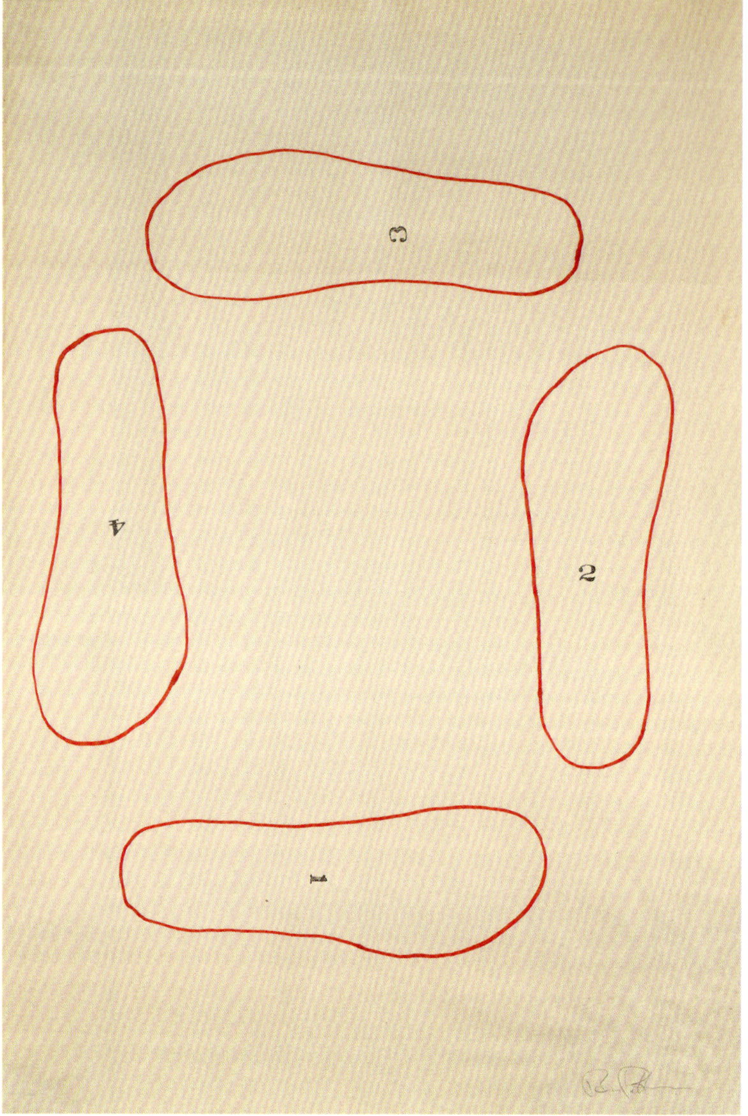

Instruction No. 1 (Steps 1–4), 1964
Ink and rubber stamp on construction paper
37⅝ × 26¾ inches (frame)
30¹¹⁄₁₆ × 20¹⁄₁₆ inches (sheet)
The Museum of Modern Art, New York;
The Gilbert and Lila Silverman Fluxus Collection Gift

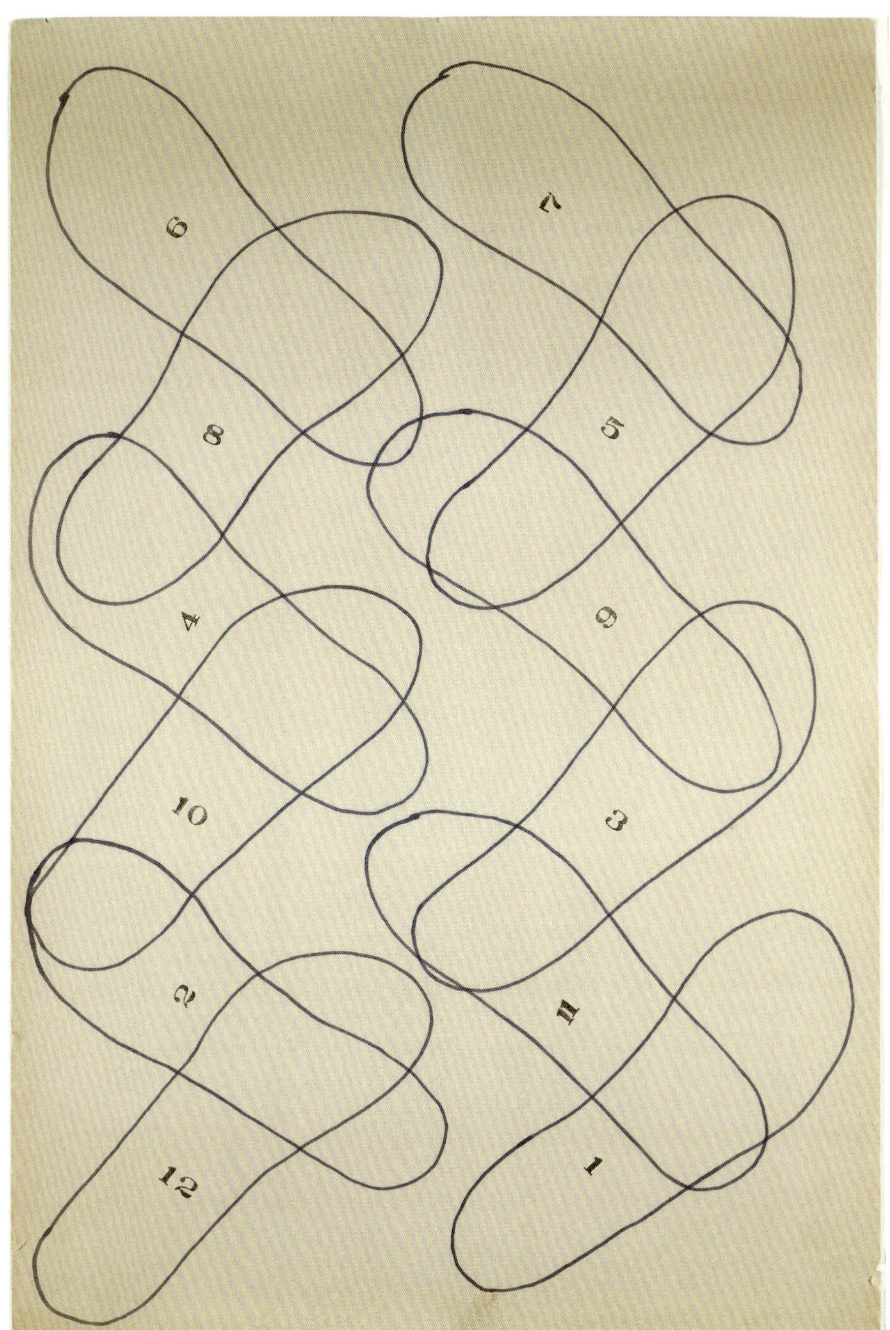

Instruction No. 1 (Steps 1–12), 1964
Ink and rubber stamp on construction paper
37⅝ × 26¾ inches (frame)
30¹¹⁄₁₆ × 20¹⁄₁₆ inches (sheet)
The Museum of Modern Art, New York;
The Gilbert and Lila Silverman Fluxus Collection Gift

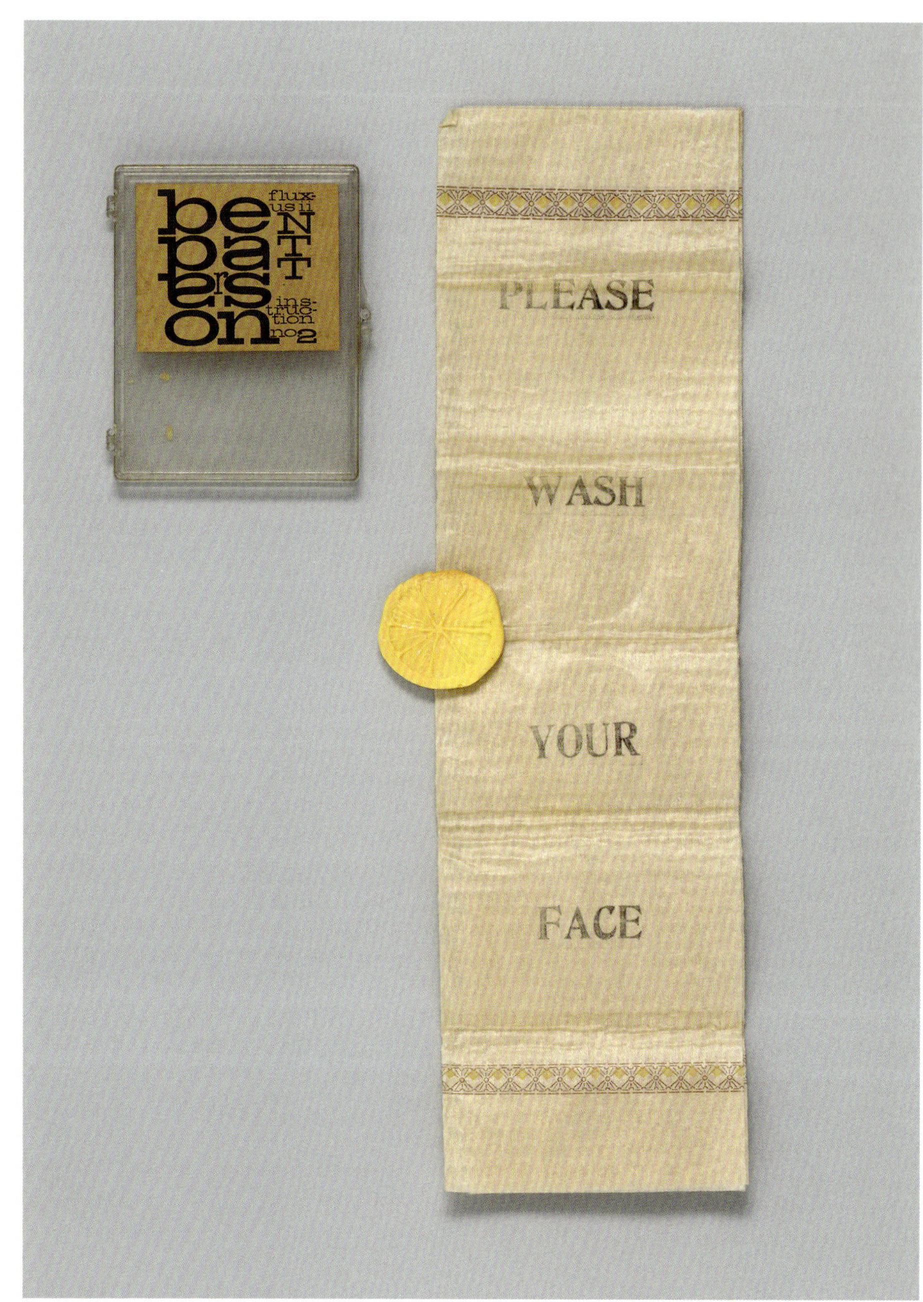

Instruction No. 2 (Please Wash Your Face), 1964
Fluxus Edition box
Plastic box, guest soap, paper hand towel with stamped ink
Box: ½ × 3¹⁵⁄₁₆ × 4¹¹⁄₁₆ inches
Unfolded towel: 16¾ × 4⁷⁄₁₆ inches
Soap: ¼ × 1¹³⁄₁₆ inches
The Museum of Modern Art, New York;
The Gilbert and Lila Silverman Fluxus Collection Gift

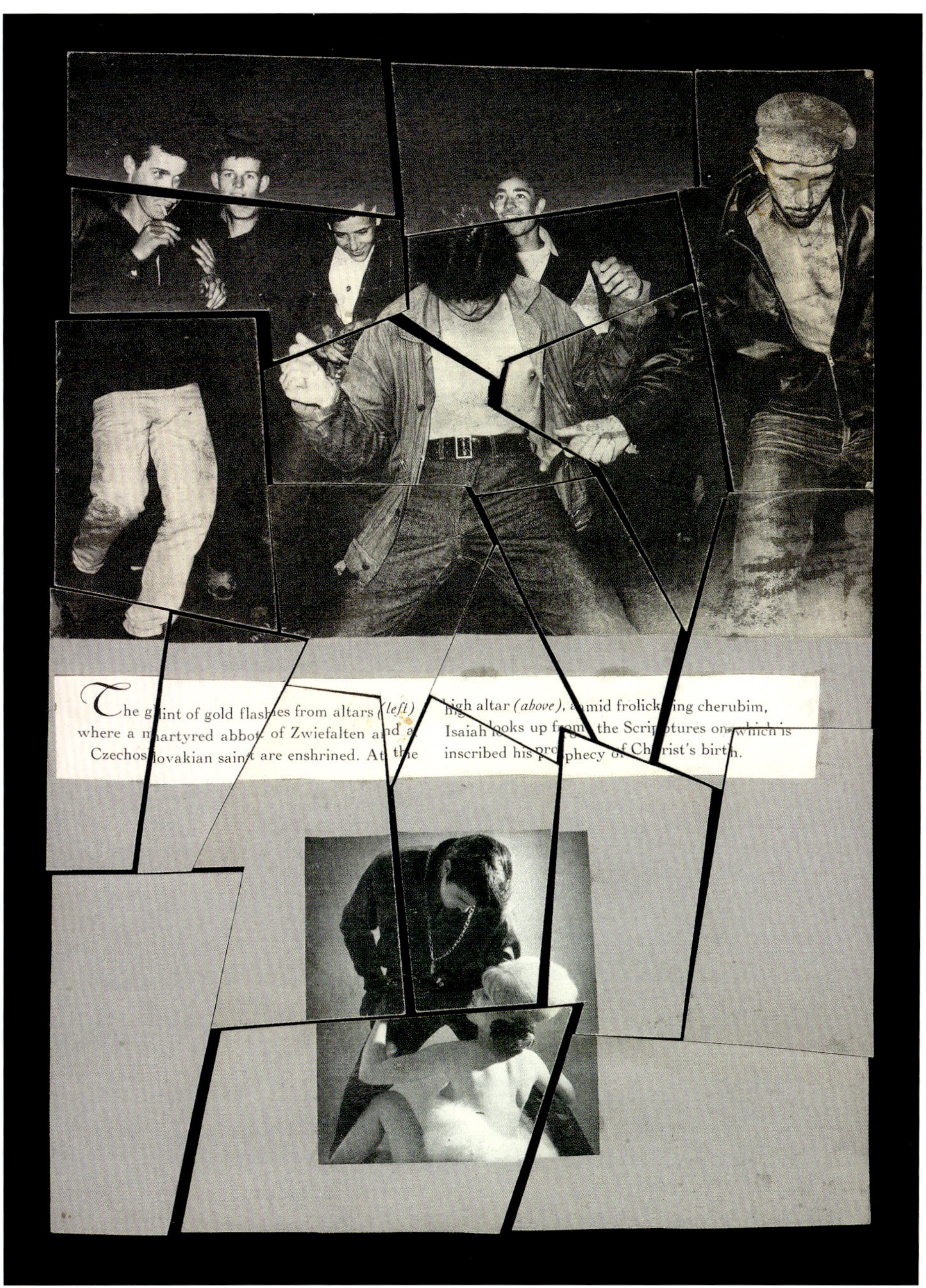

Puzzle-Poem, 1964
Collage on board, plastic bag
Bag: 14¹¹⁄₁₆ × 9⅞ inches
Puzzle-poem: 14⁹⁄₁₆ × 10¹⁄₁₆ inches
Getty Research Institute, Los Angeles

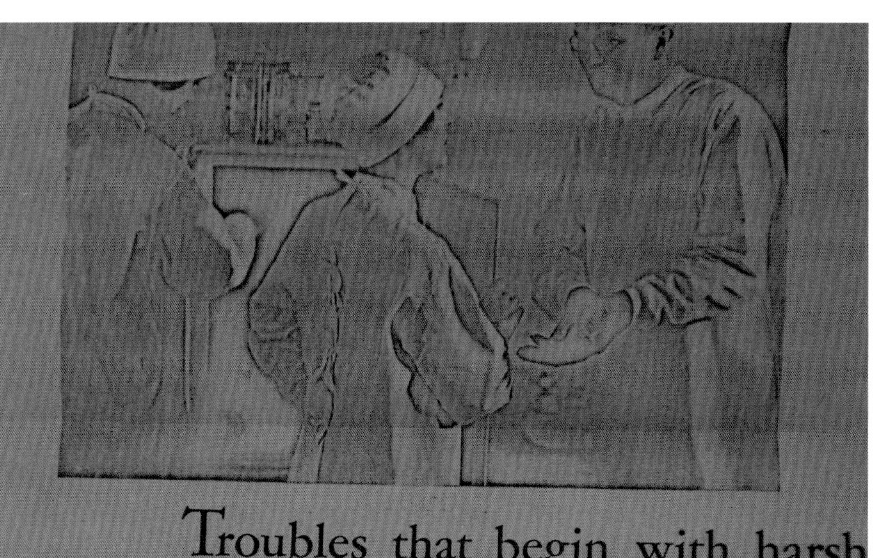
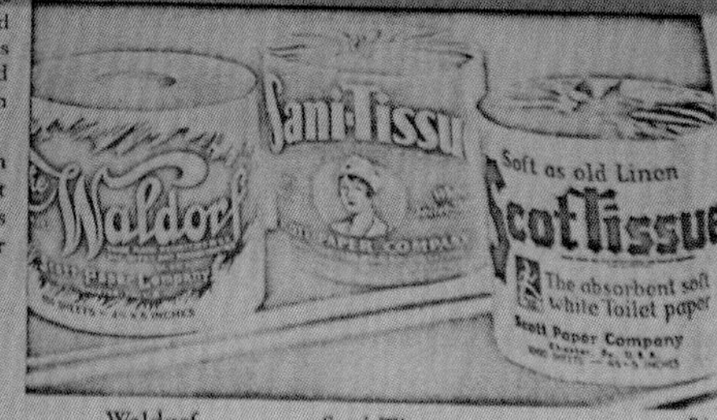

Untitled (Scott Tissue), c. 1964
Photocopy paper collage
9½ × 14 inches
Staatsgalerie Stuttgart, Hanns Sohm Archive

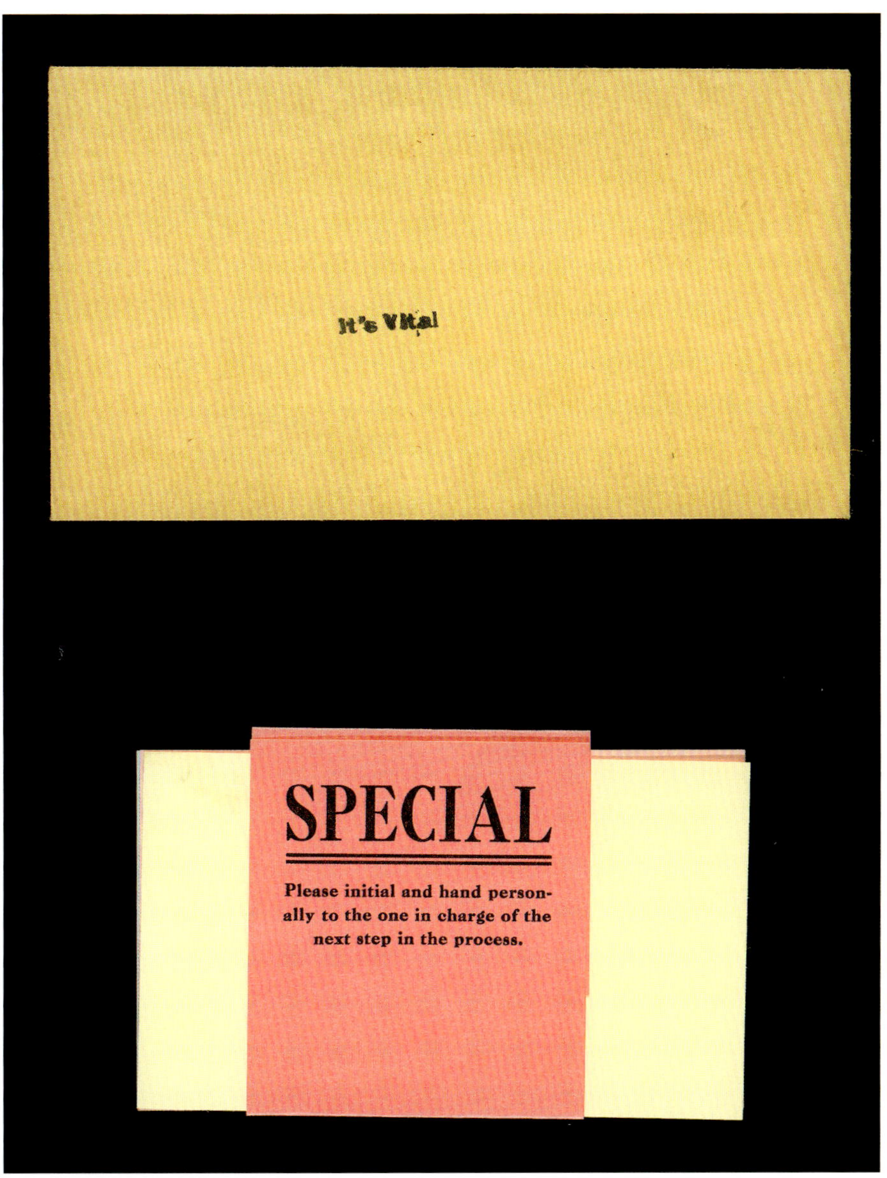

It's Vital, 1965
Ink on index card, envelope
3 cards, 2¹⁵⁄₁₆ × 4⅞ inches each
Wrapper: 3⅛ × 2¾ inches
Envelope: 3¾ × 6½ inches
Getty Research Institute, Los Angeles

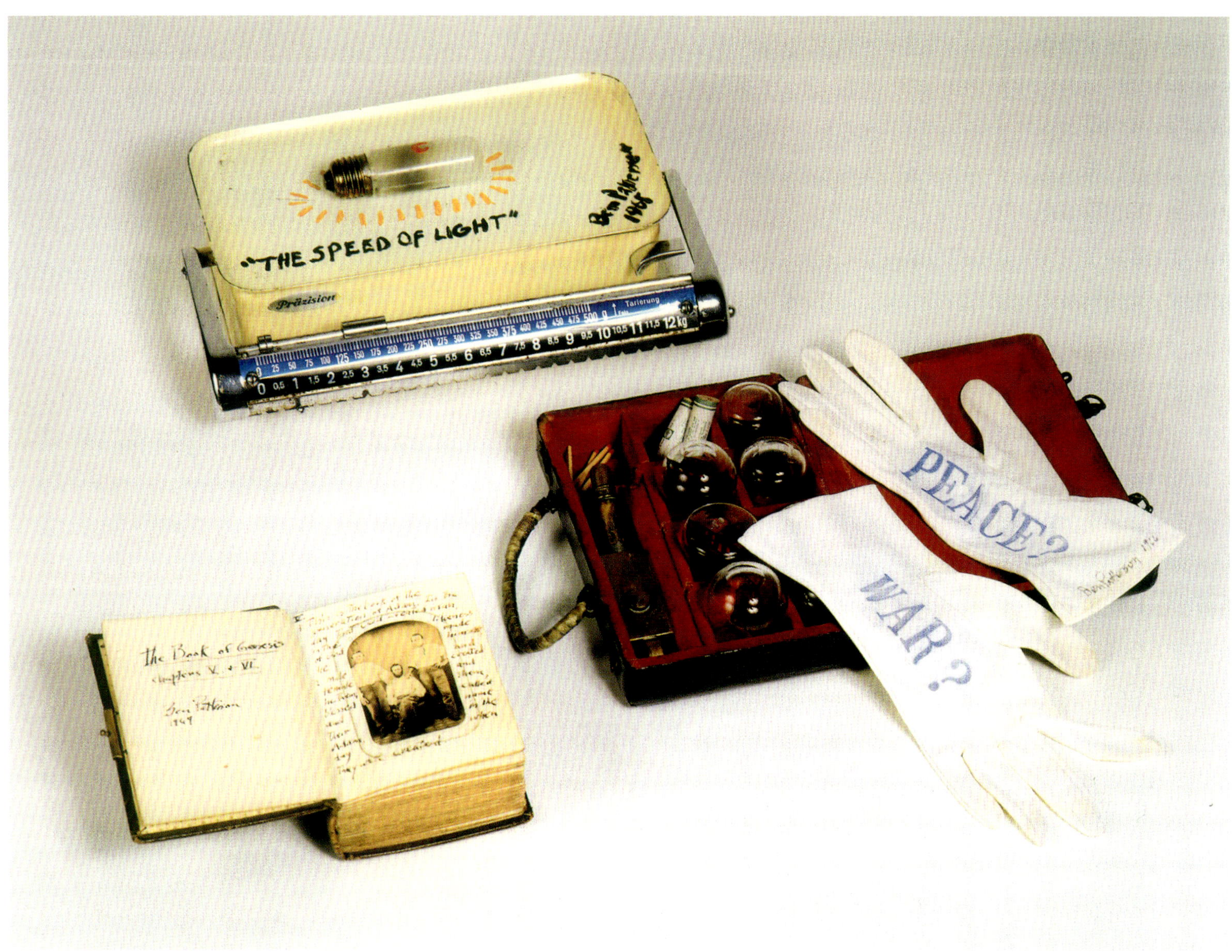

Speed of Light, 1965
Metal scale, marker, bulb, mixed media
12½ × 7½ × 3¼ inches
Collection Caterina Gualco, Genoa, Italy

The Book of Genesis, 1969
Leather antique photo book, photographs, ink
6 × 4½ × 2½ inches
Collection Enzo Gazzerro, Genoa, Italy

Valigetta, 1966
Box, antique glass bulbs, cut photo negatives, gloves, ink
6 × 8 × 3½ inches
Collection Caterina Gualco, Genoa, Italy

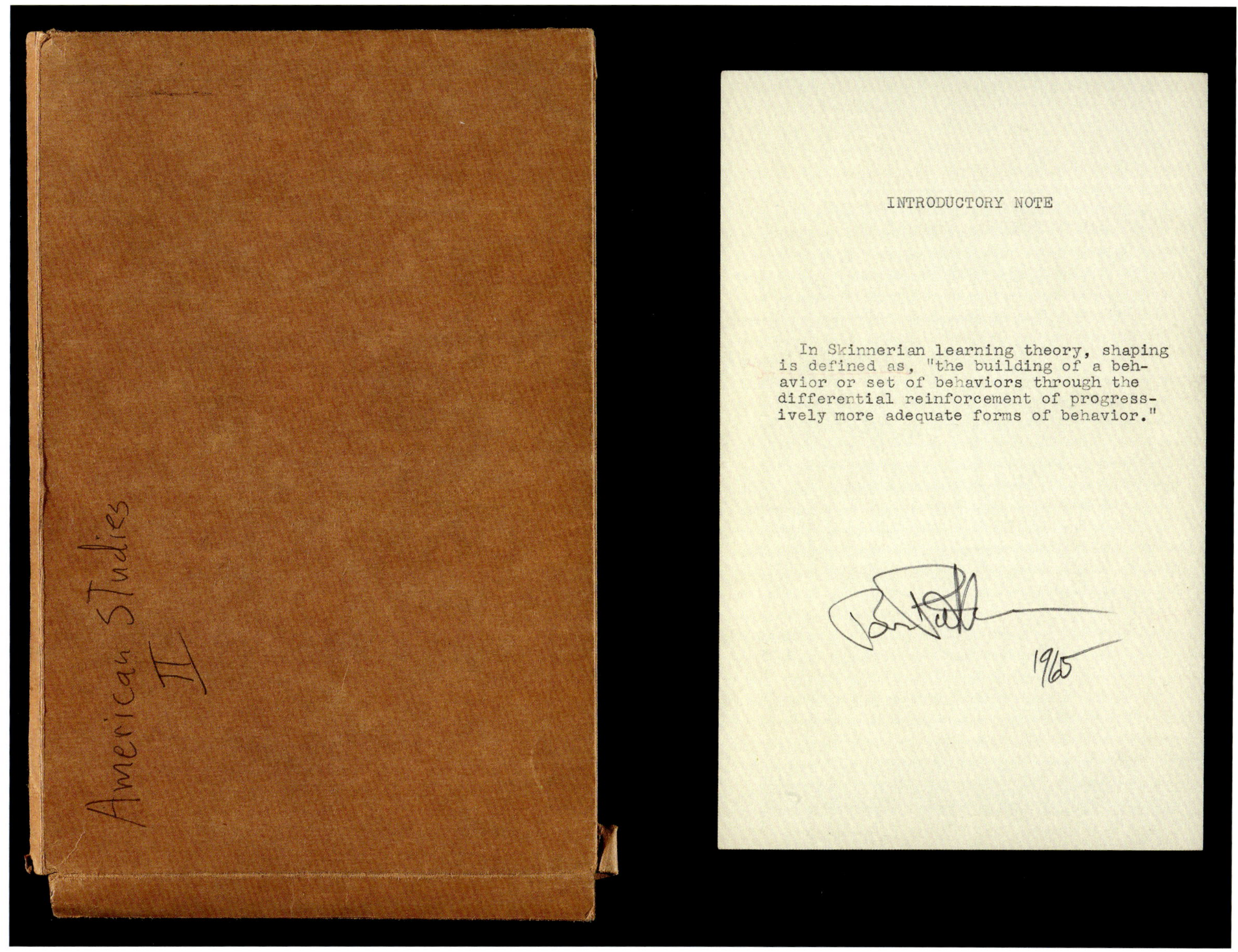

*Untitled (Introductory Note . . . In Skinnerian
Learning Theory)*, 1965
Ink and colored pencil on index card, envelope
6 cards, 8 × 5 inches each
Envelope: 5¹¹⁄₁₆ × 8⅜⁄₁₆ × 1¹⁄₁₆ inches
Getty Research Institute, Los Angeles

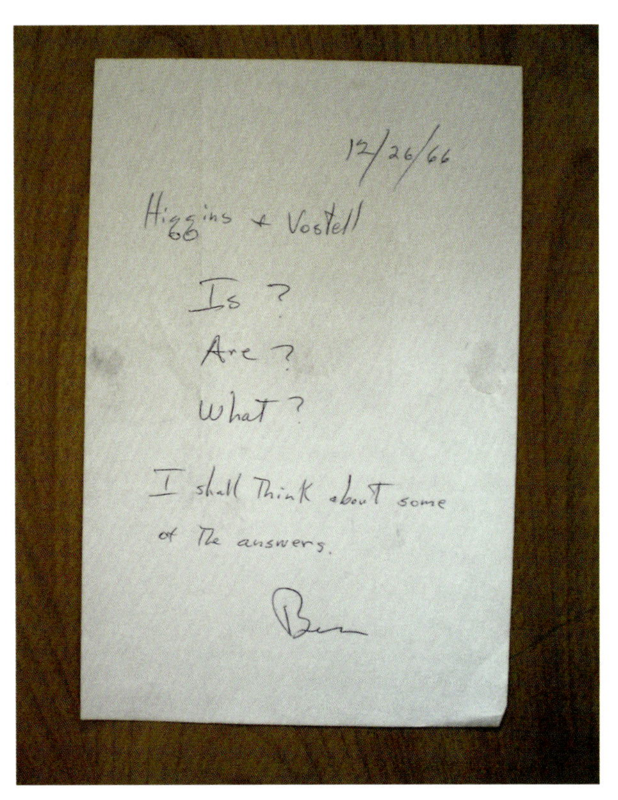

Untitled (Is Are What), 1966
Ink on paper
8 × 5 inches
Staatsgalerie Stuttgart, Hanns Sohm Archive

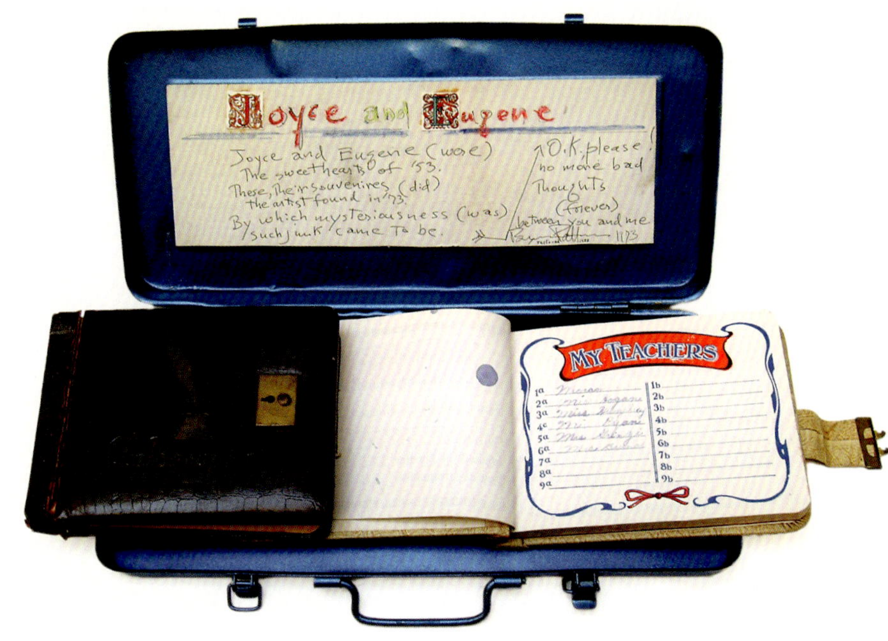

Joyce and Eugene, 1973
Aluminum box, found autograph books,
paper, ink
5½ × 12 × 2½ inches
Collection Marcel and David Fleiss,
Galerie 1900–2000, Paris

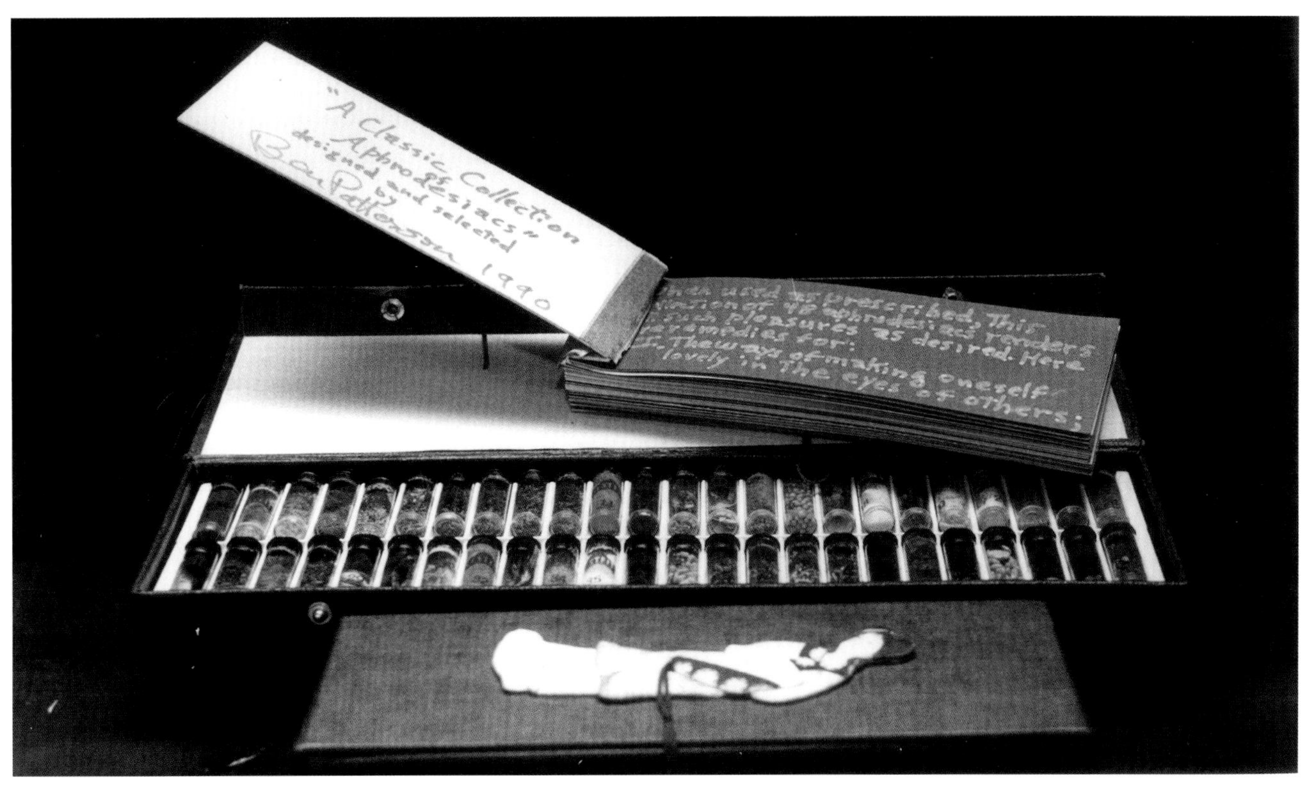

Aphrodisiacs, 1990
Cloth boxes, accordion book with text, bottles
Box 1: 13 × 3½ × 1 inches
Box 2: 8¾ × 3 × 2 inches
Collection Caterina Gualco, Genoa, Italy

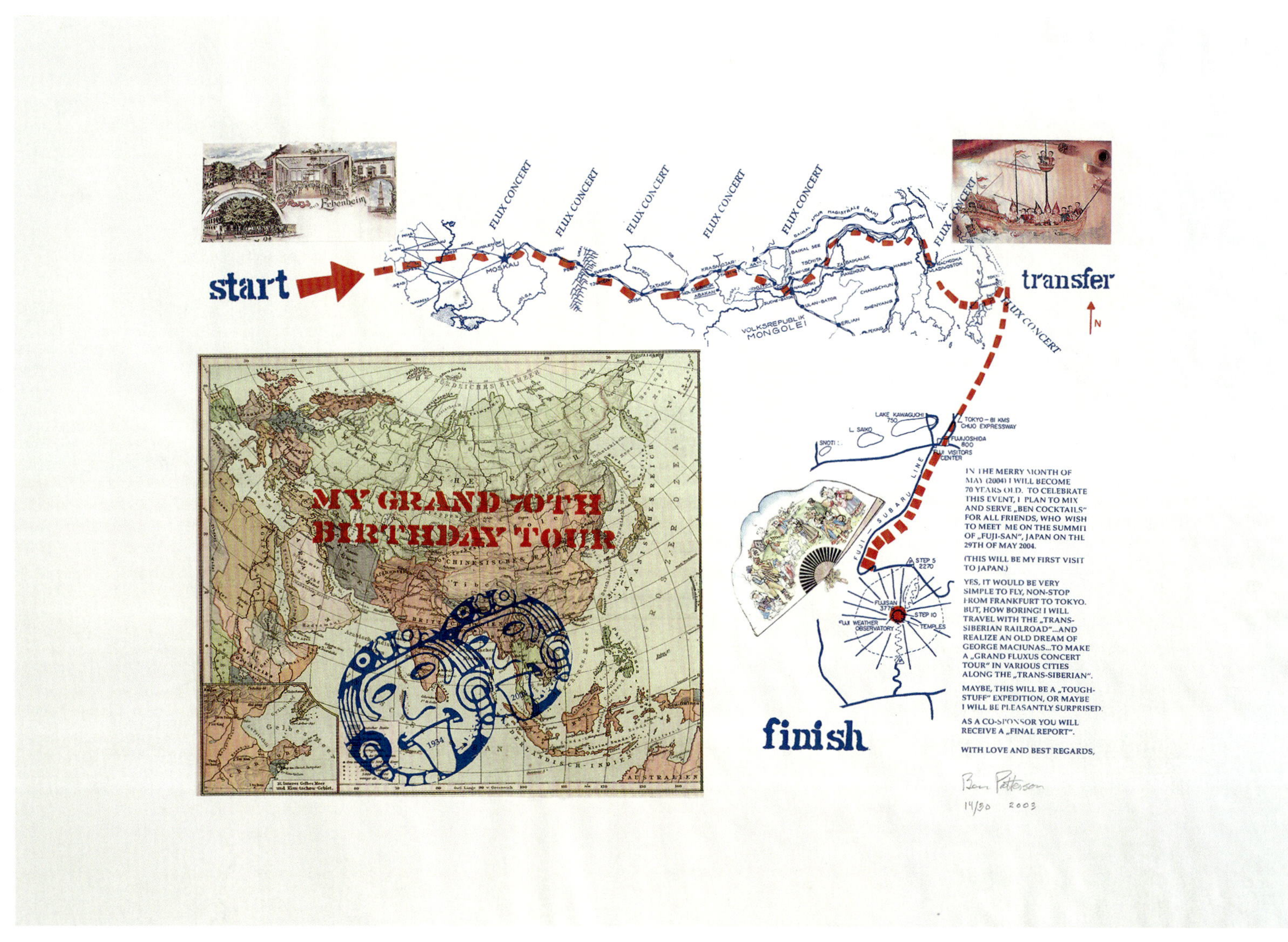

My Grand 70th Birthday Tour, 2003
Ink on paper, plastic, mixed media
5 × 14 inches
Courtesy the artist

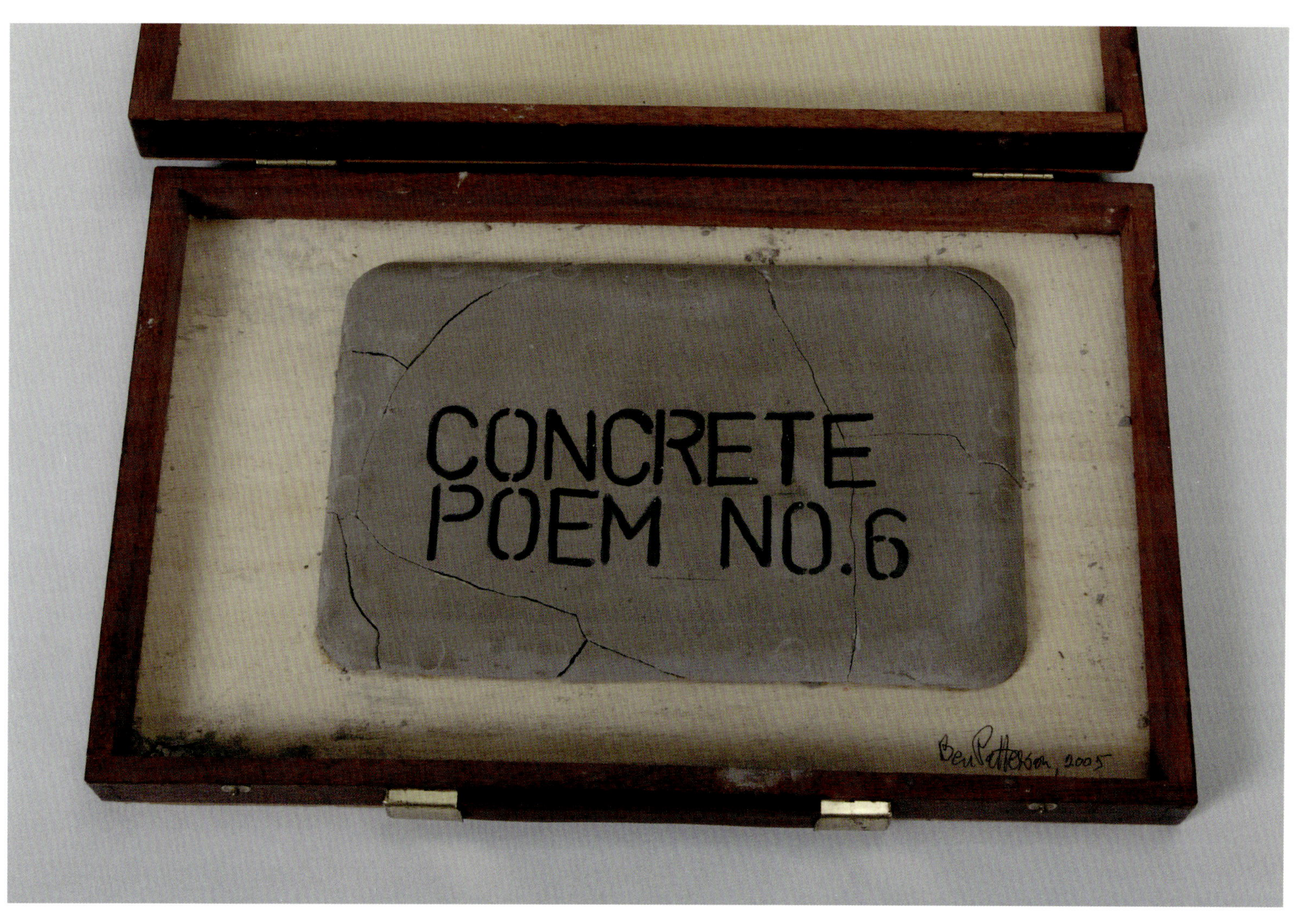

Concrete Poem No. 6, 2005
Wooden box, concrete, marker,
violin fragment, mixed media
10 × 15½ × 4 inches
Courtesy the artist

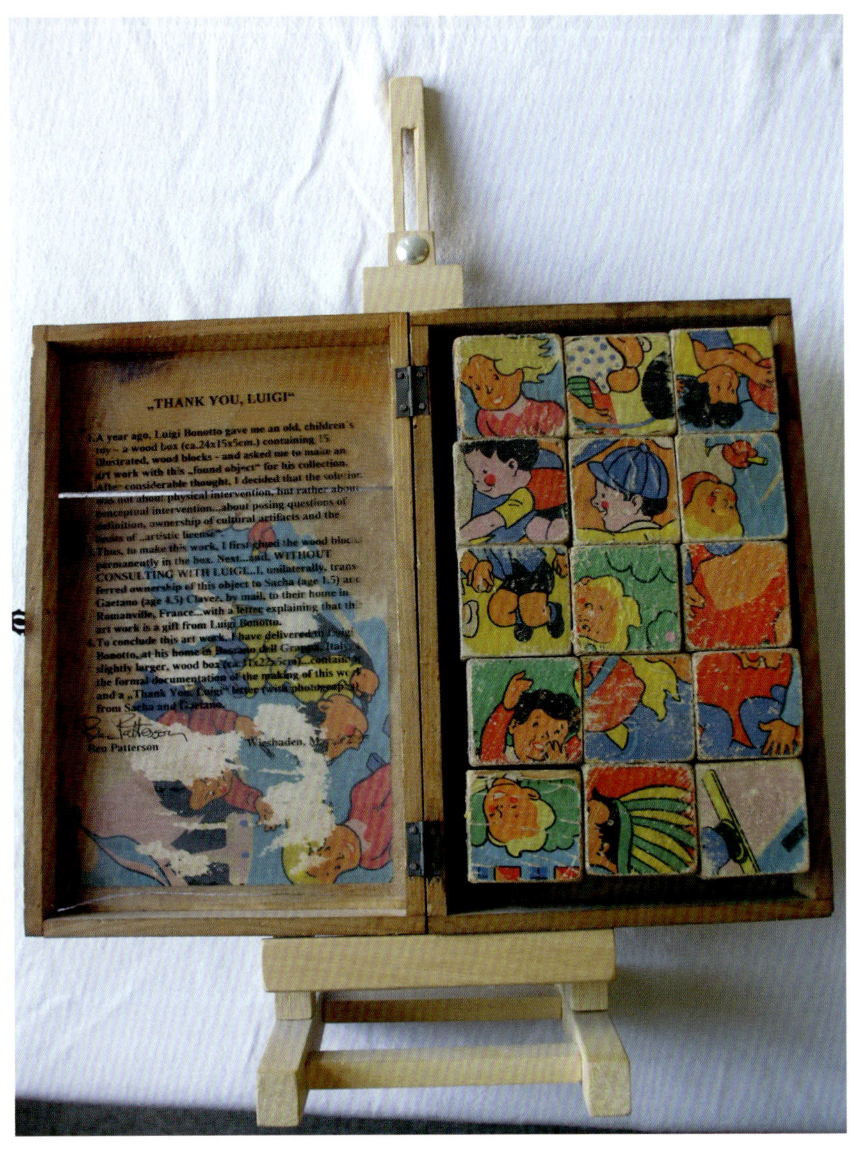

Thank you, Luigi, 2005
Wooden box, vintage children's blocks, easel, mixed media
Book: 6 × 9½ × 2 inches
Easel: 17 × 5½ inches
Collection Bertrand Clavez, Paris

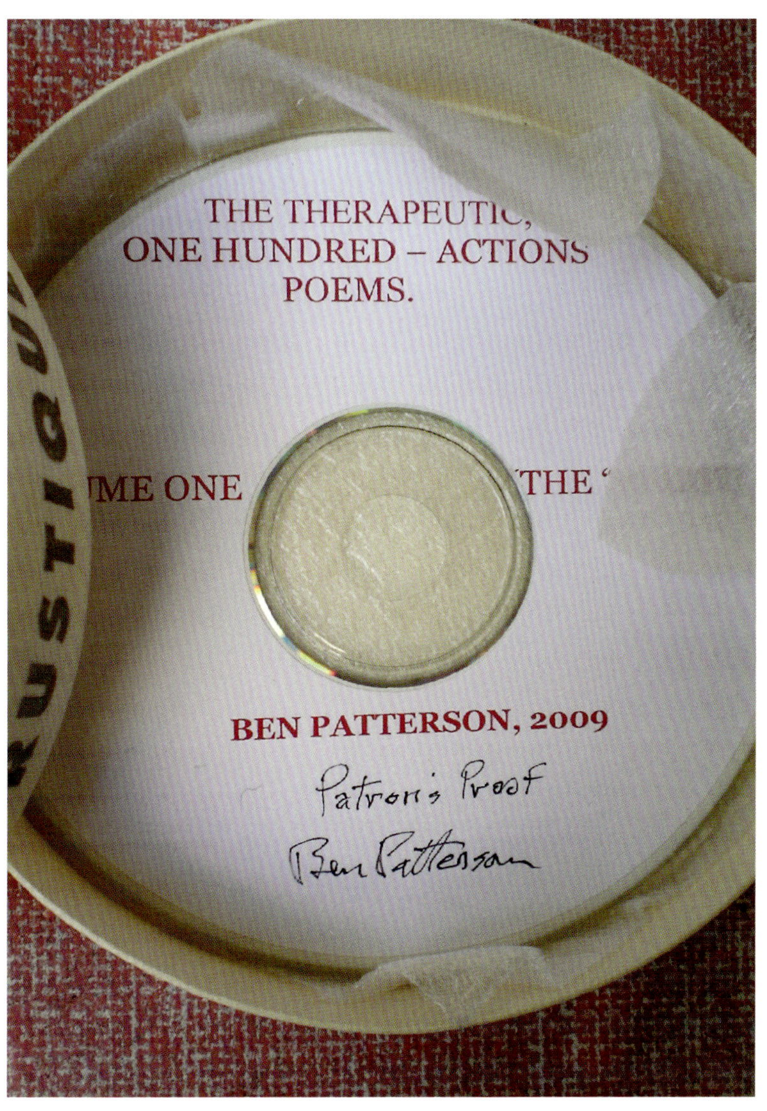

The Therapeutic: One Hundred Actions Poems, Volume A, 2009
Collage and ink on paper
28 pages, 11⅝ × 8¼ inches each
Courtesy the artist

Necessary Objects:
Paintings, Sculpture, and Installations

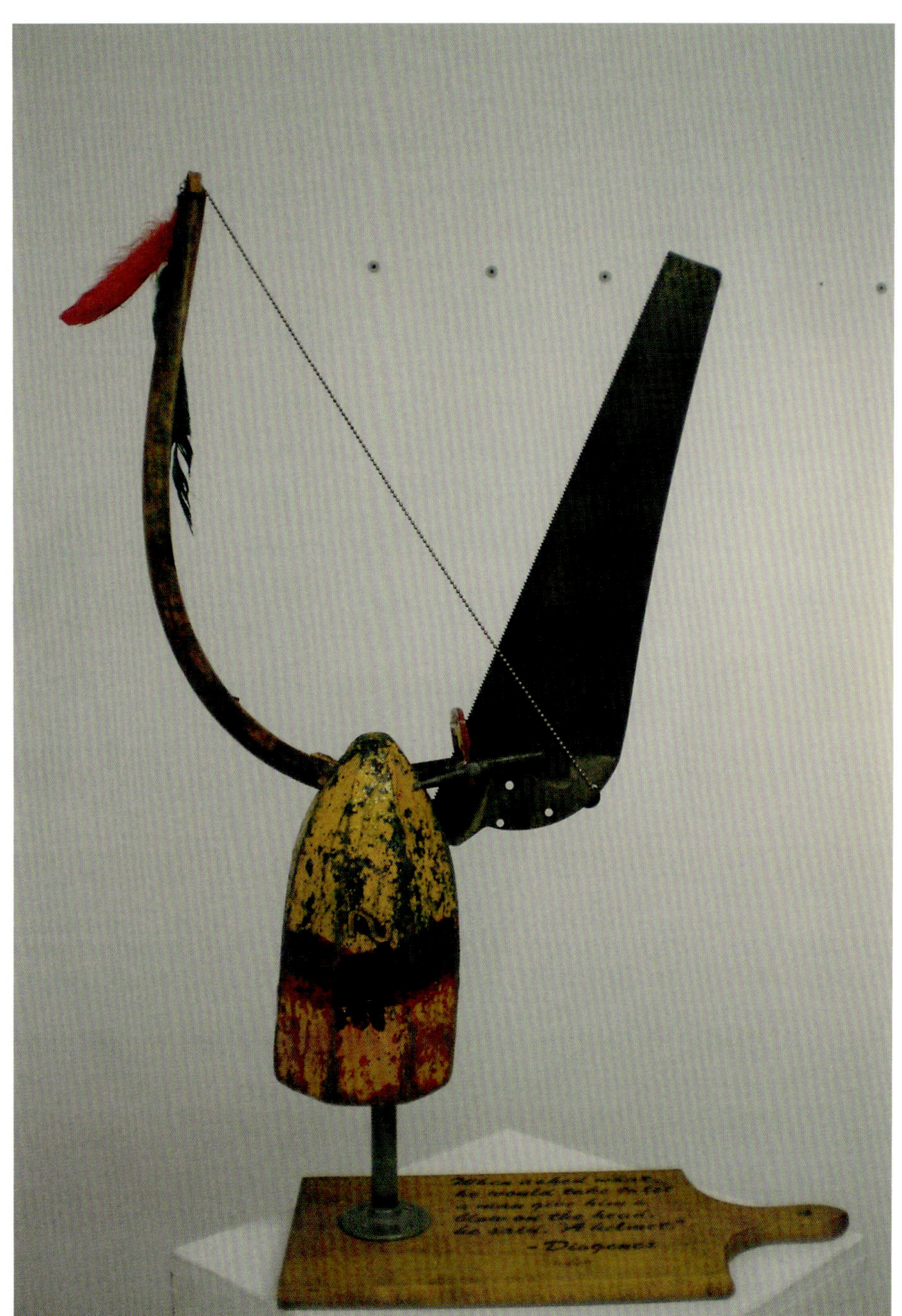

Helmut, 1975
Buoy, bread board, handsaw, mixed media
32⅜ × 18 × 5⅞ inches
Courtesy Galerie Schüppenhauer, Cologne

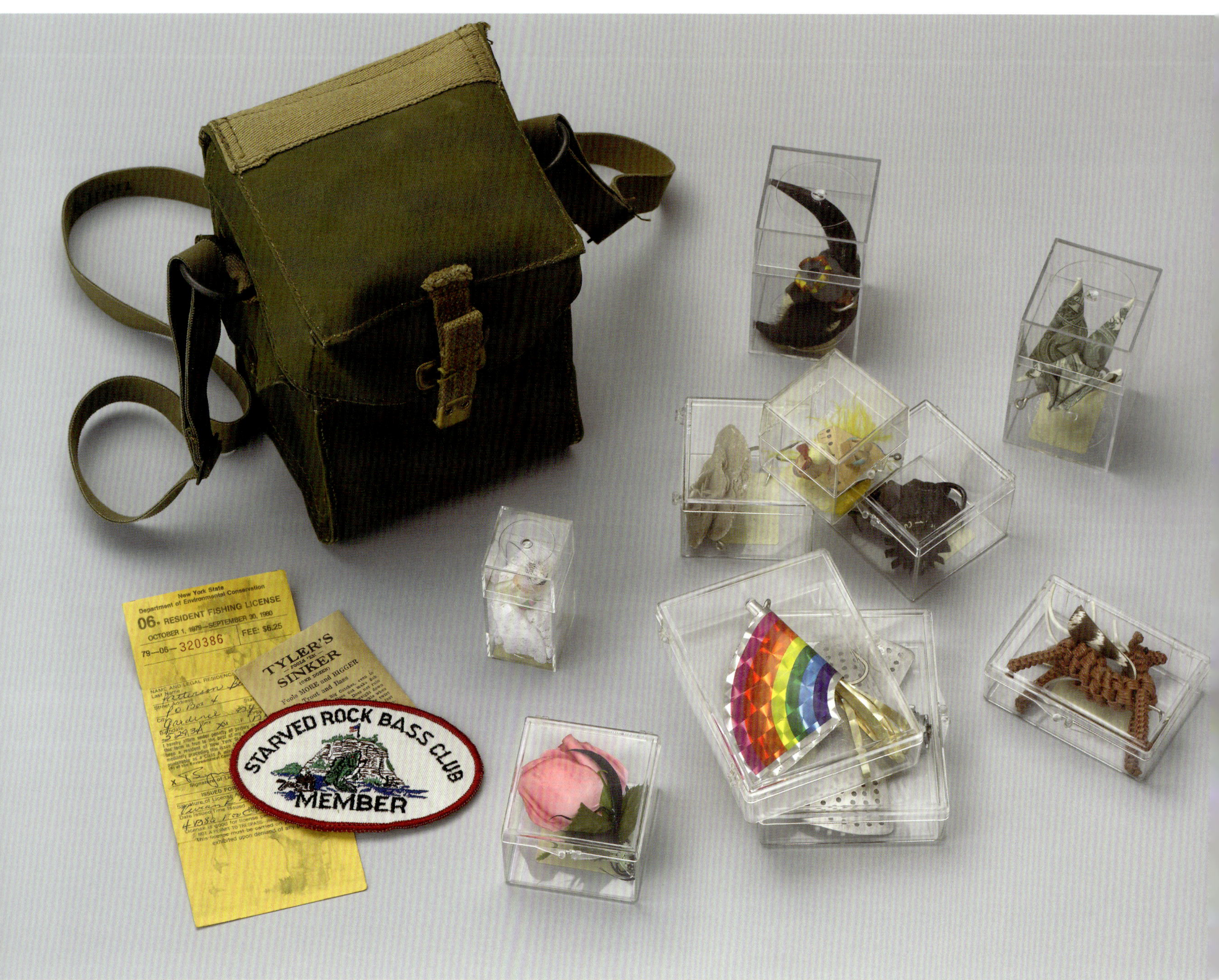
New York State
Department of Environmental Conservation
06. RESIDENT FISHING LICENSE
OCTOBER 1, 1979—SEPTEMBER 30, 1980 | FEE: $6.25
79—06— 320386
TYLER'S
SINKER
Pools MORE and BIGGER
Trout and Bass
STARVED ROCK BASS CLUB
MEMBER

Trout Bag, 1981
Canvas satchel, metal sinkers, fishing license,
10 altered fishing lures in plastic boxes
Canvas satchel: 9¹⁄₁₆ × 7⅞ × 6½ inches
10 plastic boxes, 4³⁄₁₆ × 2¼ × 2¼ inches each
Watt's Pachyderm lure: 2⁹⁄₁₆ × 2¹⁵⁄₁₆ × 4⁵⁄₁₆ inches
Green Caddis lure: 3⅜ × 2⅝ × 3⅛ inches
Brown Stonefly lure: 1¼ × 1⁹⁄₁₆ × 2¹³⁄₁₆ inches
Yellow Paumgartner lure: 1¼ × 2½ × 2¾ inches
Deerfly lure: 2½ × 2⁷⁄₁₆ × 3⁹⁄₁₆ inches
June Nymph lure: 3¹⁵⁄₁₆ × 1⅞ × 5⅛ inches
Pink Ghost lure: 1¾ × 2⅝ × 3 inches
Royal Coachmen lure: 1⁷⁄₁₆ × 3¹⁄₁₆ × 2⁷⁄₁₆ inches
Wooly Bomber lure: 1⁵⁄₁₆ × 4⁷⁄₁₆ × 2¹¹⁄₁₆ inches
Rainbow Hopper lure: ⅜ × 3⁷⁄₁₆ × 4¹¹⁄₁₆ inches
The Museum of Modern Art, New York;
The Gilbert and Lila Silverman Fluxus Collection Gift

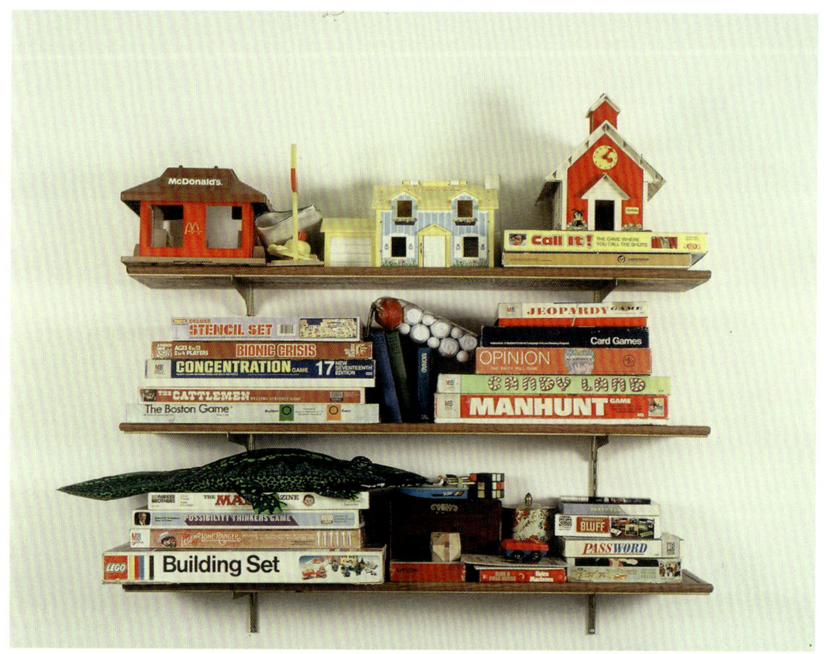

Candyland, 1988
Board games, toys, mixed media on
wooden shelves, brackets
40 × 36 × 14 inches
Courtesy the artist

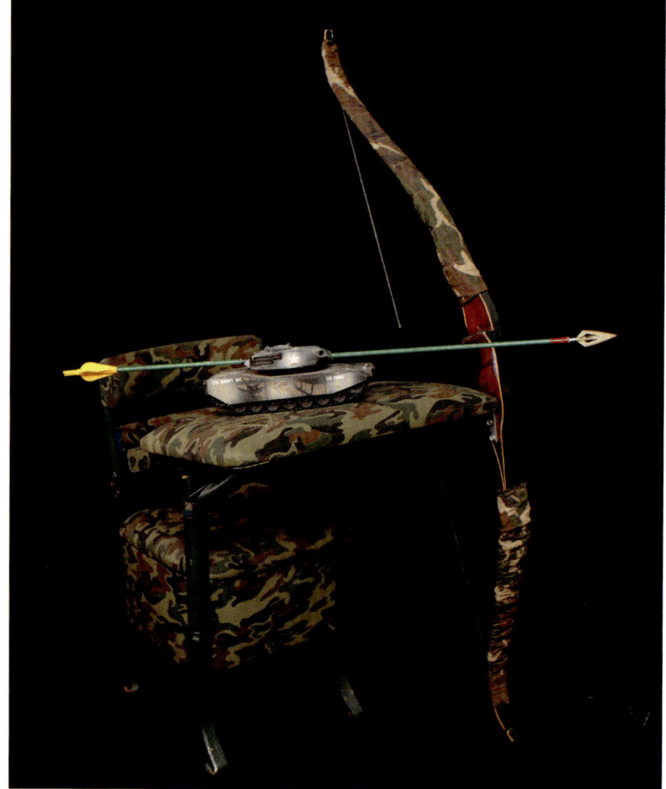

Hell on Wheels, 1988
Wooden desk, plastic, cloth, steel
36 × 40 × 24 inches
Collection Heinrich Riskin, Bad Rothenfelde,
Germany

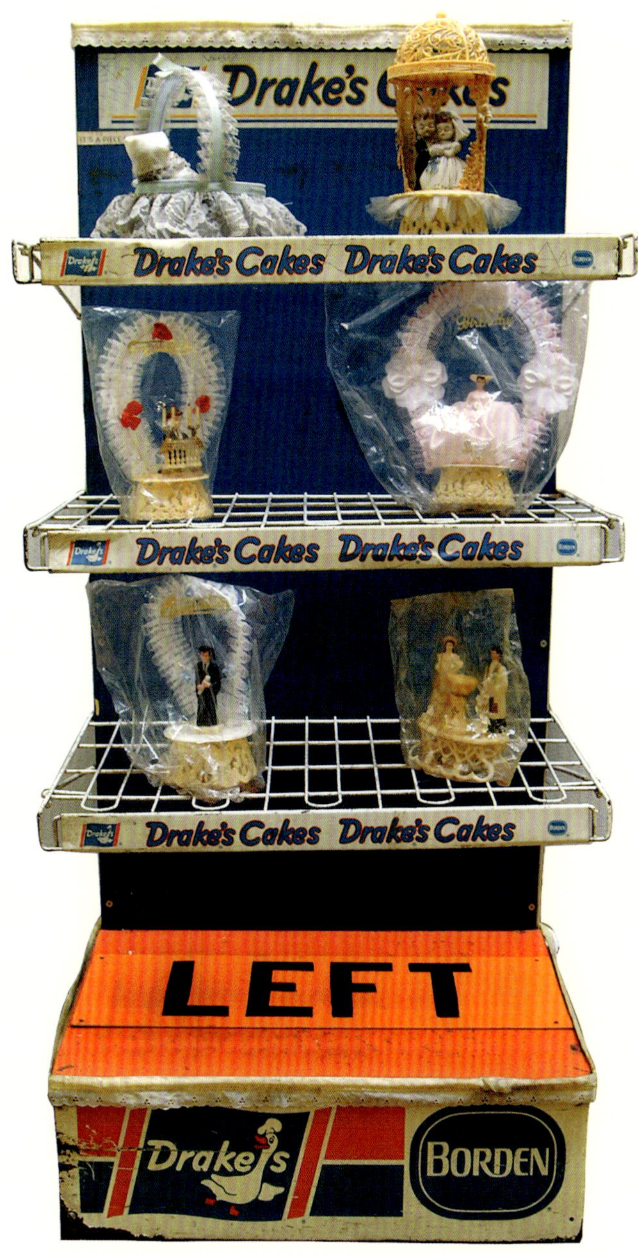

It's a Nice Piece of Cake, 1988
Metal bakery display rack, traffic sign, decorative cake toppers
55¼ × 24½ × 16¾ inches overall
Collection Marcel and David Fleiss, Galerie 1900–2000, Paris

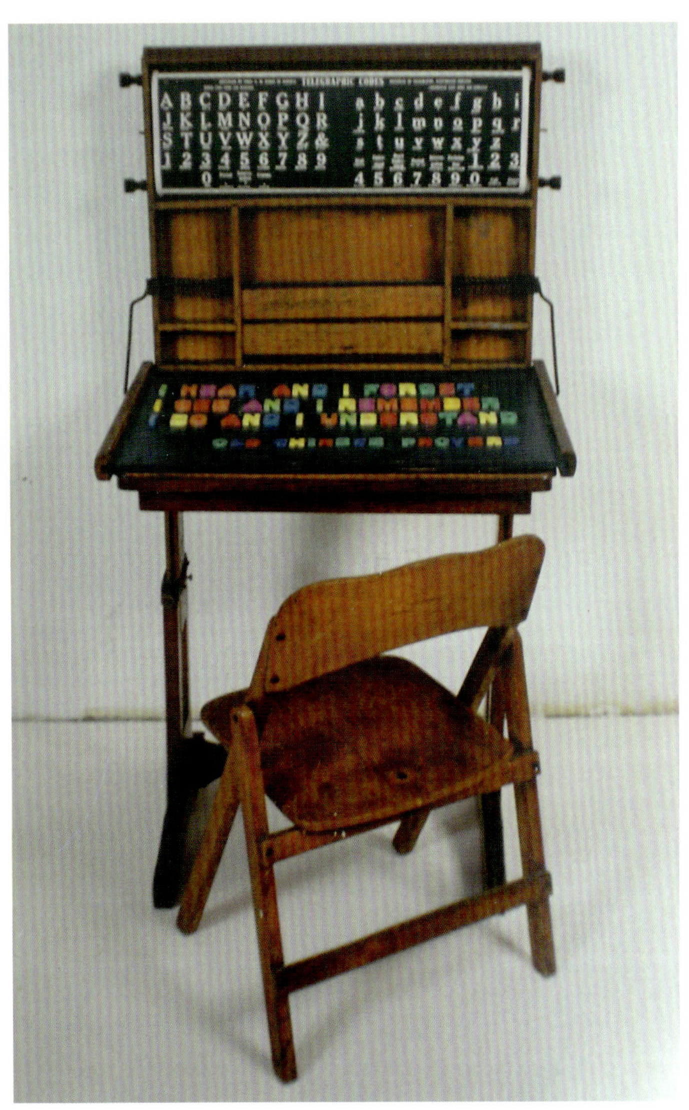

Old Chinese Proverb, 1988
Antique Chautauqua industrial art desk on stand,
mixed media
34 × 23 × 3 inches
Collection Klaus Fehlemann, Dortmund, Germany

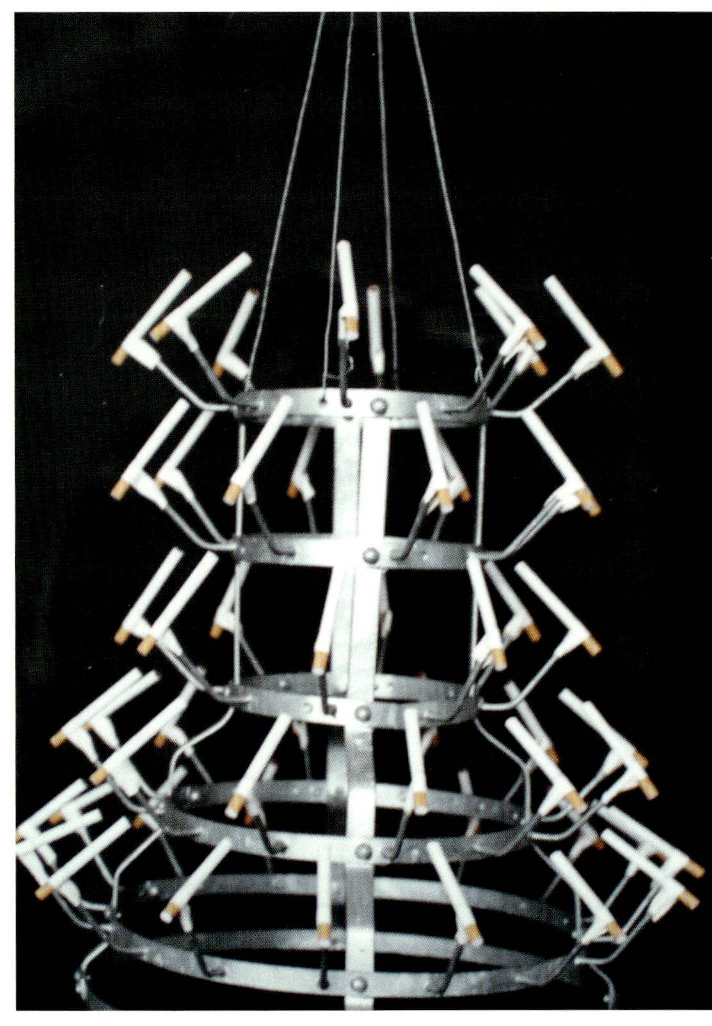

Smoker's Rights, 1988
Antique bottle rack, tape, cigarettes
27½ × 16 × 16 inches
Courtesy the artist

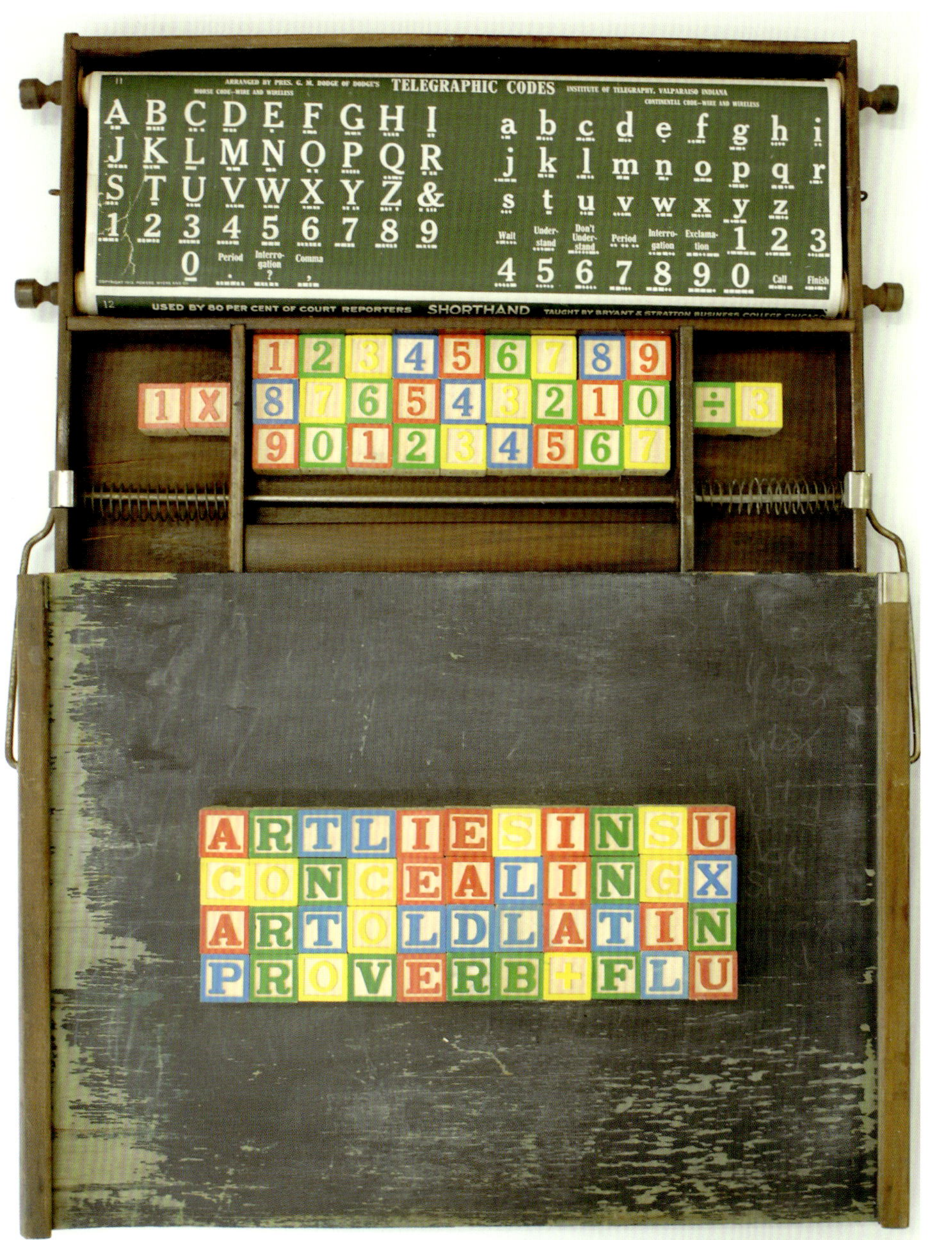

Old Latin Proverb, 1988
Antique Chautauqua industrial art desk, mixed media
34 × 23 × 3 inches
Courtesy the artist and Galerie Schüppenhauer, Cologne

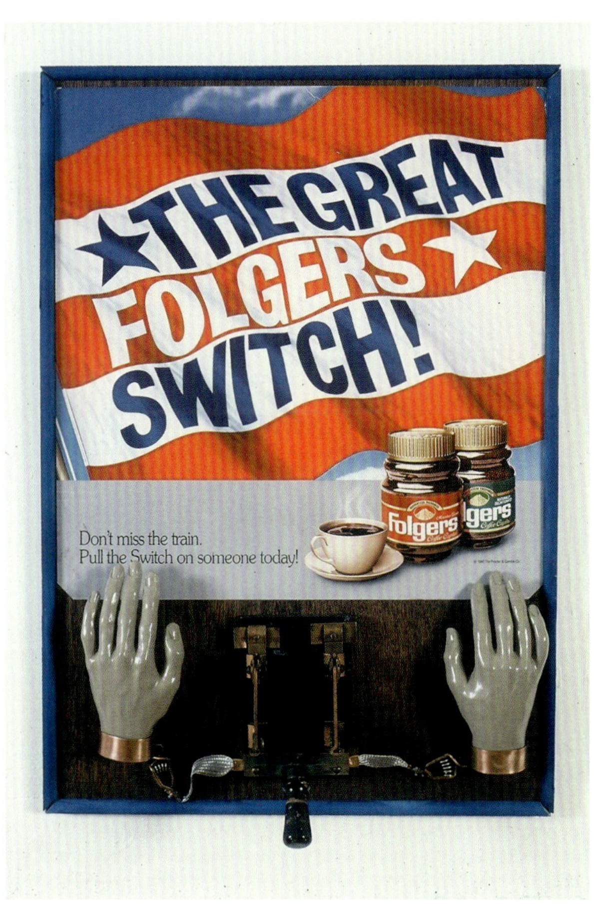

The Great Switch, 1990
Poster mounted on plywood, mixed media
26 × 24 × 2 inches
Collection Enzo Cattelani, Modena, Italy

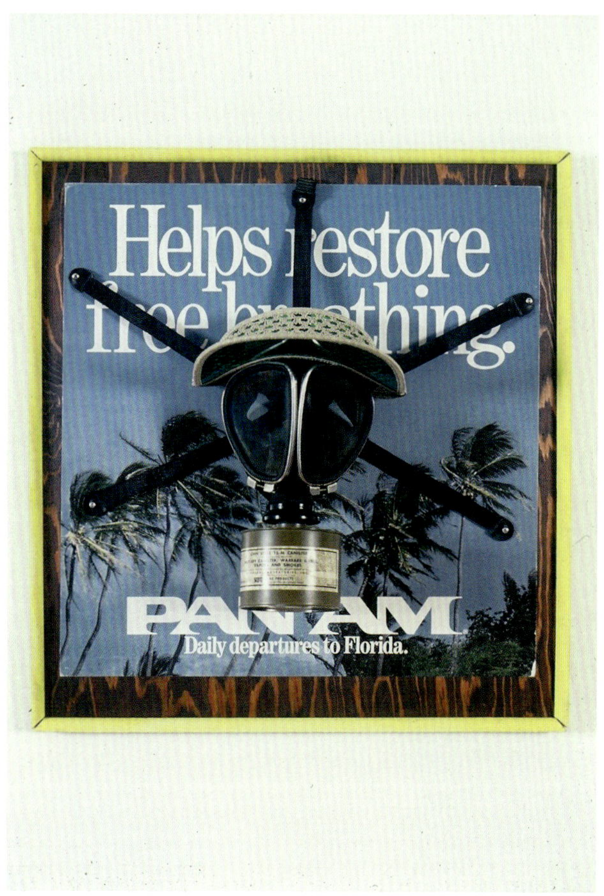

Pan Am, 1990
Poster mounted on plywood, mixed media
26 × 24½ × 3⅞ inches
Collection Enzo Cattelani, Modena, Italy

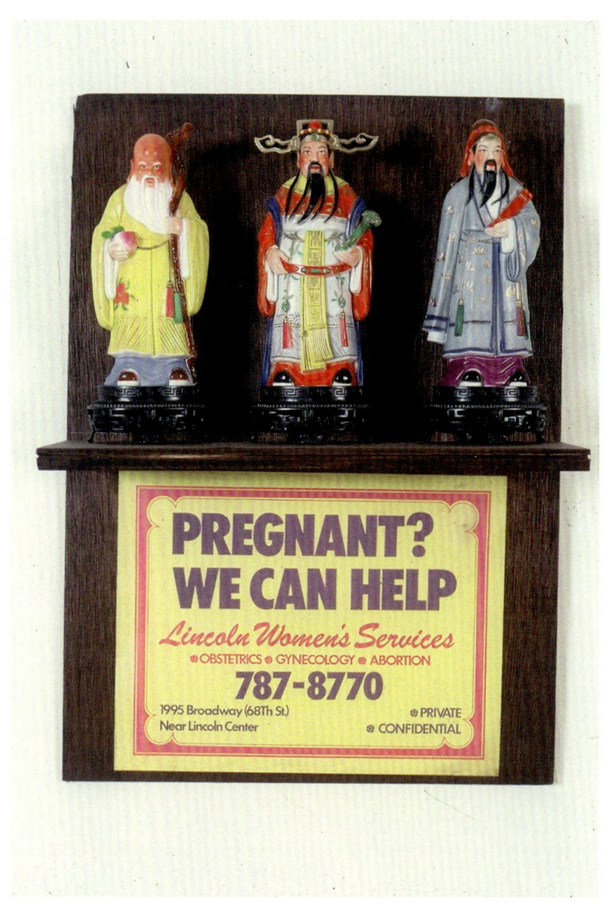

Pregnant?, 1990
Poster mounted on plywood, mixed media
25⅛ × 17¾ × 6 inches
Collection Enzo Cattelani, Modena, Italy

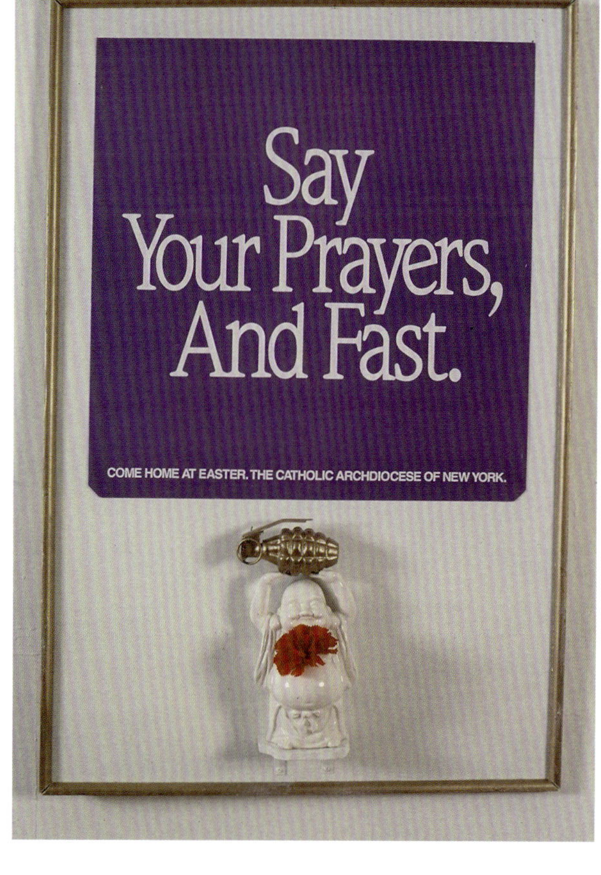

Say Your Prayers, 1990
Poster mounted on plywood, mixed media
38¼ × 25¼ × 3½ inches
Collection Enzo Cattelani, Modena, Italy

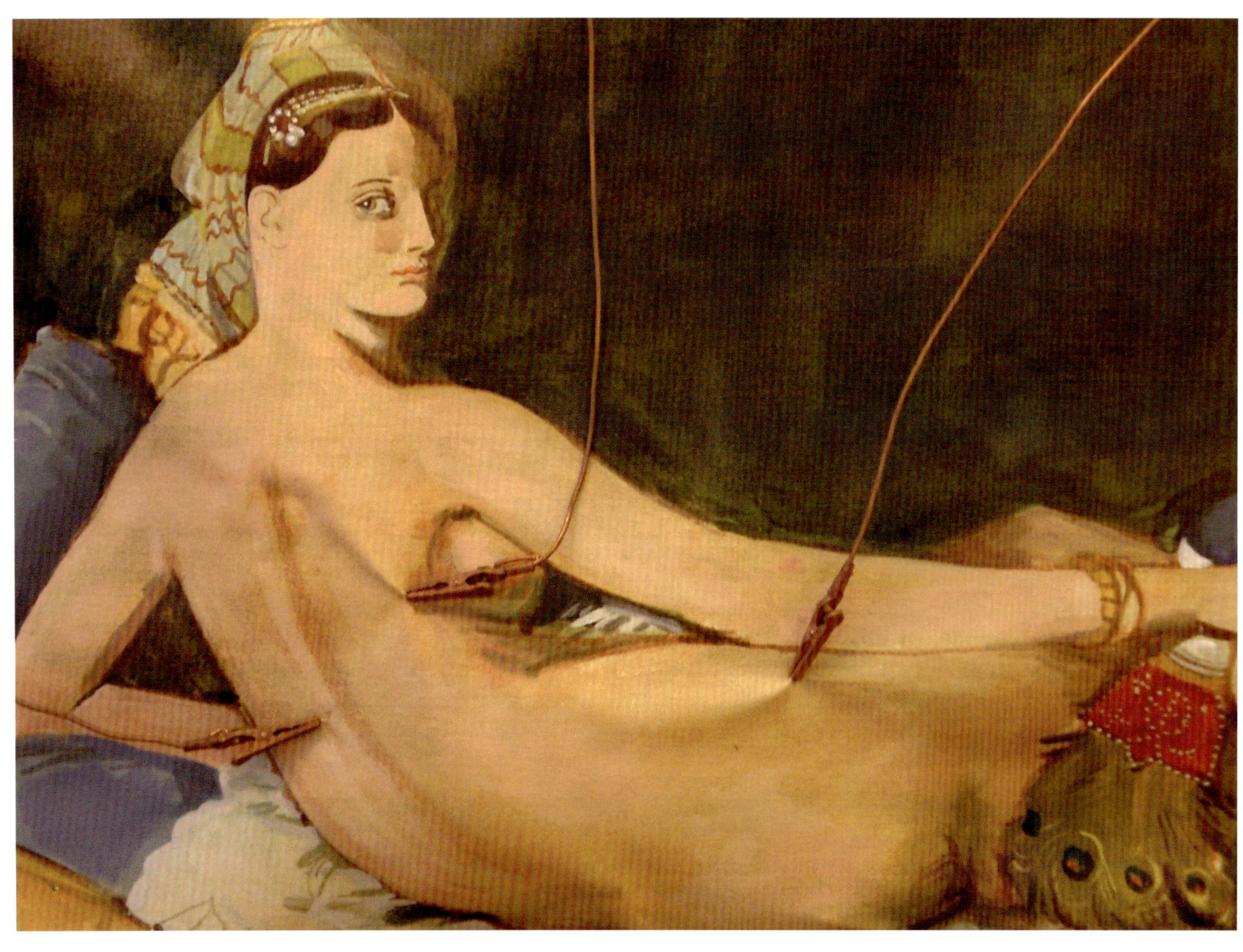

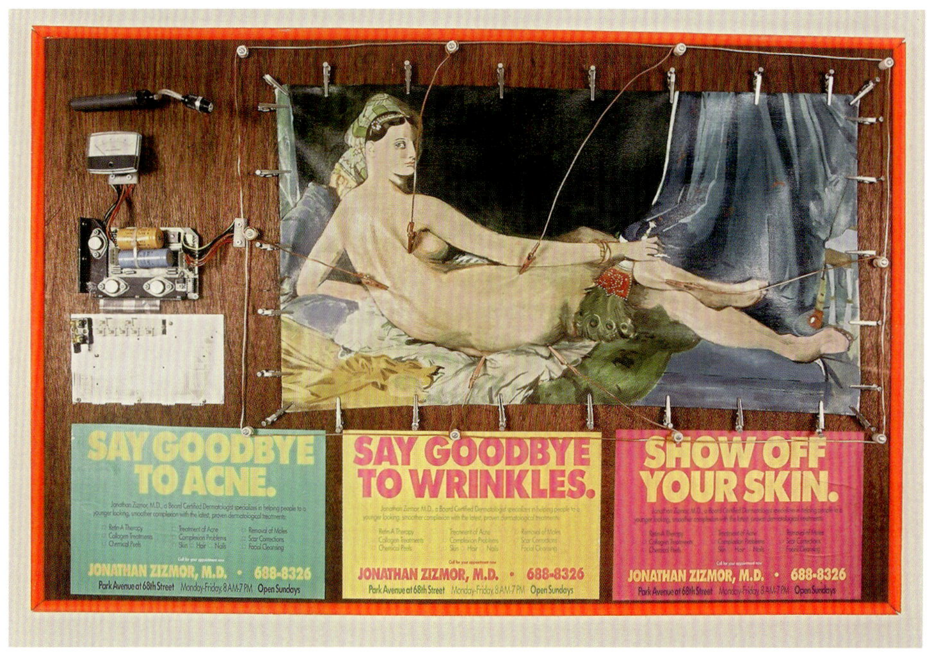

Show Off Your Skin, 1990
Collage paper and painted canvas mounted on wood, mixed media
32 × 48 × 6 inches
Collection Heinrich Risken, Bad Rothenfelde, Germany
(Detail, opposite)

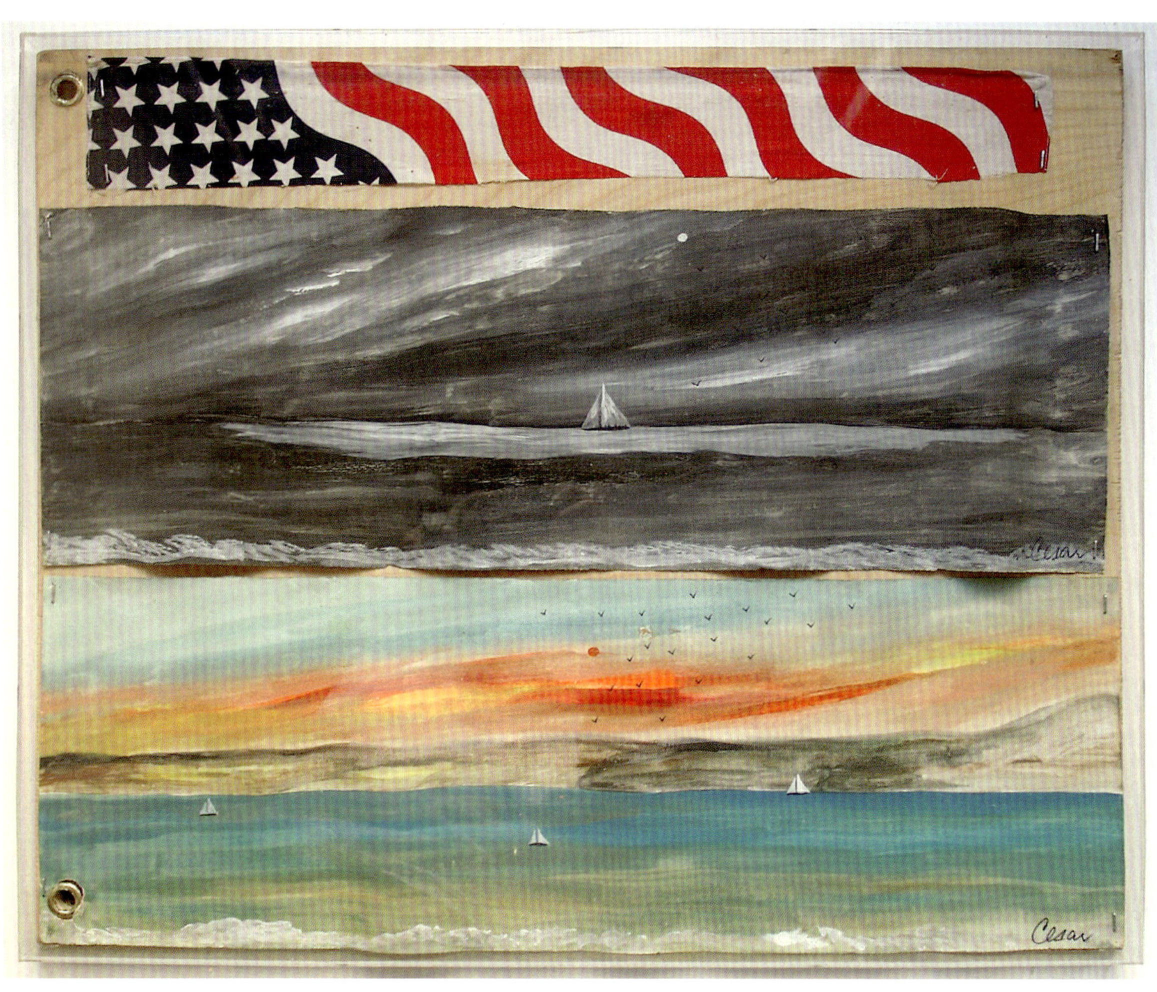

Untitled, 1990
Collage fabric and painted canvas mounted on wood
24¼ × 24⅜ × 1½ inches
Courtesy the artist and the Emily Harvey Foundation,
New York/Venice

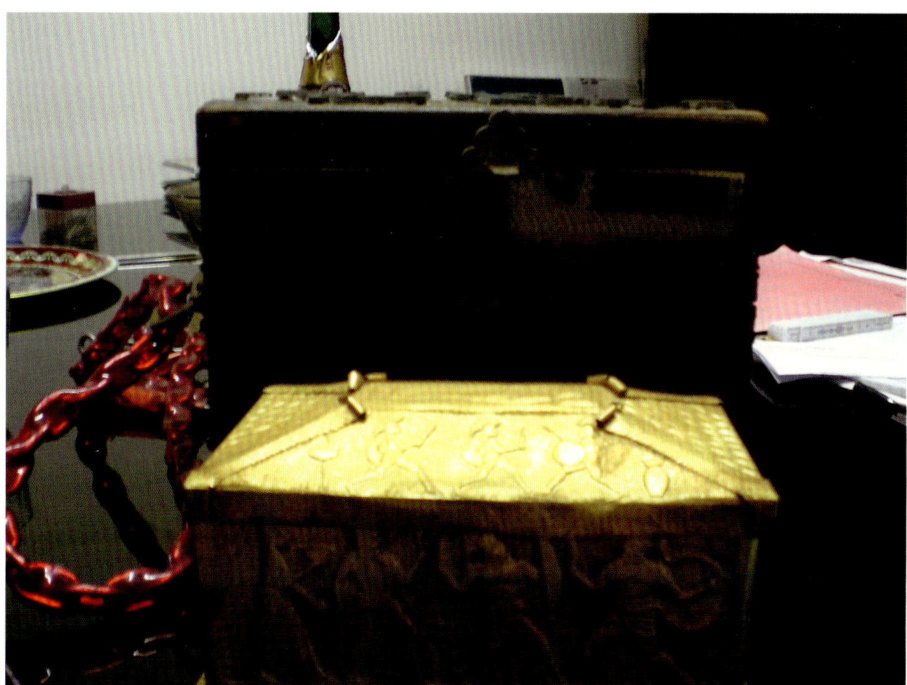

Fluxus Protected, 1991
Wood and metal boxes, cloth, chain, mixed media
7⅞ × 10¾ × 5¼ inches
Collection Enzo Cattelani, Modena, Italy

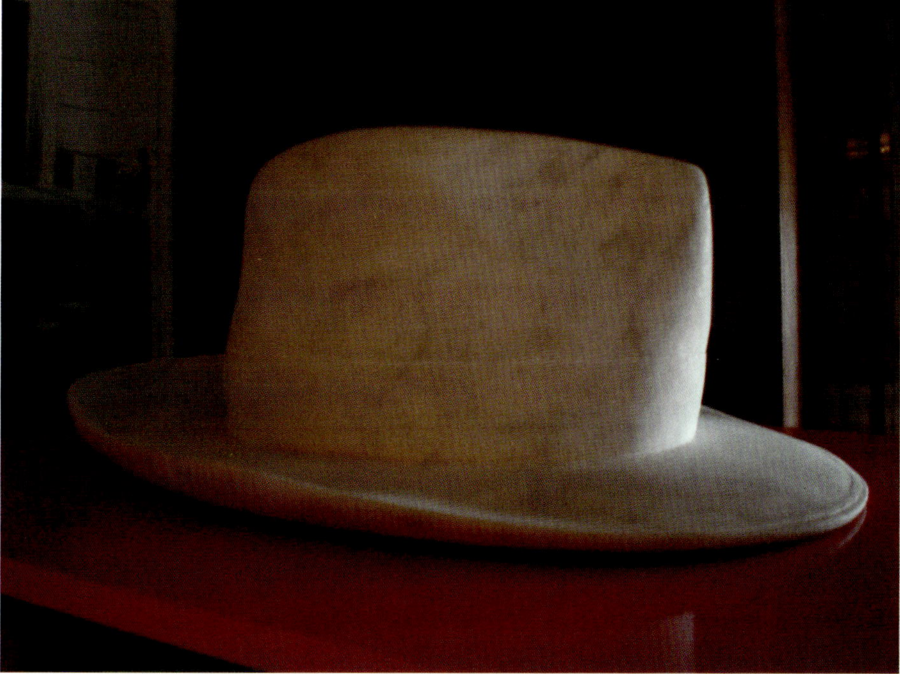

Marble Hat, 1991
Cut Carrara marble
12 × 24 × 10 inches
Courtesy the artist

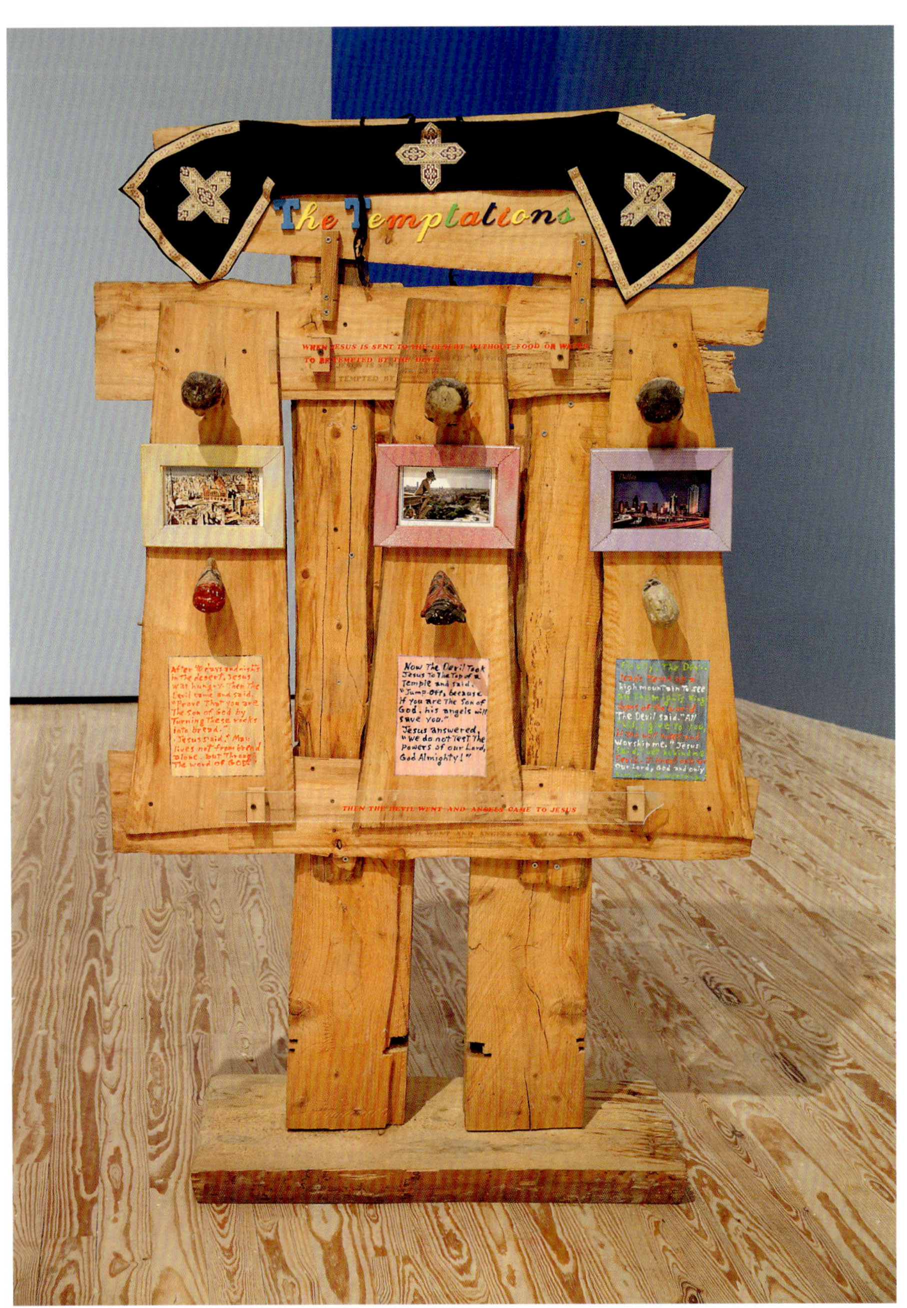

The Temptations, 1991
Wood, mixed media
66⅜ × 40 × 9¼ inches
Collection Carlo Cattelani, Modena, Italy

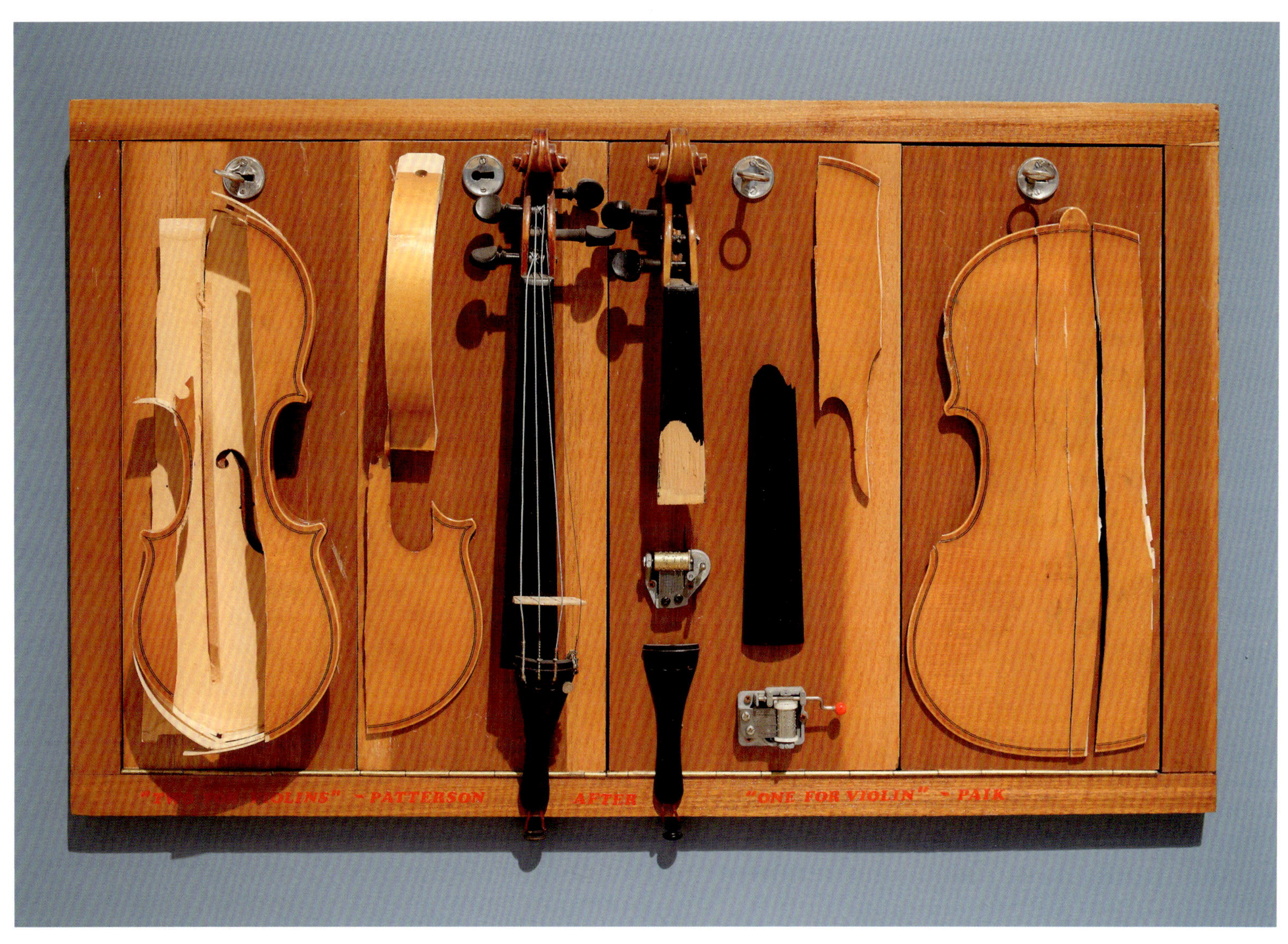

Two for Violin after Nam June Paik's
One for Violin, 1991
Broken violin, wood cabinet door, music box
31 × 19 × 4 inches
Courtesy Galerie Schüppenhauer, Cologne

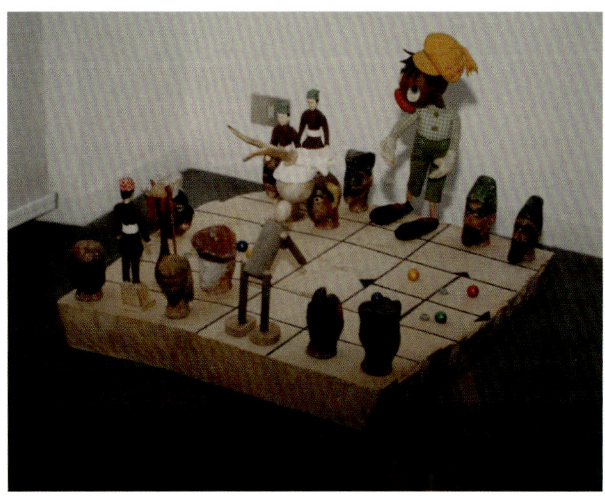

Early Chess, 1992
Wooden table, mixed media
29 × 25¼ × 24 inches
Collection Carlo Cattelani, Modena, Italy

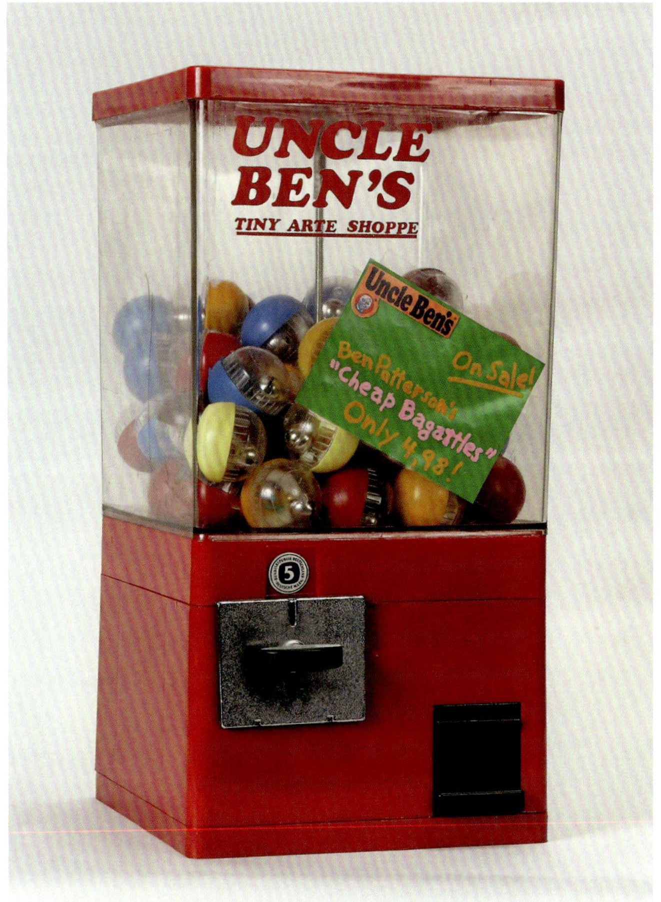

Uncle Ben's Art Shoppe, 1992
Toy-dispensing machine, plastic containers,
mixed media
19 × 10 × 9⅝ inches
Courtesy the artist

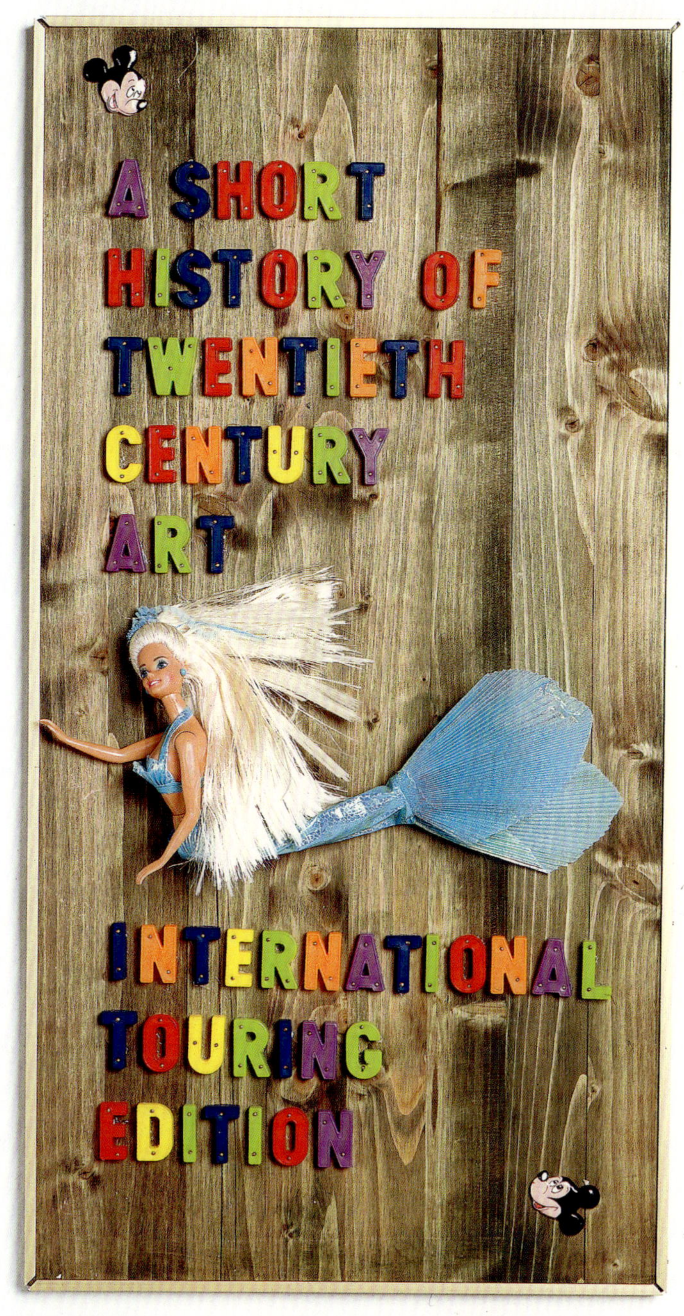

A Short History of Twentieth-Century Art, 1993
Mixed media on wood panels
5 parts, 11 × 14 × 3 inches each
Institut für Auslandsbeziehungen e.V., Stuttgart, Germany
(Right and pages 90–92)

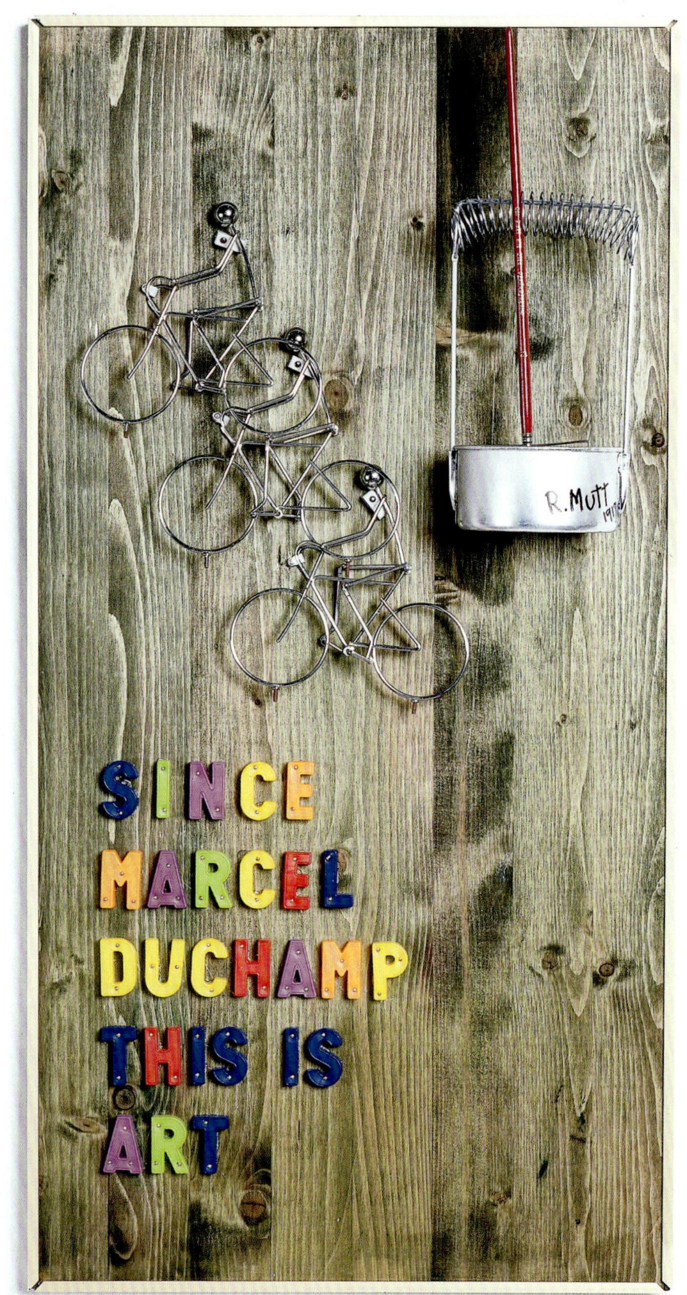
R. Mutt
SINCE
MARCEL
DUCHAMP
THIS IS
ART

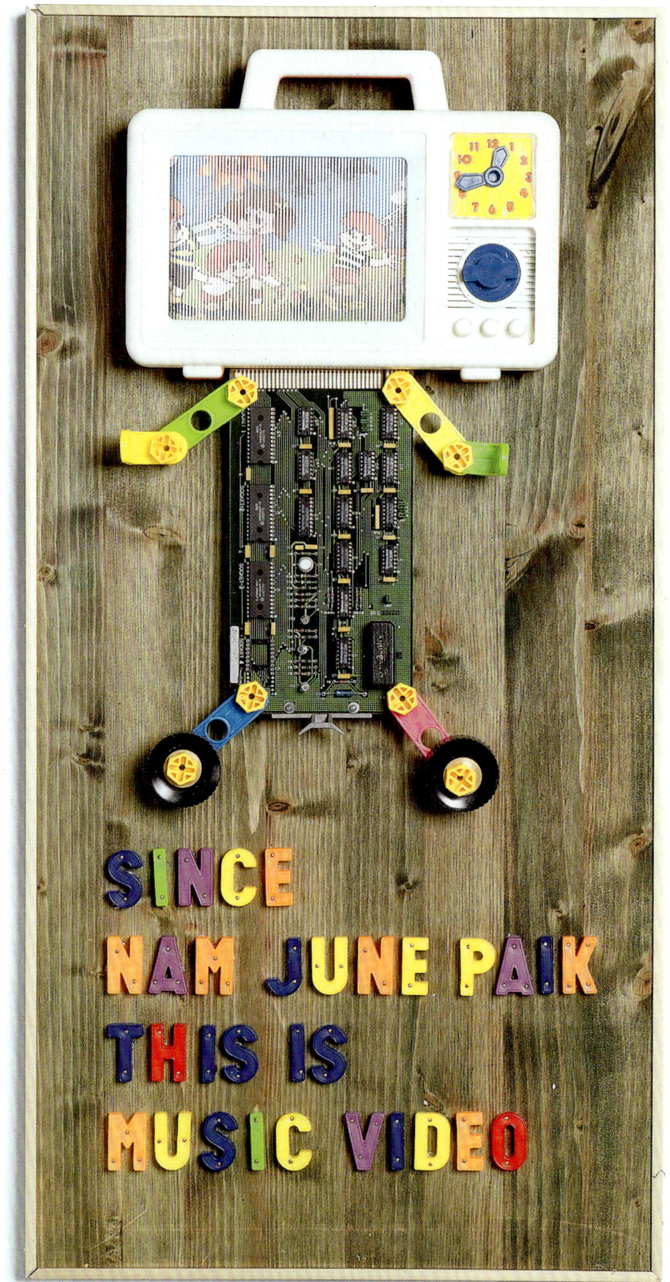
SINCE
NAM JUNE PAIK
THIS IS
MUSIC VIDEO

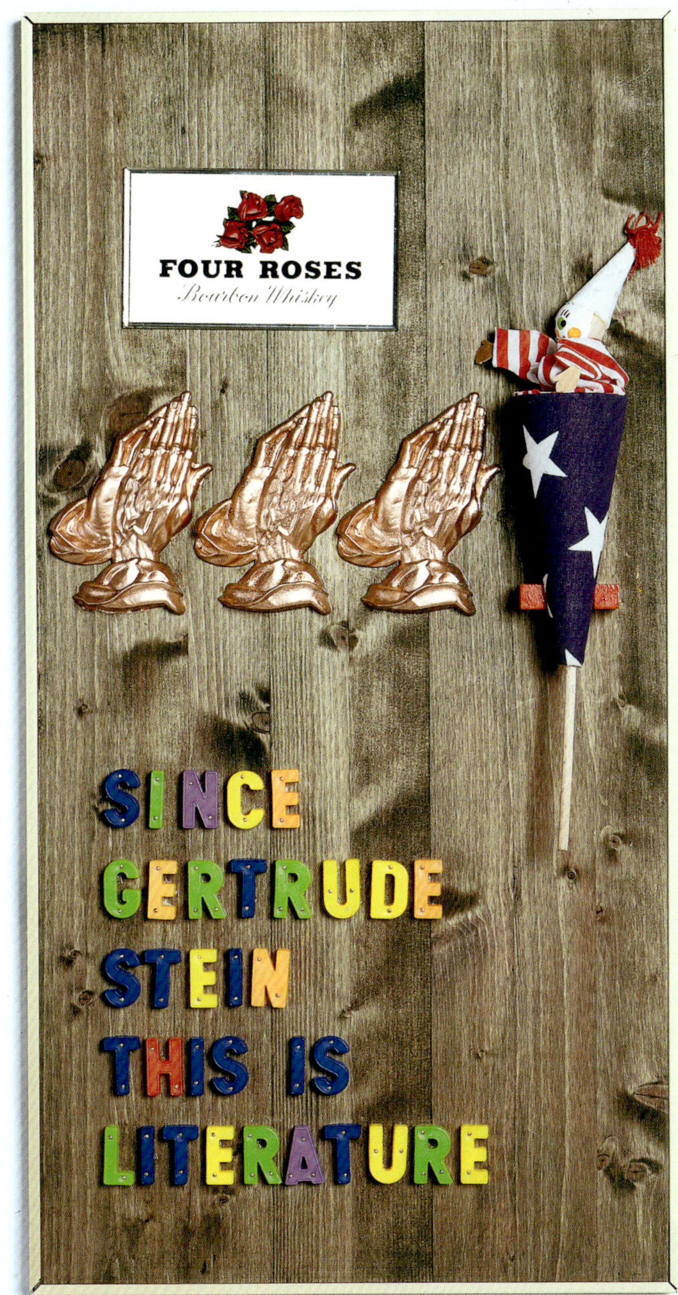
FOUR ROSES
Bourbon Whiskey
SINCE
GERTRUDE
STEIN
THIS IS
LITERATURE

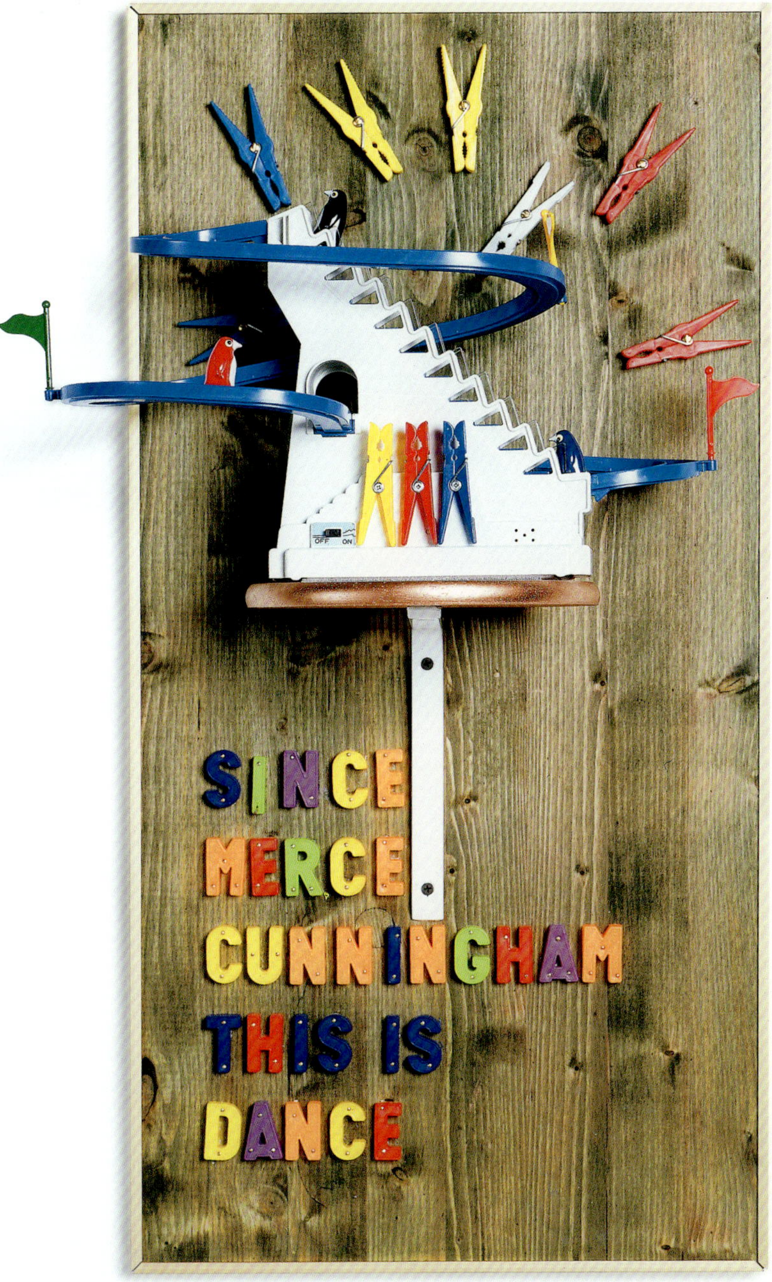
OFF ON
SINCE
MERCE
CUNNINGHAM
THIS IS
DANCE

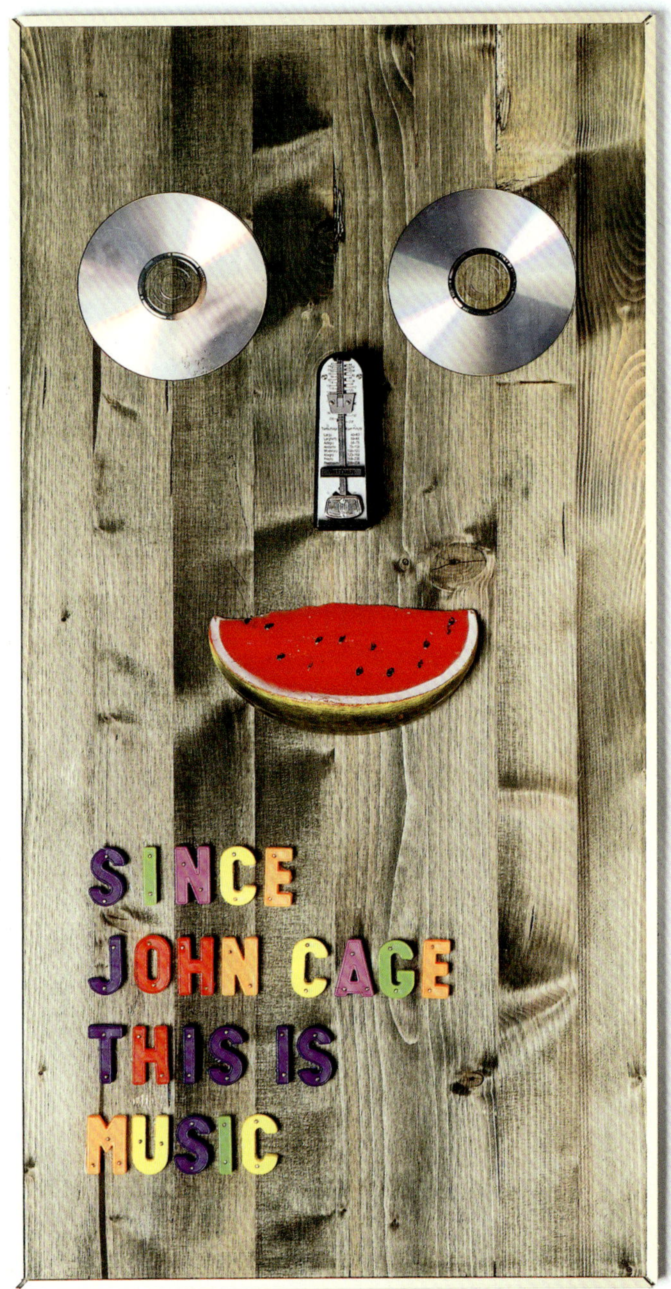

SINCE
JOHN CAGE
THIS IS
MUSIC

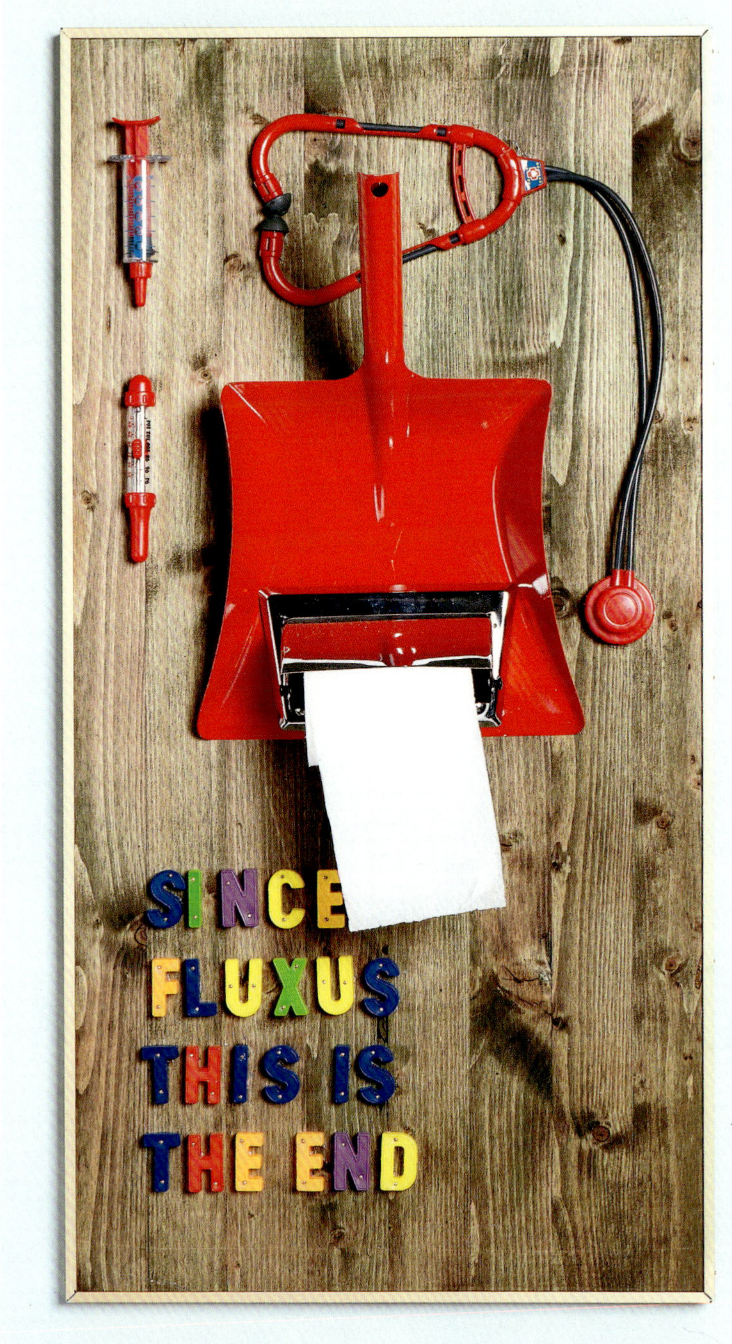

SINCE
FLUXUS
THIS IS
THE END

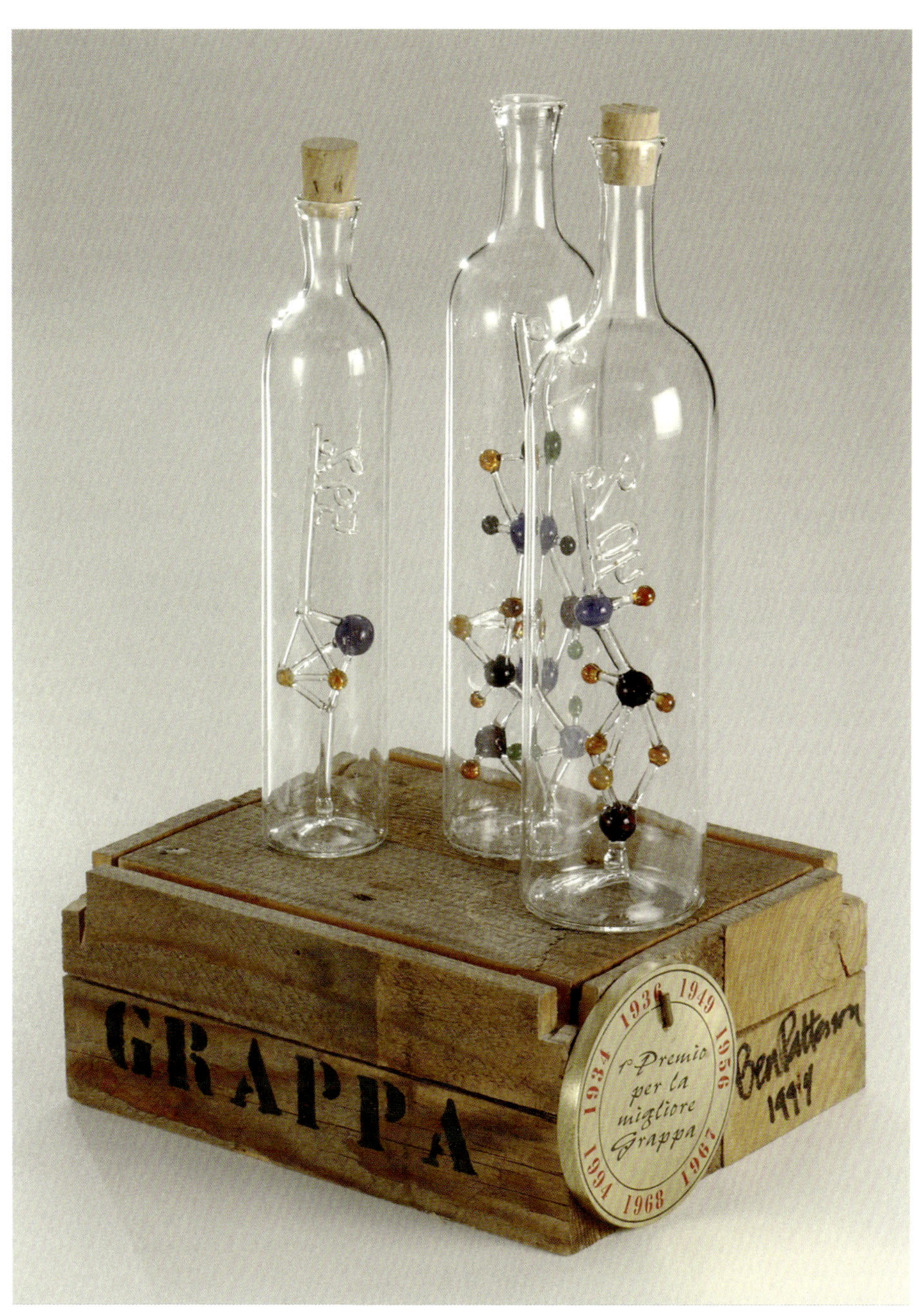

Il primo segreto della grappa, 1994
Handblown glass bottles
11½ × 2⅞ inches
Archivo Bonotto, Molvena, Italy

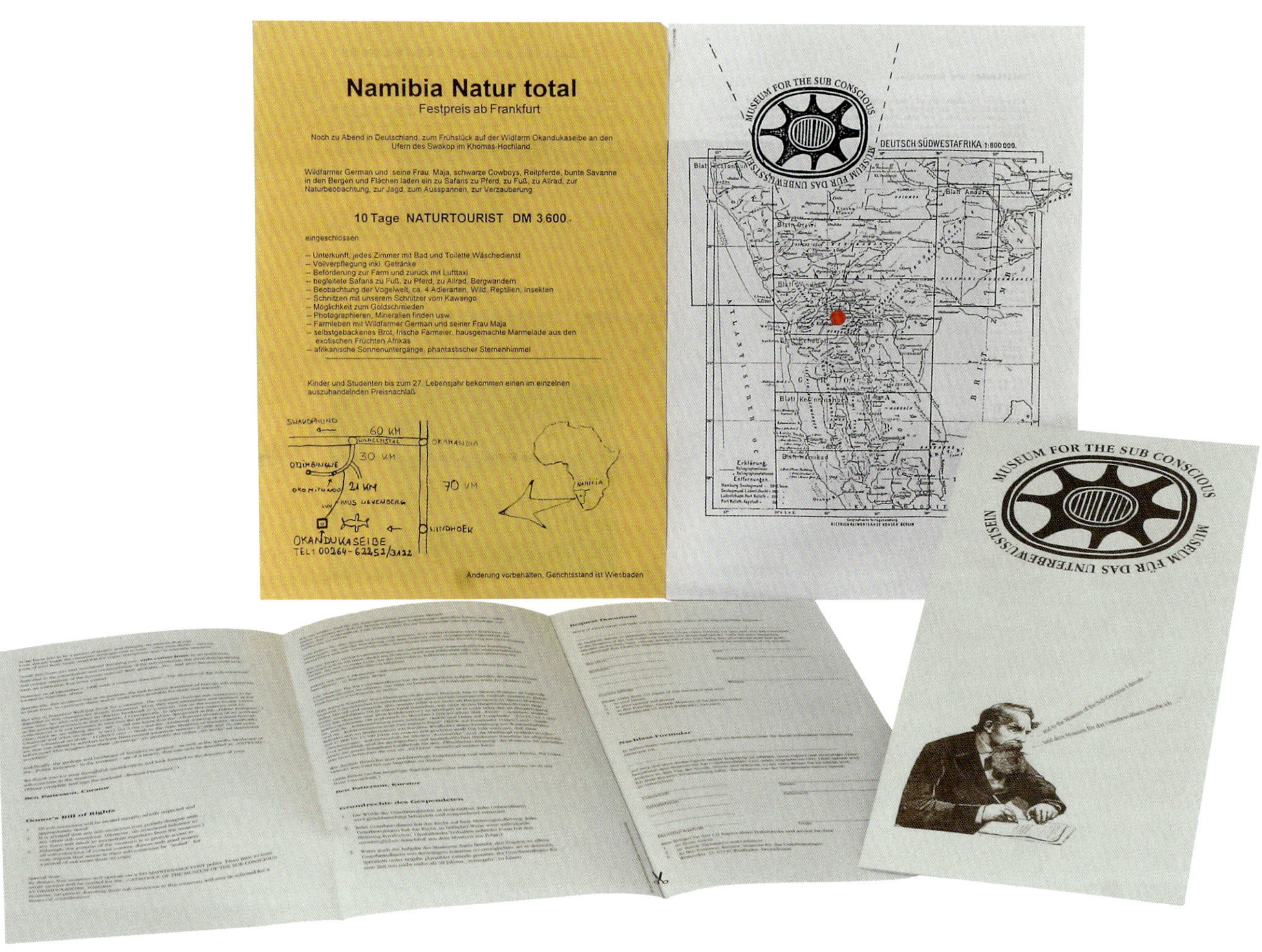

Museum of the Subconscious
(Namibia, guidelines and ephemera),
1996
Metal plaque, wooden box, mixed media
Plaque: 11 × 14 inches
Box: 12⅝ × 12⅝ × 1⅜ inches
Courtesy the artist

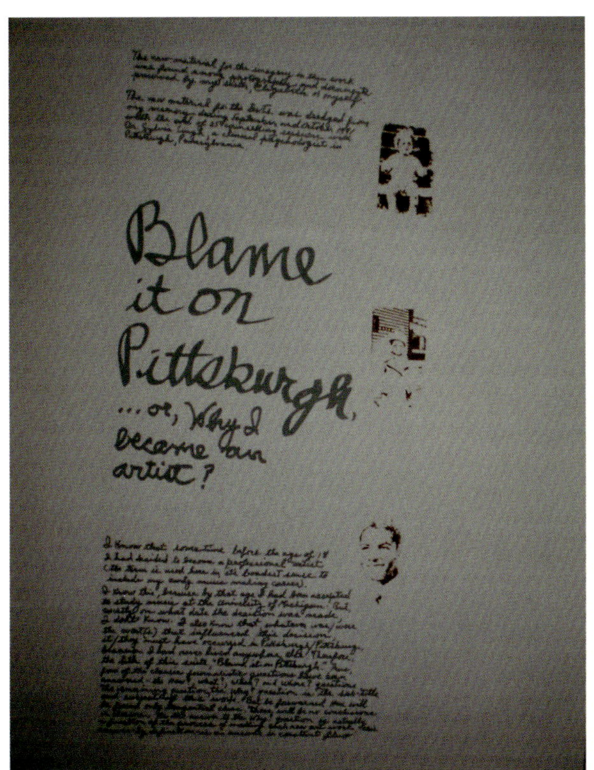

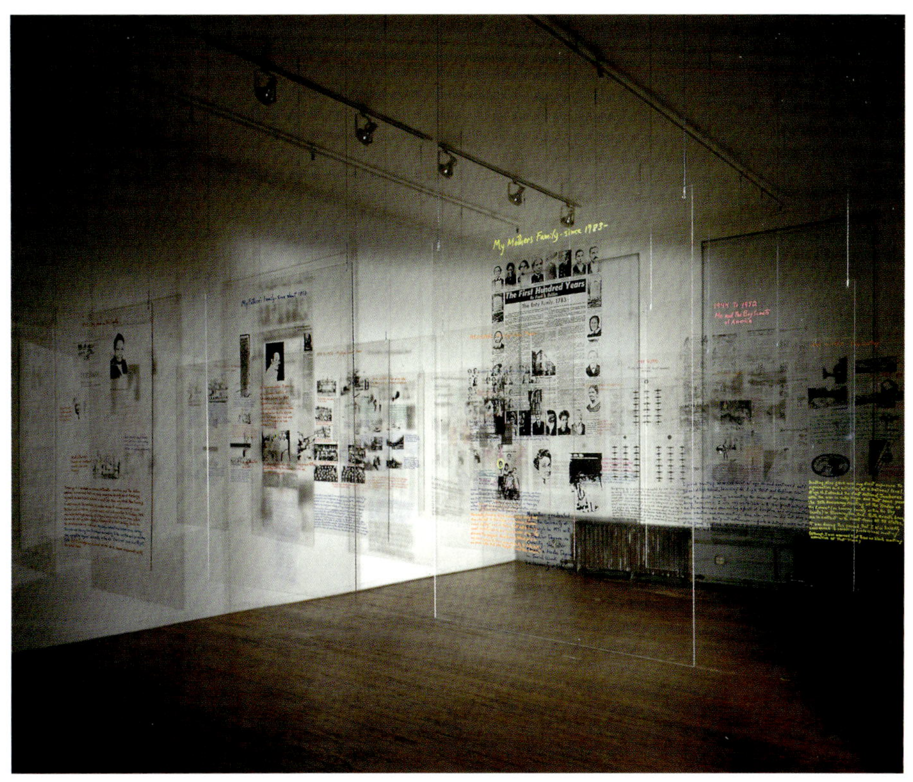

*Blame It on Pittsburgh; or, Why I
Became an Artist*, 1997
Silk screen on Plexiglas
18 panels, 59 × 39 × ¼ inches each
Courtesy the artist

Trains of Thought (Josef Hayden), 1997
Discarded train sign, wooden boxes, cassette tape player,
audiocassette, mixed media
72 × 12 × 3½ inches
Courtesy the artist

Trains of Thought (Maurice Ravel), 1997
Discarded train sign, wooden boxes, cassette tape player,
audiocassette, mixed media
72 × 12 × 3½ inches
Collection Elfi Kreiter, Wiesbaden, Germany

Trains of Thought (Verdi), 1997
Discarded train sign, wooden boxes, cassette tape player,
audiocassette, mixed media
72 × 12 × 3½ inches
Collection Elfi Kreiter, Wiesbaden, Germany

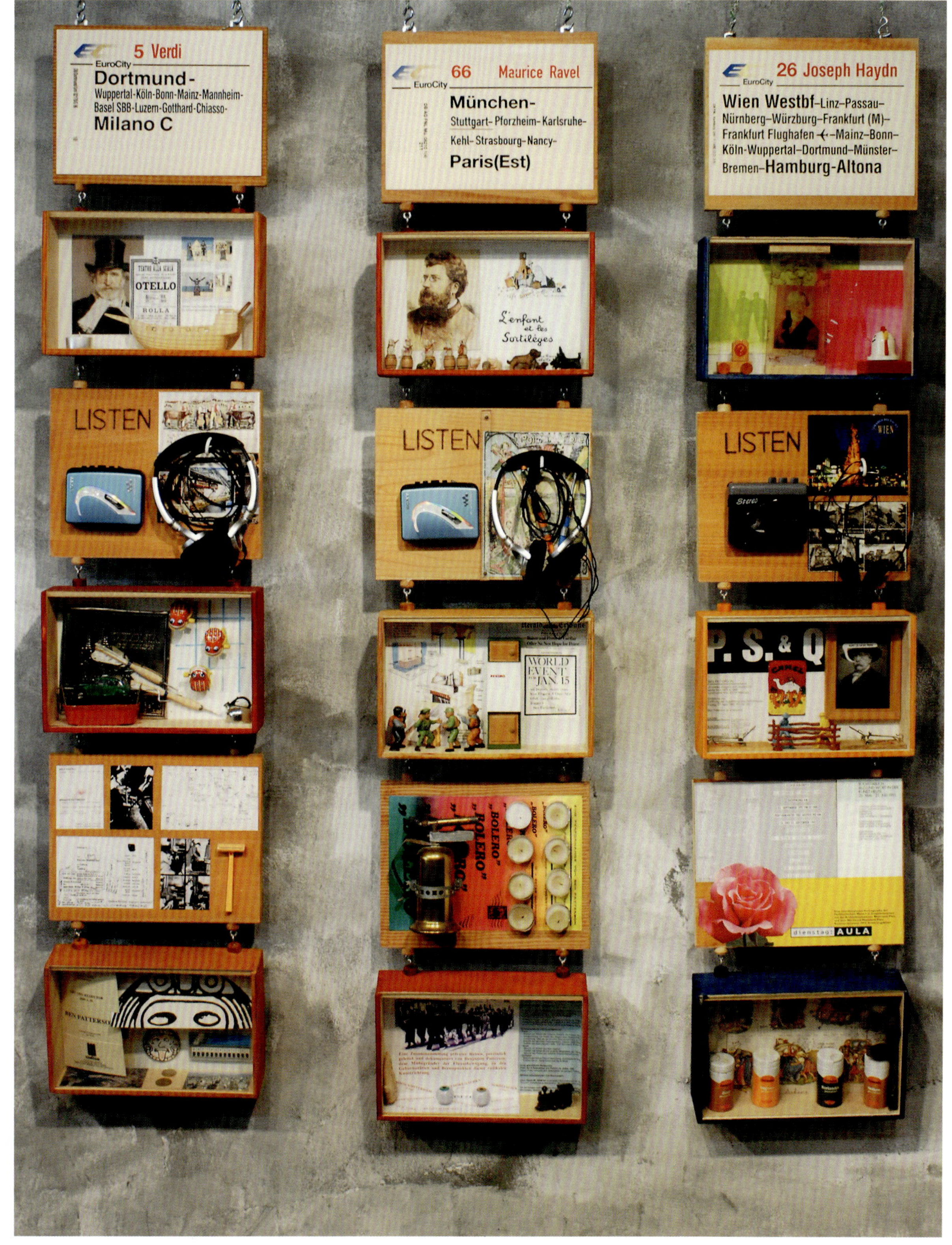
EC EuroCity   5 Verdi
Dortmund-
Wuppertal-Köln-Bonn-Mainz-Mannheim-
Basel SBB-Luzern-Gotthard-Chiasso-
Milano C
OTELLO
LISTEN
BEN PATTERSON
EC EuroCity   66 Maurice Ravel
München-
Stuttgart- Pforzheim-Karlsruhe-
Kehl- Strasbourg-Nancy-
Paris(Est)
L'enfant et les Sortilèges
LISTEN
WORLD EVENT JAN 15
BOLERO
EC EuroCity   26 Joseph Haydn
Wien Westbf-Linz-Passau-
Nürnberg-Würzburg-Frankfurt (M)-
Frankfurt Flughafen-Mainz-Bonn-
Köln-Wuppertal-Dortmund-Münster-
Bremen-Hamburg-Altona
LISTEN
WIEN
P.S. & Q
CAMEL
dienstag AULA

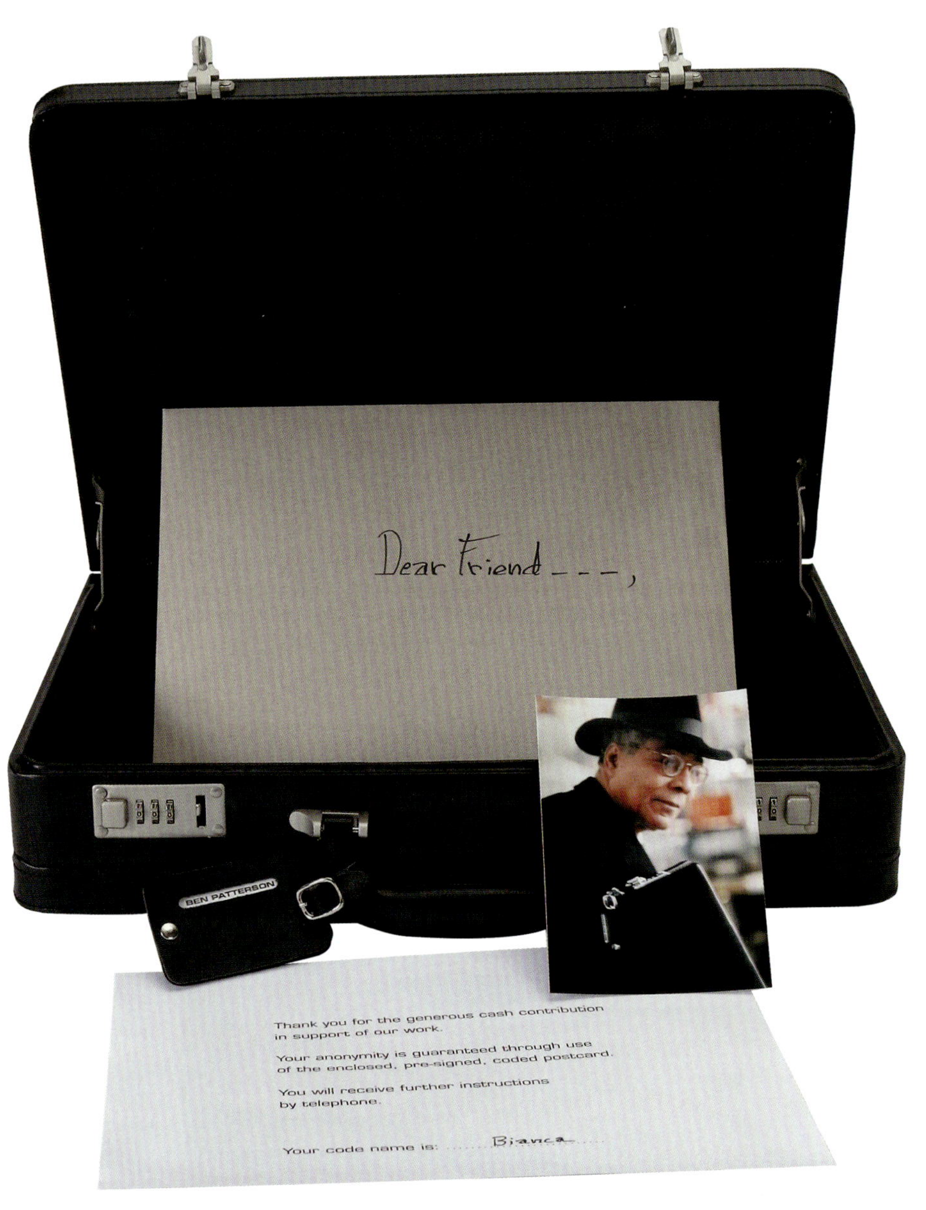

Kohler Koffer, 1999
Leather briefcase, ink on paper,
offset on paper, mixed media
14 × 11½ × 2 inches
Courtesy the artist

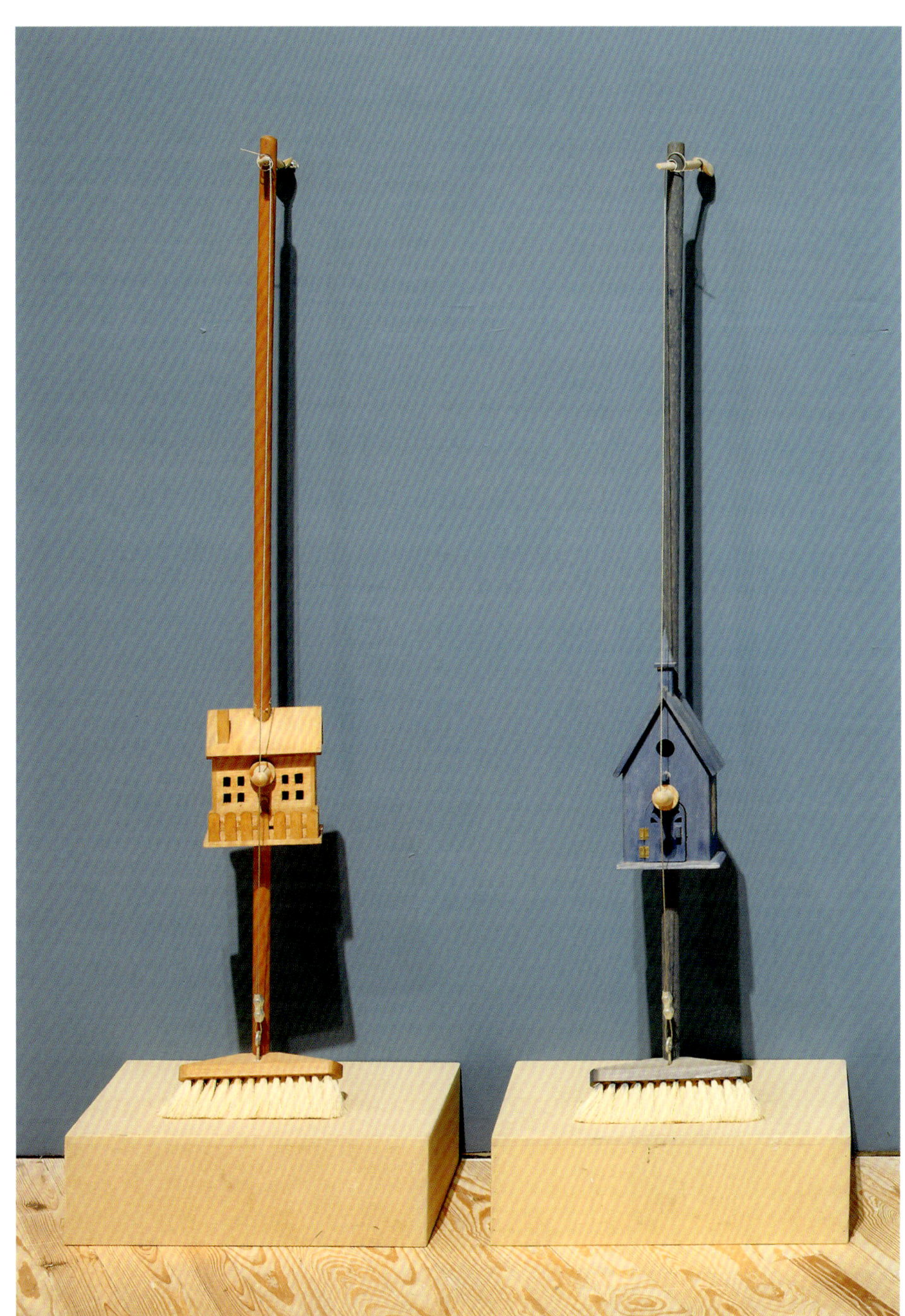

Cello (Blue), 2003
Wooden push broom, birdhouse,
metal strings, wooden spoon
53 5/16 × 10 × 5 inches
Courtesy the artist

Cello (Red), 2003
Wooden push broom, birdhouse,
metal strings, wooden spoon
53½ × 10 × 5 inches
Courtesy the artist

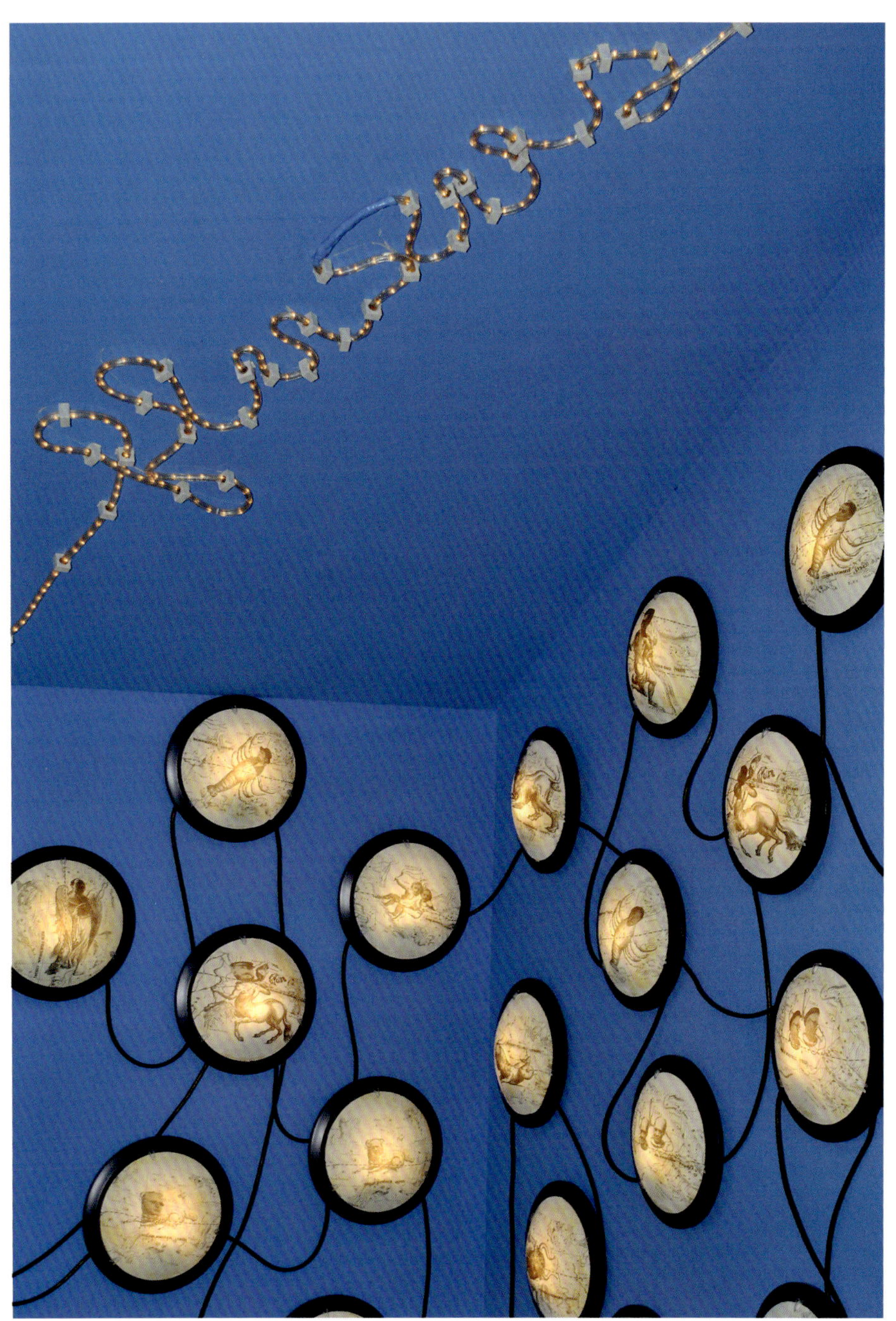

Fluxus Constellation, 2003
Silk screen on nylon, glass sconces, electrical system, tube lights
34 sconces, 23¾ × 8 × 2½ inches each
Dimensions variable
Museo d'arte contemporanea di Villa Croce, Genoa, Italy

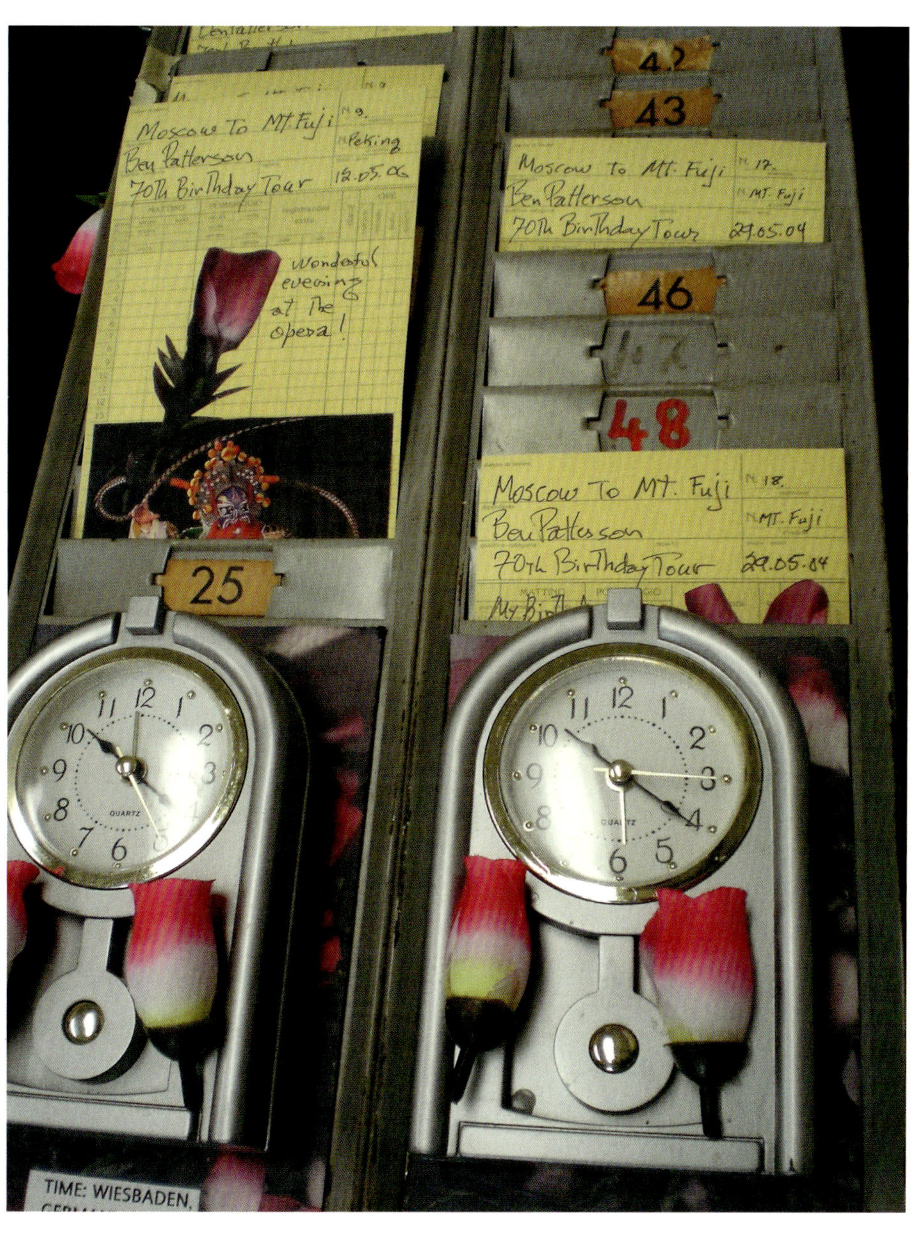

It Was Roses All the Way (My Grand 70th Birthday Tour), 2004
Metal time-card machine, ink and marker on time cards, artificial flowers, Plexiglas
40 × 20 × 10 inches
Collection Archivo Bonotto, Molvena, Italy

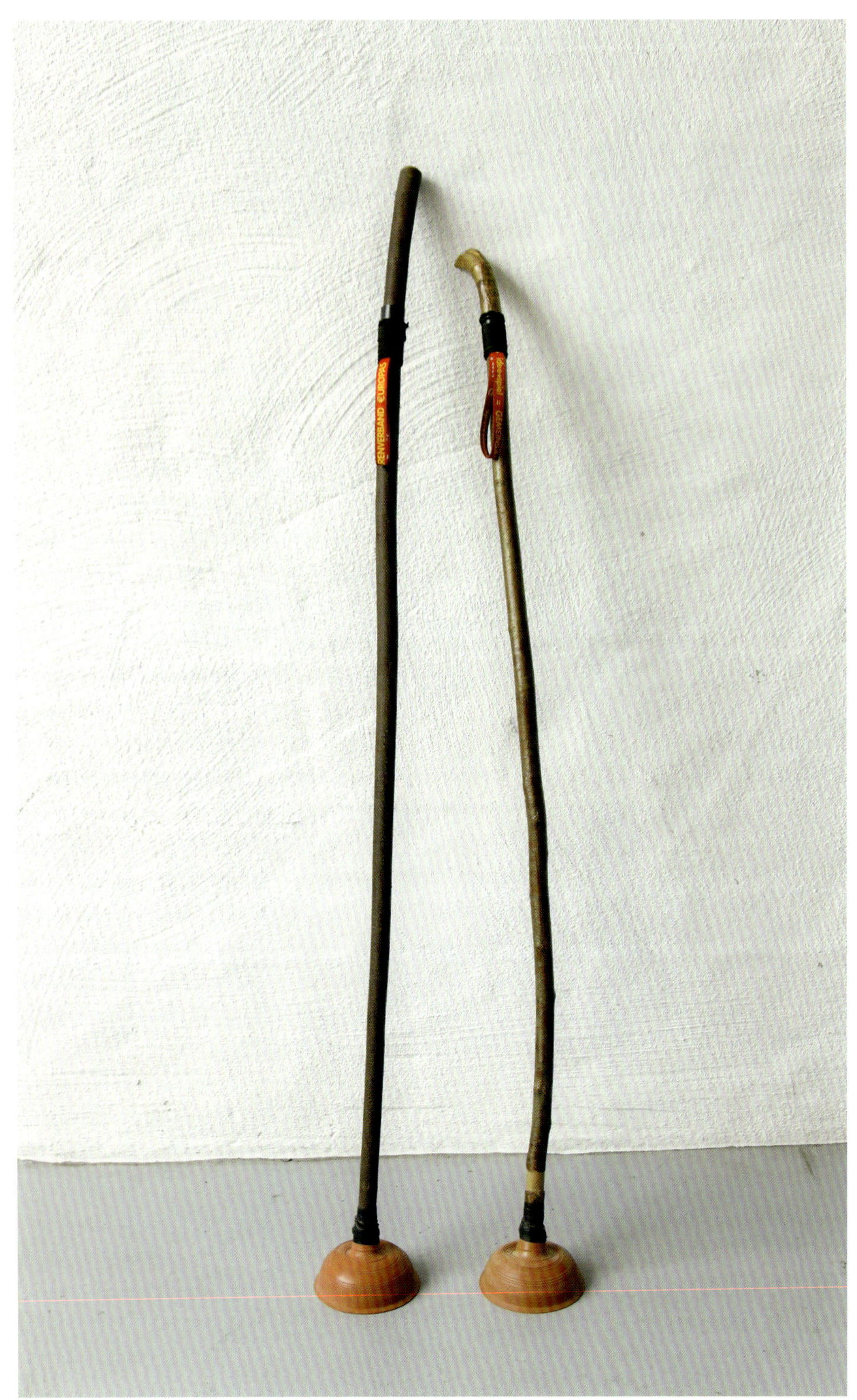

Ski Poles (from Climbing Mt. Fuji), 2004
Broom handles, rubber plungers
60 × 6 × 1 inches
Courtesy the artist

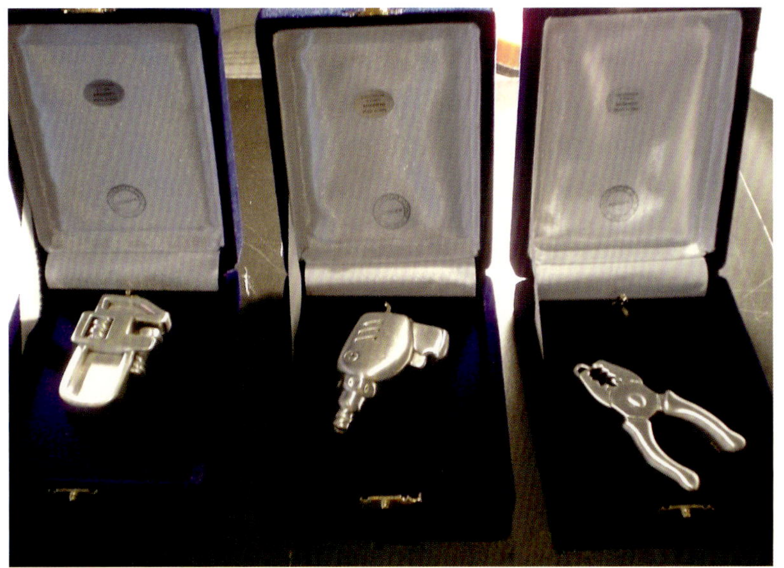

Industrial Chic (a.p.), 2007
Cast-silver toy tools, velvet jewelry boxes
6 parts, 3 × 2 × ½ inches each
Courtesy the artist

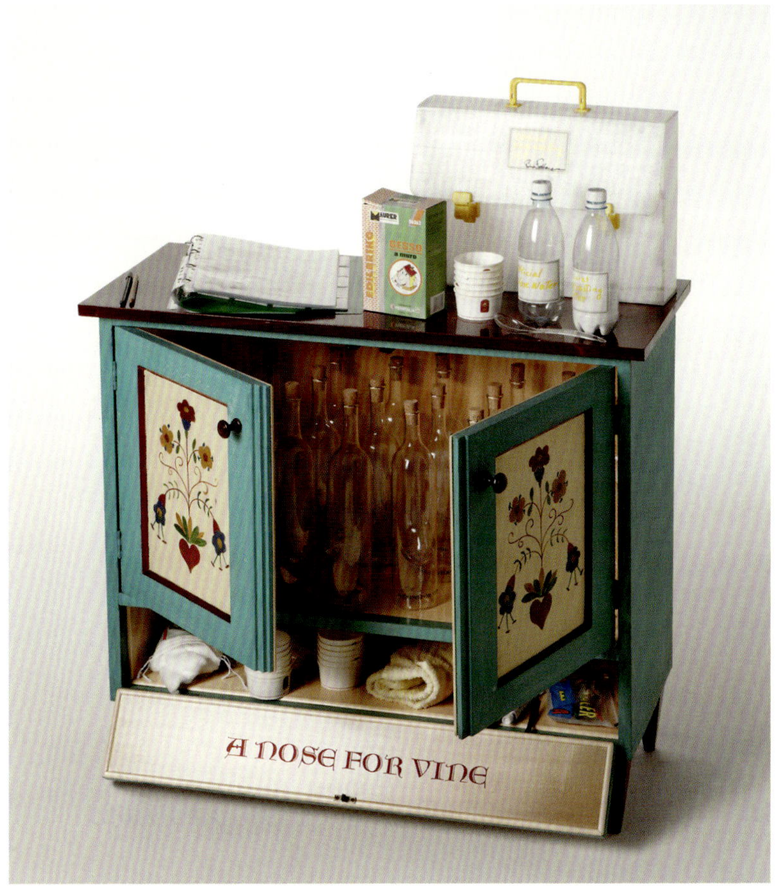

A Nose for Wine, 2008
Wine bottles with cast molding
12 bottles, 11½ × 2⅞ inches each
Collection Archivo Bonotto, Molvena, Italy

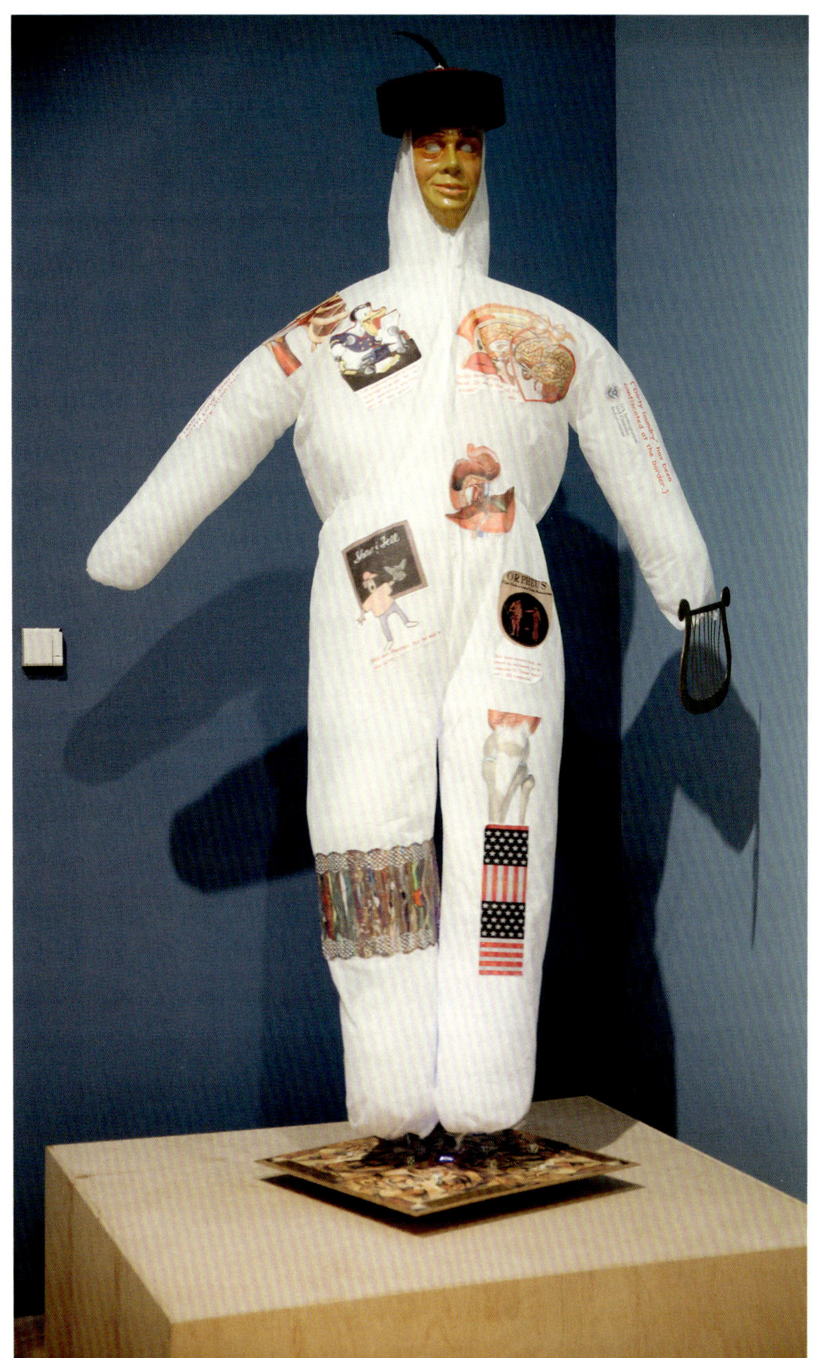

Effigy for Dick Higgins II, 2010
Effigy: paper jumpsuit, costume hat, mask, collage, mixed media
Base: collage on wood, dice, light, turntable
Effigy: 70 × 20 × 7 inches
Base: 21 × 20 × 1¾ inches
Courtesy the artist

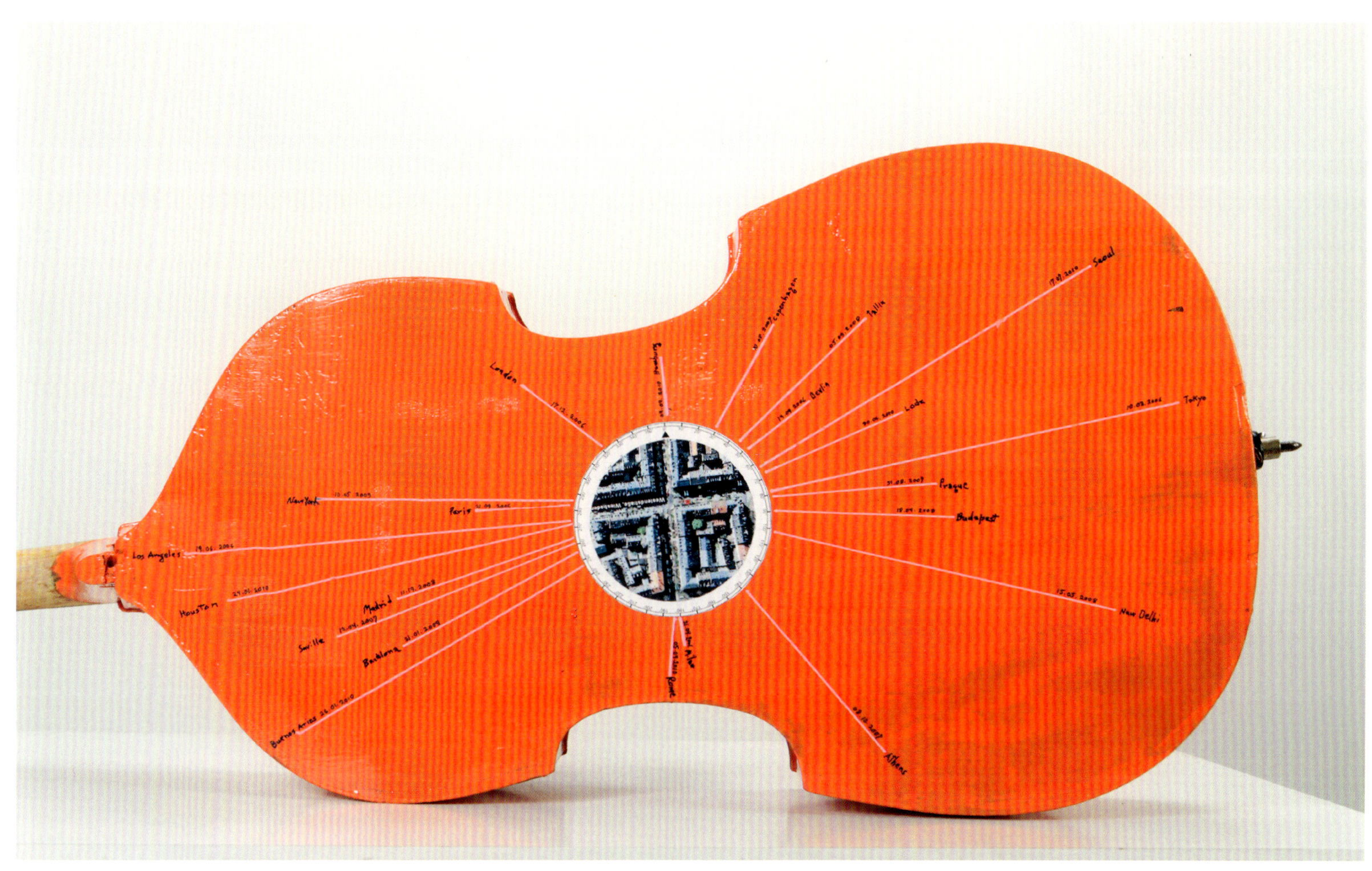

Flying Bass II, 2010
Double bass, metallic ink, metal propane
burners, mixed media
70 × 36 × 12 inches
Courtesy the artist

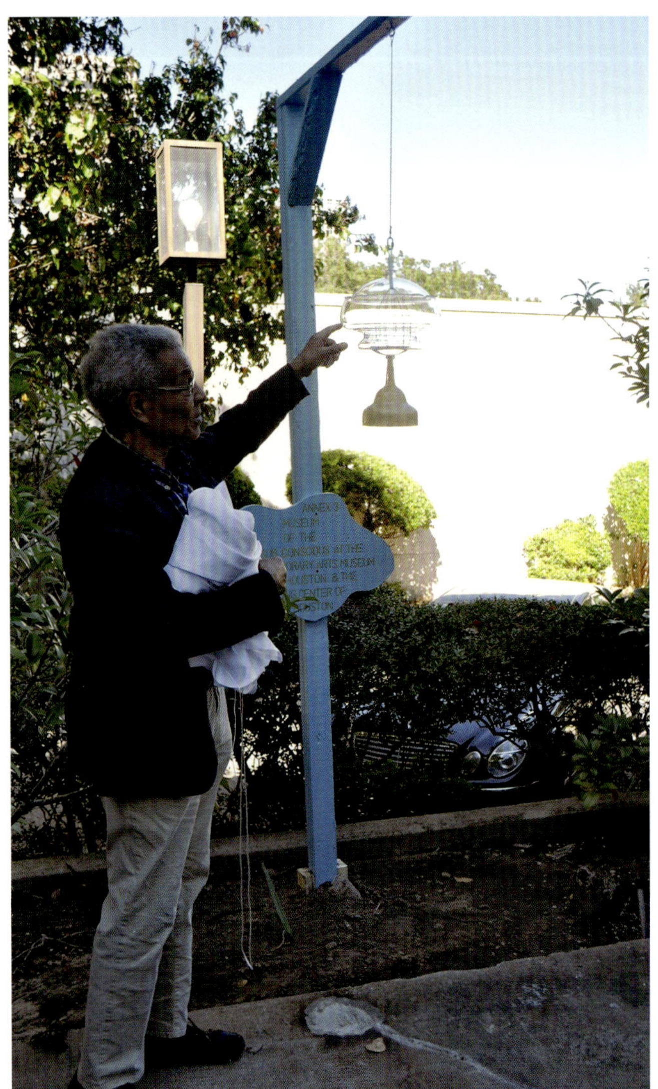

The Museum of the Subconscious—
Houston Annex, 2010
Plastic, wood, paint, mixed media
Museum: 20 × 10 inches diameter
Hanging armature: 108 × 24 × 32 inches
Courtesy the artist

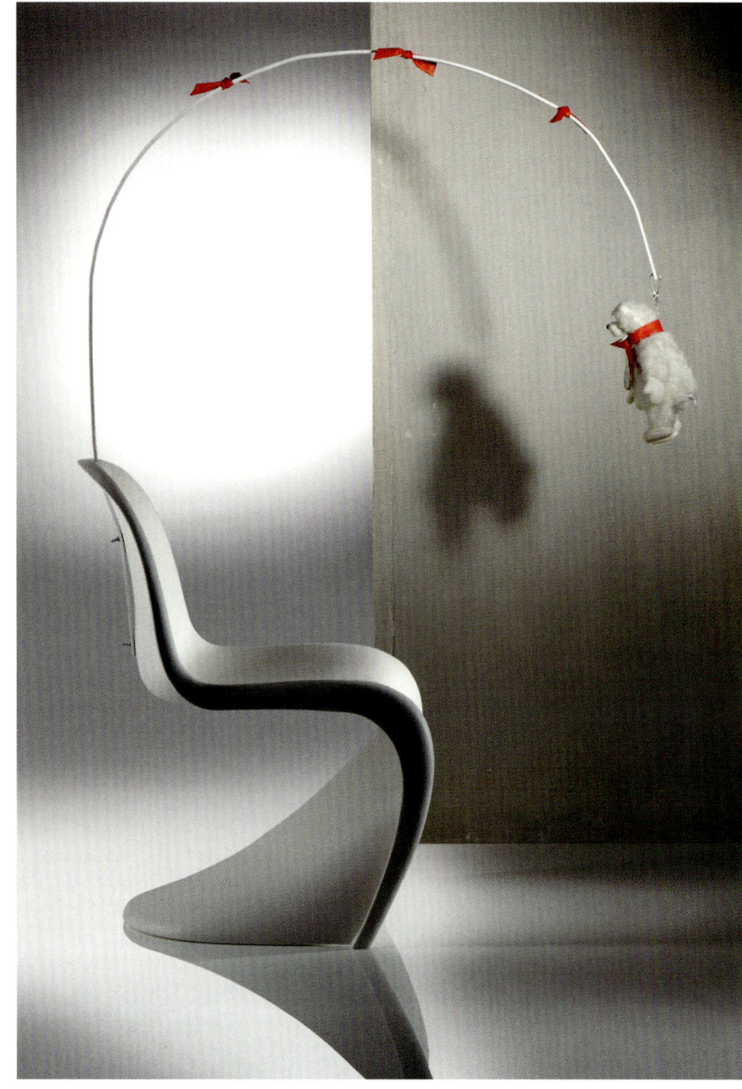

Sit Down, 2010
Pantone injection-molded plastic chair,
metal rod with stuffed bear, recorder
Chair: 35¼ × 19¾ × 23½ inches
39½ × 39¾ × 23½ inches overall
Courtesy the artist

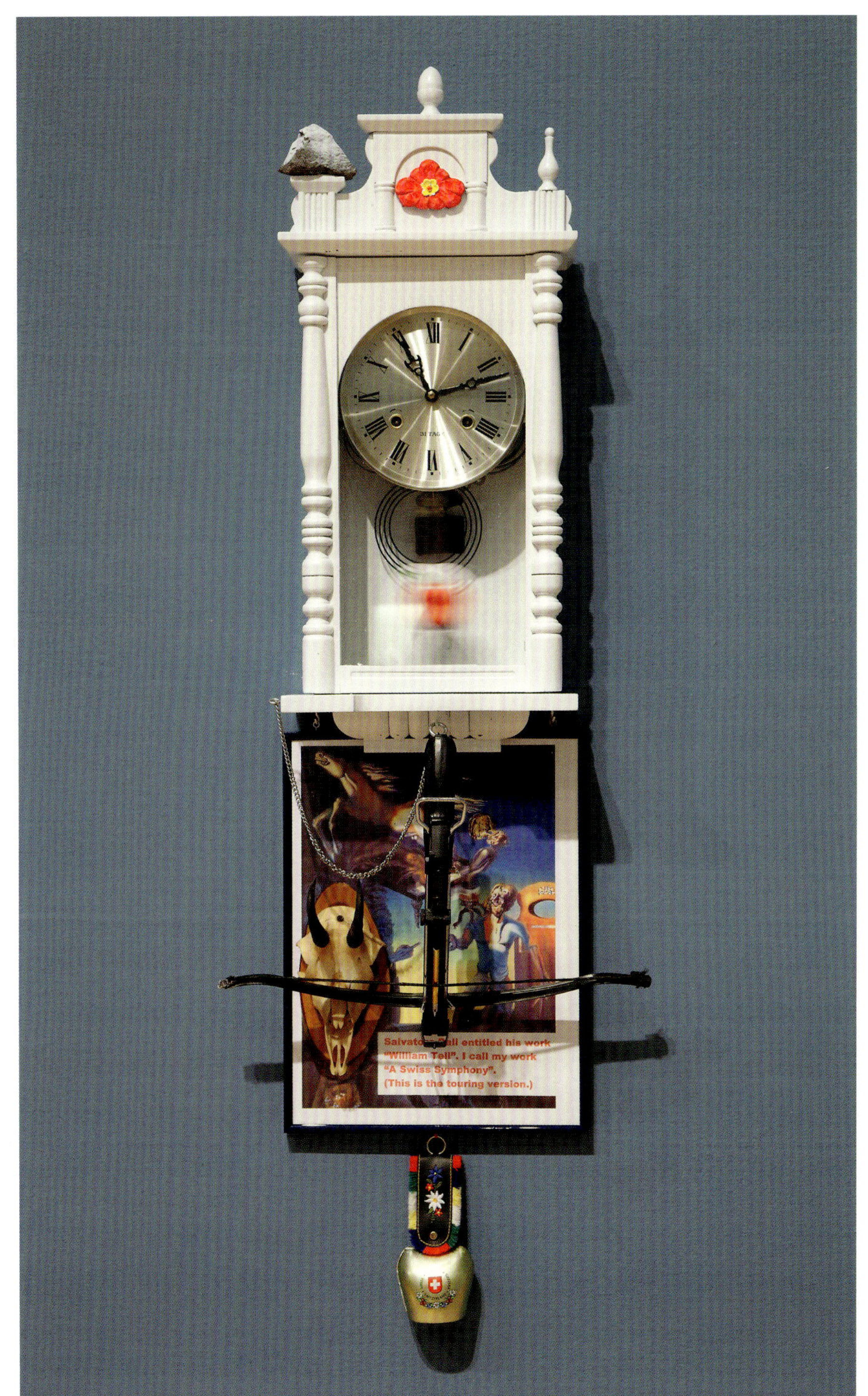

Swiss Symphony II, 2010
Wooden wall clock, collage on board, crossbow, mixed media
60 × 16½ × 5 inches
Courtesy the artist

I'm Glad You Asked Me That Question

BENJAMIN PATTERSON

Dieter Daniels suggested that he would like to do a piece on Ben Patterson in a special Fluxus issue of *Kunstforum*. He suggested an interview as an interesting format, and an appointment was arranged. During the next day, however, I began to remember how much I disliked interviews—that is, how I considered myself as a person who tends to think and speak slowly and rarely expresses himself well in interviews. So I decided to borrow one of the techniques of the manipulated political press conference and "plant" some questions for which I would have prepared answers (as in "I am glad that you asked me that question . . ."). When I informed Dieter Daniels of my intentions, he not only approved of the idea but also further suggested that I should do the whole interview of myself by myself. We reviewed the questions that I had wished to "plant," and he suggested several other general topics and specific questions that I should address. Thus the following interview with Ben Patterson, conducted by Ben Patterson in various places in Europe and America between May 1990 and February 1991.

Q: Is it true that the exhibition at Galerie Schüppenhauer last April was your first solo exhibition, not only in Cologne but also in Europe?

A: Well, yes, that is almost true. As you know, I lived in Cologne from 1960 to 1962 and was active first in the radical fringe of the "new music" scene and later in the birth of Fluxus. If the event *Ein kleines Sommerfest* at Galerie Parnass in Wuppertal in June 1962 is accepted as the "unofficial" birthday of Fluxus, then you might say that George Maciunas and I were the charter members, as we were the only performers that evening. And of course, until I returned to New York in 1963, I participated in nearly all the European Fluxus events. But during this period I thought of myself as some sort of a composer-performer (the term *performance artist* hadn't been invented yet), and most of my work was presented in the context of a Fluxus festival or concert. These works—if not exactly music—were still based primarily in time and activity, not space and color. It was only toward the end of 1962, when I was living in Paris, that I began to make visual objects, works that I called "puzzle-poems." Robert Filliou liked these works very much and offered me an exhibition of miniature "puzzle-poems" in his *Galerie Légitime*, which was located on top of his head under his hat. Since such a gallery obviously had great mobility, we decided that for the "opening" we should go to the public rather than asking them to come to the gallery. So we planned a twenty-four-hour tour of Paris by metro, by bus, and on foot, and we sent out announcements, which were in fact a map of our tour route, indicating the specific times we would be at certain locations. It was a wonderful "opening" attended by thousands of people, and we sold more than half of the exhibition (at five francs each) during the opening. Thus, to be historically correct, this event in Paris in 1962 was my first solo exhibition in Europe.

Q: I want to ask you about Paris later, but first I would like to know more about Cologne. Why did you come to Cologne? What did you do there? Whom did you work with, etc.?

A: Well, first you must know that for the previous four years I had been a professional classical double bassist (including two years in the U.S. Seventh Army Symphony Orchestra in Germany) and that during the season before

Cologne (1959–60) I worked during the day as principal double bass with the Philharmonic Orchestra of Ottawa, Canada, and experimented at night at a primitive electronic music studio in the National Research Center in Ottawa. My original plan was to spend the summer holidays visiting the major electronic music studios in Cologne, Milan, and Paris and return to Ottawa in the fall. I was especially interested to meet and perhaps work with Stockhausen. So I arrived in Cologne in time for the first concert of the International Society of Contemporary Music Festival, and after the first concert, at what I thought was an appropriate moment, I presented myself (with a letter of introduction from the German ambassador to Canada, who was also Stockhausen's brother-in-law) to Stockhausen. For better or for worse, this meeting, which lasted less than five minutes, was the beginning and the end of our working relationship. However, the next day I learned that a kind of counterfestival had been organized by Mary Bauermeister and that John Cage and David Tudor would be there to present several programs of works by the most radical of the younger American composers. It was during these counterconcerts that I met Cage and Tudor, and because I was immediately invited to be a performer in several works in the following evening's concert, I came to learn firsthand the compositions of many artists who would later become "core" Fluxus people. Needless to say, the approach to art that these compositions represented was a revelation to me and a major turning point in my artistic development. During the days of these concerts I also discovered a small international group of young artists (David Behrman from the U.S., Cornelius Cardew from England, François Biel from France, Sylvano Bussotti from Italy, Kurt Schwertzig from Austria, Wolf Vostell from Germany, and of course Nam June Paik from Korea) living in Cologne, who shared a similar excitement about such radical "experimentation." In short, when I learned a little later that a

musician's strike in Ottawa had caused the cancellation of the coming season, I was already prepared and happy to stay in Cologne.

The next year was more or less the typical life of a young artist: no money, sometimes hungry, and always in need of free or cheap housing. But there was plenty of activity, and by the end of 1961 I had participated in "radical" music festivals in Vienna and Venice and had presented at Galerie Haro Lauhus in Cologne three concerts of works I had composed during the year. (As a historical footnote it may be interesting to know that one of these concerts was for the opening of Christo's first show in Western Europe, the second was for the opening of Daniel Spoerri's first exhibition in Germany, and the third was for Wolf Vostell's first solo exhibition.) Included on these programs were two works that became standard in the Fluxus repertoire: *Paper Piece* and *Variations for Double Bass*. Also in August 1961 I presented a relatively major work in Vostell's studio: this work, which I called *Lemons*, was composed of twenty-three brief scenes, each lasting anywhere from three seconds to three minutes, with lots of darkness in between. The "score" for this work required a dancer (Gisela Olroth), a singer (William Pearson), an artist (Wolf Vostell), and a musician (myself). I believe that it was the first "happening" in Cologne.

Q: If I understood you correctly, until 1960 you were a professional classical musician. But by the end of 1961 you were creating Happenings, and a year later you were participating in the "birth" of Fluxus. I would think that this required a very rapid and radical change of aesthetics and philosophy. How was this possible?

A: Well, first—and perhaps this is more a "New World" than an "Old World" trait—I have found that many people are not always only what their business card announces them to be. As a child and through high school, I dabbled in the visual arts, literature, and music, as well as in the natural sciences, Eastern and Western philosophies, and religions. By age four I had heard, via the Metropolitan Opera radio broadcasts, every major opera at least twice. By age twelve I had read every word (not always with complete understanding) up to the letter *M* in the twelfth edition of the *Encyclopaedia Britannica.* By age sixteen I was a volunteer assistant at both the Carnegie Museum of Natural History and the Pittsburgh Zoo, working in the entomology department of the former and in the herpetology department of the latter. I also managed to find time for sports and briefly held local and regional records in several middle-distance track events. All in all, I was on my way to being a "Renaissance man." But when the serious business of university studies began, I elected music for my profession. And I also embarked on a crusade—to be the first black to "break the color barrier" in an American symphony orchestra. You must remember that this was in the 1950s, when there was still official segregation in the South and de facto segregation in most of the North and particularly in the places of high culture.

Fortunately I did have some talent, and I received excellent musical training at the University of Michigan, and so when I left the university, I was well equipped to compete with the best. But in the end, even though such a famous conductor as Leopold Stokowski fought strongly on my behalf, America was not yet ready for a black symphony musician, and so I went to Canada. My point, however, is that although before university I was exploring a wide range of subjects, media, and materials, from anthropology to Zen—all of which eventually found a place in my art—the urgency/discipline of my "crusade" kept me pretty much on a "straight line" all the way through university. In other words: although I read Joyce, Beckett, Ionesco, and the existentialists and wrote serial exercises à la Webern or silly songs à la

Virgil Thomson, I really never allowed myself the time to sit back and contemplate: "What is wrong here? What else can be done?" And although the university as a whole was still stunned by the ravages of McCarthyism, it was not an impossible place for new thoughts. Only a year after I left Michigan, Gordon Mumma (a classmate and a close friend), together with Bob Ashley, founded the Once Group and started producing amazing festivals. So the answer to your question—"How was this rapid and radical change possible?"—is that there already existed a mental background prepared to act when the circumstances and stimulation were appropriate. As it happened, circumstances and stimulation collided first in Cologne, and then I followed them, or they followed me, to Paris and later, for a few years, to New York.

But if there was ever a critical moment, it was the collision of circumstances and stimulation in Cologne at Mary Bauermeister's "counterfestival." Even now I still have a vivid memory of telling myself, when I heard the first works by John Cage, that this is the music that I had been hearing in my head for years but had never thought possible to realize.

Q: Since you raised the issue of "circumstance and stimulation," I must assume that you are not claiming to be a completely original and unique artist without antecedents or influences. If so, then tell me who do you now think were the most important influences in your development in Cologne, in Paris, in New York, etc.?

A: Hmmm . . . Well, if I were to do my American "show-biz" thing properly, I would have to start by naming my mother and father, my grandmothers and grandfathers, etc. But that is already obvious, as even a cursory look at my work suggests that I did not have an unhappy childhood. But to seriously answer the question, I am glad that you asked me only about these three cities.

In Cologne:

1. Stockhausen (negatively). The excesses of his ego-centricity revolted me so much that I eventually went into isolation for three days to ponder a more socially responsible way of making art. *Paper Piece* was the result.

2. Cornelius Cardew (positively). He embodied—for me—the highest moral ground. I had some difficulty with his collaborations with Stockhausen, but it was clear where his true feelings were. He was above all a person of great intelligence and a tireless innovator, gifted with a high tolerance and a recognition of social responsibility.

3. Wolf Vostell (positively). As he was then still bumbling around, still caught between continuing an established career as a commercial artist and an overwhelming need to be recognized as a fine artist—as well as a decent and generous "mensch"—I could only respect and deeply admire the poignancy and energy of his efforts.

4. And then of course I met John Cage, David Tudor, and Merce Cunningham first in Cologne—with all that implies.

In Paris:

1. Daniel Spoerri (positively). During my first months in Paris, I visited him in Place Contrescarpe almost daily. Over coffee and wine our conversations roamed widely and wildly. But in the end I remember three important things:

—He introduced me to Robert Filliou.

—He encouraged me to publish and distribute *Methods and Processes.*

—And he once said something like: "Ben, we are lucky. I began as a classical ballet dancer. You began as a classical symphony musician. We both learned the discipline of art elsewhere, and now that we have changed media, we are free to create without bearing the historical baggage of our first art."

2. Robert Filliou (most positively). This was as close as I think it will ever get to true artistic "brother." Our works were on adjacent, parallel tracks even before we met. Naturally, Robert's work—he being ten or more years older—was more "matured," but not only were we never competitive, but we seemed to strive to be complementary. It seemed that we each tried to adapt each new work somehow to fall more closely in line with the newest work of the other. (Perhaps this thought is just my overblown romantic tribute to a beloved comrade, but I do think a comparison of works will pass at least the first test.)

3. Jan Voss (German), Benita Sanders (Welsh Canadian), and Bob Thompson (black American) (positively). I mention these three expatriate, more or less traditional artists in one breath because they each mutually reinforced, both through their personalities and through their works, my continuing respect not only for craftsmanship but also for the solid base of continuing values that empowered their works. Yes, despite my Fluxus credentials, I still hold on to some traditional values.

In New York:

In a way my return to New York unleashed the greatest paradox of my artistic (even my overall personal) career. At that time (1963–68) *everyone* moved to New York, or came for extended visits, or already lived there. Perhaps 80 to 90 percent of Fluxus and friends could be found somewhere within thirty miles of the Empire State Building on any given day. Probably the major original magnet attracting the Europeans and Japanese was the return of George Maciunas to New York and the various activities and projects he was organizing. Later Dick Higgins's Something Else Press created excitement. But all throughout there were Charlotte Moorman's Avant-garde Festivals, the Judson Church Dancers, the Living Theatre, Happenings, "be-ins," civil rights marches,

Pop Art, and generally a very big and hotly spiced stew. "Avant-garde" (we still called ourselves avant-garde then) activity was intense and continuous. And since the "core" audience was always the same thirty or forty people (regardless of whether it was a Happening, concert, dance performance, poetry reading, or art exhibition), with a fringe of foreign visitors, everyone met everyone at least weekly, if not nightly! Thus I met everyone in or passing through New York. But curiously, with only a very few did I find a kinship that would qualify as an influence. I admired and respected the work of Jackson Mac Low, Henry Flynt, and La Monte Young, but I don't think they became major influences. Yvonne Rainer, Richard Maxfield, and Robert Morris were also impressive but not influential. The Happenings gang—Hansen, Kaprow, Whitman, Oldenburg, etc.—were already so "big time," as were William Burroughs, Allen Ginsberg, and Andy Warhol, etc., etc., etc. Yes, to varying degrees they all became friends of a sort. But now I recognize that we simply did not share the deep-rooted (albeit hidden) alienation that I lived with as the only black in this crowd.

Thus, in the end I would probably cite only Robert Watts, George Brecht, Ay-O, and perhaps Dick Higgins as influences during these years—and most likely because they approached the work through poetics rather than mathematics.

And now to complete the "chart of influences," I must mention Emmett Williams and George Maciunas, both of whom I met first in Wiesbaden. For me, Emmett is the very American Robert Filliou (and vice versa). There is a purity and sensitivity in his work that are never endangered by the gloss of pseudoformalism with which he structures his work. And since our first meeting in 1962 until today, we have remained great "drinking buddies."

In contrast, with Maciunas I must confess that I never felt that we shared anything more than a perfunctory personal relationship. Our habits and sins differed too widely. Thus it is probably not surprising that I was not greatly impressed with most of his artworks. (George was a notorious plagiarizer/"arranger" of other people's ideas.) However, a few I think are genuine "Fluxus masterpieces" (such as *In Memoriam to Adriano Olivetti*). In the end my basic problem with George was the ideological hammer with which he tried to nail together all the varied Fluxus personalities and activities into a Maciunas-controlled monolithic structure.

Despite his claims to be an anarchist, George was much more a Stalinist than a Buchanist. Nevertheless, without George, art historians today would not be able to profit by commenting on whatever it was that we were doing then under the rubric Fluxus.

Q: That reminds me of another question that I wanted to ask. What do you know about how this phenomenon came to be called Fluxus?

A: Well, I assume you are not asking about the Latin origins of the word or its standard dictionary definitions, since those are well known. So I will just give you my version of how the word got associated with the work.

"In the beginning . . ." Somewhere in the mid- to late 1950s George Maciunas, a young Lithuanian immigrant living in New York and concerned about the future of his native country, proposed to edit and publish a magazine for the Lithuanian community in the U.S. about developments in the arts, culture, and politics in the homeland, to be called *Fluxus*, which, I am told, in Lithuanian means something like "freedom." For whatever reasons, the idea did not excite the community, and George went on to do other things, including founding the AG Gallery (which, I am also told, featured heavy doses of early Renaissance music), as well as slowly becoming involved with some of the "guiding lights" of what was to become New York

Fluxus. It was this involvement that eventually led to the publication of *An Anthology*, the seminal publication documenting the advances of the leading edge of the American avant-garde at that time.

If nothing else, George M. had a great "nose," and he sniffed that herein lay a great future. Plans to edit and publish an unconventional magazine dedicated to the works of the *Anthology* artists were proposed and developed, and the title *Fluxus* was carried forward. Shortly thereafter (1961?) George transferred his residence to Wiesbaden, Germany. (Some usually reliable sources suggest an escape from loan sharks.) It seems that there George decided to produce a grand festival (five to ten days) of all that was "new" in the arts as a promotion for the release of the first issue of *Fluxus*, the magazine. The festival would be called Fluxus. It was during this time—probably early spring 1962—that I first met George, by way of an introduction from Emmett Williams. Somehow the chemistry was right at that moment, and we worked well together, not only to realize the Wiesbaden Festival but also to produce the pre-events, the Galerie Parnass Wuppertal evening, and later the Paris "Fluxus sneak preview," which I organized in conjunction with the opening of my exhibition at Robert Filliou's *Galerie Légitime.*

As you know, the greater part of the program of this Wiesbaden festival consisted of works—music, dance, film, or poetry—that (in my view) could only be called "new," as the signature date was sometime after 1950.

The really radical stuff—La Monte Young, John Cage, George Brecht, Phil Corner, etc.—represented hardly more than one-tenth of the entire festival. However, in those days, when a bunch of young people (I don't think any of us were over twenty-five years old) presented "new" culture in Wiesbaden by attacking a Steinway grand piano with ax, hammer, saw, screwdriver, etc., baby, that was *news!*

And thus Phil Corner's *Piano Activities* and my *Variations for Double Bass* got front-page print and early evening television news coverage throughout the country. But since this was done in the name of art, and therefore had to be considered seriously, what was the "news handle"? How do we pigeonhole this business? Until then, what is now known as Fluxus did not know what it was—or even if it was enough to claim a new designation. So the German news media decided that the overall festival title, Fluxus, not having been applied previously to any other art movement, was available (without copyright restrictions) to be applied to the actions of these "crazy young artists" (who must be somebodies, since the festival was taking place in the Municipal Theater of Wiesbaden). Thus this hardly even loosely associated collection of artists from Japan to Yugoslavia (most of us knew at best 30 percent of the names and 10 percent of the works, and maybe 5 percent of us had actually met flesh to flesh) was formalized, more or less overnight and without prior approval, into a "new art movement" called Fluxus! In short, we became Fluxus because the German press/media couldn't find a better term to describe "awful."

Q: Hmmm, interesting information. But now I would like to ask about Fluxus the political animal. First, of course, is the question, Was Fluxus political?

A: Of course, more or less, not only, certainly, and perhaps. (A hard "yes" or "no" could not be Fluxus.) I have given this answer because, given that Fluxus included so many nations, how could a singular answer be possible?

Let's start by remembering that "seminal works" of Fluxus—whether created in Europe, the U.S., or Japan—happened between 1958 and 1962. This was a period of great political upheaval in the U.S., which willingly or unwillingly found reflections in many places elsewhere in the world. It was a time (according to me) when no artist should "sit on the fence." But in general I think Fluxus did sit on the fence. True, many of the Fluxus artists during that time were very willing to "confess" to harmless friends that they were really anarchists, communists, socialists, and/or something or other in that direction. But I must state that I never got a telephone call from "Fluxus Central" asking me to join next Saturday's "March on Washington"—for any purpose. (Although other organizations, which knew me only as a "likely" telephone number, called regularly. And, yes, I did march—not every weekend but enough to get a good taste of tear gas.) Nevertheless the demonstration against the performance of Stockhausen's *Originale* at Carnegie Hall and Henry Flynt's picketing of MoMA stirred up storms of sufficient strength to encourage George Maciunas to pronounce his first "excommunication." What a silly business! (What are the concerns represented here?)

Despite all Maciunas's protestations as well as his own political leanings, Fluxus was never really political. All it really did with its reputation for radical aesthetics was to provide a safe refuge and masks for a bunch of well-meaning artists.

Yes, I was disgusted, and yes, the lack of support for civil rights and antiwar efforts was an important factor in my subsequent "retirement" from the art scene. But please know that I have been talking only with reference to the American/New York Fluxus scene. Perhaps the European scene was a little different. But then what are the risks if racial prejudice has not yet raised its ugly head or if you are only a spectator to a distant war? Basically I don't think that Fluxus had the formal capacity to be political. The simplicity of the one-line gag aesthetic, as dictated by George M., may have had some validity in attacking overblown cultural illusions, but the form simply had no capacity to deliver even a moderately sophisticated political message. From this perspective, I think Fluxus may have been a great mistake, although many or most Fluxus artists were "on the left" and I think/know that they wanted to confront the issues. But while there may well be one or more simple answers to complex problems, "the work" must have the capacity to manifest more complex answers when it becomes clear that the simple answer is not working.

Q: Let's use that answer as a lead-in to a few questions about your own work. I assume from the above that you consider it important for an artist to be socially critical and even overtly political. Yet your work seems to depend heavily on humor, kitsch, and toys. How do you think you can address life's serious questions with these materials?

A: Well, from the beginning humor or fun was a very prominent element of Fluxus, especially for the Americans. A lot of us, I believe, started out to have nothing less than some irreverent good fun, debunking what we considered the pretentions of "high art"/culture. Bob Watts was amused by the idea of trying to lure "flying saucers" to land on his farm by setting up automobile hubcaps as flying-saucer decoys.

Although Dick Higgins titled his piece *Danger Music No. 2*, I am sure he thought it would be "fun" to have his head shaved in public. It was certainly fun to stick a finger into one of Ay-O's boxes. Likewise I hope Phil Corner intended us to have fun wrecking the piano in Wiesbaden, because I certainly did. And there were all the funny pieces by Emmett Williams, and even the performances of my *Lick Piece* were always more funny than erotic. And above all there was always George Maciunas, the master of slapstick and the one-line gag.

In Europe there was something else afoot. Humor, yes. But not so direct as in the U.S. Satire and irony and other more complex forms of humor played a larger role. Beuys or Tomas Schmit found the best line. In Japan the humor was infected with Zen, or maybe the other way around.

Yes, I think we were all serious about our work, but we did not feel that work expressing "seriousness" was either the best or only path. To answer your question directly, from my point of view I do believe that "life's serious questions" (as well as politics) begin with art. Art establishes a cultural foundation from which all else proceeds. Naturally one can approach this problem from many directions—dogmatically, didactically, minimally, etc. But personally, when making art (and therefore culture), I prefer to use humor as it often provides the path of least suspicion/resistance for the implanting of subversive ideas. Remembering, as I mentioned before, that I grew up as a black in an America of legalized racial segregation, which allowed few means of protest (please know that we blacks used satirical humor as a protest form). This is best exemplified in one of my works exhibited at Galerie Schüppenhauer, titled *Educating White Folks*. In this piece I quote a black folk story, which goes like this: "The appropriation for the Negro school was used for the white school. The superintendent explained this to the Negro principal, who of course couldn't make a direct protest. So he said, 'The one thing we need most of all is educated white folks.'" So that is where I come from.

Q: It seems that the iconography of your work depends almost exclusively on "found objects"—often cheap, familiar, and kitschy. The result is that the message or content of your works appears not only very direct but also quite simple. If this is true, do you feel that this "simplified" iconography limits your development of more subtle subjects and ideas?

A: Well, yes. The iconography does often depend on cheap, familiar, and kitschy materials. But there are differences between: (a) the simple physical presence of an object and (b) the cultural context from which it has been appropriated and (c) the ways that the object-cum-icon relates to other object-icons, texts, or images appearing in a particular work. For starters, as an eternal optimist, I believe that life can, or at least could, be simple. Next, I am not convinced that if there is something to be said it gains profundity through obscurity. On the one hand, there are certainly such things as mysteries, and they are wonderful subjects for study, but I don't find that a "mystical" treatment of a mystery (such as the mystery of death) does much to either advance understanding or inspire awe. On the other hand, toys and kitsch are instruments for measuring how much we have trivialized life. In the end the types and qualities of the objects that I have used for iconographical purposes limit me only in the rigor required to find precise and meaningful solutions to their relatedness—both internally and externally.

Q: There is another question that I want to ask about your work. It is about "craftsmanship." Compared with other American Fluxus artists—let's say George Maciunas, Bob Watts, or George Brecht—your work, if you will excuse me for saying so, seems often "unfinished" or even crude. Is this intentional or only because you are lazy?

A: Well, I don't think that I am lazier than most people. But it is true that my work does not have a "high-gloss" finish. I could fall back on the excuse that I was never trained as a visual artist and have only recently started making objects again, after a twenty-five-year "vacation." But that is not the issue. You may remember that even my early performance work, which depended on my training as a musician, often seemed roughshod and "in process." So you may conclude that my low-tech approach is intentional. Although I admire craftsmanship, I don't think that the kind of technically flawless (if such is really possible) work is consistent with an overview that accepts that the haphazard and even chaos are part of the acceptance of life. And in the end I think that works of "flawless craftsmanship" intentionally or unintentionally give the observer/viewer the "easy way out" of reacting to the superficial qualities of the work without engaging whatever more substantial discourse may be present.

Q: Okay, I have only one final question. Your first works—those created in Cologne and Paris—were what we now might call "conceptual art" or "performance art." That is, they were based in time, language, gestural, and acoustic events, and the end product had no material permanence. In fact, I understand that these works were informed by a strong antimaterialistic bias. Now you are making works that have a physical permanence: they are exhibited in galleries, have acquired commercial value, and are available to be sold and bought. Why? Have you rejected your original idealism?

A: Well, there are several parts to the answer of this question. First, I, like most of humanity, must labor by hand or mind for my daily bread. And during the first twenty years, when Fluxus was at best a fringe phenomenon, it held few or no commercial opportunities sufficient to support a family. (I did have a family to support.) That has changed somewhat during these last years.

Second, you are correct, at least with respect to my work, that it was informed by an antimaterialistic bias. But that does not mean that I did not wish (rather than expect) that the work would be a means to earn a livelihood. To be perfectly honest, there was little to find in my early work to be commercialized. Works like *Methods and Processes* were very slippery, meant to infiltrate at a near-subliminal level and then exit, leaving behind little or no trace/evidence that a foreign matter had entered and tweaked a bit of your mind.

So as you can imagine, that kind of work had very limited commercial possibilities. Now, of course, the work is "art history," and original copies have some commercial value. It is also true that my early objects (the "puzzle-poems," for example) were intentionally designed to have no or little intrinsic, commercial value—and to be cheaply reproducible. But quite frankly, even if the "content" of the work could have been "packaged" in a form having greater commercial value, at that time (and I think all of us were ready to sell) there was no one with money interested in what Fluxus was doing. Thus, for the most part we ended up exchanging our works with other like-minded and equally moneyless souls. Now, of course, there is a bit of a market for Fluxus, and being the lazy human being that I am, it is only natural that I now try to see if it is not easier to earn my livelihood by making silly objects rather than by working as a bureaucrat in a boring office.

Q: Finally, do you agree that Fluxus is dead now that Maciunas is dead?

A: The final truth is that Fluxus—however laudatory our various initial pronouncements may have been—was never much more than a pragmatic episode (not even a collective), which floundered into a circumstance rich enough to accommodate a very wild but also very focused bunch of 1960s radical artists. Without George Maciunas the various strains of Fluxus would have probably disappeared as "early attempts" at this or that recent art form (Pop Art, Minimalism, Conceptual Art, Mail Art, etc., etc., etc.). But because of George Maciunas, not only is the Fluxus legacy still alive, but it is also dead.

As a nonbeliever, I have no idea about how George M. may or may not be enjoying "life after death." But I do believe not only that Fluxus has survived George but also that now that it is finally free to be Fluxus, it is becoming that something/nothing with which George should be happy!

In Search of Benjamin Patterson: *An Improvised Journey*

GEORGE E. LEWIS

Benjamin (Ben) Patterson. Born 1934 in Pittsburgh, Pennsylvania. I wish I knew Ben Patterson. In a way, I've been searching for him all my life, even though he was always and already there. I'll explain that in a moment, but I should say at the outset that the work being performed by this article somewhat exceeds my original intent to examine Patterson's work in terms of contemporary ideas about improvisation.

There's a long tradition in jazz of referring to musicians by their first names, shortened first names, or nicknames. Insiders—musicians and listeners but not necessarily the general public—refer confidently to Miles and Duke and Hawk and Bud and Trane. Although Ben Patterson's life and work did not have much to do with jazz, at least according to the standard portrayals, Fluxus narratives also asserted first-name familiarity with alacrity. The stories always seemed to invite you to imagine (or wish) that you yourself had been on the Fluxus scene.

There was another Ben—Ben Vautier—whose e-mail listserv I was on for years. I have no idea who put me on his list, but as a longtime denizen of several experimental music scenes, I enjoyed being able, on an irregular basis, to keep up with the doings of George and Shigeko and Emmett and Alison and so on. These e-mails presented lots of stories, more than a few complaints, and a strong, celebratory sense of community.

So many Fluxnarratives—like the narratives of its predecessor movement, the Beats—trade on the familiar: personal stories and histories, sometimes with a point or edge, sometimes not. During my early years in New York, the mid-1970s, I would sit placidly—by turns mystified, fascinated, nonplussed, and here and there a bit bored—as older artists who knew the principal players in the drama—or, as I found out later, were players themselves—told Fluxus stories that never made the books but that "everyone" somehow knew. I was flattered to be there since I am considerably younger than the Fluxus originators, and I don't think they're taking on new members—or rather, we want our own clubs and our own names anyway.

George Maciunas's 1967 mapping of Fluxus and its relationship to the avant-garde presented the exoskeleton of a socio-artistic network concerned with the production of knowledge—oral, written, graphic—about itself.[1] This epistemologically centered identity-formation project is central to many art movements, but the degree to which Fluxus publicly articulated this kind of networked affinity consciousness is particularly noteworthy. It is this sense of affinity that produces art, movements, and genre membership, and the oral histories I absorbed in those bar and backstage sessions not only constituted valuable preparation for the textual histories and collegial connections I encountered later but also whetted my appetite for actually meeting this mysterious black figure, Ben Patterson.

A later reason why I wanted to get to know Patterson in some way—at least historically, if not personally—is that a fair amount of my current scholarly direction casts a critical, contextualizing eye upon the frequent discrepancies between scholarly and popular histories of experimentalism and what artists actually experienced in and around those experimental art worlds. This isn't quite the same thing as reading a history of the period and complaining, "That's not the way it happened"; rather, what is of concern here is an analysis of mediation, critically examining differences between what James Scott would call "public" and "private" transcripts.[2]

Another reason why I wanted to get to know Patterson is more personal. I've been associated for many years with the Association for the Advancement of Creative Musicians, an influential African American musical avant-garde that is roughly contemporaneous with Fluxus. As I noted in my book on this musical collective, "AACM musicians updated and revised a model pursued by black classical composers, an important group of creative music-makers who, I maintain, have been all but ignored by the major black cultural critics and public intellectuals who have come to prominence since 1980"—composers like Tania Leon, Hale Smith, T. J. Anderson, and Alvin Singleton, who, like Patterson, pursued more or less conventional Western classical music training.[3]

Now this working-class, grassroots experimental music movement appears not only in otherwise whiteness-imbued historical accounts of experimental music but also in canonical histories of African American music. In contrast, black music scholar Dominique-René de Lerma's review of the 1971 edition of Eileen Southern's now-canonical survey text, *The Music of Black Americans*, notes that Patterson isn't even listed in the index.[4] Even more oddly, a review of the literature finds that although Fluxus is mentioned in at least one of the major surveys on African American art, its sole black exponent and arguable cofounder, Benjamin Patterson, was somehow overlooked.[5] A computer search finds that the canonical *Black Music Research Journal* never mentions him in more than a quarter-century of excellent scholarship on music of all types, including my own article in the journal.

On the other side of the tracks (so to speak), Patterson fares somewhat better, but a curious tandem of display and erasure dominates his presence. While he is invariably mentioned in nearly every prominent account of the movement,[6] his work is seldom the focus, either in the critical writing on Fluxus or in the first-person Flux-reminiscences. Perhaps the most extensive and diverse edited collection of Patterson's early works is to be found in the book *Fluxus Codex* (1988), edited by Jon Hendricks, and a comparatively substantial review of his later works, including color reproductions of his objects and installations, can be found in a volume published in Brazil in 2002.[7]

A more typical example is Ken Friedman's 1998 book *The Fluxus Reader*, which makes only modest mention of Patterson; an article by Dick Higgins in the volume briefly recounts a Patterson street event on the edge of a red-light district in New York's Times Square as "one of the more successful Fluxperformances."[8] Even as a 1997 *TDR* article claims, "There's no denying it: Fluxus was an inclusive operation," invoking Patterson to corroborate the further claim that "there were probably more women and artists of color associated with Fluxus than with any other previous grouping of artists in Western art history,"[9] as far as I have been able to determine, few critical or historical articles on Patterson's work have been published.

Thus we might say (uncharitably, to be sure) that when it comes to Fluxhistory, Benjamin Patterson functions as the Spook Who Sat by the Door,[10] a metonym prominently positioned by well-meaning scholars (and possibly colleagues) to retroactively bolster the movement's diversity bona fides. While imputations of racism would be simplistic and unwarranted, to pretend that issues of race do not invade historiographies and personal narratives of experimentalism would be needlessly (or willfully) naive, particularly given the general lack of attention to issues of race in scholarly histories of the avant-garde. In fact, the dogged investment in liberal theories of color blindness articulated in most commentary on the period contrasts markedly with recent scholarship in many other fields.[11] As a consequence, before examining Patterson's work in the context of improvisation, it might be useful to take a virtual tour of the artist's early history.

Formative Years

Benjamin Patterson's background was superficially similar to those of many white experimentalists whose crucial formative years spanned the 1950s and 1960s. As a child, he listened assiduously to classical music, particularly opera, and pursued postsecondary classical music study in composition and double bass performance at the University of Michigan, where he went to school with composer Gordon Mumma.[12]

After Patterson graduated from college in 1956, according to his own account, "I also embarked on a crusade—to be the first black to 'break the color barrier' [and play] in an American symphony orchestra.... But in the end, even though such a famous conductor as Leopold Stokowski fought strongly on my behalf, America was not yet ready for a black symphony musician, and so I went to Canada."[13] During his initial brush with expatriate life, Patterson performed as a contrabassist with the Halifax Symphony Orchestra and the Ottawa Philharmonic Orchestra, and also became involved with electronic music, working in Ottawa with Canadian pioneer Hugh Le Caine and performing his own experiments.[14]

Here Patterson's activity diverges from the normative white experimentalist biography; moreover, it is precisely at this point that one could say that Fluxus's prehistory becomes bound up with race. As a start, let us say that, in the event, the U.S. classical world's contemporaneous rejection of black Americans as performers proved fortuitous; had matters been otherwise, Patterson might have ended up buried at the side of the stage behind the cellos, with no time to create visual works, installations, compositions, or "events." The composer himself hinted at this in 1991, describing his symphonic Jackie Robinsonism as a distracting cross he forced himself to bear: "My

point, however, is that although before university I was exploring a wide range of subjects, media, and materials, from anthropology to Zen—all of which have eventually found a place in my art—the urgency/discipline of my 'crusade' kept me pretty much on a 'straight line' all the way through university."[15] Another divergence from the standard experimental music biography was Patterson's stint in the United States Army, in which he performed, not with "army bands," as one finds on many pre-Vietnam jazz resumes, but with the Seventh Army's Symphony Orchestra in Germany.

From this point, divergences abound. For instance, while the literature on black American artistic expatriates to Europe concentrates largely on the French experience, in 1960 we find Patterson in Cologne, where after an encounter with Karlheinz Stockhausen, he met John Cage, David Tudor, La Monte Young, and George Brecht at Mary Bauermeister's studio events (the Fluxus equivalent of Minton's Playhouse), experiencing a moment of self-realization that one might compare with Charlie Parker's legendary chili house epiphany: "Even now I still have a vivid memory of telling myself . . . that this is the music that I had been hearing in my head for years but had never thought possible to realize."[16]

Staying in Cologne, Patterson met Emmett Williams, Daniel Spoerri, Nam June Paik, Cornelius Cardew, and others, and he began working on new ways of making music. "At some point or other," Patterson recounted in 2001, "George Maciunas fell into our lives and the Wiesbaden Festival happened"—the signal event that announced the name Fluxus to the larger worlds of art and music, and arguably rendered Patterson a founding member of the movement.[17]

At least part of the reason for Patterson's modest presence in histories of experimental art making might well be laid at the composer's own door. Where he appears, his biographies are laconic, even cryptic. Jürgen Becker and Wolf Vostell (the latter a card-carrying Fluxus art-ist) list him in their 1965 survey, but in that volume's set of self-submitted biographies, one notes the contrast between the expansive Nam June Paik and the drily fac-tual Patterson:

> Name: Benjamin A. Patterson, Jr.
> Height: 180 cm.
> Weight: 77 kg.
> Wears glasses. Excellent health. Married
> (2 children).[18]

What follows is a medieval-style, basically nonnarrative chronicle, a set of annals presenting dates that may or may not be important, followed by a modestly presented list of publication and performance venues. That's all.

> 1934: Born on May 29, in Pittsburgh, Pa.
> 1952: Penn High School (Pittsburgh, Pa.)
> 1956: University of Michigan (Bachelor of Music)
> 1956–60: Contrabassist with Halifax Symphony
> Orchestra; U.S. Army 7th Army Symphony
> Orchestra; Ottawa Philharmonic Orchestra
> 1960–62: Lives, writes, and performs in Cologne
> and Paris

By his own account, Patterson was active in Fluxus from 1962 to 1967 and "semi-active" after that. A 1990 self-biography lists Patterson as working at the New York Public Library in 1963, getting a master's degree in library science at Columbia University in 1967, and "retiring as an artist in the late 1960s to pursue an 'ordinary life.'"[19]

During his "retirement," Patterson engaged deeply with creating new cultural infrastructures for African American and other artists of color. A 1970 article by Dominique-René de Lerma identified Patterson as a former president of the Society of Black Composers,[20] and in March 1972 the composer participated in a panel discussion titled "Music in Black America" at the Music Educators National Conference in Atlanta, alongside Wendell Whalum, then chair of the music department at historically black More-house College.[21] Patterson helped to develop the Com-poser in Performance programs for the New York State Council on the Arts, as well as serving as chair of the Department of Performing and Creative Arts at Staten Island Community College. He served as general man-ager of the Symphony of the New World (an ensemble devoted early on to fostering ethnic and gender diver-sity in symphony orchestras, including both performers and composers) and as director of development for the Negro Ensemble Company.[22]

Methods and Processes (1)

Patterson's text pieces are usually grouped under the general heading of what are now known as "event scores," said to be pioneered in the early 1960s, in particular by La Monte Young, Yoko Ono, and George Brecht, whose Fluxus work is generally seen as being emblematic of the early possibilities of the medium.[23] Critic Liz Kotz focuses on the poetics of text scores:

> Rather than pulverizing language into sonorous fragments, the scores focus on the instructions themselves as poetic material. This alternate poetics, of deeply prosaic everyday statements, comprised of short, simple, vernacular words, presented in the quasi-instrumental forms of lists and instructions, emerges in the postwar era as a counter-model to the earlier avant-garde practices of asyntacticality, musicality, and semiotic disruption. . . . Physically modest and de-skilled, these "scores" represent an artistic practice driven by but also counter to the recording and reproductive technologies that would increasingly restructure sound and language in the postwar era.[24]

While many of Patterson's text scores incorporate a freely significative poetics, unlike Brecht's works, they neither necessarily valorize the everyday nor situate events at a threshold point between performance and its environment. Rather, some of these works perform a more traditional role of asking listeners and performers to locate themselves in interaction with sonorous experience. As French critic Nicolas Feuillie stated in 2002: "Benjamin Patterson maintains about his concept of 'events' that the instructions require special involvement by the interpreters. Rather than an art that is distracting or soothing, and in contrast to the uniquely playful aspect that such 'events' may seem to have in general, he affirms their essentially personal dimension, the character of lived experience that enriches those who create them, and the immediacy that their apprehension requires—a demand that abandons the very notion of art."[25]

Further, these Patterson pieces differ from other Fluxus scores, later conceptual art/music pieces, and traditional scores in that their realization cannot take place in the imaginary; to be perceived at all, they must be performed—physical, real-world action must be asserted. The consequences of that action must be experienced, and no attempt is made to anticipate or control audience or environmental response or orientation to time, memory, or history.

Writing in 1964, Patterson himself declared: "I demanded of an experiencer (not a passive viewer or listener) to act in the position of performer, interpreter and even as creator in the event. I was not concerned about stimulating retinas or eardrums, but instead to make that which would address the integration of experience and relevant capabilities."[26] A 1991 "interview with himself" first published in German translation in the journal *Kunstforum International* (the original English version is included in the present volume) provides perhaps the most extensive critical autoethnography of Patterson's

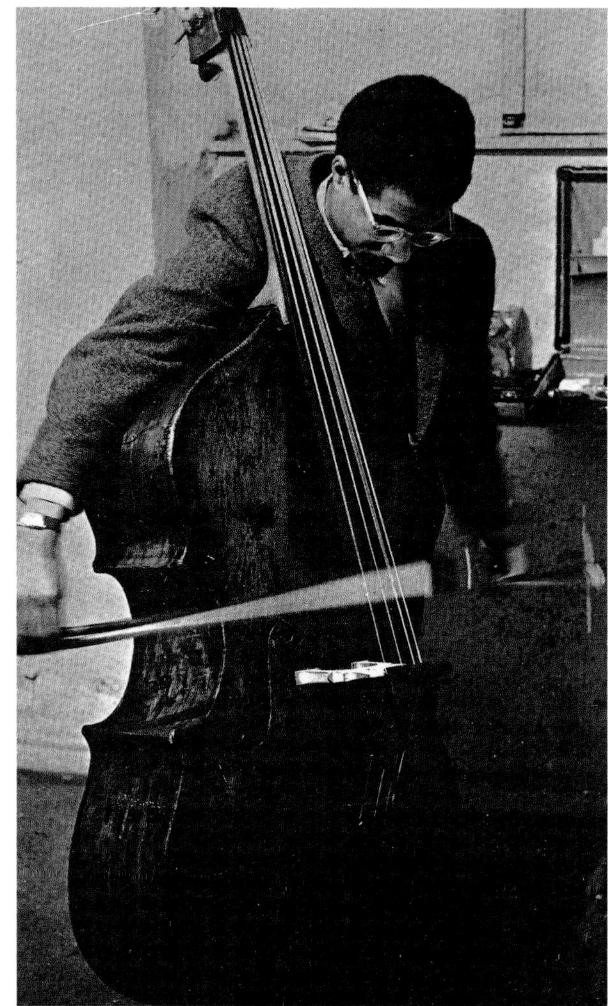

Patterson performing *Variations for Double Bass* (1961) in 1962

view of his early works. "But during this period," he related, "I thought of myself as some sort of a composer-performer (the term *performance artist* hadn't been invented yet), and most of my work was presented in the context of a Fluxus festival or concert. These works—if not exactly music—were still based primarily in time and activity, not space and color."[27]

Fluxus artists were inordinately fond of including themselves on taxonomically articulated lists and genealogies. Patterson appears on nearly all the lists, but the nature of his presence varies. The composer's own list comes in the form of a piece, *Constellations of the First Magnitude* (2002), rendered as a sample of Renaissance visual cosmology, complete with astrological signs.[28] Patterson's self-produced narratives are relatively modest in scope and number, and like many African American artists working in whiteness-imbued art worlds, he may well have realized that he would be obliged to write himself back into his own history.

Typically Patterson performs this historiographical function with a certain modesty and self-effacement that, alternatively, could be viewed as a strategy of masking. In 2001 he noted the relation between a certain whimsy and playfulness that his work evoked and "the old saying that you catch more flies with honey than with vinegar, which has something to do with the African American that I am . . . the standard Amos and Andy situation of getting through difficult situations with humor with more smile on your face is one of the things I learned as a survival technique."[29]

The comment seems to add new dimensions to the context within which Fluxus humor has been presented. Indeed, critic Kristine Stiles saw cryptic references to race in Patterson's use of coffee grounds in the text score of his 1964 *First Symphony*:

FIRST SYMPHONY
One at a time members of audience are questioned,
"DO YOU TRUST ME?" and are divided left and
   right, yes
and no.
the room is darkened.
freshly ground coffee is scattered throughout
   the room.[30]

Queried by the critic, Patterson himself was less sanguine about this interpretation: "I must admit that I do not remember being so consciously aware of . . . racial impli-

cations when I made this work. Of course, I knew I was a Negro (the terminology in those days) and quite a bit about racism and how it was affecting my life. But, consciously, I really did not understand how deeply racism affected my work. Obviously, subconsciously a lot was happening."[31] For Patterson, the centerpiece of *First Symphony* was the use of the "pop" sound of opening a can of coffee on stage in the dark as a means of provoking audience anxiety: "[It was] a sound familiar to many people (male and female) at that time thru military experience or 'civil rights' marches (it is the sound of opening the container of a smoke, percussion or tear-gas grenade)."[32] Nonetheless, Stiles is reluctant to embrace Patterson's disclaimer, concluding that "issues of race found both overt and covert expression" in his work and that, in *First Symphony*, Patterson "seemed to confront his predominantly white, avant-garde audience with its veneer of sophistication, that gloss that thinly cloaks deep and unresolved racial conflict."[33]

What seems equally plausible upon further reflection, however, is that the composer expected even a normatively white audience for avant-garde work to recognize and respond to the sounds of protest demonstrations, including the ominous sounds of lethal authority. In this way, rather than being narrowly focused on confronting and thereby centering the experience of whiteness, Patterson was using sound to universalize the experience of social protest, something experienced by citizens of all races at the time.

This is not to say that Patterson avoided confrontation with race in his work. In his 1991 self-interview, he notes that he prefers to use humor "as it often provides the path of least suspicion/resistance for the implanting of subversive ideas."[34] His assertion of this method in one piece could be seen as a precursor of Adrian Piper's even more pointedly ironic participation work of 1982, *Funk Lessons*.[35] As Patterson described it: "This is best exemplified in one of my works exhibited at Galerie Schüppenhauer, titled *Educating White Folks*. In this piece I quote a black folk story, which goes like this: 'The appropriation for the Negro school was used for the white school. The superintendent explained this to the Negro principal, who of course couldn't make a direct protest. So he said, "The one thing we need most of all is educated white folks."' So that is where I come from."[36]

The possibility that Patterson was uninterested in having the reception of his work overdetermined by race may have accounted for his embrace of Europe, as with so many other nineteenth- and twentieth-century African American artists. This account appears to be supported by Sally Banes's quotation of a 1964 article by Dick Higgins, whom she characterized as "someone indignant against prejudice": "Patterson married and went [from Germany] to France, as he had gone from the U.S. before, where he did not want to be a 'negro artist' but just one Hell of a good one and, among other things, a negro. Only James Baldwin and Benjamin Patterson have ever attained that proportion."[37]

Nonetheless, to the extent that simply being "a negro" automatically announced race in a whiteness-valorizing art world, one could reasonably expect that race and its naturalizations would come dangerously close to overdetermining the responses of critics, audiences, and even colleagues. Thus, even Higgins felt able to publicly declare in 1964 that, before meeting Patterson, he suspected that he was black, apparently just from reading his 1962 book *Methods and Processes*: "Actually Patterson's way of using periodic repeats and the blues feeling that this produced being so ingrained and natural struck me so much that when he first sent me a copy of methods and processes I wrote to him and guessed he was a negro."[38] In this light, it is not difficult to imagine that Patterson's use of the "survival technique" of humor involved both musical and collegial aspects.

The Role of Improvisation

Patterson's early pieces are often composed of three main elements: (1) a set of materials, physical and/or temporal; (2) performance instructions and process elaboration; and (3) limit and ending conditions. A typical example is his famous *Paper Piece* (1960), in which performers create a variety of sounds using paper bags. The piece could be presented as public and interactive, and as the score notes, "dynamics are improvised within natural borders."[39]

[Materials]

5 performers
instrumentation:
15 sheets of paper per performer approximate size
of standard newspaper, quality varied, newspaper,
tissue paper, light cardboard, colored, printed
or plain.
3 paper bags per performer; quality, size and
shape varied

[Performance instructions and process
elaboration]

procedure: A general sign from a chairman will
begin the piece. Within the following 30 seconds
performers enter at will.
By each performer, 7 sheets are performed
SHAKE
BREAK—opposite edges of the sheet are grasped
firmly and sharply jerked apart
TEAR—each sheet is reduced to particles less than
1/10 size of the original . . .

dynamics are improvised within natural borders of
approximate ppp of TWIST and fff of POP! . . .

each performer previously selects, arranges,
materials and sequence of events.

duration: 10 to 12 1/2 minutes . . . . The piece ends when the paper supply is exhausted.

Early on, Patterson saw openings in avant-garde music for improvisative modes of encounter. "In the series of Bauermeister," he recalled, "I met John and David and Cage's earliest work and recordings such as Radio Music, so I introduced myself and he asked me to perform with them the next night. And it was like a duck taking to water, and it was so natural for improvisation."[40] In contrast, Fluxus cofounder George Maciunas felt compelled to differentiate between Fluxus composers and Fluxus improvisers. By this time the art world had forgotten the late nineteenth-century origins of Western music's proscription of improvisation and was in thrall to the working out of the "Quiet Revolution" that attempted to erase the historical and cultural processes that preceded improvisation's fall from grace.[41]

For Maciunas, the prevalence of improvisative practices in the new movement seemed to imply the need for new modes of encounter and dissemination. "Generally, there are very few Europeans doing compositions, so few I really can't think of anyone," he wrote in a 1962 letter to George Brecht. "Maybe [Robert] Filliou and . . . [Wolf] Vostell and [Daniel] Spoerri. The last 2 do not write down their happenings but improvise on the spot so I can't tell you or send their things to you. Of non Europeans best are NJ Paik, Ben Patterson, Emmett Williams, Paik again does not write down his compositions, but a few simple ones I can describe."[42]

The possibility that the binary opposition between improvisation and composition might constitute a merely vestigial remnant of Western music's post-Romanticism occurred to few at this time, at least publicly. In any case, Patterson, who did not study with Cage, seemed unfazed by that community's suspicion of improvisation, and the

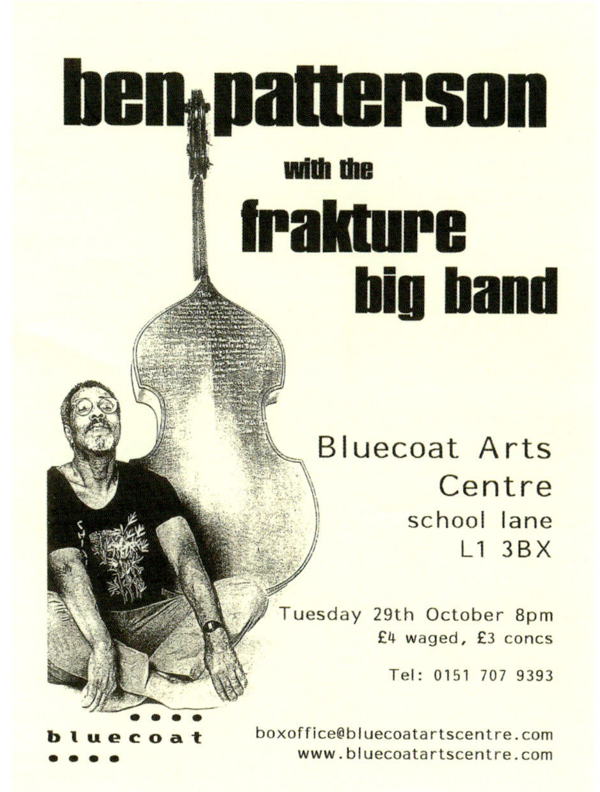

Poster for Patterson performance in Liverpool, 2002

improvisation-composition binary evidently lacked the moral force commonly assumed for it at the time. Thus, in a decided difference from Cagean aesthetics, a performance of *Paper Piece* could be Dionysian or Apollonian according to mood, and at least from the evidence of a 1999 performance of the work,[43] the tendency was clearly toward the former. Moreover, despite Patterson's initial negative reaction to Stockhausen, the pieces resemble the older composer's notion of composer control more than that of Brecht or Young.[44]

The only other African American who has been associated with Fluxus was the innovative avant-garde jazz-identified singer Jeanne Lee. As historian Eric Porter has it: "Lee was briefly married to and collaborated with sound poet David Hazelton and worked with other artists affiliated with sound poetry, Fluxus, and Happenings. She became interested in sound poetry's dedication to conveying emotional meaning through intonation, communicating via non-verbal utterances, and connecting poetry to bodily movement and sensation. Lee was also drawn to the experimentalism, ritual, audience participation, and iconoclasm associated with Fluxus and Happenings."[45]

For the most part, however, the canonical literature on Fluxus has been careful to distance the movement from jazz. The closest affinity to jazz runs through saxophonist La Monte Young, whose background in jazz was well known, albeit commonly portrayed as an aspect of his past that has little to do with the scope of his career.[46] Nonetheless, Porter argues that Lee's notion of the relation between performed sound and the environment connects jazz with Fluxus, in that it "suggests a commitment to human interactivity during the creative process that creates non-hierarchal relationships among performers and audience members and invites the audience to participate in the creation of meaning around the performance. It is an ethos that can be found in the work of Fluxus and Happenings participants, as well as that of African American improvisers such as members of the AACM, and multi-instrumentalist Marion Brown, on whose *Afternoon of a Georgia Faun* Lee performed."[47]

Similarly, a communal interaction with the audience is audible on the archival live recordings of Patterson's 1961 *Variations for Double Bass* and *Duo for Voice and a String Instrument*. Sudden silences are punctuated by unusual and evocative sounds, both great and small, and members of the gallery audience are talking, laughing, and freely applauding Patterson's performance efforts, as in a jazz bar. Moreover, photos of performances of *Variations* from 1962 and 1989 (see p. 199) indicate that the piece was as much visually as sonically articulated.

A deceptively complex example of improvisation from *Methods and Processes* uses materials from the environment itself—in this case, a bakery:

> enter bakery
> smell
> leave
> enter second bakery
> smell
> leave
> enter third bakery
> smell
> leave
> continue until appetite is obtained.[48]

The piece asks participants to interact with a potentially large number of bakeries but gives a limited set of instructions as to how that interaction is to be performed. In Cagean terms, this is a moment in the score that would ideally be "indeterminate with respect to performance," but in everyday-life terms, innumerable small acts, performed in the spirit of the piece, require indeterminacy to live alongside agency in ways that cannot be conflated with what Cage called "the dictates of ego."[49] These small acts include not only physical motion and decision making as to timing but also self-reflection, attention, and evaluation with regard to the experience itself—elements that, after all, are explicitly called for in the piece and that draw upon essentially universal human tendencies and capabilities.

The notion of improvisation subsumes all these acts and in the end constitutes a much better descriptor of the actual affective worth of performance. As Patterson notes, "My pieces, as they appear on paper, have neither material nor abstract value." Rather, for Patterson, "They can only achieve value in performance, and then only the personal value that the participant himself perceives about his own behavior and/or that of the society during and/or after the experience. (In fact, any piece is just this: a person, who, consciously, does this or that. Everybody can do it.)"[50]

What Now?

Patterson returned to active Fluxduty in 1988, around the time of a general recrudescence of interest in Fluxus. Besides his important sound and music works, he was also a printmaker and a painter, and he created sculptures ranging from the ubiquitous Flux-box form to room-size installations that have been exhibited in solo and group shows and performances around the world.

In the interim, digital compact discs had become a prime contemporary form for sonic dissemination, one far more tractable and less expensive to produce and distribute than the bulky analog vinyl discs of the 1960s. New recordings began to appear, such as the seven-part *Liverpool Song Lines* from 2002 and 2003's hilariously thought-provoking *Surveying Western Philosophy Using China Tools*,[51] as well as archival recordings and new performances of Patterson's acknowledged classic works, such as *Variations for Double Bass, Duo for Voice and a String Instrument*, and *Paper Piece*.[52]

Patterson's 2002 recording of his work *The River Mersey* indicates that his commitment to improvisation has not slackened. The piece combines periodic repetitions of R & B–style audio, spoken event instructions, elements of *Duo for Voice and a String Instrument*, and audibly jazz-identified performance of a graphic score.[53] While such scores can function as sites for the improvisative act's signature combination of indeterminacy, agency, history, and memory, one might observe, as I have noted elsewhere, that "once a graphic score migrates conceptually beyond the communities in which it originated, however, the metatext that it represents inevitably becomes

transformed. In that sense, either the graphic score or the improvisation can become a site for asserting affinities with, or articulating fealty to, a received tradition. . . . The future history of any graphic score or improvisation will be partly oral, partly aural as mediated through recording, and partly related to the texts that musicians, scholars, and journalists have produced about it."[54]

The River Mersey shows us that the sound of any realization of a graphic or textual score fortuitously transcends the composer and the contemporaneous environment at the time of its original conception. Thus embedded in the histories of its current performers and audiences, the scores can remain alive, resisting any notion of "historically correct performance" as they remain responsive to the vicissitudes and necessities of the creative social moment. In this way, each performance can be unique and "original" with respect to time and space. Indeed, a major trope of Benjamin Patterson's work concerns simply staying alive—to possibility and to experience.

I once saw singer Richie Havens on a television show; the host of the show, noting that it had been a long time since mainstream media audiences had seen Havens, asked him if he had a message for the public.

"Tell them I'm still here," came the reply.

NOTES

I wish to thank Valerie Cassel Oliver for access to a partial text of Benjamin Patterson's *Methods and Processes.*

1. This Fluxus mapping is reproduced in Hannah Higgins, *Fluxus Experience* (Berkeley and Los Angeles: University of California Press, 2002), 79.

2. See James C. Scott, *Domination and the Arts of Resistance: Hidden Transcripts* (New Haven: Yale University Press, 1990).

3. George E. Lewis, *A Power Stronger Than Itself: The AACM and American Experimental Music* (Chicago: University of Chicago Press, 2008), xlv.

4. Dominique-René de Lerma, "Review: The Music of Black Americans: A History," *Notes* 28 (September 1971): 43–44. The oversight continues in the third edition. See Eileen Southern, *The Music of Black Americans: A History,* 3rd ed. (New York: W. W. Norton, 1997).

5. See Sharon F. Patton, *African-American Art* (New York: Oxford University Press, 1998). Richard J. Powell's compact history mentions performance art but not Fluxus, while Samella Lewis's 2003 survey mentions neither. See Richard J. Powell, *Black Art: A Cultural History* (London: Thames & Hudson, 2002), and Samella Lewis, *African American Art and Artists,* 3rd ed. (Berkeley and Los Angeles: University of California Press, 2003). Also see Lewis, *Power Stronger Than Itself.*

6. That is, except for Wikipedia (http://en.wikipedia.org/wiki/ Fluxus, accessed May 7, 2009), but Patterson could fix that himself.

7. Jon Hendricks, ed., *O que é Fluxus? O que não é! O porquê?* (Rio de Janeiro: Centro Cultural Banco do Brasil; Detroit: Gilbert and Lila Silverman Fluxus Collection Foundation, 2002); Jon Hendricks, ed., *Fluxus Codex* (Detroit: Gilbert and Lila Silverman Fluxus Collection; New York: Harry N. Abrams, 1988).

8. Dick Higgins, "Fluxus: Theory and Reception," in *The Fluxus Reader,* ed. Ken Friedman (Chicester, West Sussex, and New York: Academy Editions, 1998), 234.

9. Kathy O'Dell, "Fluxus Feminus," *TDR* 41 (Spring 1997): 43.

10. The reference is to Sam Greenlee's classic tale, in which the central trope explored in Ralph Ellison's classic novel *Invisible Man* is reimagined by way of the character of "Freeman," a CIA-trained African American who becomes a mole in Chicago's social services system, combining his training with his "invisibility" to covertly destabilize and subvert white dominance. See Sam Greenlee, *The Spook Who Sat by the Door* (Detroit: Wayne State University Press, 1990).

11. One recent exception is Sally Banes's work on the New York avant-garde scene of the early 1960s. Even though I have critiqued Banes's approach elsewhere, her work stands out among scholars of her generation for its relatively forthright treatment of race, which otherwise seems relegated to nonissue status in most published critical commentary on experimentalism in music. See Sally Banes, *Greenwich Village, 1963: Avant-garde Performance and the Effervescent Body* (Durham, N.C.: Duke University Press, 1993). For a critique of Banes, see Lewis, *Power Stronger Than Itself,* 79–84.

12. Judith A. Hoffberg, "Ben Patterson in Los Angeles: A Flux-Interview," *Umbrella* 24 (2001): 79.

13. Benjamin Patterson, "I'm Glad You Asked Me That Question," in this volume; originally published in German translation as "Ben Patterson: Ich bin froh, daß Sie mir diese Frage gestellt haben," ed. Dieter Daniels, *Kunstforum International* 115 (September–October 1991): 166–77.

14. Ibid. Also see Hoffberg, "Ben Patterson in Los Angeles," 79.

15. Patterson, "I'm Glad You Asked."

16. Hoffberg, "Ben Patterson in Los Angeles," 79.

17. Ibid.

18. Jürgen Becker and Wolf Vostell, ed., *Happenings, Fluxus, Pop Art, Nouveau Réalisme: Eine Dokumentation* (Hamburg: Rowohlt, 1965), 445.

19. Achille Bonito Oliva, ed., *Ubi Fluxus ibi motus, 1990–1962* (Milan: Mazzotta, 1990), 245.

20. Dominique-René de Lerma, "Black Music Now!," *Music Educators Journal* 57 (November 1970): 29.

21. "Report on MENC Atlanta," *Music Educators Journal* 58 (February 1972): 27.

22. Oliva, *Ubi Fluxus,* 245.

23. See Liz Kotz, "Post-Cagean Aesthetics and the 'Event' Score," *October,* no. 95 (Winter 2001): 61.

24. Ibid., 61–62.

25. Nicolas Feuillie, ed., *Fluxus dixit: Une anthologie,* vol. 1 (Dijon: Presses du réel, 2002), 187; translation by the author.

26. Benjamin Patterson, "Bekenntnis," in Becker and Vostell, *Happenings, Fluxus, Pop Art,* 241; translation by the author.

27. Patterson, "Ich bin froh," 167; translation by the author.

28. Hendricks, *O que é Fluxus?,* 162.

29. Hoffberg, "Ben Patterson in Los Angeles," 81.

30. Quoted in Kristine Stiles, "Between Water and Stone— Fluxus Performance: A Metaphysics of Acts," in *In the Spirit of Fluxus,* by Elizabeth Armstrong et al. (Minneapolis: Walker Art Center, 1993), 79.

31. Quoted ibid.

32. Ibid.

33. Ibid.

34. Patterson, "I'm Glad You Asked."

35. See the discussion of this equally didactic work in Adrian Piper, *Out of Order, Out of Sight: Selected Writings in Meta-Art 1968–1992,* vol. 1 (Cambridge, Mass.: MIT Press, 1999).

36. Patterson, "I'm Glad You Asked."

37. Banes, *Greenwich Village, 1963,* 206.

38. Higgins, quoted ibid., 206. See also Benjamin Patterson, *Methods and Processes* (Paris: Privately printed, 1962).

39. The score is reproduced in Geoffrey Hendricks, ed., *Critical Mass: Happenings, Fluxus, Performance, Intermedia, and Rutgers University, 1958–1972* (New Brunswick, N.J.: Rutgers University Press, 2003), 51. Also see Hendricks, *Fluxus Codex,* 444.

40. Hoffberg, "Ben Patterson in Los Angeles," 80.

41. See Robin Moore, "The Decline of Improvisation in Western Art Music: An Interpretation of Change," *International Review of the Aesthetics and Sociology of Music* 23 (June 1992): 61–84. Also see George E. Lewis, "Improvising Tomorrow's Bodies: The Politics of Transduction," *E-misférica* 4 (November 2007), http://www.hemi.nyu.edu/ journal/4.2/eng/en42_pg_lewis. html.

42. Quoted in Kotz, "Post-Cagean Aesthetics," 31n68.

43. See Ben Patterson, *Early Works,* Alga Marghen, 1999 (compact disc).

44. For a discussion of the differences between the two composers' understandings of event scores, see Kotz, "Post-Cagean Aesthetics," 77. In this light, the well-known debate between Cage and Young on this issue becomes a matter of situating the locus of compositional control, rather than a philosophical discussion of free will.

45. Eric Porter, "Jeanne Lee's Voice," *Critical Studies in Improvisation/ Études Critiques en Improvisation* 2, no. 1 (2006): 2.

46. The trope of the "former jazz musician" is common in the experimental music literature. As I have written elsewhere, the trope embodies "a double reflection: the engagement itself wards off charges of elitism, while the discourse frames involvement with jazz as a form of youthful indiscretion" (Lewis, *Power Stronger Than Itself,* 587n193).

47. Porter, "Jeanne Lee's Voice," 5–6.

48. Patterson, *Methods and Processes.*

49. See John Cage, "Composition as Process: Indeterminacy," in *Silence: Lectures and Writings by John Cage* (Middletown, Conn.: Wesleyan University Press, 1974), 35–40.

50. Patterson, "Bekenntnis," 241; translation by the author.

51. *Liverpool Song Lines* appears on Ben Patterson, *Liverpool Soundworks, Volume One,* Audio Research Editions, 2002 (compact disc). *Surveying Western Philosophy Using China Tools* appears on Ben Patterson, *Liverpool Soundworks, Volume Two,* Audio Research Editions, 2003 (compact disc).

52. Recordings of these works appear on Patterson, *Early Works.*

53. See Patterson, *Liverpool Soundworks, Volume Two.*

54. George E. Lewis, "Improvisation and the Orchestra: A Composer Reflects," *Contemporary Music Review* 25 (October–December 2006): 431.

Fluxus: Unimaginable Without Benjamin Patterson

JON HENDRICKS

Ben Patterson has had an enormous role in Fluxus. His presence and work dominated the very first Fluxus concert in Wuppertal, Germany, at Galerie Parnass on June 9, 1962, an event titled Kleines Sommerfest: Après John Cage. Two of Patterson's works were performed. *Duo for Voice and a String Instrument* (1961), with William Pearson, was a seemingly improvisational noise music work with two voices: Pearson's vocal intonations and Patterson's double bass, attacking, repelling, and embracing each other's sounds. The second work, *Variations for Double Bass* (1961), became an iconic Fluxus work that was later performed in numerous Fluxus concerts and festivals.

Patterson, a classically trained musician, used his antique double bass in as many irreverent ways as seemed possible. In fact, *Variations for Double Bass* was scored not in a traditional way with musical notations but as a textual score. Two of the notations:

IV.
Place a number of wooden and plastic spring-type clothespins on strings several inches above bridge in such a manner that they rattle and/or produce odd tones. arco; tremolo; trills and/or long tones.

X.
perform pianissimo, medium and short tones arco with mute

The sounds were delicious, assaulting the well-dressed upper-crust German audience. The actions produced laughter and bewilderment.

I doubt very much that anyone present, other than the Fluxus artists on the program, had ever experienced anything as unconventional. Fortunately, the director of the gallery, Rolf Jährling—an architect in the town with a vibrant curiosity and love of the new, who had traveled throughout the United States, even visiting Black Mountain College—arranged to have photographs and a sound recording made of this Fluxus event, which preserves the experience so that visitors to Patterson's exhibition in Houston were able to see and hear what took place that night.

In 1962 in Paris, Patterson self-published an important collection of his scores, titled *Methods and Processes*. The publication contained several works that became Fluxus classics, including *Lick Piece* (1962; p. 132), performed for the first time in New York in the spring of 1964 at the Fluxhall, 359 Canal Street, during Fully Guaranteed 12 Fluxus Concerts. Benjamin Patterson, Robert Watts, and others covered artist Letty Eisenhauer's naked body with a Reddi-wip type of whipped cream from aerosol cans as she watched with a bemused expression on her face. In one of Peter Moore's photographs of this process, Patterson's score *Instruction No. 1* is visible on the floor underneath his flip-flop-clad foot—as though he were performing two of his compositions simultaneously.

The piece probably most associated with Fluxus is *Paper Piece*, written in 1960 and performed in nearly every Fluxus festival from the fall of 1962 onward. The Fluxus interpretation of the work generally involved large pieces of paper hanging in front of the stage and artists standing behind, making holes, at times performing other works such as Nam June Paik's *Young Penis Symphony* (1962), in which performers put either their fingers or their penises through the holes, throwing programs or Fluxus scores through the holes made in the paper curtain, then breaking through the paper and extending it out over the audience.

Patterson had written a somewhat more structured score for *Paper Piece*, which was exhibited in Houston. Some of the sounds included in the score associated with paper are "shake," "break," "tear," "crumple," "rumple," "bumple," "rub," "scrub," "twist," "poof," and "pop." Patterson's action music was among the most radical of the time and helped to define Fluxus as both humorous and outrageous, an affront to cultural normalcy.

George Maciunas, the visionary Lithuanian American artist who was the conceptual instigator of Fluxus and its primary theoretician and organizational planner, was invited to Wuppertal at the suggestion of Nam June Paik. Paik, another major Fluxus artist, had been invited by the Galerie Parnass director, Rolf Jährling, to organize an event for the opening of a summer exhibition of Art Informel at the gallery. Remarkably, among the list of painters and sculptors was none other than "Hulbeck-New York." "Hulbeck" of course was Richard Huelsenbeck, one of the several founders of Dada at the Cabaret Voltaire in Zurich in the spring of 1916, forty-six years earlier.

Paik felt that he didn't have enough time to prepare an event, so he suggested Maciunas. Things start, and Maciunas's plan for the event that early summer was the first public manifestation of Fluxus. The invitation card lists Benjamin Patterson (USA-Paris) together with George Maciunas (USA) on top, as though to imply that the two were the artistic presenters of this Après John Cage soirée and the sole performers—indeed, the printed program lists only four works:

Einführung: Neo-Dada in New York Maciunas
Chefredacteur der neuen Kunst-zeitschrift FLUXUS
Variation für contrabass Patterson
Duo Patterson
Lippen Musik Maciunas

However, the copy of the program invitation card in the Silverman collection has holographic notations by

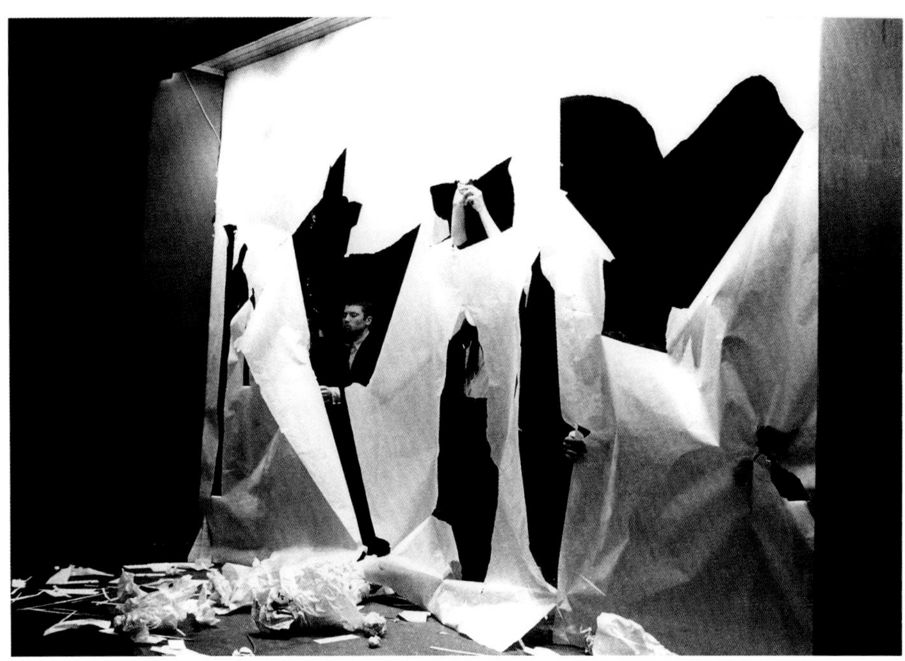

Performance of *Paper Piece*, Hypokriterion Theater, Amsterdam, 1963

both Maciunas and Rolf Jährling. Maciunas has enlarged and changed the program: number 2 becomes number 3, and number 3 becomes number 2 with Pearson's name (added by Jährling). Then Maciunas adds a number 5, "*Ear Music*—Terry Riley" and number 6, "*Constellation No. 2*—Dick Higgins" and changes the title of his work under number 4 from *Lippen Musik* to *Homage to Adriano Olivetti*. A number 7 is added in Maciunas's handwriting, "Tribut/Jed Curtis," with some additional notes in Jährling's hand. Maciunas adds the names— "Caspari," "Kosugi," "Jed Curtis USA," [not readable], "Alvermann O," "Thomas" [Tomas Schmit], and "Nam Jun Paig" [Nam June Paik]—thus creating a Fluxus cabaret sampler.

Maciunas's text read by Arthur C. Caspari in German at the beginning of the program is clearly a manifesto laying out the territory of Fluxus. In addition, Maciunas wrote and published the "Brochure Prospectus" for Fluxus, which was distributed to the guests for the very first time,

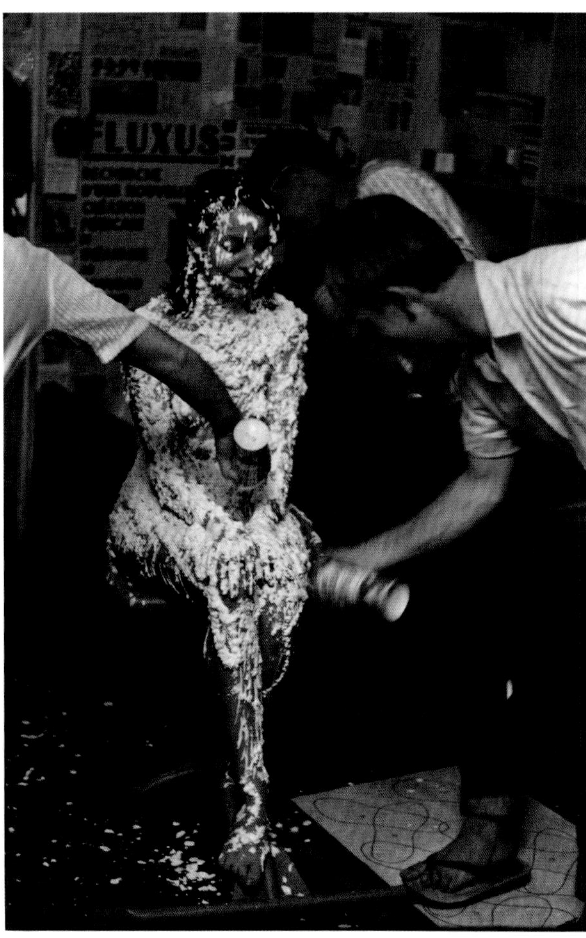

Performance of *Lick Piece*, Canal Street loft, New York, 1964; photograph by Peter Moore

and Maciunas's designed announcement card cube for *An Anthology* was also handed out—people used the cubes as bracelets and can be seen in photographs holding the brochure.

These were the beginnings, the very beginnings of Fluxus. And Benjamin Patterson was present—not as a spectator but as a featured performer. His presence would be felt as the movement evolved, throughout that year and the next, in concerts and publications, in Europe, and in New York on Maciunas's return to the United States at the end of 1963. When one studies programs from these early years of Fluxus, one can see the importance of Patterson's work.

A week after the Galerie Parnass concert, on June 16, 1962, in the Kammerspiele in Düsseldorf, during a concert organized by Nam June Paik and George Maciunas titled Neo-Dada in der Musik, Patterson's *Paper Music* and *Disturbance from Lemons* were performed. On July 3, 1962, during Sneak Preview: Fluxus on the streets of Paris, organized by Robert Filliou and Patterson to coincide with the opening of Patterson's exhibition at the Galerie Girardon, Patterson's *Paper Piece* and *Variations for Double Bass* were performed. On September 9, at the Städtisches Museum, Wiesbaden, during Fluxus internationale Festspiele neuester Musik, Patterson performed *Variations for Double Bass*. And on September 16, for the same festival in Wiesbaden, Patterson performed two works: *Septet from Lemons* (1961) and *Overture I and II* (1961). On October 24, 1962, at the Institute of Contemporary Arts in London, in conjunction with the Festival of Misfits, Patterson's *Paper Piece* was performed. *Paper Piece* was performed again on November 23, 1962, at Festum Fluxorum/Musik og Anti-Musik det Instrumentale Teater at the Nikolaj Kirke, Copenhagen. In the same festival, this time at the Alle Scenen, Copenhagen on November 25, *Solo for Dancer* (1961) was performed. On November 26, back at the Nikolaj Kirke, *Septet* and the world premiere of *Pond* (1962) took place. On December 3, at the American Students and Artists Center in Paris, during Festum Fluxorum poésie, musique et antimusique événementielle et concrète, *Paper Piece* was performed. The next day, Patterson performed *Variations for Double Bass*, and on the December 6 concert of the festival, he performed two pieces from *Methods and Processes*. The next year, on February 2 and 3, in Düsseldorf at the Staatliche Kunstakademie, in a concert organized by George Maciunas and hosted by Joseph Beuys, *Paper Piece*, *Septet from Lemons*, and *Pond* were performed.

In 1966 Maciunas prepared Fluxus versions of Patterson's scores, which were simplifications and pared-down instructions from the more precise and elegant scoring that Patterson used. These simplifications were typical of Maciunas's approach to work for Fluxus concerts and to distribute publicly for others to perform. They are reproduced here to give a sense of how performers might have interpreted Patterson's work for Fluxus concerts in which Patterson was not the performer.

Ben Patterson
PAPER PIECE
Improvisation with paper.
Ben Patterson

SEPTET (FROM "LEMONS")
7 kettles, each equipped with different whistle in nozzle is fitted over nozzle with balloon. As water is boiled balloons inflate while whistles play. Three performers shoot at balloons with pistols or darts or bows or arrows.

Ben Patterson
VARIATIONS FOR DOUBLE BASS
17 variations are performed such as:
locating pin of bass over location of performance on a map, attaching clothespins on strings and rattling them, agitating strings with comb, corrugated board, feather duster or chain, eating edibles from peg box, posting a letter through the f hole, etc., etc., etc.

Ben Patterson
POND, for 4, 8 or 12 performers.
Performer voices repetitive sounds after a jumping mechanical frog enters his zone on a charted floor. Score.

Published in *Fluxfest Sale* (Winter 1966).

This is just to demonstrate Patterson's important participation in those first crucial months and the initial manifestations of Fluxus. During this time, his scores were published in *KWY*; in *Décollage*; in Jürgen Becker and Wolf Vostell's *Happenings / Fluxus / Pop Art / Nouveau Réalisme*; in the *Fluxus Preview Review*; in the Fluxus newspapers nos. 1 and 2; and in *Four Suits*, published by Something Else Press.

Benjamin Patterson is an iconoclast, a provocateur, a trickster. He is someone who makes you smile and engages your mind. All the things that an artist should be. All the things that a good artist should be. He is those things.

Methods and Processes:
Scores, Actions, and Happenings

(Paper Piece)
-1-

3' Bags will be performed

"Poot" - inflate with mouth
"Pop!"

Dynamics should be improvised within the natural borders of
the approx ppp of the "twist" and the fff of
the "Pop!"

Each performer will have previously selected and arranged
his own materials and sequence of events. Arrangement
of the sequence of events may concern not only the
general order — No. 1 "shake", "Break", "Tear", No 2 "Poot",
"Pop" — the inner orders may also be considered — "Tear",
"shake", "Break", IT is advisable to mark the method
of performance on each sheet

Benjamin Patterson
Köln 1960

"Paper Piece"
for 1 to 5 performers

Instruments   15 sheets of paper per performer approx size of double-page
newspaper, quality varied - newspaper, tissue paper, cardboard,
colored, printed or plain
3 paper bags per performer, size, shape, quality varied

Duration   Between 12.5 minutes and 10 minutes

Procedure   a signal from a chairman will begin the piece; within the following
30 seconds each performer enters at will. The piece ends when
the paper supply is exhausted
7 - sheets will be performed
"shake"
"Break" - the edges of the sheet are grasped and sharply jerked
apart
"Tear" - each sheet should be reduced to particles less than 1/10
the size of the whole sheet
approx 1 minute per sheet
5 - sheets will be performed
"crumple"
"Rumple"
"Bumple" - the paper is bumped together between the hands
approx 30 seconds per sheet.
3 - sheet will be performed
"Rub"
"Scrub"
"Twist" - the paper is twisted tightly until a squeaking
sound is produced. Approx. 30 seconds per sheet

Paper Piece, 1960
Ink on paper, envelope
8¾ × 6⅞ inches
The Museum of Modern Art, New York;
The Gilbert and Lila Silverman Fluxus Collection Gift

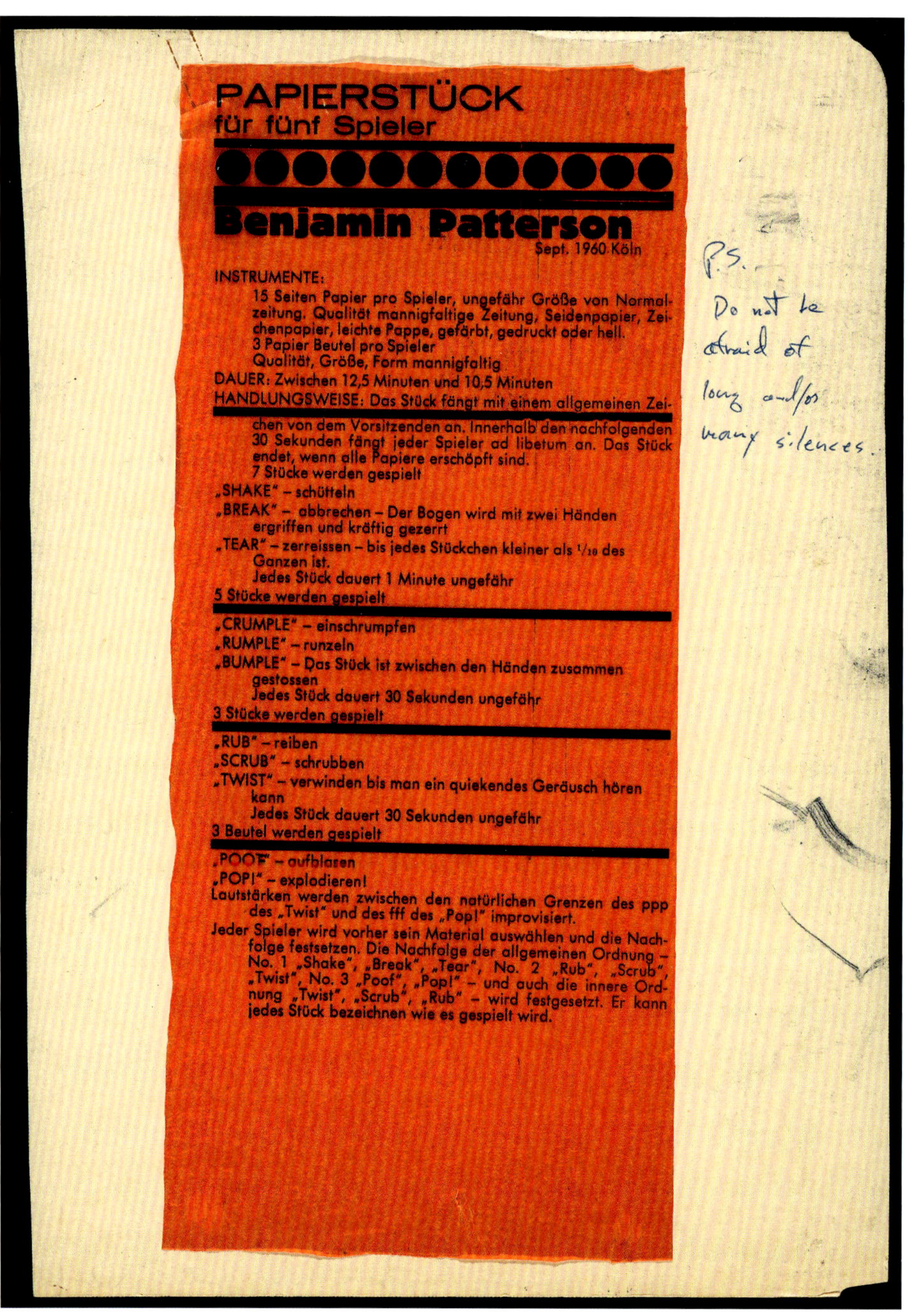

Papierstück für fünf Spieler,
from *Ich bin schön*, 1960
Ink on paper
11 × 8⅛ inches
Getty Research Institute, Los Angeles

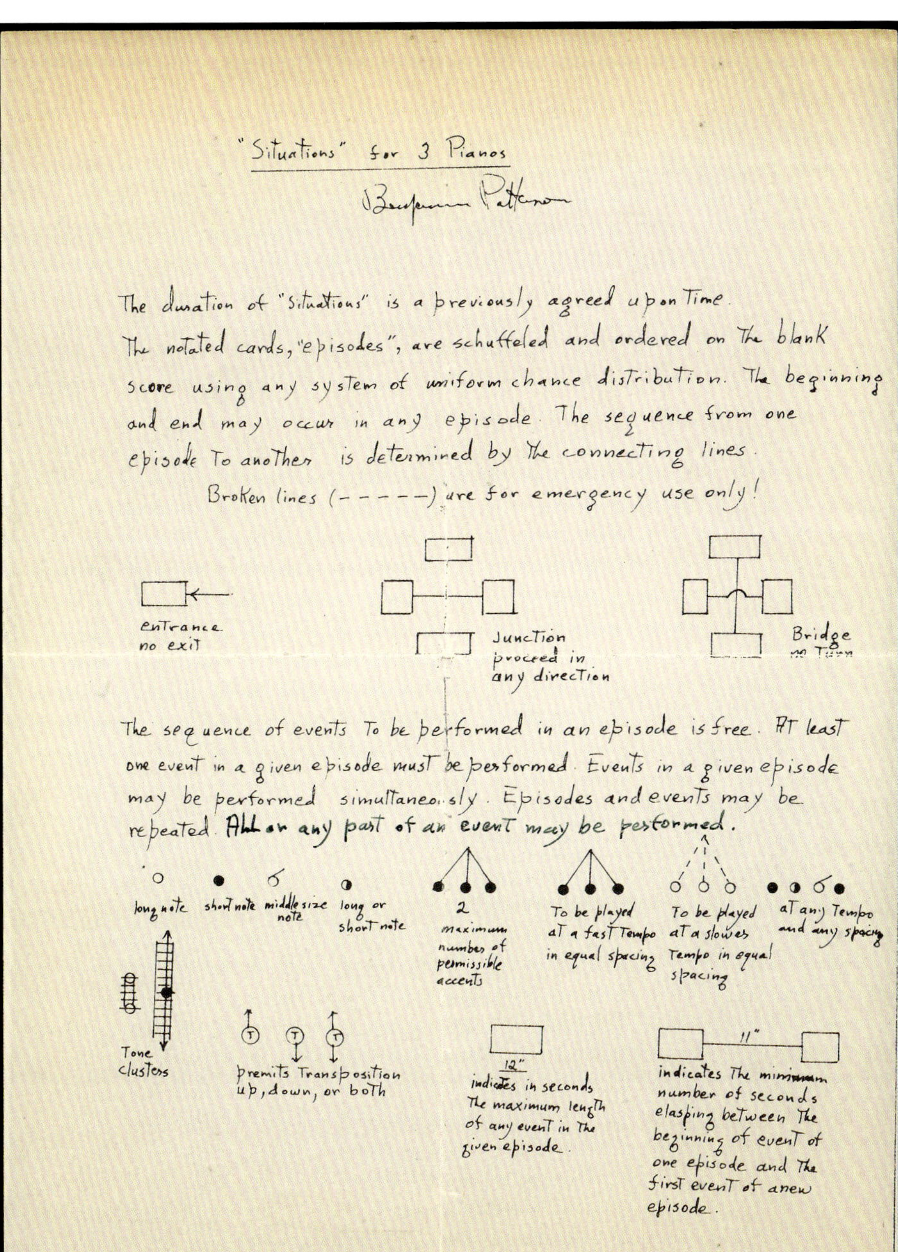

"Situations" for Three Pianos, 1960
Ink on composition paper
2 pages, 11 × 8¼ inches each
Getty Research Institute, Los Angeles

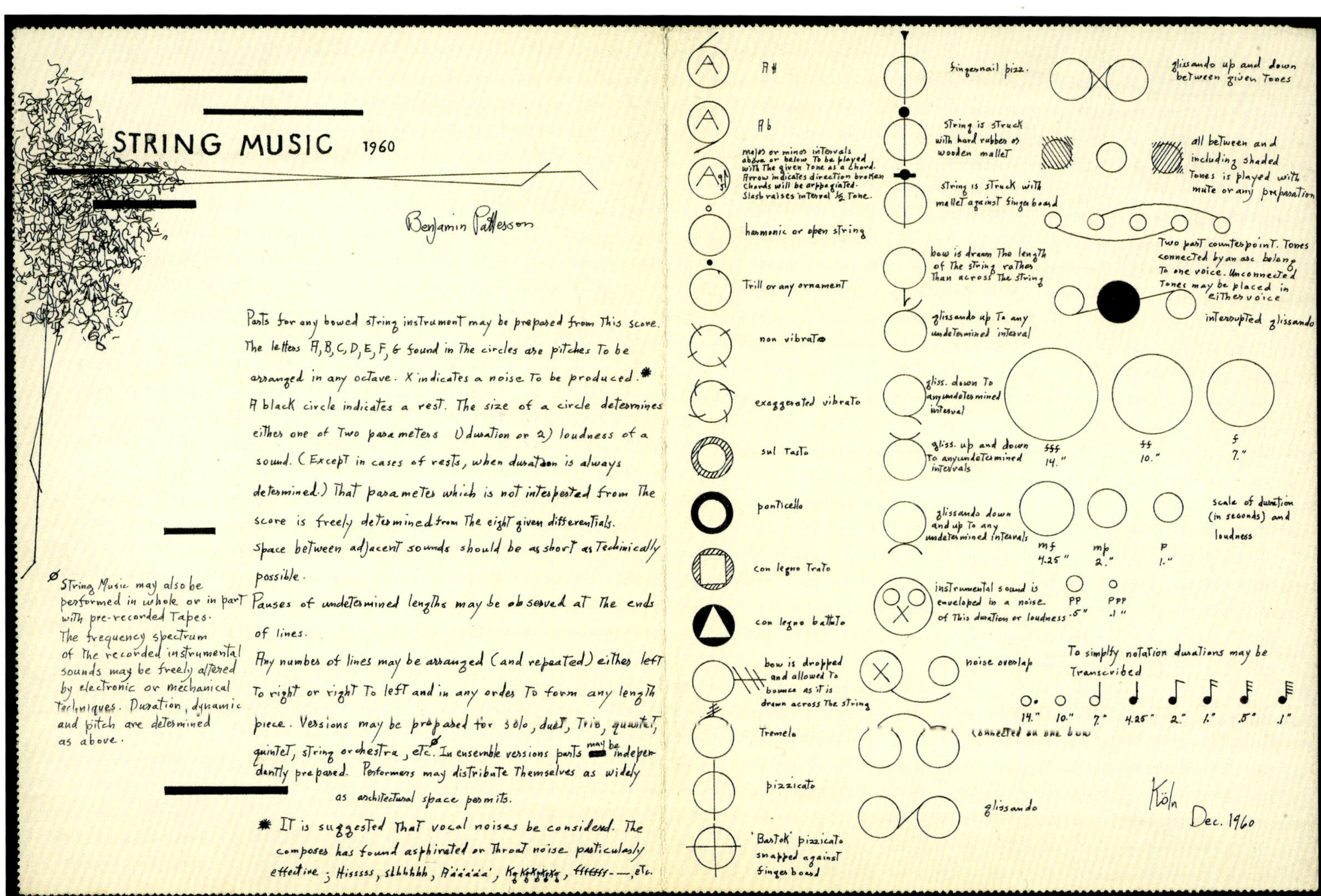

String Music, 1960

Ink on watercolor paper

Instructions: 10¹³⁄₁₅ × 16 inches

Graphic score, page 1: 10¹³⁄₁₆ × 16 inches

Graphic score, page 2: 11¹³⁄₁₄ × 15¹¹⁄₁₆ inches

Graphic score, page 3: 10¹³⁄₁₆ × 16 inches

Getty Research Institute, Los Angeles

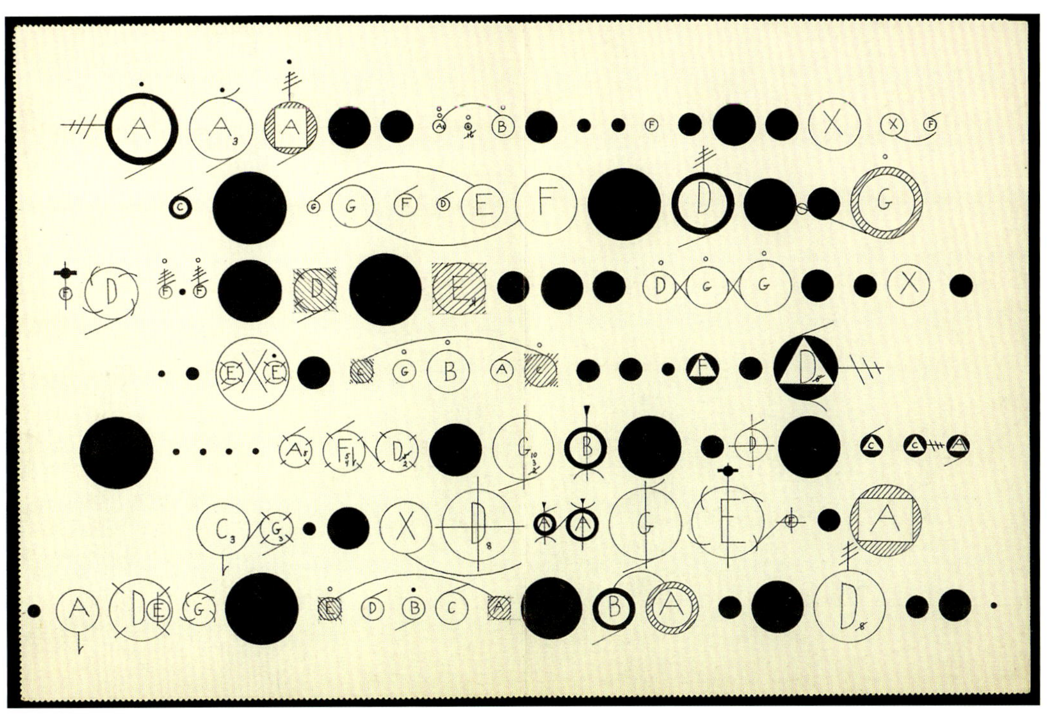

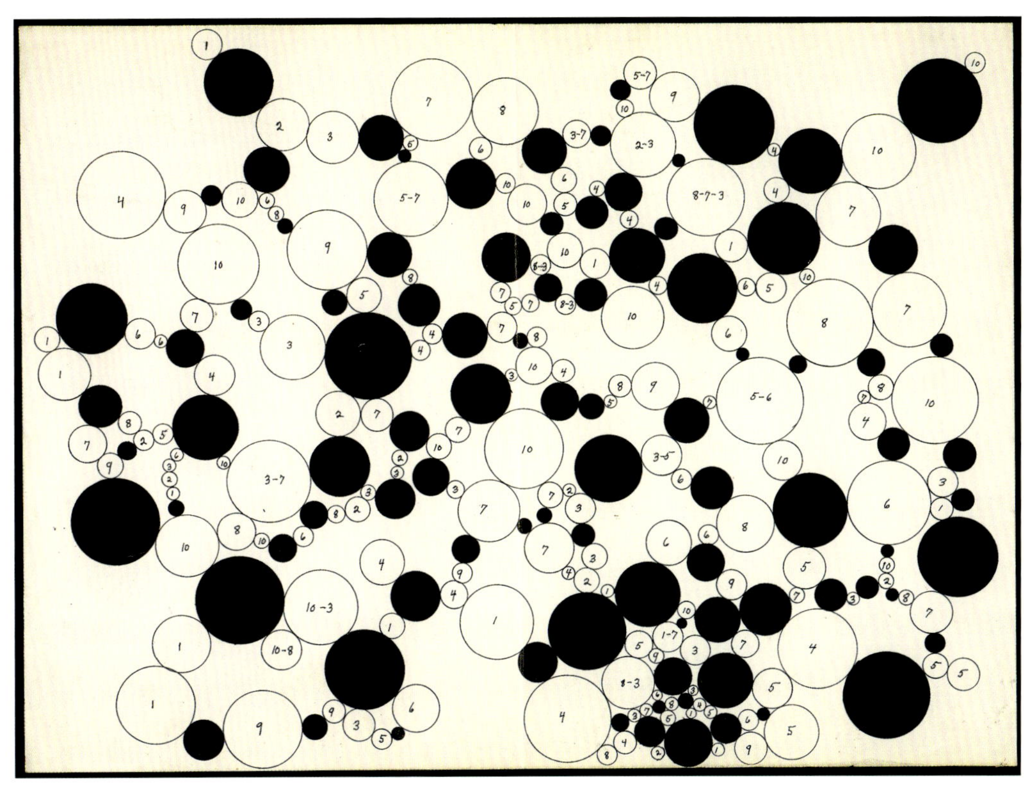

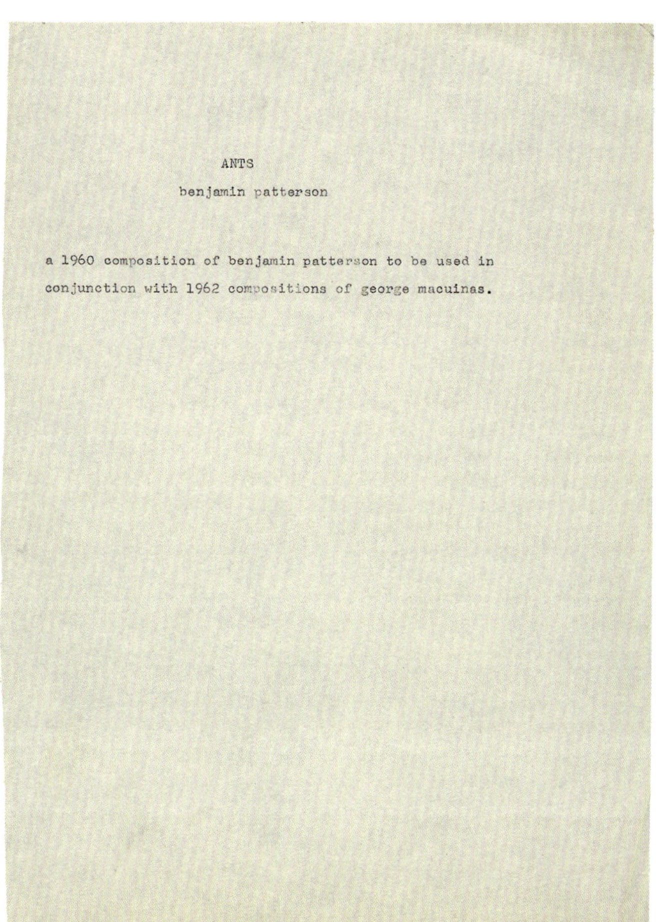

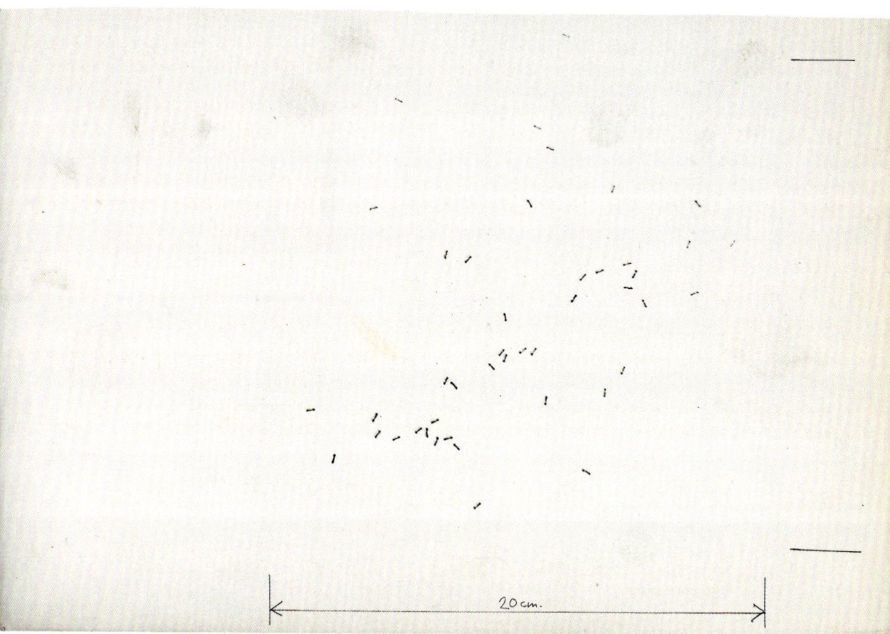

Ants, 1960–62
Ink on paper, black-and-white photographs
Photograph: 8⅛ × 11¾ inches
Photograph: 8¼ × 11¾ inches
Sheet: 10¹⁵⁄₁₆ × 7¾ inches
Getty Research Institute, Los Angeles

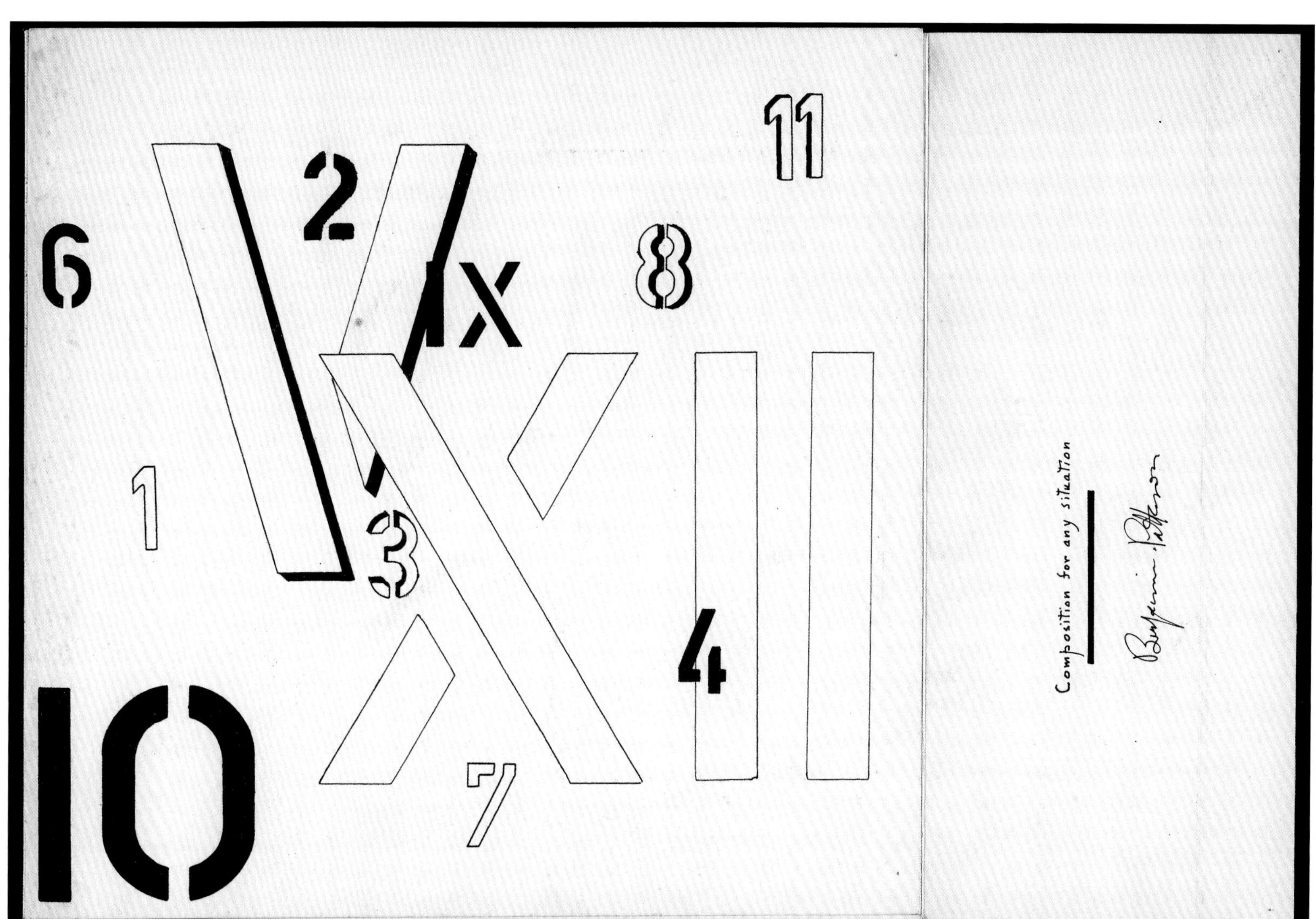

Composition for Any Situation, 1961
Ink on paper
8¼ × 8¼ inches
Getty Research Institute, Los Angeles

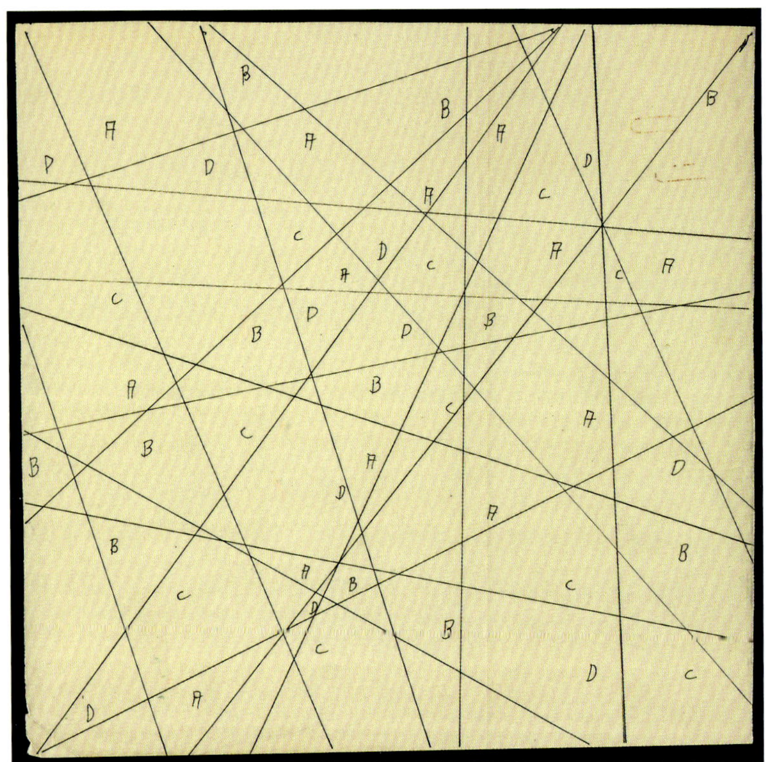 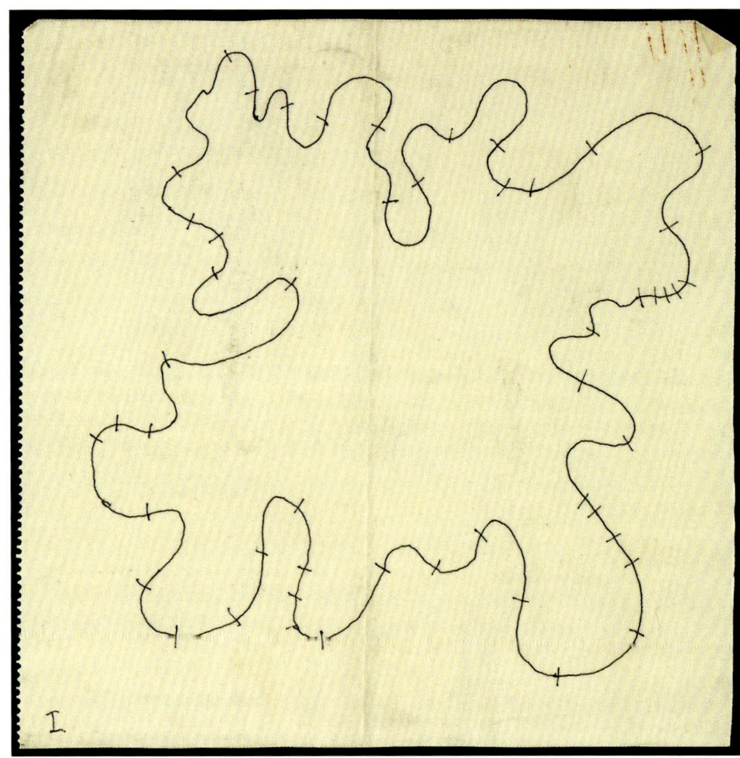

Décollage Piece for Wolf Vostell, 1961 (detail)
Ink on paper and vellum
Score, page 1: 6⁷⁄₁₆ × 6¼ inches
Score, page 2: 6¼ × 6⅞ inches
Getty Research Institute, Los Angeles

a disturbing composition

a soloist will perform a decided upon number of visual,
acoustic, olfactory, tactual, caloric, etc. disturbances
during the course of any concert, play, lecture, etc.
distribution of disturbances is determined by chance or choice
without regard to other contents of program.
disturbances in general are brief.
they may be performed on stage, in audience, outside hall,
underground, etc.

paris, 1961

A Disturbing Composition, 1961
Typed ink on paper
10⅞ × 7¹³⁄₁₆ inches
Getty Research Institute, Los Angeles

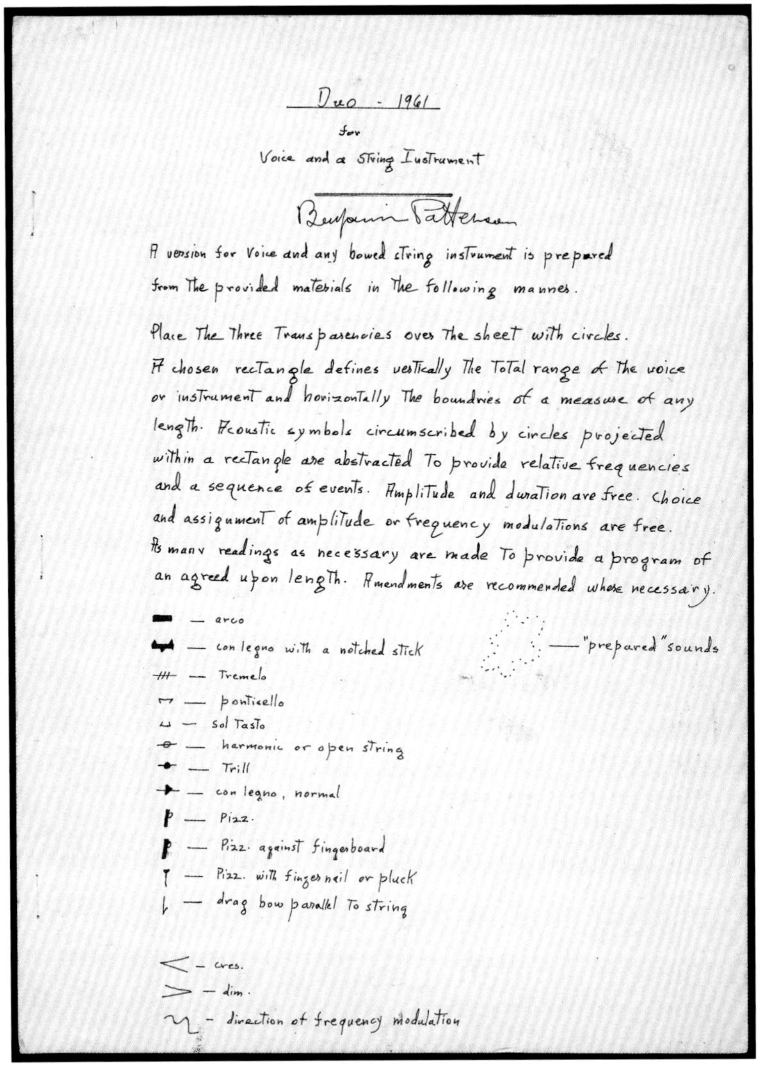

Duo - 1961

for

Voice and a String Instrument

Benjamin Patterson

A version for Voice and any bowed string instrument is prepared
from the provided materials in the following manner.

Place the three transparencies over the sheet with circles.
A chosen rectangle defines vertically the total range of the voice
or instrument and horizontally the boundries of a measure of any
length. Acoustic symbols circumscribed by circles projected
within a rectangle are abstracted to provide relative frequencies
and a sequence of events. Amplitude and duration are free. Choice
and assignment of amplitude or frequency modulations are free.
As many readings as necessary are made to provide a program of
an agreed upon length. Amendments are recommended where necessary.

— arco
— con legno with a notched stick
— Tremelo
— ponticello
— sol Tasto
— harmonic or open string
— Trill
— con legno, normal
— Pizz.
— Pizz. against fingerboard
— Pizz. with fingernail or pluck
— drag bow parallel to string

— "prepared" sounds

— cres.
— dim.
— direction of frequency modulation

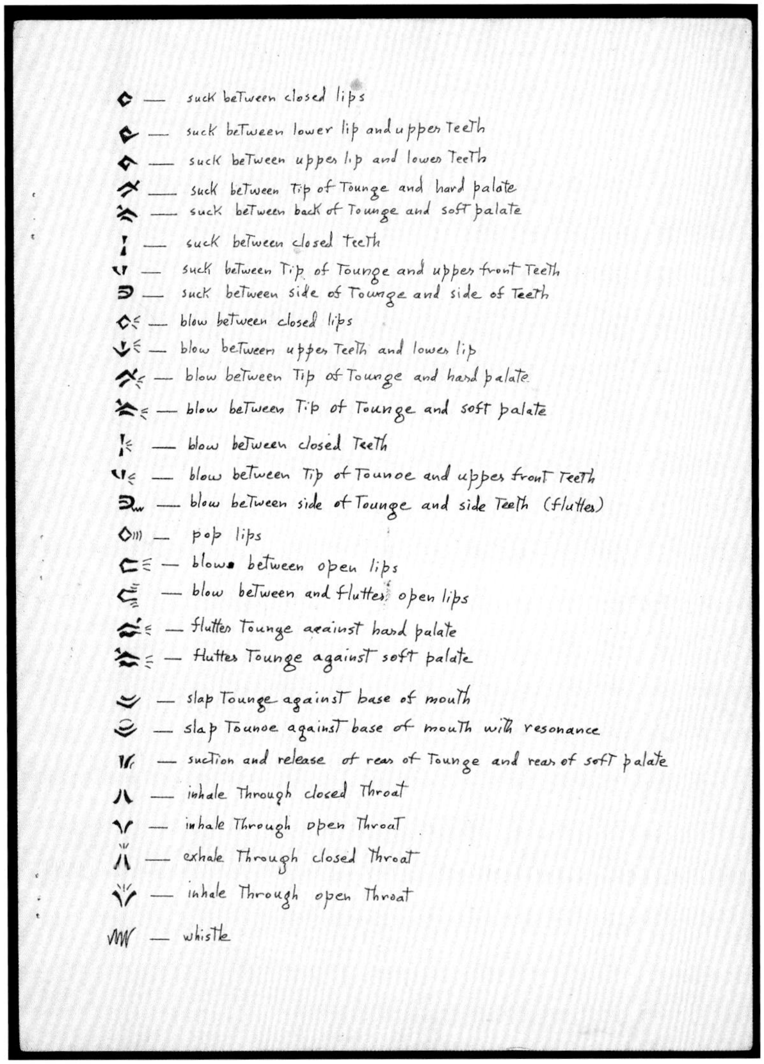

— suck between closed lips
— suck between lower lip and upper teeth
— suck between upper lip and lower teeth
— suck between tip of tounge and hard palate
— suck between back of tounge and soft palate
— suck between closed teeth
— suck between tip of tounge and upper front teeth
— suck between side of tounge and side of teeth
— blow between closed lips
— blow between upper teeth and lower lip
— blow between tip of tounge and hard palate
— blow between tip of tounge and soft palate
— blow between closed teeth
— blow between tip of tounge and upper front teeth
— blow between side of tounge and side teeth (flutter)
— pop lips
— blow between open lips
— blow between and flutter open lips
— flutter tounge against hard palate
— flutter tounge against soft palate
— slap tounge against base of mouth
— slap tounge against base of mouth with resonance
— suction and release of rear of tounge and rear of soft palate
— inhale through closed throat
— inhale through open throat
— exhale through closed throat
— inhale through open throat
— whistle

Duo for Voice and a String Instrument, 1961 (detail)
Black and colored ink on paper and transparency
Instructions: 2 pages, 11¹¹⁄₁₆ × 8¼ inches each (above)
Transparency: 11⅜ × 8¼ inches (opposite)
Getty Research Institute, Los Angeles

144

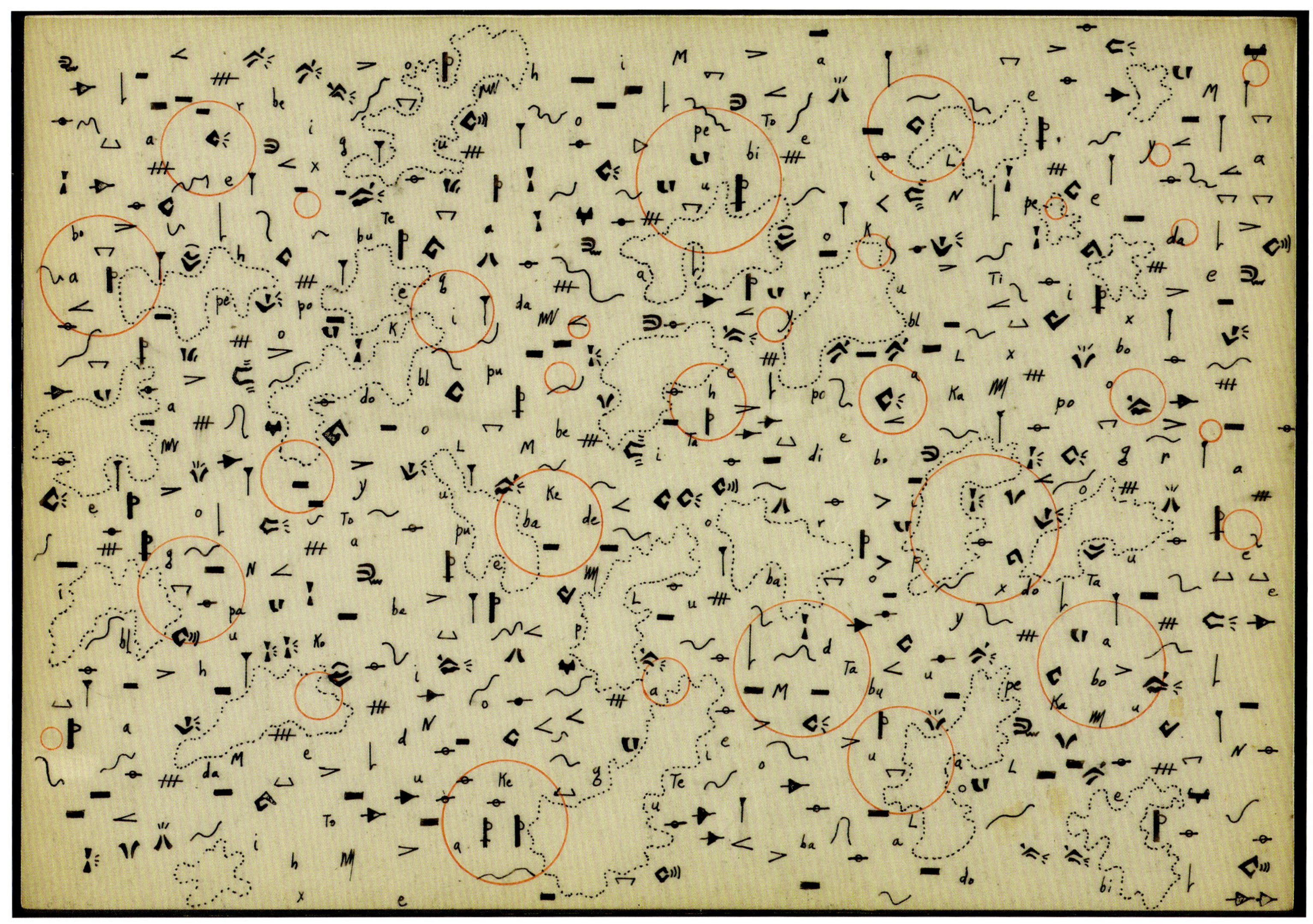

```
                    overture
                  (version II.)

preparations:
a noise-maker¹·⁾ wrapped²·⁾ and sealed³·⁾ is placed in a
small container⁴·⁾. this container is wrapped and sealed and
placed in a larger container. the larger container is wrapped
and sealed and placed in a still larger container; etc..
time, space, and expense determine the number of containers,
wrappings and sealings.

performance:
a performer unseals, unwraps and opens containers. two musicians
standing on either side of the unwrapper produce alternately
the lowest possible tones on (1.) a bass brass-wind instrument
and (2.) a large gong or tam-tam. coincident with the opening
of each container, the musicians perform a long tone in
ensemble. as the noise-maker is unwrapped, the two musicians
perform a very long tone in ensemble.
after a pause the unwrapper performs a single long tone with
the noise maker.

     1. a simple device to be blown, such as a tube with
          an obstruction, producing a"white-noise" is prefered.
     2. wrappings are of paper, cellophane, leather, cloth,
          wood, metal, plastic, etc.
     3. sealings are of wax, glue, zippers, buttons, nails,
          ropes, tape, locks, nuts and bolts, etc.
          (knives, scissors, wrenches, blow-torches, cork-screws,
           bottle-openers, surgical instruments, etc. are used
           to open sealings.)
     4. containers are boxes, barrels, baskets, caskets,
```

```
                    -2-
                (overture, version II.)

suitcases, punch bowls, safes, garbage trucks, storerooms,
grottos, etc.



                                    paris, 1961
```

Overture, Overture (Versions II and III), 1961
Ink on paper
10⁹⁄₁₆ × 8¼ inches
Getty Research Institute, Los Angeles

                         overture
                       (version III.)

preparations:
see version II. substitute a "canned"woman's laugh for noise
maker.1.), 2.)

performance:
a performer unseals, unwraps, and opens containers. turn off
laugh when"canning" device is unwrapped.

        1. laugh is"canned" on small transistor tape-recorder
           or similar device.
        2. device should be wrapped in such a manner that
           laugh is inaudible at beginning.

Ursula Girardon   23 boulevard Pasteur, Paris 15   tel. FON 53-41

                20:30 heures   25 Mars 1962

                    "PORTRAIT OF EGG"

                   Benjamin Patterson

20:30.5 heures   bifth of EGG

                  emerges, breathing through snorkel, reading by
                  candle light, wearing turtle-neck sweater and
                  diving mask...

20:33   "   EGG, consumer

                  prepares sandwich from cut, grounded, sanded, sawed
                  brazed, boiled, raw, seasoned (spices, oils, nut,
                  bolts, etc.) and unseasoned breads, fruits,
                  vegetables, meats, nuts, etc... he eats...(1.)

20:35.1   "   EGG, rationalist

                  analysis, measures, calculates and describes
                  algebraiclly dimensions, directions, distances,
                  angles, weights, etc. of objects, articles,
                  persons, etc...(2.)

20:39.7   "   death of mother of EGG

                  ...moment of reverent silence...

20:40   "   EGG, orator

                  oration of spits, spats, sputters (3.) to audience
                  of paper (4.)...

20:44   "   snapshot of EGG, june 11, 1961

                  ...as virtuoso of double-bass (5.)

20:50.6   "   EGG as Niki de Saint Phial

                  ...astonishing septet (6.) "and bound in brotherhood..."

20:59.9   "   degenerate pastimes diversions of EGG

                  (through "furry door"), ravishes (sitting on toilet)
                  (covered with...) girl...is flushed. (7.)

21:06   "   EGG acheives immortality

                  ...on stilts (dark room), lights candles (8.), rings
                  bell, blows whistles (9.), exits deep hole (10.)
                  or garden wall... is photographed ("blitz" lighting)
                  during candle ceremony...

Portrait of an Egg, 1961
Ink on paper
10⁹⁄₁₆ × 8³⁄₁₆ inches
Getty Research Institute, Los Angeles

SEPTET

benjamin patterson

preparations:

small quantities of water are placed in each of seven
whistling tea kettles. a rubber ballon is fitted over the
whistle of each kettle in a manner that does not hinder whistling.

performance:

kettles are placed on individual heating devices, arranged in
a row, and water is brought to boil.
as many as three performers seated at a reasonable range from
kettles explode inflating ballons in any sequence with pellets
shot from a gas or air pistol, darts or bow and arrows.

   1. determine quantities of water to avoid simultaneous
      boiling.
   2. whistles are of differing frequencies.
   3. performers may smoke, comverse, read, eat, play cards,
      etc. while awaiting boiling of water.
   4. aim carefully

cologne, 1961

Septet from Lemons, 1961
Ink on paper
11 × 8 inches
Getty Research Institute, Los Angeles

<u>Solo</u>

Décollage Piece – 1961

for Wolf Vostell.

———

A collage, mass of 1 to x layers, is prepared on each of four surfaces, A, B, C, D. Choice of materials is free — paper, wood, metal, stone, plastic, liquids, eatables, etc.   A program of events – décollaging actions①— is prepared from the given materials in the following manner. Place the three Transparent squares, I, II, III, over the larger non-Transparent square. The intersections along the continous line [square I.] suggest a succession of single events, décollaging actions, within a time continium of any pre-determined length. The passage of this continium through various lettered and unlettered areas of the non-transparent square determines the surface on which events are performed, the number of events on a given surface, the occurance of rests [unlettered area], the relative duration of events and rests and the sequence of events and rests from point y to point z within the time continium. The acoustic amplitude of an event and any alterations of this amplitude are determined from the projections of squares II. and III

within the given area of the non-transparent square. Choice and assignment are free. Improvise where necessary.   As many readings as necessary are made to provide a program of any length. May be performed with "Paper Piece" – 1960.

Benjamin Patterson

Köln   April, 1961

① A décollaging action is a removing of a portion of a collage. Technique is free — Tearing, cutting, sawing, grinding, sanding, chisling, scraping, burning, eating, etc.

Décollage Piece for Wolf Vostell (handwritten iteration), 1961
Typed and colored ink on paper (verso/recto)
10⅞ × 11 inches
Getty Research Institute, Los Angeles

```
PAVANE FOR FLUTES

     benjamin patterson


a flute (transverse or vertical) and a music stand on which
is found a graphically symbolized 1, 2, or 3 tone musical
motive are placed at a point midway between a chosen entrance
and exit.
a child, as young as possible, enters and interprets on flute
the assigned motive as well as possible, replaces flute (on
stand) and exits. a second child enters, interprets, exits;
a third child, etc.. as many children as possible.
as many flutes and stands and differing motives are used as
                                      1.)
there are separate entrances and exits.    all children
perform on all flutes. as many cycles as possible are performed.
shy children should not be excluded.


   1. an entrance for one flute may serve as an exit
      for another flute and vice versa.




               paris, 1961
               rescored; pittsburgh,1962
```

Pavane for Flutes, 1961–62
Ink on paper
11 × 8⅛ inches
Getty Research Institute, Los Angeles

VARIATIONS FOR DOUBLE-BASS

benjamin patterson

pitches, dynamics, durations and number of sounds to be
produced in any one variation in this composition are not
notated. (in the first performance by the composer a graphic
score derived from ink blots was used as a guide; however,
there are many other satisfacory solutions.)

I.

unfold world map on floor. circle with pen, pencil, etc. city
in which performance is being given. locate end pin of bass
in circle.

II.

using four different toy whistles, animal or bird imitators or
calls, etc. tune strings of bass as well as possible.

III.

produce a number of arco, quasi-webern sounds.

IV.

place a number of wooden and plastic spring-type clothespins
on strings several inches above bridge in such a manner that
they rattle and/or produce odd tones. arco; tremelo, trills
and/or long tones.

V.

weave strips of gold-face paper through strings in space
between bridge and fingerboard. fasten four colorful plastic
butterflies to strings over gold paper. performing normal,
"bartok" and/or "fingernail" pizzicati, catapult butterflies
from strings.

-2-

VI.

fasten clamps ("C" claps, woodworking, etc. of various sizes)
over playing area on each of the four strings. flip clamps
with fingers in such a manner that they rebound between
adjacent strings.

VII.

place small objects of metal (paper clips, hair pins, etc.)
on each string in various positions above bridge. perform
double-stops, arco and/or pizzicato.

VIII.

holding bass by fingerboard upside-down, balance on scroll.

    1. rub object of rubber (suede-leather brush, etc.) over
       strings

    2. rub, crumbling to small pieces, large piece of cellotex
       over strings

    3. roll narrow wheeled furniture caster slowly down from
       endpin over tailpiece, bridge, G string and into pegbox
       (caster may squeak)

IX.

holding bass right-side-up perform long tones and double stops
with two bows (right and left hand)

X.

perform pianissimo, medium and short tones arco with mute

XI.

agitate strings with following materials

    1. comb (as with hair; may employ mirror)

    2. corrugated cardboard

Variations for Double Bass, 1961–62
Ink on paper
5 pages, 11 × 8¼ inches each
Getty Research Institute, Los Angeles

3. newspaper holder (wooden sticks as used in libraries)
   filled with tissue paper, newspaper, cellophane, toilet
   paper, tinfoil, etc.
4. feather duster (red)
   (should bridge be misaligned by vigorous agitation of 3.,
   reposition with hammer before feather dusting 4.)

XII.

(optional)

lay bass on side. slap and knock with flat and knuckles of hands

XIII.

place bass on stand, in a corner, or on a chair

1. fan with japanese or spanish hand fan and blow with
   mouth over strings
2. place inside bass one end of flexible tube to which is
   attached a ballon.(f-hole) fasten pump or mouth to other
   end and inflate ballon. detatch pump, attach whistle and
   allow ballon to deflate blowing whistle.

XIV.

(may overlap above)

pull "chain" (previously prepared) of various threads, cords,
strings, ropes, shoelaces, plastic, insulated electric wiring,
and/or old rags out of bass through f-hole. "chain"may be
replaced again inside through opposite f-hole.

XV.

peg-box previously prepared with a) filling of small pieces
of wire, colored paper, plastic, metal or b) eatibles and
covered with unobtrusive black paper.

1. open hole in paper cover with corkscrew, drill, knife,

saw, and/or scissors.
2. clean out foreign material with dining fork (eat)
3. choose texts or pictures from newspaper, magazine, etc.
   crumple and place in peg-box.
4. replace paper cover and tape closed.

XVI.

pull silk stocking over scroll and fasten with garter around
neck above saddle. set on chair, peg-box (toe) down and place
rose between strings under bridge.

XVII.

address, write message (reading aloud) and stamp picture postcard.
post in f-hole.

cologne, 1961
revised pittsburgh, 1962

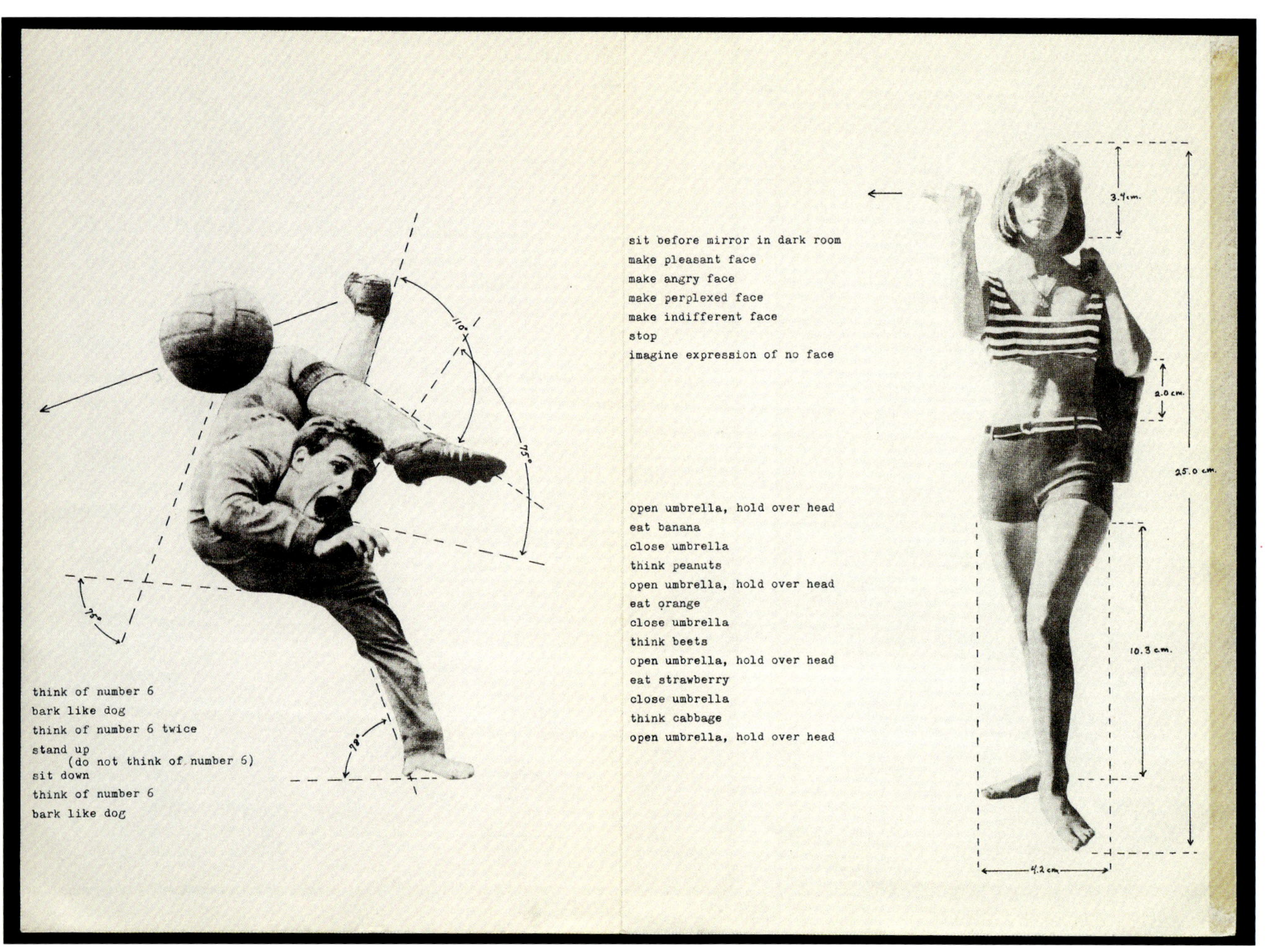

Methods and Processes, 1962 (detail)
Printed ink on paper
10¹¹⁄₁₆ × 7⅜ × ¹⁄₁₆ inches
Getty Research Institute, Los Angeles

"POND"

benjamin a patterson

a grid (dimensions about 6feet by 6 feet), coordinates (Q, A,
E) and time ranges are chalked on floor of performing area. (see
chart)

each of 8 performers is assigned an area, (I-VIII)(area consists
of three adjacent columns in their whole lengths) and is entrusted
a mechanical animal ("wind-up" toy, suggesting such animals
found in or around a pond; frogs, etc.)

each performer takes an attending position at the head of any
column within his area and upon a signal from a director begins
counting silently from zero to the number he has selected from
the time range (10-20, etc.) assigned to his area. upon reaching
this number he releases "frog" into an adjacent column facing
pond center. should a "frog" move into, through or stop in a
column which is being attended, the responsible performer will,
if necessary, stop counting and reply immediately with response
assigned to the column. (Q.-Question, A.-Answer, E.-Exclamation).
this response will be repeated, intoned and accented in a manner
exhibiting the general characteristics of natural animal calls.
it will continue until "frog" exits the column (performer may
then begin again counting from zero) or director signals end
of performance.

    a Question (Q.) will have 3 syllabes and loudness level
        "soft"

    an Answer (A.) will have 2 syllables and loudness level
        "moderate"

"POND"

-2-

    an Exclamation (E.) will have 1 syllable and loudness level
        "loud"

performers each ahve free choice of texts, language and/or
dialect. exit of a"frog" from a personally attended column allows
a performer to change position to attend another column within
assigned area. however, each performer is limited to 2 changes
of position during a performance. should a second "frog" enter
a column already occupied, the response may be transfered to
new "frog".

performance ends a) when all "frogs" have halted in unattended
columns, b) all "frogs" exit and halt beyond boundries of grid,
c) combination of a) and b), d) upon a signal from director
(used only to end infinite-response situations.)

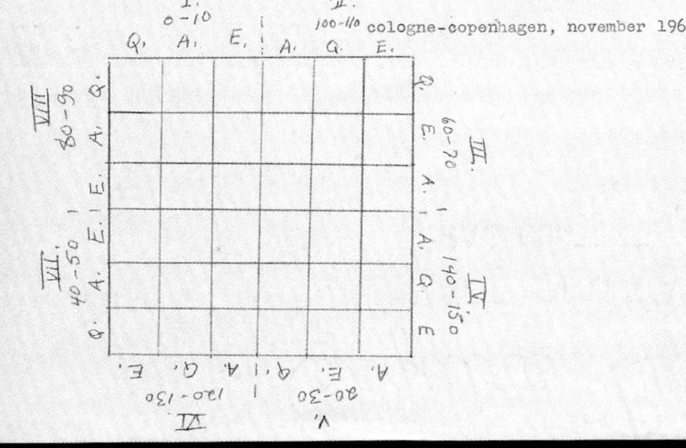

Pond, 1962
Ink on paper
2 pages, 10⁹⁄₁₆ × 8³⁄₁₆ inches each
Getty Research Institute, Los Angeles

SOLO FOR DANCER

benjamin patterson

a pulley is hung from ceiling. a rope, both ends reaching floor,
is hung through pulley. dancer ties loop in one end of rope,
lays self on floor face down, up, left, or right (or all four
possibilities), places feet (or foot) through loop and hoist
self using free end of rope. dance may end upon achieving
ceiling, failure of a pre- or indetermined number of attempts,
or exhaustion.

wiesbaden, june 1962

A VERY LAWFUL DANCE

for ennis

benjamin patterson

a traffic light, with or without special pedestrian signals
is found or positioned on street corner or at stage center.

performer(s) waits at real or imaginary curb on red signal,
alerts self on yellow signal, crosses street or stage on
green signal. achieving opposite side, performer(s) turns,
repeats sequence. a performance may consist of an infinite,
indetermined or predetermined number of repetitions.

wiesbaden, june 1962

Two Dances: "Solo for Dancer" and
"A Very Lawful Dance for Ennis," 1962
Ink on paper
3 pages, 11 × 8 inches each
Getty Research Institute, Los Angeles

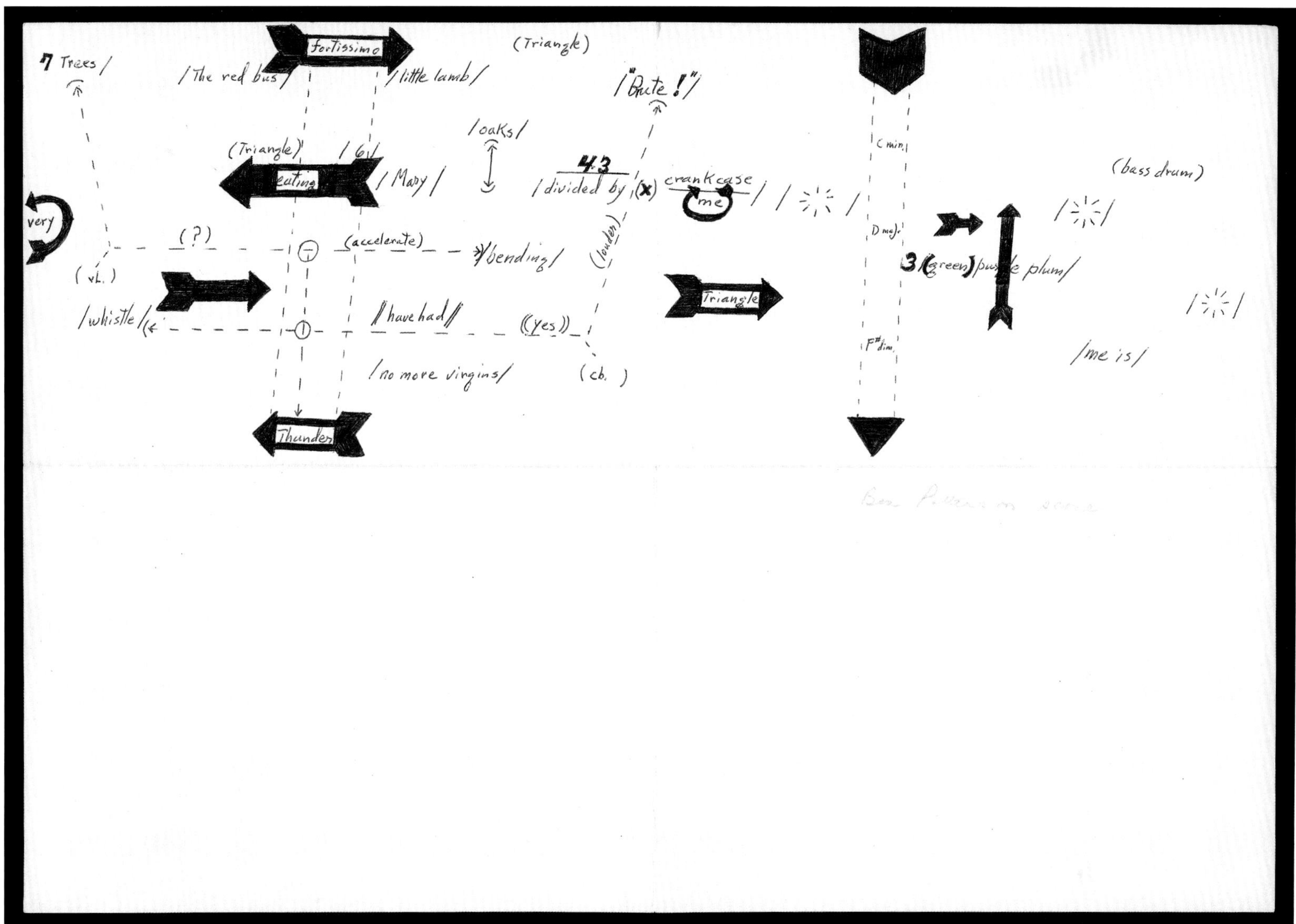

7 Trees /
/ The red bus /
fortissimo
/ little lamb /
(Triangle)
/ "Brute !" /
/ oaks /
(Triangle)
/ 6 /
eating
/ Mary /
43
/ divided by / (X)
crankcase
me
(bass drum)
C min.
very
(vl.)
(?)
(accelerate)
/ bending /
(louder)
D ma).
3 (green) purple plum /
(vl.)
/ whistle /
/ have had /
((yes))
Triangle
F# dim.
/ me is /
/ no more virgins /
(cb.)
Thunder

Untitled (handwritten iteration of *Variations
for Double Bass*), c. 1962
Ink on poster for Fluxus internationale Festspiele neuester Musik
16½ × 11¾ inches (unfolded); 5⅞ × 8¼ inches (folded)
Getty Research Institute, Los Angeles

                    for Pyla

                 A BITING PIECE
                      I.

         (The following text is read aloud before activity begins.)

         "An old man cutting and laying a hedge in one of our lanes with
         whom we stopped to chat one day, told us something of his life's
         work. Besides general farm work and hedging and ditching, he
         had the job in the spring time of shortening the lambs' tails
         by biting them off. He showed us how his teeth were worn down
         by the process, and well they might be, for frequently he had
         bitten off as many as three hundred tails in a day. He declared
         that this was by far the safest and most sanitary method of
         operation. This old man compared the youth of the present day
         with those of his own time, saying that today young people have
         no idea of what real poverty is nor of the frugal conditions in
         which his generation had been brought up."

              (Mona Clyde Clinch: "The story of Blisworth, Northamptonshire")

                      II.

         Performers (3 or more) form a row, backs to audience, attitude
         semi-squat - head forward, buttocks protruding, hands on knees
         providing support - are found at one extreme of performing area.
         First performer (A) moving behind other performers, bites each
         on buttocks as he passes and takes new position at end of line.
         Second performer (B), beginning after being bitten by A, repeats
         activity, biting C and successive performers in row, and takes
         a new position at end of row. Thus each performer in row recreates
         the activity, continuing in leap-frog fashion until opposite
         extreme of performing area is achieved, ending piece.

                           New York, 1963

                    "TOUR"

         PERSONS ARE INVITED AND MEET AT DESIGNATED TIME AND
         PLACE TO COMMENCE TOUR.
         AFTER METHODS AND GENERAL CONDITIONS OF TOUR ARE
         EXPLAINED, PARTICIPANTS ARE FITTED WITH BLINDFOLDS
         OR SIMILAR DEVICES AND LED THROUGH ANY AREA OR AREAS
         OF GUIDES' CHOICE(S).
         DURATION EXCEEDS 45 MINUTES.
         SUFFICIENT AND RESPONSIBLE GUIDES ARE PROVIDED.

                    APRIL, 1963   NEW YORK

A Biting Piece (for Pyla), 1963
Ink on paper
13 × 8½ inches
Getty Research Institute, Los Angeles

Tour, 1963
Ink on paper
11 × 7⅞ inches
Getty Research Institute, Los Angeles

```
(you're standing, perhaps drinking)                      beat-
                                                         beat-
close your eyes                                          beat-
                                                         beat-
sit down
                                                         Go Man!
(there's a good boy on bass; he's warming up)           Go Man!

you come along                                           stop

                                                         stop

                                                         stop

alright, now start to slow down                          (your shoe's
                                                         are new and
(that's right, beat's getting faster, you're to slow down)  the sky's
                                                         blue)!
let go; relax
                                                         beat-
(there, that's better; beat's still getting faster, you're   beat-
                                                         beat-
        slowing down)                                    beat-

(nice, eh?)                                              Go Man!
                                                         Go Man!
bells start to ring
                                                         jump
(sunday morning)
                                                         jump
all time mixing up, faster and slower, faster and slower
                                                         jump
mixing up, mixing up
                                                         (money's honey
faster and slower, faster and slower                     and we're
                                                         all runny)!
(add colors-like blue, yellow, pink)
                                                         beat-
(smoke, too, if you like)                                beat-
                                                         beat-
mixing up, faster and slower, blue, yellow, pink, smoke, beat-

        ringing (WOW! WOW! WOW!)                         moving faster,
                                                         moving faster,
(that's just fine!)
                                                         come Along!

                                                         come Along!

alright, had enough?                                     beat-
                                                         beat-
stop                                                     beat-
                                                         beat-
(now, when you hear the gong, open your eyes, sun's going to
                                                         Go Man!
  be shining, your shoes'll be new, sky'll be getting blue  Go Man!

  and everything, everything is going to be a lot, lot better,(damn your
                                                         mamie, make it
  O.K.?)                                                 with Annie)!


                                                         beat-
now, try it                                              beat-
                                                         beat-
well, there, what do you think about that?               beat-

want to try it again?                                    Go Man!
                                                         Go Man!
ok, close your eyes
                                                         laugh man, you
sit down
                                                         gotta laugh

                                                         man, laugh man
                                                         ...
```

Untitled (You are standing, perhaps drinking), c. 1963
Ink on paper
13 1/16 × 8 1/4 inches
Getty Research Institute, Los Angeles

FIRST SYMPHONY

One at a time members of audience are questioned,
"DO YOU TRUST ME?" and are divided left and right, yes
and no.
the room is darkened.
freshly ground coffee is scattered throughout the room.

May, 1964
New York City

First Symphony, 1964
Ink on paper
10½ × 16¹⁄₁₆ inches
Getty Research Institute, Los Angeles

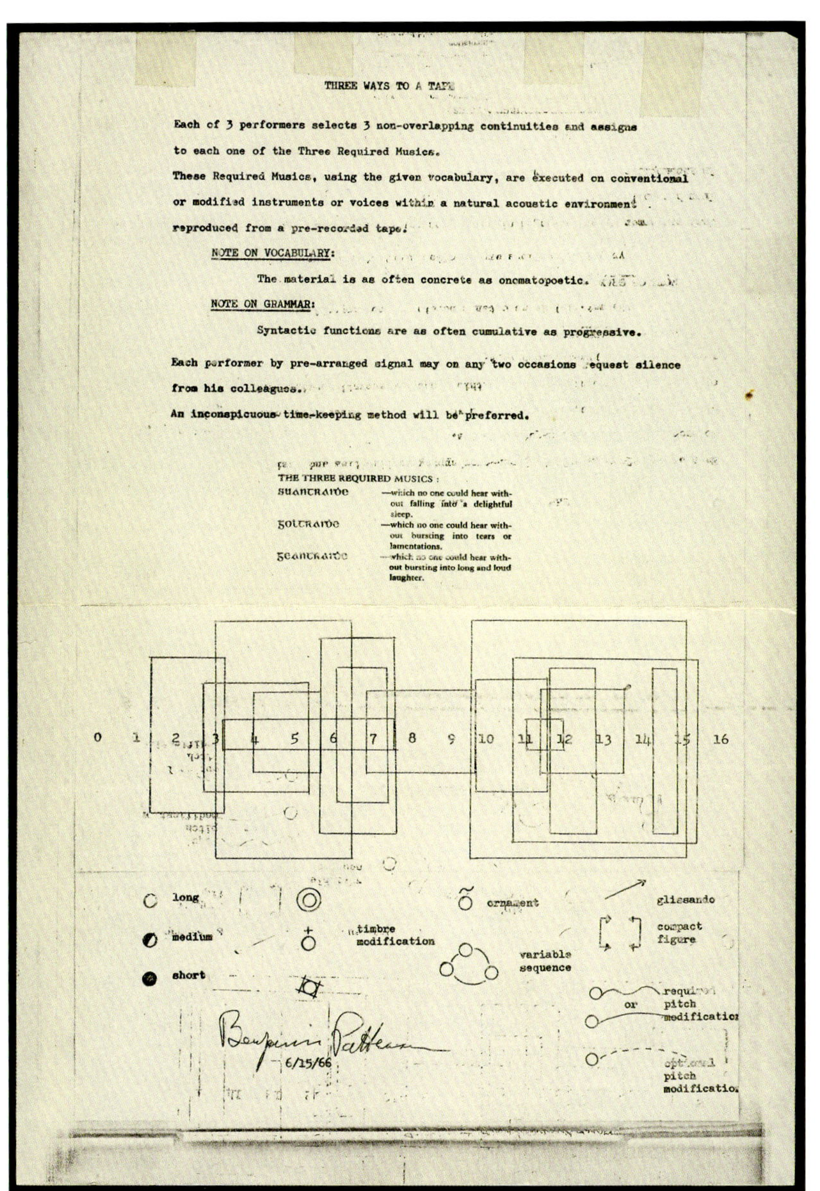

THREE WAYS TO A TAPE

Each of 3 performers selects 3 non-overlapping continuities and assigns
to each one of the Three Required Musics.

These Required Musics, using the given vocabulary, are executed on conventional
or modified instruments or voices within a natural acoustic environment
reproduced from a pre-recorded tape.

NOTE ON VOCABULARY:

The material is as often concrete as onomatopoetic.

NOTE ON GRAMMAR:

Syntactic functions are as often cumulative as progressive.

Each performer by pre-arranged signal may on any two occasions request silence
from his colleagues.

An inconspicuous time-keeping method will be preferred.

THE THREE REQUIRED MUSICS :

SUANTRAIDE —which no one could hear without falling into a delightful sleep.

GOLTRAIDE —which no one could hear without bursting into tears or lamentations.

GEANTRAIDE —which no one could hear without bursting into long and loud laughter.

Three Ways to a Tape, 1966
Ink on paper
14 15/16 × 10 inches
Getty Research Institute, Los Angeles

Das Bahnhof Requiem, 1995 (detail)
Ink and collage on paper
Instructions: 2 pages, 11½ × 8⅛ inches each
Score: 4 pages, 10½ × 15½ inches each
Courtesy the artist

"THE THREE OPERAS"

        (a work by Ben Patterson
         based on music by
         Bizet-"Carmen";
         Puccini-"Madame Butterfly"; and
         Wagner-"Tristan and Isolde".)

Foreword: These instructions for the performance of "THE THREE
          OPERAS" represent my most recent thoughts about this
          work. Historically, this work spans more than three
          decades. The "stage-action" for "TRISTAN AND ISOLDE"
          was originally a discrete "event/happening", first
          published in Paris, 1961. Wagner's music, the chop-
          sticks, and the rice were added only in 1992. "CARMEN"
          came to life as a unique work in 1989. "MADAME BUTTERFLY"
          was created to fill the "perceived" gap between "CARMEN"
          and "TRISTAN AND ISOLDE" for the first performance of
          "THE THREE OPERAS" in Seoul, Korea, 1992.

          At the first performance in Seoul, Korea, I only saw
          this as three nice, but unrelated works. The public
          reaction to this performance was a great educatiom for
          me. The public saw a unity that I had not yet seen.

          Since then, of course, I aware of this "unity". Still,
          the big question remains: "What does it all mean?"

          Ben Patterson

          Wiesbaden, 1997

The Three Operas, 1997 (detail)
Ink on paper
5 pages, 11⅝ × 8¼ inches each
Courtesy the artist

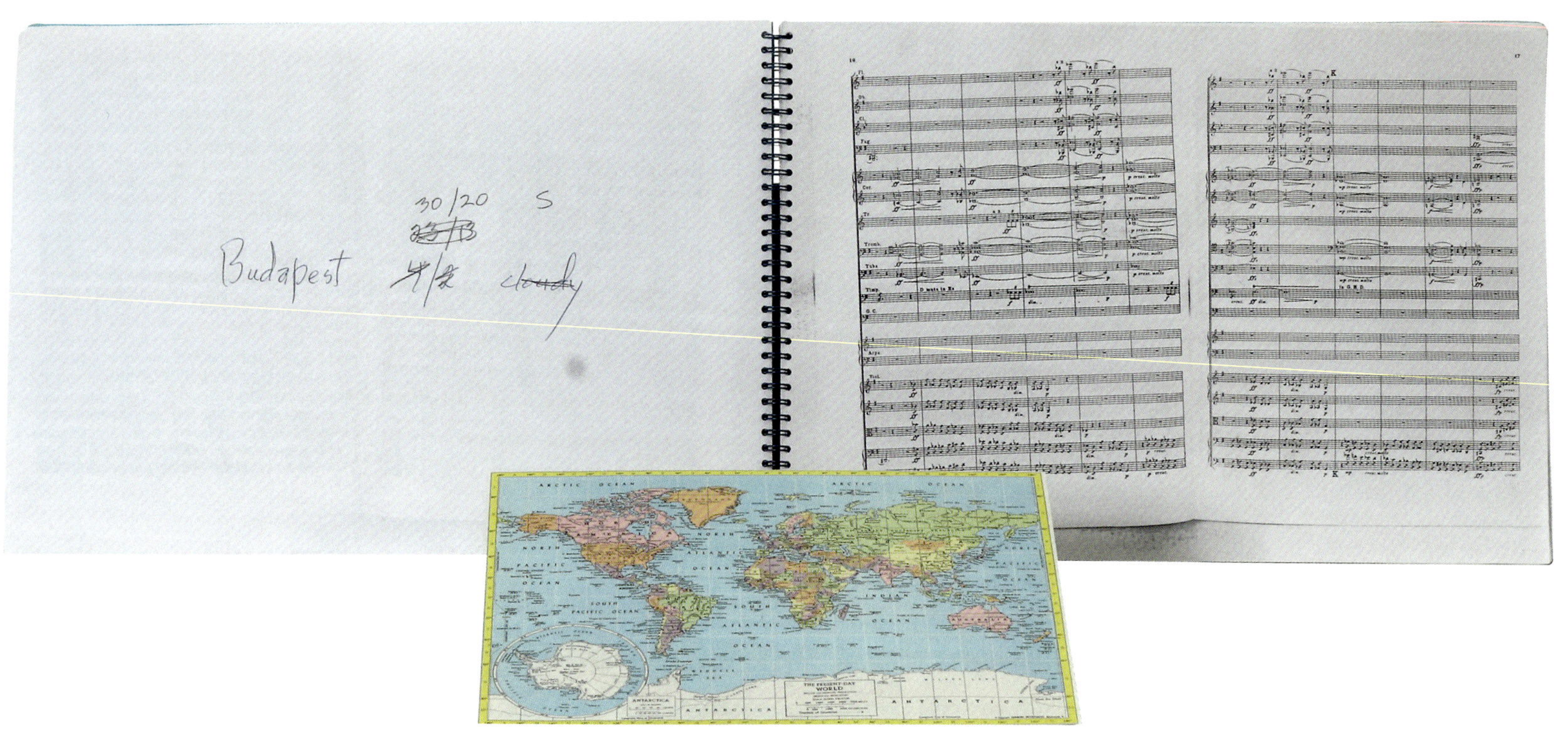

World Weather, 1997
Spiral-bound music composition notebook,
ink and color markers on paper, world map
11⅝ × 8¼ inches
Courtesy the artist

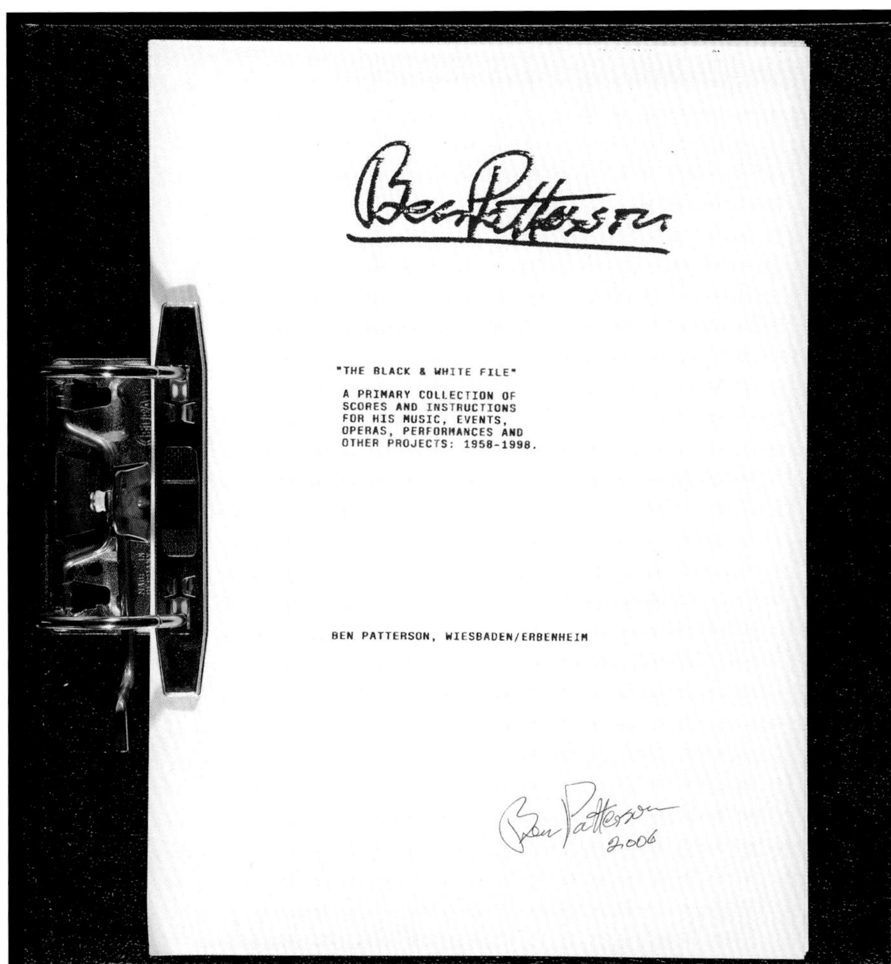

Benjamin Patterson: "The Black and White File":
A Primary Collection of Scores and Instructions
for His Music, Events, Operas, Performances,
and Other Projects: 1958–1998, 1999
Photostat paper in black binder
12½ × 11⁷⁄₁₆ × 1⅞ inches
Courtesy the artist

File includes the following scores and actions:
Paper Piece, 1960
Ants, 1960–62
Duo for Voice and a String Instrument, 1961
Lemons, 1961
Overture, Overture (Versions II and III), 1961
Septet from Lemons, 1961
Pavane for Flutes, 1961–62
Variations for Double Bass, 1961–62
Pond, 1962
Portrait of an Egg, 1962
Sneak Peek, 1962
Solo for Dancer, 1962
A Very Lawful Dance for Ennis, 1962
A Biting Piece for Pyla, 1963
Examination, 1963
First Symphony, 1964
How the Average Person Thinks about Art, 1983 (4 pages)
I Visited the U.S.A., 1987
Artists' Greeting, 1988 (5 pages)
Critical Encounters, 1988
Signature No. 1, 1990
Signature No. 2, 1991
Bolero, 1994
Das Bahnhof Requiem, 1995 (7 pages)
On the Road with Al . . . a Gedächtnisperformance für Al Hansen,
1996 (2 pages)
A Simple Opera, 1996 (7 pages)
The Future Makes Progress, 1997 (7 pages)
Some "Found Objects"—Quotations—Recently Discovered by
Benjamin Patterson, 1997
The Three Operas, 1997 (*Carmen,* 1990; *Madame Butterfly,* 1993
[2 pages]; *Tristan und Isolde,* 1961–93)
World Weather, 1997
The Creation of the World, 1998 (3 pages)
How to Make Art: Benjamin Patterson's Foolproof Methods, 1998

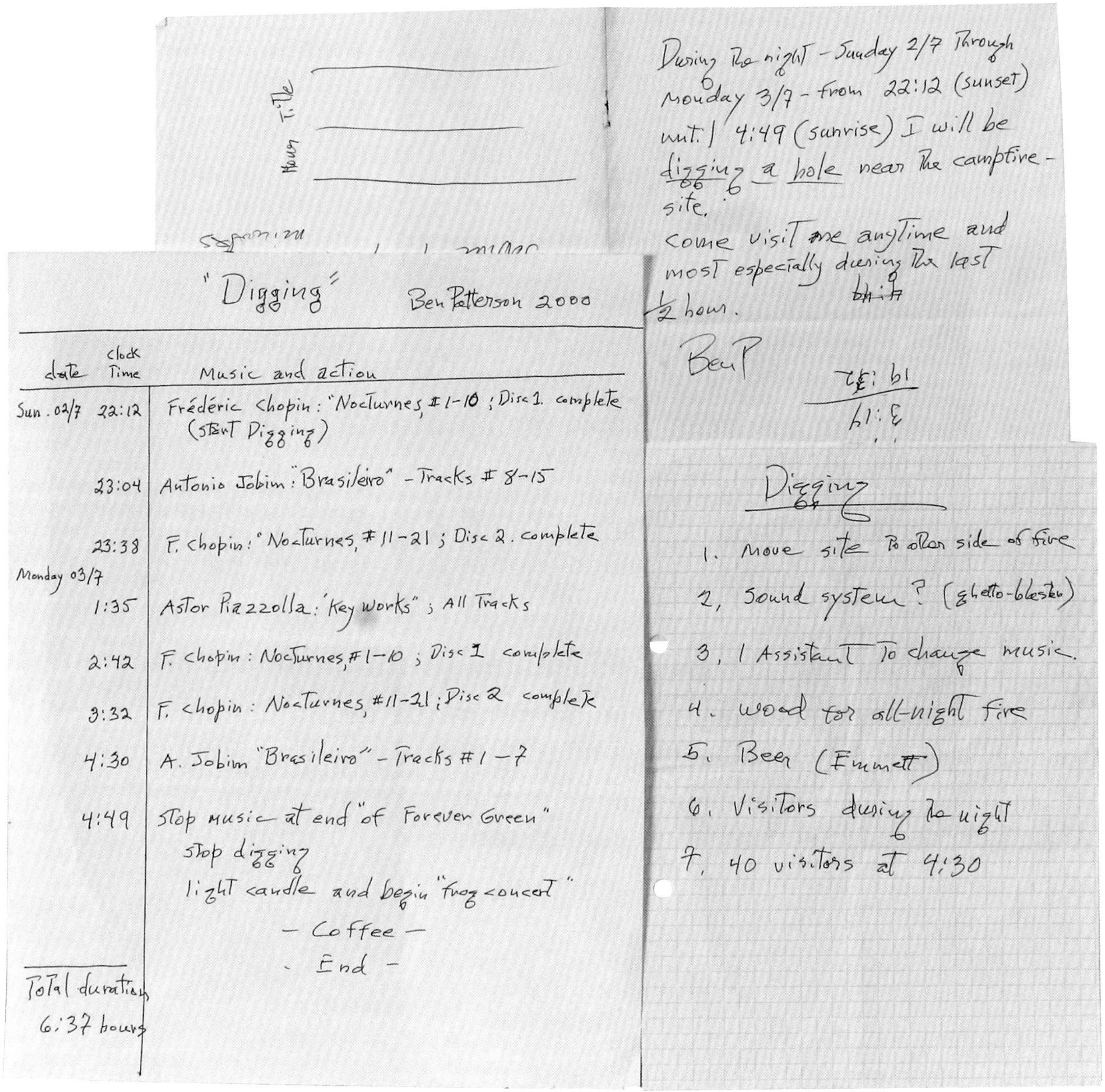

"Digging" Ben Patterson 2000

date	clock Time	Music and action
Sun. 02/7	22:12	Frédéric Chopin: "Nocturnes, #1-10; Disc 1. complete (start Digging)
	23:04	Antonio Jobim "Brasileiro" - Tracks # 8-15
	23:38	F. Chopin: "Nocturnes, #11-21; Disc 2. complete
Monday 03/7	1:35	Astor Piazzolla: "Key works"; All Tracks
	2:42	F. Chopin: Nocturnes, #1-10; Disc 1 complete
	3:32	F. Chopin: Nocturnes, #11-21; Disc 2 complete
	4:30	A. Jobim "Brasileiro" - Tracks #1-7
	4:49	Stop music at end "of Forever Green" stop digging light candle and begin "Frog concert" — Coffee — — End —

Total duration 6:37 hours

During the night — Sunday 2/7 through Monday 3/7 — from 22:12 (sunset) until 4:49 (sunrise) I will be digging a hole near the campfire-site.

Come visit me anytime and most especially during the last ½ hour.

Ben P

Digging
1. Move site to other side of fire
2. Sound system? (ghetto-blaster)
3. 1 Assistant to change music.
4. Wood for all-night fire
5. Beer (Emmett)
6. Visitors during the night
7. 40 visitors at 4:30

Digging, 2000
Ink on paper
4 sheets, 10⅝ × 8⅛ inches each
Courtesy the artist

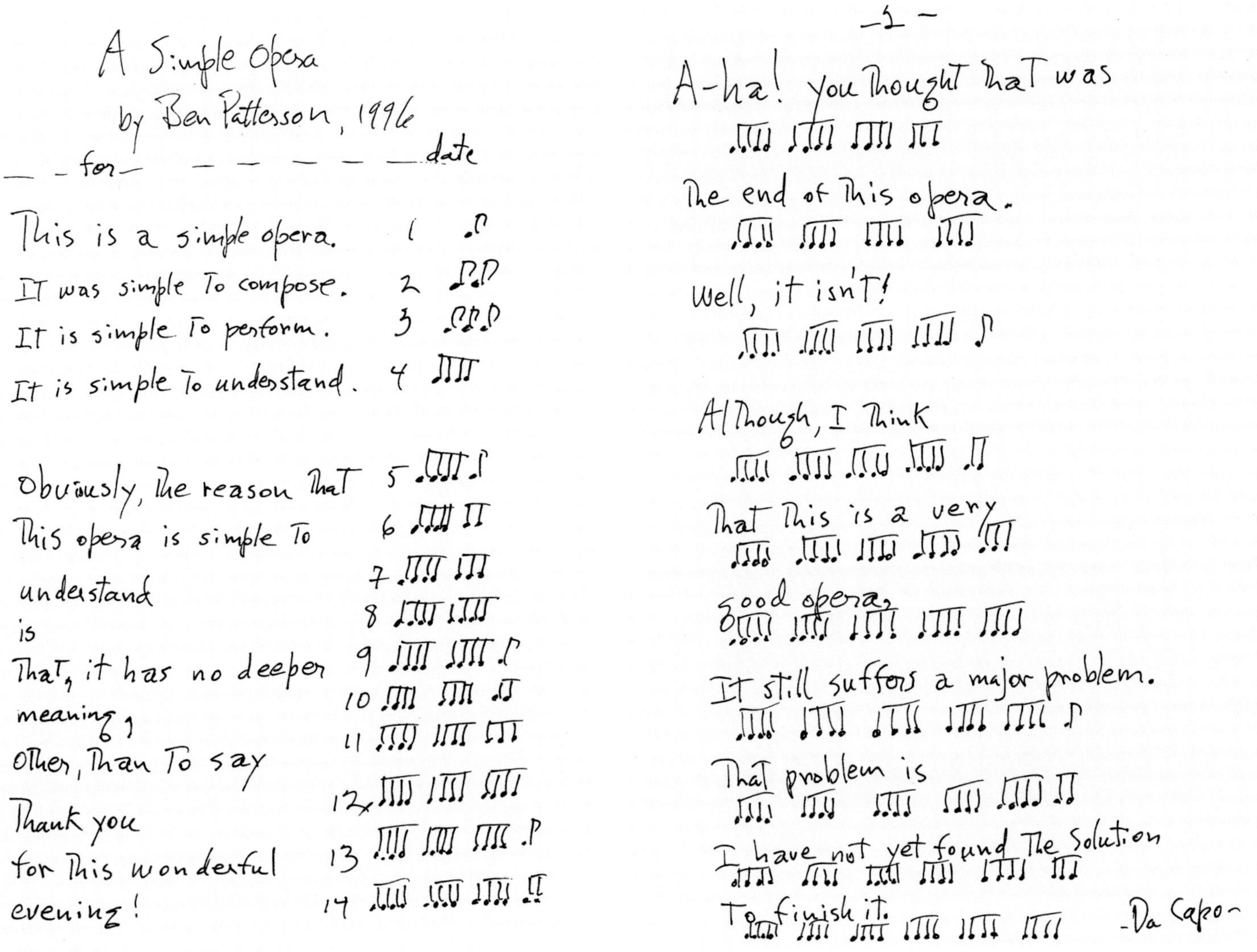

A Simple Opera
by Ben Patterson, 1996
_ - for _ _ _ _ _ _ date

This is a simple opera.   1
IT was simple To compose.   2
It is simple To perform.   3
It is simple To understand.   4

Obviously, The reason That   5
This opera is simple To   6
understand   7
is   8
That, it has no deeper   9
meaning,   10
Other, Than To say   11
Thank you   12
for This wonderful   13
evening!   14

- 2 -

A-ha! you Thought That was

The end of This opera.

Well, it isn'T!

Although, I Think

That This is a very

good opera,

It still suffers a major problem.

That problem is

I have not yet found The Solution

To finish it.   -Da Capo-

A Simple Opera, 2001
Ink and collage on paper
11⅝ × 8¼ inches
Courtesy the artist

„This is my Tone"

Ben Patterson, 2005

To introduce this work, may I tell you a true story told to me (Ben Patterson) in 1975 by
Robert Mann, who at that time was the first violinst of the Juilliard String Quartet.

This story took place around 1967-1968, when the <u>U.S.A.</u> and the <u>U.S.S.R.</u> were still
conducting a „cultural Cold War" to win the „hearts and minds" of „Third World
countries". In this context the U.S.A., Department of State sent numerous, high-profile
performing arts ensembles on tour throughout the world. Thus, the Juilliard String
Quartet was sent on a two-week tour to West Africa. After concerts in the several
capitals and major cities of Ghana, Nigeria, Congo, etc., the Quartet discovered – much
to their surprise – that the final concert would be in a true, tribal, Bantu village...deep in
the „bush". Arriving at the village, they found their suspicions confirmed: the setting
was somewhere between a Hollywood „safari film" and a 1930´s ethnological
documentary film. Of course, the first question the Quartet asked themselves was,
„What do we have in our repertoire to play for this audience?" Finally, they decided on
honesty...which meant to present those compositions, for which, at that time, their live-
performances and recordings enjoyed world-wide acclaim. So sitting in the open, under
an African moon, circled by several hundred villagers, in front of the chieftain´s hut, the
Juilliard String Quartet performed Beethoven´s three „Rasumowsky Quartets", Opus 59.

According to Robert Mann, the extraodinary circumstances inspired the Quartet to
present their „best-ever" performances of these three quartets. Finishing the last notes of
the concert, each member of the Quartet felt, that they had finally achieved a truely
transcendental interpertation of these great Beethoven compositions. However,...and
greatly disturbing for the Quartet members...was the complete lack of any apparent
reaction – negative or positive - by the audience...no applause, no stapping of feet, no
presentation of flowers or anything else to suggest that they appreciated this
extraordinary performance! The villagers simply stood up with saddened faces, milled
around silently for a while, and then finally sat down to begin the festive meal ending this
event. The members of the Quartet were seated next to the chieftain...and so, after some
polite conversation and after an appropriate amount of food and drink had been
consumed, Robert Mann dared to ask the chieftain about this public relations disaster.
Robert Mann explained that the the Quartet members thought that they had just presented
their „best-ever" performance of these quartets...and that they were surprised that the
villagers, apparently did not appreciate their efforts.   The chieftain, gazing into the
distance - not wishing to present bad news, eye-to-eye, replied: „My people feel great
sympathy for you. They see that you are already so old, and they feel sad that you have,
not yet, found your tone."

....
POSTSCRIPT:
To understand this reply by the chieftain, it is necessary to understand a few basic
principles of the polyphonic music of the Bantu tribes of West and Central Africa:

My Tone, Your Tone, His Tone,
Her Tone, 2005 (detail)
Ink on white and colored paper
6 pages, 11⅝ × 8¼ inches each
Courtesy the artist

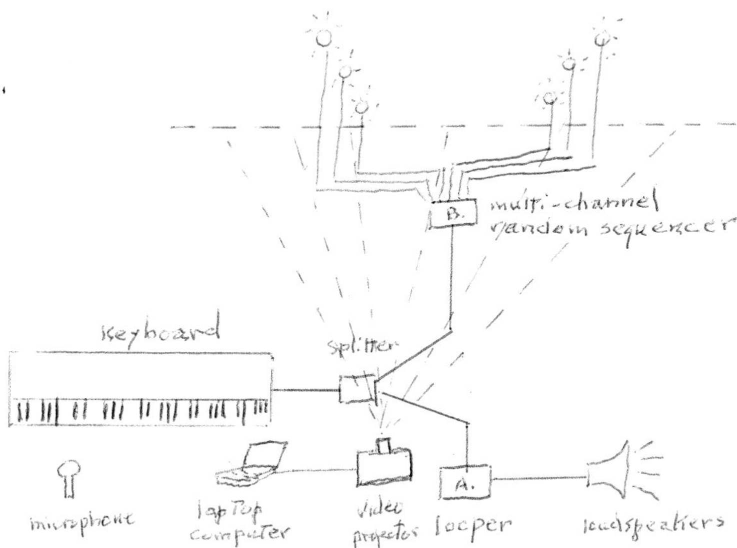

A Fluxus Elegy (Audiovisual Performance),
c. 2006
Ink on paper
7⅞ × 11⅞ inches
Courtesy the artist

"Ants...revisited"
Ben Patterson, 2010

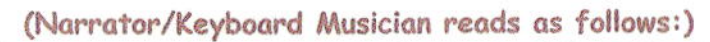

(Narrator/Keyboard Musician reads as follows:)

"The story of this composition begins in July 1960. Discovering an "ant hill" in a garden in Düsseldorf, I believed I had found a new approach to aleatoric music. I scooped-up a bunch of these ants, dumped them into the center of a sheet of paper and then made 6 photographs over a period of 10 minutes, recording the new positions of the ants at each of these 6 moments. I transferred these "random" dots (ants) to pages of blank music staffs, expecting interesting "music". A try-out on my double-bass was quite disappointing. (Only much later did I realized that what I had discovered was a "method",…and of course, a "method" is not "music".) Thus, this first attempt was abandoned and placed in the "future projects" file.

Four years later…1964 in New York, I opened this file again and published "Ants II, a composition to be used in conjunction with any 1962 composition of George Maciunas." To date, I know of no public performance of this version.

Now, 50 years later we have "Ants Revisited"…based on recent scientific behavioral studies of the methods of communication among ants. In this version, I have assumed that the original ants organized their escape from that sheet of paper, primarily communicating with pheromones (in this score represented by an accumulating cloud of long tones) and secondarily with stidulations (the intermittent rasping or clicking sounds). One original photograph has served as a reference for determining time and pitch relationships. The resulting "composition" is not a true transcription of the original traffic of pheromones and stidulation signals between those ants, but rather a presumptive, acoustic model based on the remaining evidence.

Ants Revisited, 2010
Ink on paper
3 pages, 11⅞ × 16½ inches each
Courtesy the artist

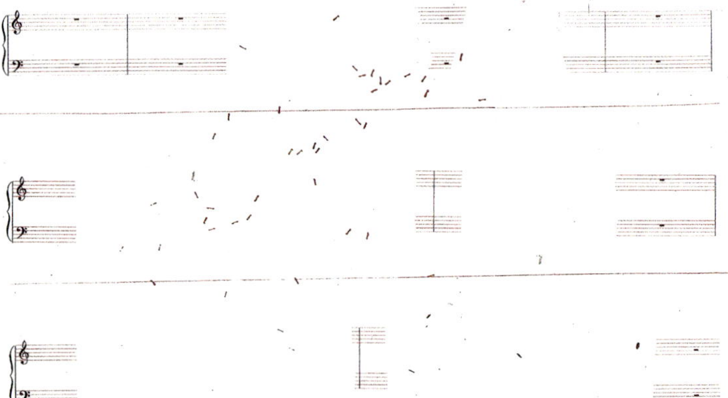

The keyboard starts the piece. Reading from left to right, top to bottom the spatial distribution of the ant images suggest time intervals and pitches to be performed by depressing and taping down the appropriate keys, creating an accumulating "acoustic cloud", which continues until the end of the piece.

Clickers and Rasps (stidulations)

Ten performers are equipped with devices, which make clicking and/or rasping sounds. Each performer is assigned one line (from a to j) from the graphic below. At some point in time during the third system (to be signalled by the keyboard player), the clickers and raspers (guided by the graphic below, representing the stidulations of 10 different tree-hopper ants) enter and begin producing "stidulations." These stidulations, combined with the "pheromones cloud", continue until the keyboard player signals the end of the piece.

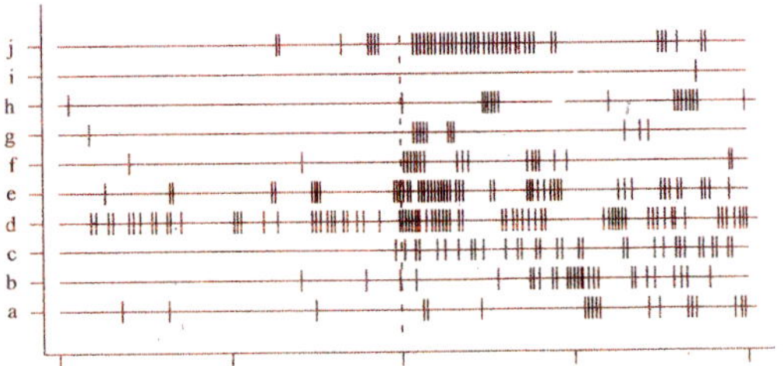

The duration of a performance of this work may, or may not be pre-determined.

"Duo for Voice and a String Instrument"
arranged for
Voice and String Quintet

Notes to the score:

For this arrangement 16 sets of "calls and responses" have been prepared.
The voice "calls" and the quintet "responds". In a few sets the voice
"comments" during the "response".
All or any number of sets may be performed in any order. The
numbering on each set is for purposes of identification only.
Amplitude, duration and frequencies are open to interpretation. A set may be
performed in a loud, dense, aggressive manner, or in a quiet, pointillist,
reserved manner, or in any other manner.
In the parts for the quintet, symbols which appear in the space between two
staffs may be performed by either one or both musicians.
The wavy solid lines indicate the modulation of a continuing sound. The
dotted, amoeba-like forms indicate where the instrument is "prepared" (mute,
paper clip on a string, etc.) to perform all or some of the immediately
surrounding symbols.
Admendments are recommended where necessary (to make music).

Ben Patterson
Oct. 18, 2010
Wiesbaden

Duo for Voice and a String Instrument Arranged for Voice and String Quintet, 2010 (detail)
Ink on paper
Instructions: 11¾ × 8¼ inches (folded), 11¾ × 24⅞ inches (unfolded)
Score (16 pages): 8¼ × 11¾ inches (folded), 8¾ × 23¼ inches (unfolded)
Courtesy the artist

16.

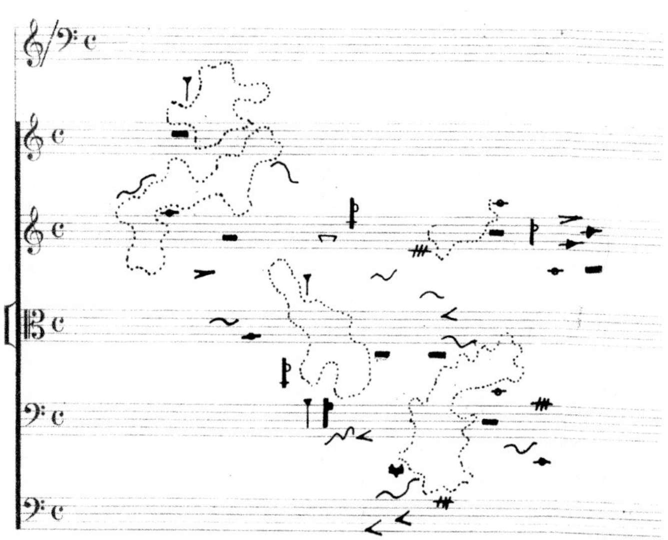

"GIVE ME A BREAK!"   Ben Patterson, 2010

Seven sections (hereafter called "jams") of notations and performance instructions are provided, as well as, an assortment of necessary "tools". A performance may consist of one or more jams in any order and of any duration.

1. A performance begins with a background PA system, virtual, hard rock "beat",... which continues (even bridging jams) until the end of the performance. Patterns, tempi and volume of this beat may or may not change during the course of a performance. Source of the "beat" may be a CD, synthesizer, keyboard or other. From time-to-time, any/all performers may "ride" live on top of this beat. Use supplied samples or create others.

2. At an appropriate moment (after the "beat" is established) the "background text" (A) for a selected jam is read by one performer. (When performing multiple jams, these texts may be read always by the same performer, or each performer, in a sequential order, may read one or more of these texts.)

3. Next, the "trick text" (B) for this jam is read by all performers in unison. (see Note 1.)

(The "background text" (A) can be read in a dry, academic style. The "trick text" (B) can be read in a rhythmic "rapper" style. Microphones are provided for each reader.)

4. Performers then attempt to perform the trick(s) on their instruments (simultaneously or in any sequence), focusing on acoustic results. (See Note 2. below) Instruments are amplified (contact microphones?) and a "looper" captures interesting "acoustic events". "X" number of interesting "events" are captured and "looped" to create a "cloud" of accumulating density. At the end of each jam, this "cloud" may end abruptly or fade away. (Ideally, there is a looper for each instrument controlled by the performer and the output mix is controlled by whoever has a free hand. However, there are other solutions.)

Note 1: In most jams, the trick text (B) provides instructions for the performance of several tricks. A single trick may be selected to be performed by all in unison, or several tricks may be selected to be performed individually or by all, simultaneously or in sequence. All trick texts are read simultaneously.

Note 2: A tonal range and/or a part of an instrument may be notated to suggest where, on the instrument, the trick should be performed. Notated tones or chords may or may not be performed. BEWARE: follow the "trick texts", rather than the images, which may or may not accurately illustrate the trick.

Note 3: Live-video capturing of details of the performance and projected onto a large screen on, or near the stage can enhance the experience.

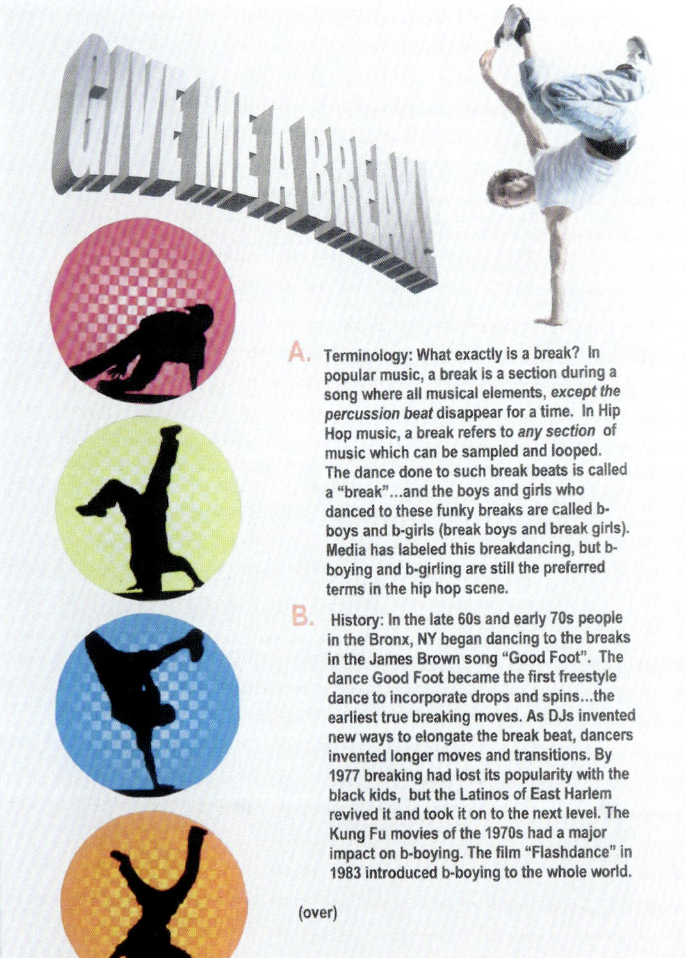

A. Terminology: What exactly is a break? In popular music, a break is a section during a song where all musical elements, *except the percussion beat* disappear for a time. In Hip Hop music, a break refers to *any section* of music which can be sampled and looped. The dance done to such break beats is called a "break"...and the boys and girls who danced to these funky breaks are called b-boys and b-girls (break boys and break girls). Media has labeled this breakdancing, but b-boying and b-girling are still the preferred terms in the hip hop scene.

B. History: In the late 60s and early 70s people in the Bronx, NY began dancing to the breaks in the James Brown song "Good Foot". The dance Good Foot became the first freestyle dance to incorporate drops and spins...the earliest true breaking moves. As DJs invented new ways to elongate the break beat, dancers invented longer moves and transitions. By 1977 breaking had lost its popularity with the black kids, but the Latinos of East Harlem revived it and took it on to the next level. The Kung Fu movies of the 1970s had a major impact on b-boying. The film "Flashdance" in 1983 introduced b-boying to the whole world.

(over)

Give Me a Break, 2010
Ink on paper
12 pages, 16⅜ × 11½ inches each
Envelope: 17½ × 12¾ inches
Courtesy the artist

B. Technique. The four primary techniques of breaking are:

1. *Toprock,* which is any string of steps performed from a standing position. Given the great variety of possible steps, *Toprock* is usually the entry dance to start a set and the foremost display of style.

2. *Downrock,* which describes any movement on the floor with the hands supporting the dancer as much as the feet. Basic *downrock* is done entirely with the hands and feet dancing the classic 6-step or 3-step.

3. *Power moves,* which are acrobatic moves requiring momentum and physical power. The breaker is generally supported by an upper body part, while the rest of the body spins or rotates. Notable examples are the windmill, swipe, head spin, back spin and flares.   AND,

4. *Freezes,* which are stylish poses in which the body is balanced in the air using only the hand(s), elbow(s), shoulder(s) or head. Notable examples are the pike, flag, headstand, k-kick and frog splashs. Freezes can be linked into chains or "freeze ladders" and often signal the end of a b-boy set.

OK! So now it is time that we GIVE YOU A BREAKS!

 The score below provides for six sets of breaks of which any or all may be performed in any order. Performers should begin each set with *top rock,* transitioning into *downrock,* followed by a few *power moves* and ending with the *freeze* illustrated in the score. Illustrated instructions for selected *top rock, down rock* and *power moves* are provided on a separate page. Performers are free to create their own moves and transitions within the general outlines of a particular technique. Use the Power Ranger and/or the small wooden figure to dance these breaks.)

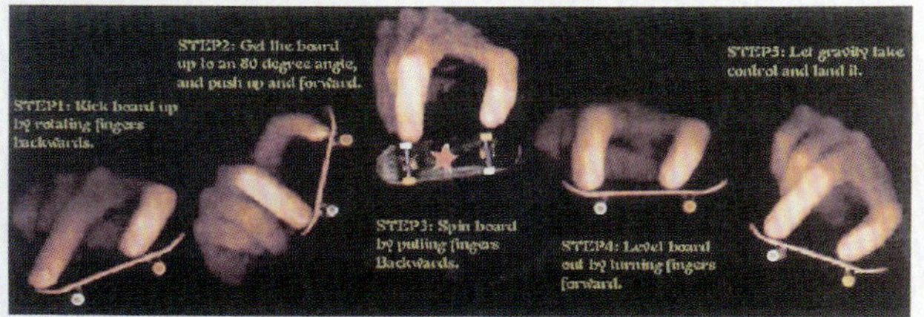

IT'S FINGERBOARD TIME!

A. A Fingerboard is basically a down-scaled skateboard. Most authorities consider the 1985 documentary film, "Future Primitive", featuring a homemade fingerboard built from cardboard, coffee stirrers and Hot Wheels axles, as the "public birthday" of fingerboarding. Now, 25 years later, fingerboarding is a $500+ million industry. Born in the USA, fingerboarding now enjoys greater popularity in Europe with annual contests, fairs, workshops and prominent placement on the shelves of even the most conservative toy stores. You need confirmation? Check "You Tube".

B. For a warm-up, we will all "build and ride" an Ollie...the foundation for all other fingerboard tricks.

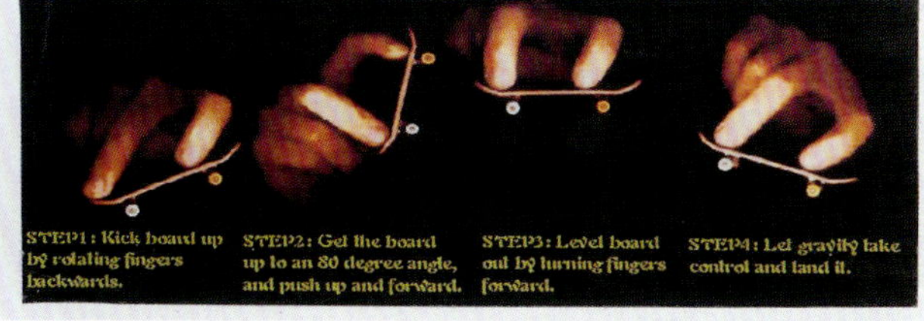

Notes on Fluxus/
Notes on an Ordinary Life

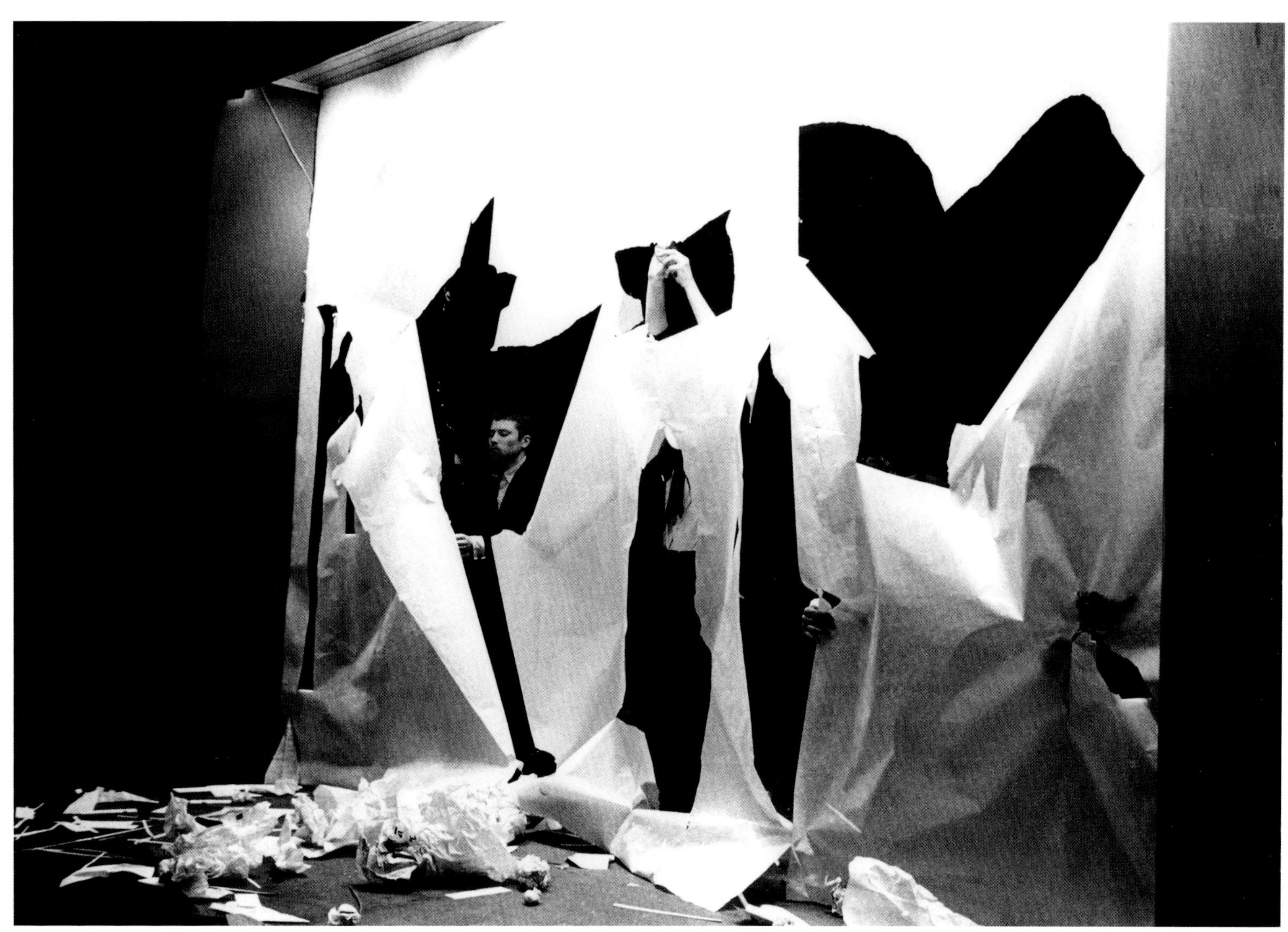

Performance documentation for *Paper Piece*,
1960
Performed at Hypokriterion Theater, Amsterdam, June 23, 1963
Gelatin silver print (photograph by Oscar van Arpken)
7⅞ × 11 inches (unframed)
20 × 17 inches (framed)
Archivo Bonotto, Molvena

lemons

benjamin patterson

23

scenen

für

tänzerin

sänger

musiker

maler

14.

juli

1961

20.30 uhr

köln

spichernstr. 18

bei

vostell

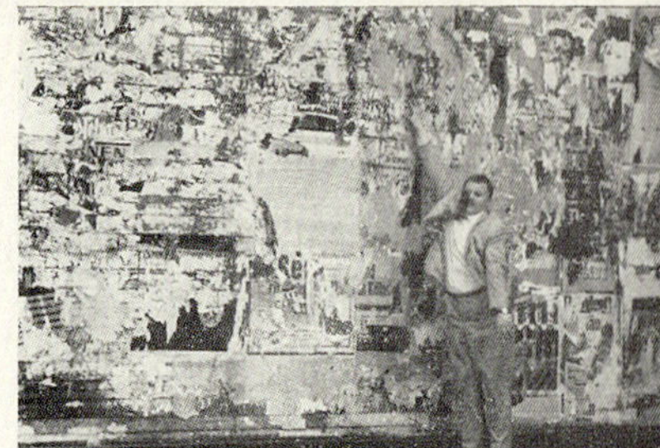

benjamin patterson

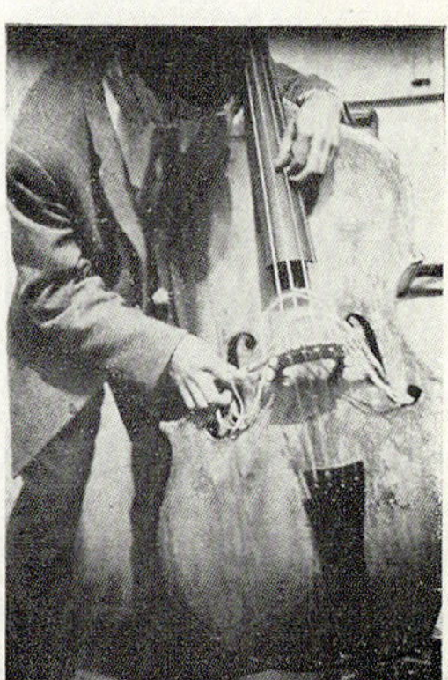

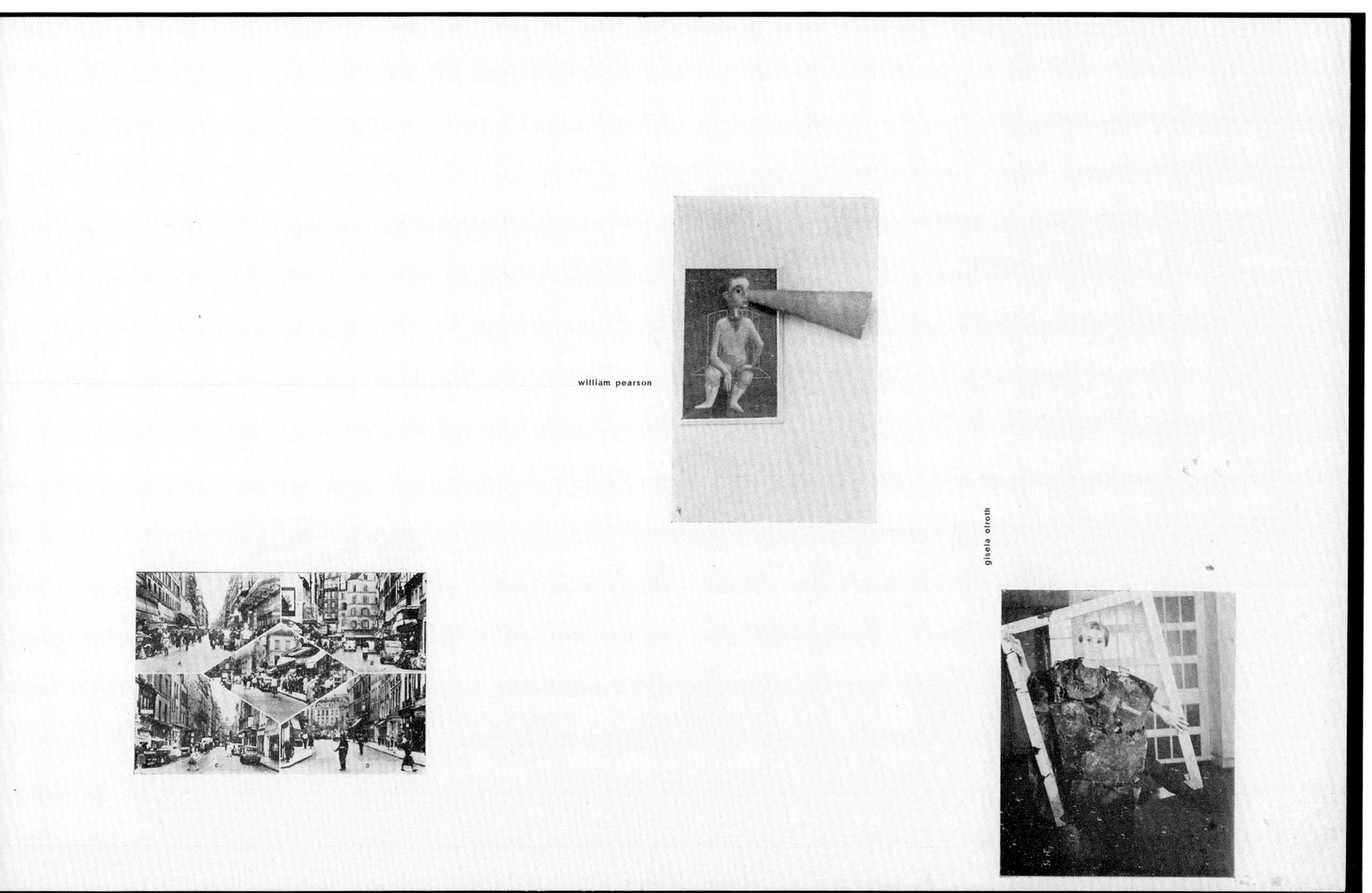

Performance documentation/brochure for
Lemons: Benjamin Patterson, 1961
Offset on paper
8⁷⁄₁₆ × 27¼ inches (unfolded)
Getty Research Institute, Los Angeles

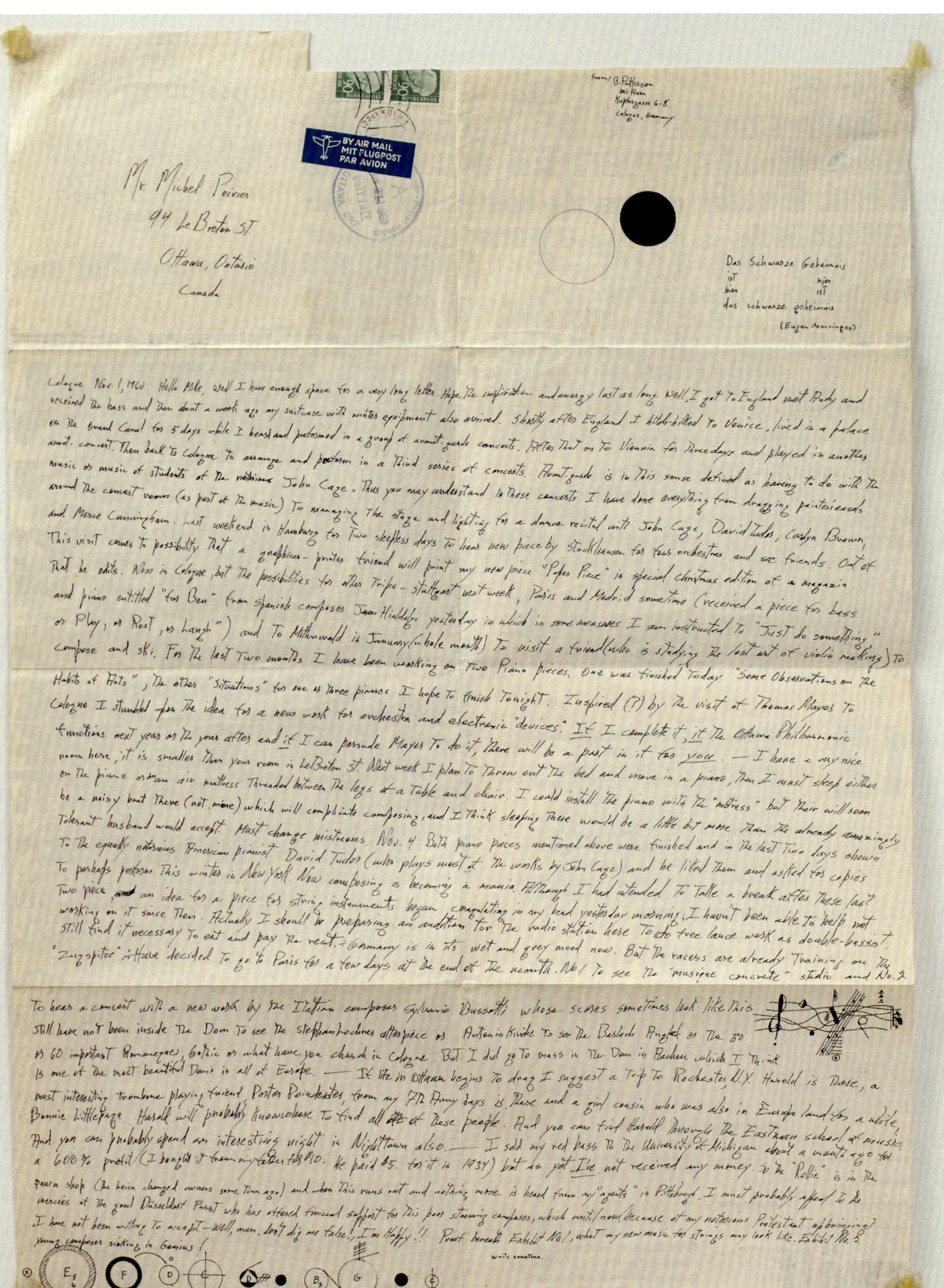

Letter from Benjamin Patterson
to Michael Porier, 1960
Ink on paper (verso, poster)
22⅝ × 16⅜ inches
Courtesy the artist

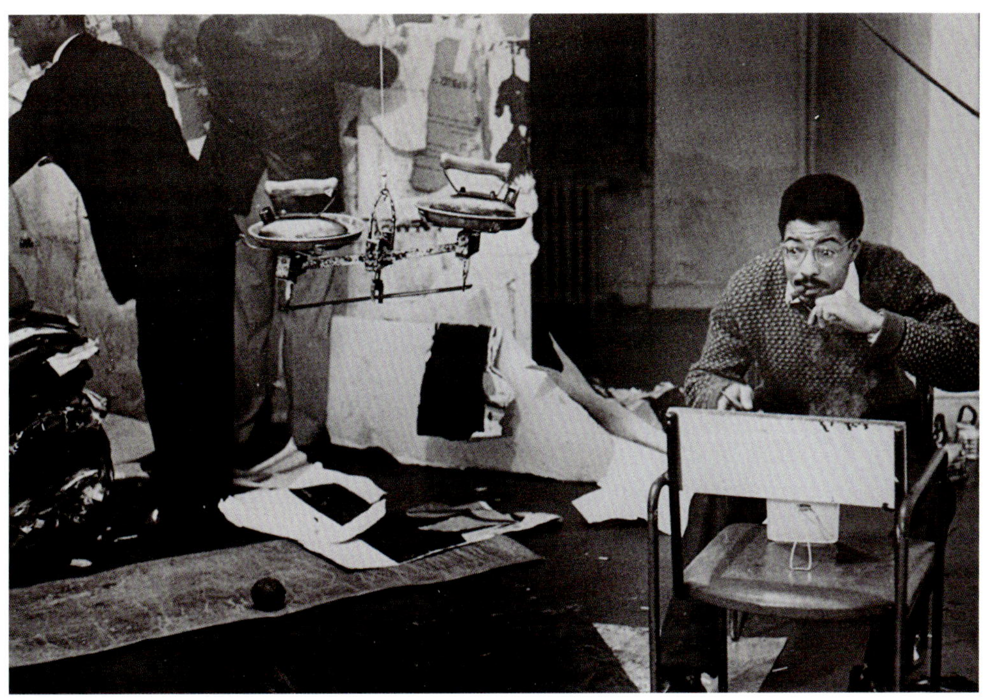

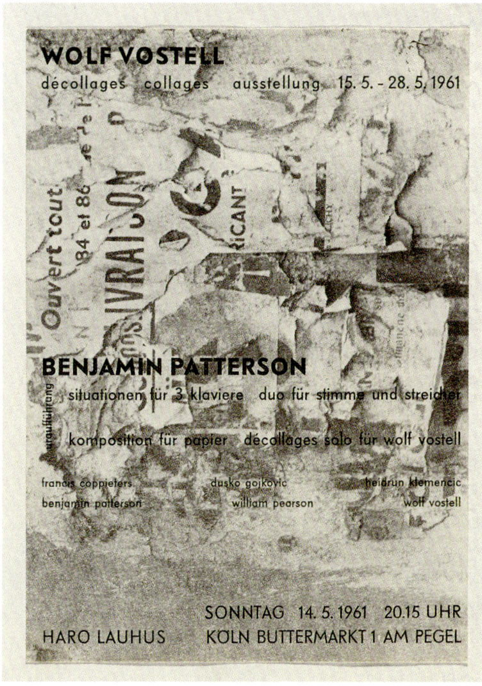

Performance documentation for *Décollage Piece for Wolf Vostell*, 1961
Black-and-white photograph
8 × 11 inches
Photographer unknown
Getty Research Institute, Los Angeles

Performance documentation for *Wolf Vostell: Décollages, Collages, Ausstellung 15.5–28.5.1961*, 1961
Offset on paper, mounted on paper
8¼ × 5¾ inches (sheet)
10⁹⁄₁₆ × 8¼ inches (mount)
Courtesy the artist

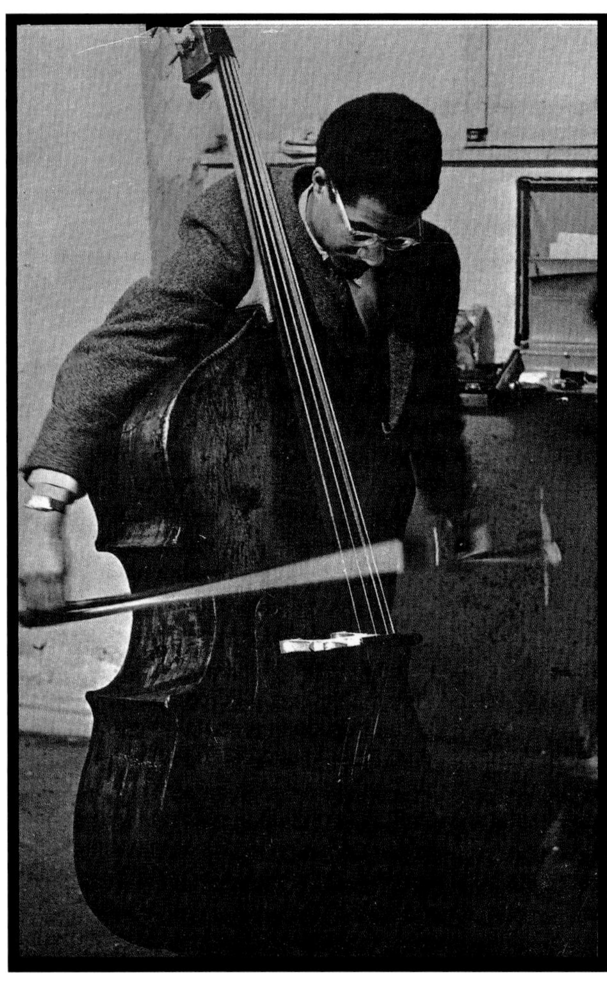

Performance documentation for *Variations for
Double Bass*, 1961
Performed by the artist at Kleinen Sommerfest/Après John Cage,
Galerie Parnass, Wuppertal, Germany, June 9, 1962
Gelatin silver prints (photograph by Rolf Jährling)
2 prints, 9¹⁵⁄₁₆ × 7¹⁵⁄₁₆ inches each
2 prints, 13¾ × 10⅞ inches each
The Museum of Modern Art, New York;
The Gilbert and Lila Silverman Fluxus Collection Gift

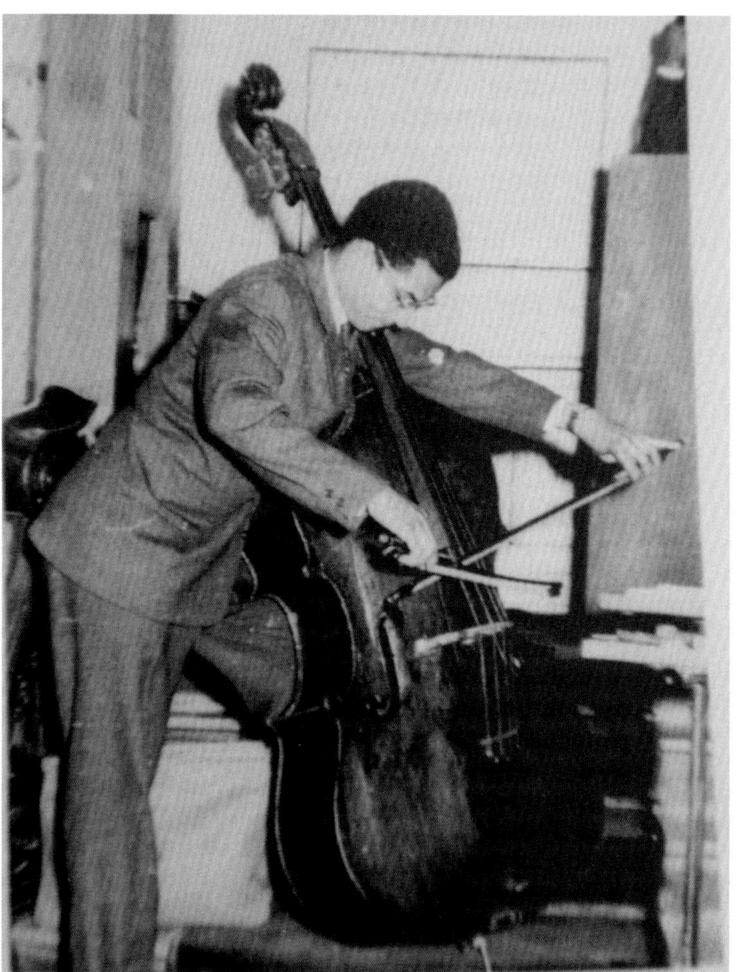

Performance documentation for *Duo for
Voice and a String Instrument*, 1961
Performed by the artist at Kleines Sommerfest/Après John
Cage, Galerie Parnass, Wuppertal, Germany, June 9, 1962
Gelatin silver print (photograph by Rolf Jährling)
8 × 10 inches
Getty Research Institute, Los Angeles

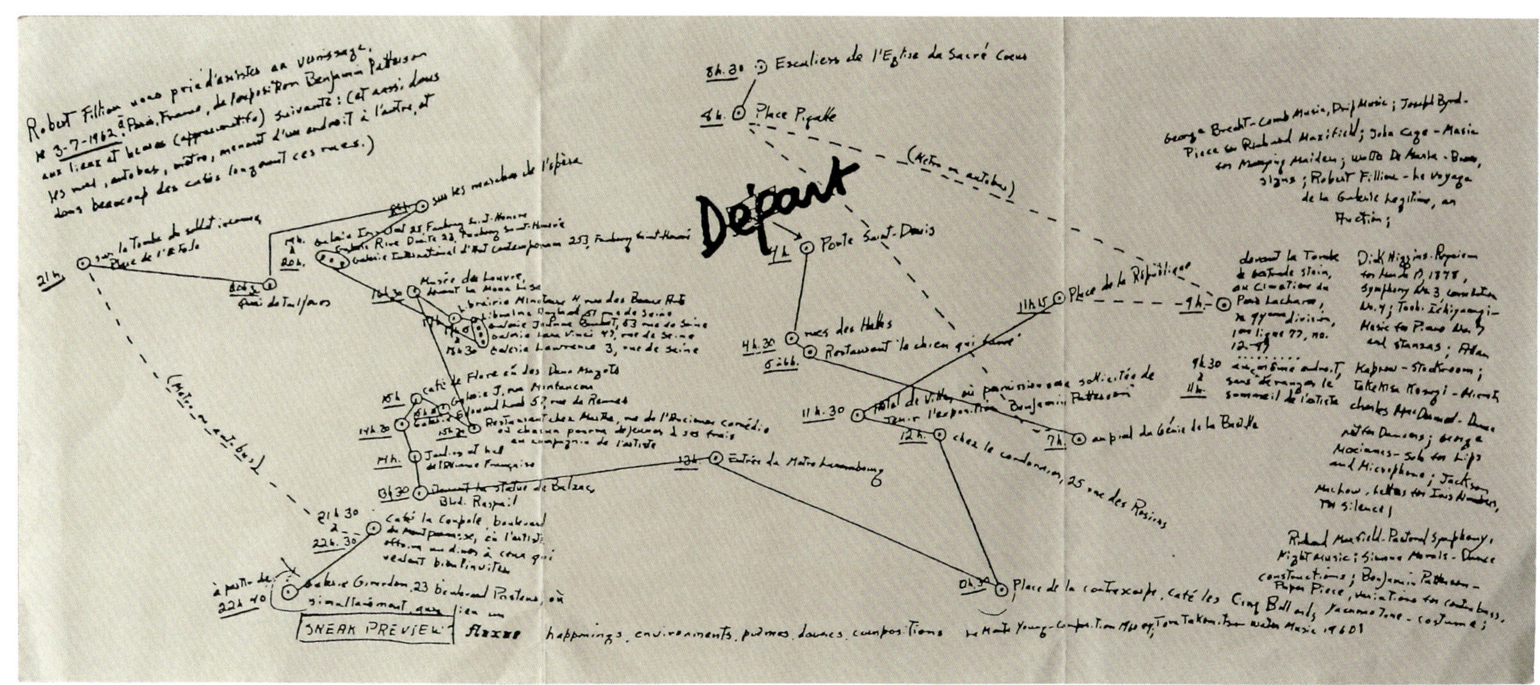

Performance documentation/brochure for
Sneak Peek: Fluxus, Happenings, Environments,
Poems, Dances, Compositions at Galerie
Girardon, 1962
Offset on paper with ink and postage stamp
7⅞ × 18⁷⁄₁₆ inches (unfolded)
The Museum of Modern Art, New York;
The Gilbert and Lila Silverman Fluxus Collection Gift

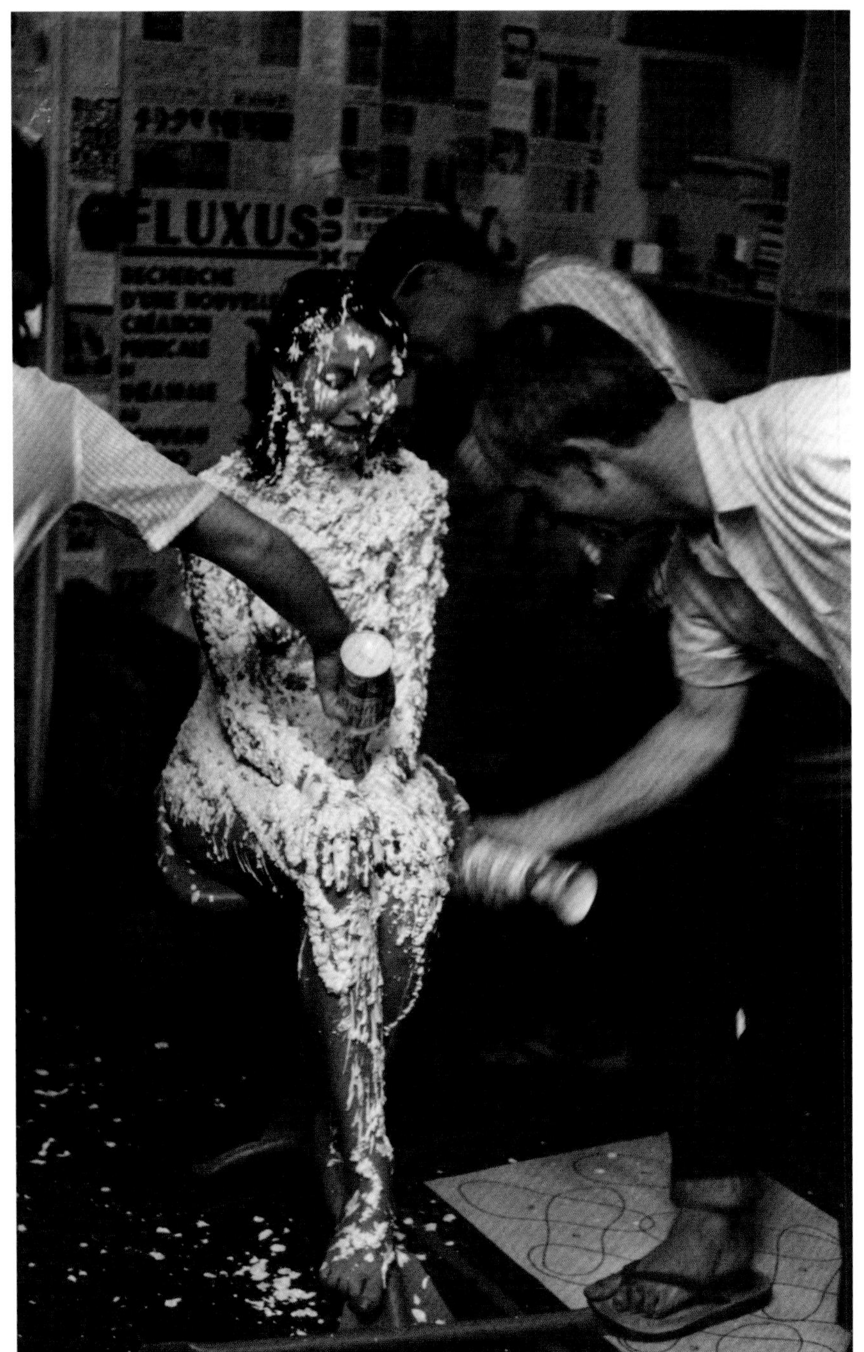

Performance documentation for *Lick Piece*, 1962
Performed by Letty Eisenhauer and unidentified individual at
Fully Guaranteed 12 Fluxus Concerts, Canal Street, New York,
May 9, 1964
Gelatin silver print (by Peter Moore)
9³⁄₁₆ × 6⁵⁄₁₆ inches; 18¹¹⁄₁₆ × 14¹¹⁄₁₆ × 1½ inches (framed)
The Museum of Modern Art, New York;
The Gilbert and Lila Silverman Fluxus Collection Gift

FLUXUS *INTERNATIONALE FESTSPiELE NEUESTER MUSiK

IM HöRSAAL DES sTäDTiSCHEN MUSEUMS, WiESBADEN

SAMSTAG 1. SEPT. 1962 14:30 UHR — KONZERT NR.1, KLAVIER KOMPOSITIONEN - U.S.A., K.E.WELIN UND F.RZEWSKI - PIANISTEN. JOHN CAGE: 31'57.9864"/PHILIP CORNER: KLAVIER TATIGKEITEN (FÜR EIN KLAVIER UND VIELE SPIELER) & FLUX & FORM NR. 7 & 14 / TERRY RILEY: KONZERT FÜR 2 PIANISTEN UND TONBAND / T.JENNINGS: KLAVIER STÜCKE / JED CURTIS: KLAVIER STÜCK / GRIFITH ROSE: 2. ENNEAD / DICK HIGGINS: CONSTELLATION NR.1(FÜR 2 KLAVIERE UND 3 RADIOS) / LA MONTE YOUNG: "566" FÜR HENRY FLYNT & KLAVIER STÜCKE FÜR DAVID TUDOR NR.2 / GEORGE BRECHT: FÜNF KLAVIER STÜCKE 1961 UND DREI KLAVIER STÜCKE 1962

SAMSTAG 1. SEPT. 20:00 UHR — KONZERT NR.2 KLAVIER KOMPOSITIONEN - JAPAN, K.E.WELIN - PIANIST. TOSHI ICHIYANAGI: MUSIK FÜR KLAVIER NR.1 BIS NR.7 / YORIAKI MATSUDAIRA: INSTRUKTIONEN FÜR KLAVIER / SHINICHI MATSUSHITA: MOSAIKEN / YOKO ONO: EIN STÜCK UM DEN HIMMEL ZU SEHEN / KEIJIRO SATO: CALIGRAPHY / YUJI TAKAHASHI: EKSTASIS / TORU TAKEMITSU: KLAVIER ENTFERNUNG UND ÜBERGANG / YASUNAO TONE: KLAVIER TON MIT TONBAND / GEORGE YNASA: PROJECTION ESEMPLASTIC I, II UND III

SONNTAG 2. SEPT. 14:30 UHR — KONZERT NR.3, KLAVIER KOMPOSITIONEN - EUROPA, K.E.WELIN - PIANIST. K.H.STOCKHAUSEN: KLAVIERSTÜCK IV / G.LIGETI: TROIS BAGATELLES / G.M.KOENIG: 2 KLAVIER STÜCKE / KONRAD BOEHMER: KLANGSTÜCK & POTENTIAL / JAN MORTHENSON: COURANTE / LARS J.WERLE: GRILLER FÜR PIANIST / MICHAEL VON BIEL: EIN BUCH FÜR DREI / DIETER SCHNEBEL: REACTIONS (KONZERT FÜR EINEN INSTRUMENTALISTEN & PUBLIKUM) & VISIBLE MUSIK FÜR 1 DIRIGENTEN UND 1 INSTRUMENTALISTEN.

SONNTAG 2. SEPT. 20:00 UHR — KONZERT NR.4, KLAVIER KOMPOSITIONEN - EUROPA, F.RZEWSKI - PIANIST. JACQUES CALONNE: QUADRANGLES SUIVIS DE FENETRES ET BOUCLES / PAOLO EMILIO CARAPEZZA: 9o CIELO / GIUSEPPE CHIARI: GESTI SUL PIANO / SYLVANO BUSSOTTI: POUR CLAVIER, 5 KLAVIER STÜCKE FÜR DAVID TUDOR & PER TRE (FÜR EIN KLAVIER UND 3 PIANISTEN) / FREDERIC RZEWSKI STUDIEN & TRÄUME / LUCIER: ACTION MUSIC FOR PIANO BOOK I / MACCHI: TITONE / MARCHETTI MUSIK

SAMSTAG 8. SEPT. 20:00 UHR — KONZERT NR.5, KOMPOSITIONEN FÜR ANDERE INSTRUMENTE UND STIMMEN - U.S.A., GEORGE BRECHT: KARTENSTÜCK FÜR STIMMEN / JOHN CAGE: SOLO FÜR STIMME (2) 1960 / PHILIP CORNER: PASSIONATE EXPANSE OF THE LAW / DICK HIGGINS: CONSTELLATION NR.4 & NR.7 / TERRY JENNINGS: STREICHQUARTETT / PHILIP KRUMM: MUSTER (FÜR STREICHQUARTETT) / JACKSON MAC LOW: BUCHSTABEN FÜR IRIS NUMMERN FÜR DIE STILLE UND DANKE - EINE ZUSAMMENARBEIT FÜR LEUTE / TERRY RILEY: UMSCHLAG 1960 (FÜR STREICHQUARTETT) / EMMETT WILLIAMS: EIN ZWEIFELHAFTES LIED IN VIER RICHTUNGEN FÜR 5 STIMMEN / GEORGE BRECHT: STREICHQUARTETT / LA MONTE YOUNG: KOMPOSITION 1960 NR.7 (FÜR STREICHQUARTETT)

SONNTAG 9. SEPT. 14:30 UHR — KONZERT NR.6, KOMPOSITIONEN FÜR ANDERE INSTRUMENTE UND STIMMEN - JAPAN, TOSHI ICHIYANAGI: STANZEN & PILE / KENJIRO EZAKI: BEWEGLICHE PULSE & DISCRETION / YORITSUNE MATSUDAIRA: EIN STÜCK FÜR SOLO FLÖTE / YASUNAO TONE: ANAGRAMM FÜR STREICHE / YOKO ONO: DER PULS /

SONNTAG 9. SEPT. 20:00 UHR — KONZERT NR.7, KOMPOSITIONEN FÜR ANDERE INSTRUMENTE UND STIMMEN - EUROPA, MICHAEL VON BIEL: STREICH MUSIK / GEORGE MACIUNAS: SOLO FÜR STIMME UND MIKROPHON / GRIFITH ROSE: STREICHQUARTETT / FREDERIC RZEWSKI: SOLILOQUY (FÜR VIOLINE) UND THREE RHAPSODIES FOR SLIDE WHISTLES / BENJAMIN PATTERSON: VARIATIONEN FÜR KONTRABASS /

FREITAG 14. SEPT. 20:00 UHR — KONZERT NR.8, KONKRETE MUSIK & HAPPENINGS - U.S.A., JOSEPH BYRD: ZWEI STÜCKE FÜR RICHARD MAXFIELD, 1960 / JOHN CAGE: VARIATIONS / GEORGE BRECHT: KARTENSTÜCK FÜR OBJEKTE, TRÖPFELNDE MUSIK, KERZEN STÜCK FÜR RADIOS & SOLO FÜR EINEN BLÄSER / JED CURTIS: GAVOTTE, ALLEMAND, UND GIGUE / DICK HIGGINS: GEFÄHRLICHE MUSIK NR.2 UND GRAPHIS 82 / JACKSON MAC LOW: EIN STÜCK FÜR SARI DIENES / TERRY RILEY: OHR STÜCK (FÜR PUBLIKUM) /

SAMSTAG 15. SEPT. 20:00 UHR — KONZERT NR.9, KONKRETE MUSIK & HAPPENINGS - JAPAN, TOSHI ICHIYANAGI: MUSIK FÜR ELEKRISCHE METRONOM & IBM MUSIK / K. AKIYAMA: EINE GEHEIM METHODE / TAKENHISA KOSUGI: MICRO I & MANODHARMA I / YOKO ONO: ZWEI STÜCKE / YASUNAO TONE: TAGE, NUMMER & UNTERREDUNG / GEORGE YNASA: MUSIQUE CONCRETE UND AOINOUE /

SONNTAG 16. SEPT. 20:00 UHR — KONZERT NR.10, KONKRETE MUSIK & HAPPENINGS - INTERNATIONAL, NAM JUNE PAIK: SIMPLE / PIERRE MERCURE: STRUCTURES METALLIQUES NR.3 / NAM JUNE PAIK: HOMMÂGE À JOHN CAGE / ETUDE FOR PIANOFORTE UND SONATA QUAZI UNA FANTASIA / DIETER SCHNEBEL: SICHTBARE MUSIK FÜR EINEN DIRIGENTEN / MACIUNAS: IN MEMORIAM FÜR ADRIANO OLIVETTI / BENJAMIN PATTERSON: SEPTET AUS "LEMONS" UND OVERTURE (2. DARSTELLUNG) / GEORGE BRECHT: WORD EVENT

22. SEPT. 14:30 UHR — KONZERT NR.11, TONBAND MUSIK UND FILME - U.S.A., JOHN CAGE: FONTANA MIX, MUSIC FOR THE MARRYING MAIDEN / LA MONTE YOUNG: ZWEI TÖNE / STAN VANDERBEEK: FILMEN / DICK HIGGINS: REQUIEM FOR WAGNER THE CRIMINAL MAYOR

22. SEPT. 20:00 UHR — KONZERT NR.12, TONBAND MUSIK - U.S.A., RICHARD MAXFIELD: HUFTEN MUSIK / RADIO MUSIK / DAMPF / PASTORAL SYMPHONY / PERSPECTIVES / NACHT MUSIK

SONNTAG 23. SEPT. 14:30 UHR — KONZERT NR.13, TONBAND MUSIK UND FILME - JAPAN, KANADA. TOSHI ICHIYANAGI: KAIKI / NOBUTAKA MIZUNO: TONBAND STÜCK / TORU TAKEMITSU: VOCALISM A-I & WASSER MUSIK / YASUNAO TONE: COSTUME UND WARANIN / GEORGE YNASA: AOI-NO-UE / TESHIGAHARA: FILM / YOJI KURI: HUMAN ZOO / OSHIMA: FILM / HANI: FILM / ISTVAN ANHALT: COMPOSITION NR.4 / CIONI CARPI & L. PORTUGAIS: POINT ET CONTREPOINT (FILM) / MAURICE BLACKBURN: JE (FILM) /

SONNTAG 23. SEPT. 20:00 UHR — KONZERT NR.14, TONBAND MUSIK - FRANKREICH, "LES PREMIERES DECOUVERTES": P.SCHAEFFER: ETUDE AUX CASSEROL P.HENRY: MUSIQUE SANS TITRE / P.ARTHUYS: NATURE MORTE À LA GUITARE / A.HODEIR: JAZZ ET JAZZ / "RECHERCHES RECENTES": L.FERRARI: ETUDE AUX ACCIDENTS & TÊTE ET QUEUE DU DRAGON / F.B. MACHE: PRÉLUDE / E. CANTON: ETUDE / J. HIDALGO: ETUDE / B. PARMEGIANI: ETUDE / F. BAYLE: TREMPLINS & LIGNES ET POINTS / M. PHILIPPOT: AMBIANCE II / P. CARSON: ETUDE / P. SCHAEFFER: SIMULTANÉ CAMEROUNAIS /

EINTRITTS-KARTEN — FÜR JEDES KONZERT DM 3 / FÜR EIN ABONNEMENT (14 KONZERTE) DM 20 / FÜR STUDENTEN DM 1.50 — EINTRITTSKARTEN SIND AM EINGANG ZU ERHALTEN ODER DURCH: VORVERKAUF AM HAUPTBAHNHOF, WIESBADEN

FLUXUS * EINE INTERNATIONALE ZEITSCHRIFT NEUESTER KUNST, ANTIKUNST, MUSIK, ANTIMUSIK, DICHTUNG, ANTIDICHTUNG, ETC.

Poster designed by George Maciunas for Fluxus Internationale Festspiele neuester Musik, Hörsaal des Städtischen Museums, Wiesbaden, Germany, September 1–23, 1962/1992 (reprint)
Offset on paper
16¼ × 15⁹⁄₁₆ inches
Courtesy the artist

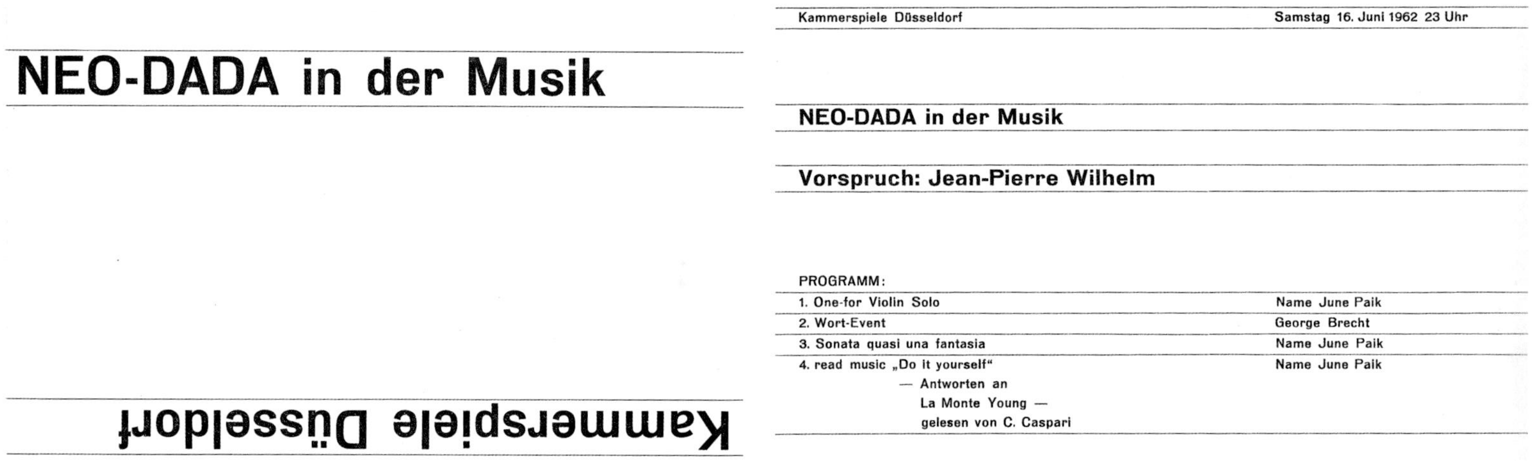

NEO-DADA in der Musik

Kammerspiele Düsseldorf

Kammerspiele Düsseldorf	Samstag 16. Juni 1962 23 Uhr

NEO-DADA in der Musik

Vorspruch: Jean-Pierre Wilhelm

PROGRAMM:

1. One-for Violin Solo	Name June Paik
2. Wort-Event	George Brecht
3. Sonata quasi una fantasia	Name June Paik
4. read music „Do it yourself"	Name June Paik
— Antworten an	
La Monte Young —	
gelesen von C. Caspari	

Program for Neo-Dada in der Musik, 1962
Offset on paper
7 × 8 inches (folded)
7 × 16 inches (unfolded)
Courtesy the artist

467 central park west
new york 25, n.y.
june 16, 1963

dear, daer O.E.W. (eeeeeeeeeeeeeee...*

i am so happy to see that you are being active in the wine and
cheese land. new york is also being as much or more than its
usuallly busy self. saw dick higgins wonderful film "flaming
city" this weekend. YAM day was quite a thing. dick and allyson
have proball-ly(¢) have given you a play-by-play of this already.
in any case i am just recovered enough to think they i may do
something after-all again someday. (now thinking about a piece
which might be call "CEREMONY".)

would like to attempt my final exam (done for YAM)? i would be
very happy to see your results if they are mailable.

DEFINE AND ELABORATE UPON THE PURPOSE OF THIS EXAMINATION.
            (one hour)

thus far dick and alley-son have contributed outstanding papers.

have Robert and Marianne really gone to denmark? what is the
address?
so there i have not only sent the score but written my longest
letter in the last two years also...., so you write too.

            love and lisses ß   Ennis walks!

Dear Ben: Thanks for your letter & "N.Y. Public library Event" — its even better when you come from 42 st. entry. Try to get free lance graphic jobs – that may increase your income. The library job however is less tiresome.
GET IN CONTACT WITH GEORGE BRECHT. He is organizing festi YAM festival now & Festum Fluxorum in Autumn. He likes your work very much. He lives in N.J. but comes frequently to town.
Now about news up here:
Paris was badly sabotaged by that #⊚ Lambert. I sent him 1000 posters, all kind of materials etc. & instead of doing some promotion he sent invitations ONLY TO HIS OWN EVENING. All he had to do is stuff our program (which he had) in the same envelopes he was sending out. RESULT: empty (or almost so) hall during the 1st. 6 concert and jammed during Lamberts evening. All people like Jouffroi, Girard etc. etc. where very dissapointed of having not known & missed Fluxus festival. Jouffroi even said it was a catastrophy. Anyway, Gherasim Luca was in our concerts every day & was the only one to who really enjoyed every moment. (another enjoying it was the superintendent). Keith Humble was not very helpfull at all & got even overly- concerned over the piano when we played La Monte's 566. Your septet came out very well with the Danish kettles. The guys who where supposed to help never showed-up (nor your kettles). We had funny adventures on the way to Paris (I mean Emmett & myself) The chevy completely fell apart near Verdun. (fully loaded with junk & electronics. So we had it towed to Verdun. Slept over in town and next day (1st. day of festival) found there where no trains to Paris. Gotterdemerung! what to do! So we TAKE TAXI (and say to Paris please). Anyway it cost 200 NF to get there & we got there 1 hour before concert. All in panic there, but concert went on allright. Spoerri & Filliou still think we do Gags — nothing else. They just cant comprehend George Brecht's Haiku type events. — it's much to simple for them. They need theatrics — artificiality. I think the french are on the way out. (maybe their Europaneism prevents them to acquire asiatic mentality). So we lost again in Paris, but not as badly as Wiesbaden. Next weekend we go to Düsseldorf. Beuys arranged 2 concerts in Ahademy which we'll pay for everything — so for once we shall not loose money.
I BOUGHT A GOOD CONTRA BASS FOR $15 !!!! at Air Force junk house. So I can perform your variations, (I hope I can do them right). I acquired all the equipment, including bird whistles etc. I also had a box built (with compartments) into which fit ALL FLUXUS CONCERT INSTRUMENTS. & ACCESSORIES. Had your kettles specially made from funnells like this.

So these kettles now fit very nicely into this FLUXUS SUITCASE. (also 10 radios, frogs, ping-pong balls etc. etc.)

KEEP COMPOSING & KEEP SENDING YOUR STUFF OVER. ALSO → SEND COMPLETE LEMONS So I can type them on IBM. Fluxus I is all at printer for past 3 weeks, BUT HE IS SLOW !!

Letter to Benjamin Patterson from George Maciunas, 1963
Ink on paper
10⅜ × 7⅞ inches
Getty Research Institute, Los Angeles

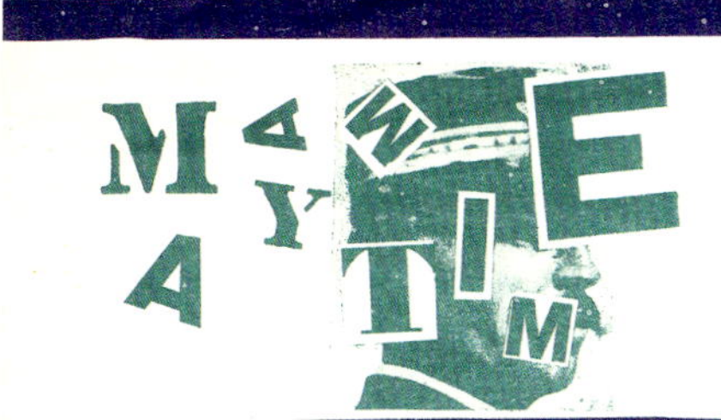

THE SMOLIN GALLERY (19 East 71st Street, NYC RH 4-3929) will be a source of information for activities listed on this calendar, will carry publications, scores, and related materials, & will arrange special shows at the gallery throughout the month.

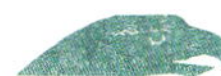

AL HANSEN'S SILVER CITY AT GROUND ZERO will evolve at Canal Street & Broadway, NYC

THE BILLY LINICH SHOW featuring *works of Eric Brun ("Man in Space" - Billy Linich / "Space in Man" - La Monte Young) Anthony Cox * The Dancing Stars of James Waring * The Developing of Michael Katz * Some Appearances by Remy Charlip, Rufus Collins * Special Mystery Star Malka Safro.   DISAPPEARING IN THE NEIGHBORHOOD

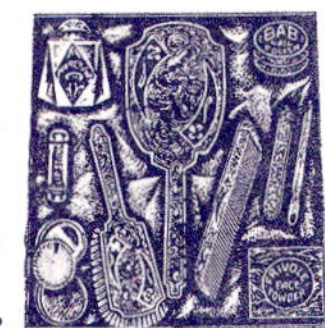

THRU MAY

1 W CLOCK DAY
- Locate a clock. Make soup with the hands.
- shoes

GROUP SHOP SOUP OPENING AT SMOLIN'S
many things by many people

3 SAY y ES TO EVERYTHING

2 Street Events
Two paintings by Dick Higgins
1. Keep our city clean
2. Paint the town red

EXHIBIT
(on the shelf)

A VERY LAWFUL DANCE
7 PM at the Times Bldg
(Ben Patterson)

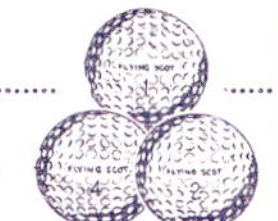
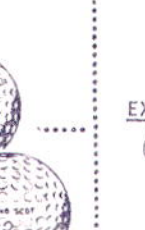
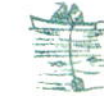
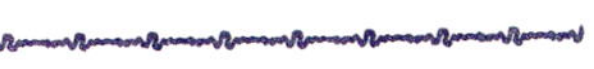

4 Hole (a sculpture)
Walk backwards all day Saturday.

Mary Ashley
(1962)

CHAIR (Robert Ashley)
SCULPTURE FOR A SIX DAY WEEK

FIRST DAY: Select a wooden chair and decorate it as beautifully as you can.

5 SECOND DAY: Break the chair into pieces
and seal all of the pieces into
the smallest possible cardboard box

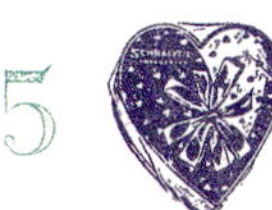

6 An aspect of Philip Krumm's UNIVERSAL EVENT:
- variations on the MANHATTAN COCKTAIL

THIRD DAY: Decorate the cardboard box as beautifully as you can

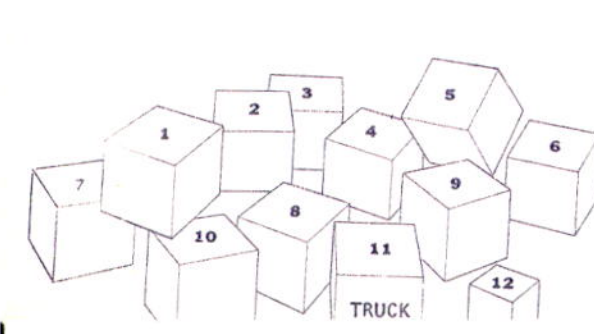

T 7 U

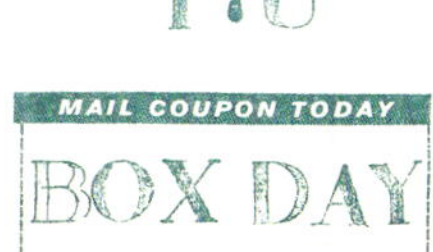

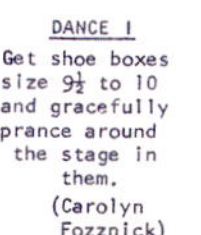

DANCE I
Get shoe boxes size $9\frac{1}{2}$ to 10 and gracefully prance around the stage in them.
(Carolyn Fozznick)

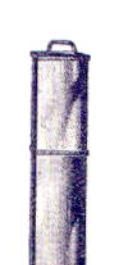

AT THE SMOLIN GALLERY

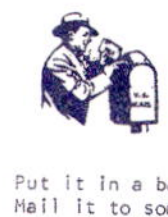

Put it in a box Mail it to some one you've never met.

Mailer for Yam Day Festival, 1963
Offset on paper
22⅞ × 8⅜ inches
Courtesy the artist

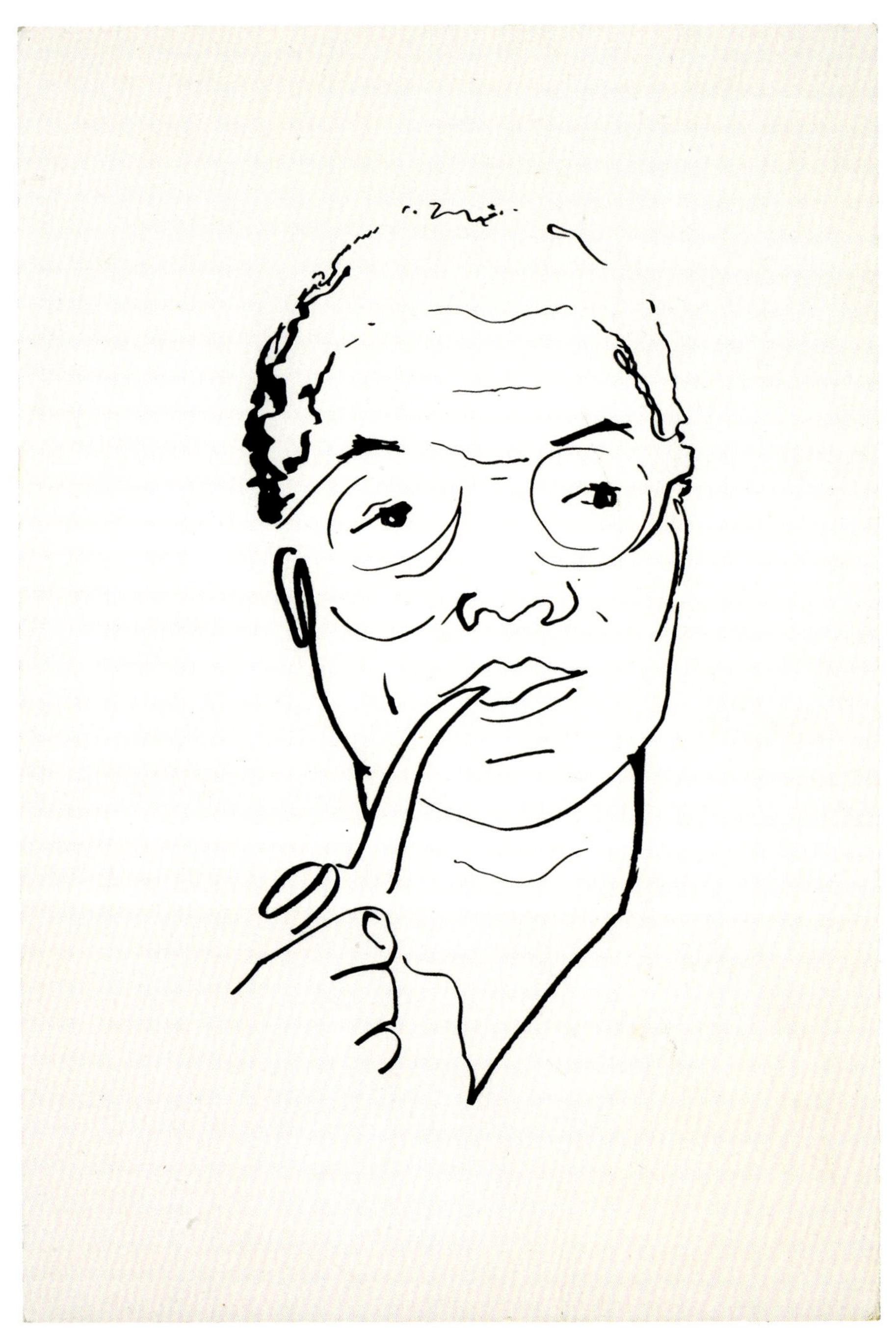

Photograph of Patterson portrait sketched
by Alison Knowles for brochure announcing
The Four Suits, c. 1965
Gelatin silver print
6⅞ × 4½ inches
Getty Research Institute, Los Angeles

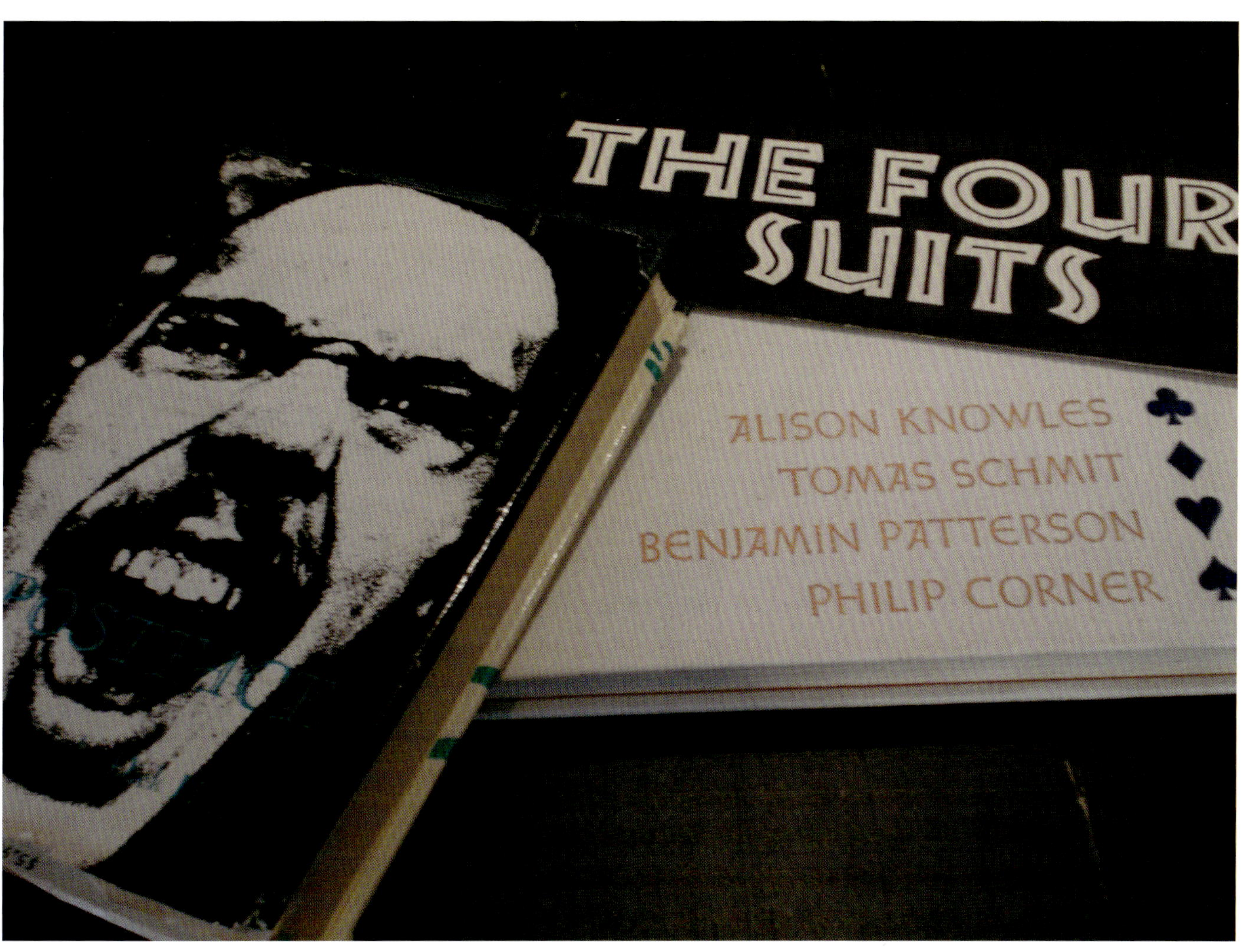

Jefferson's Birthday/Postface, 1964
The Four Suits, 1965
Publications edited by Dick Higgins
Offset on paper
Brochure: 11 × 14 inches (folded)
Book: 9½ × 6⅜ × 1⅛ inches
Book: 8¼ × 5⅞ × 1⅛ inches
Published by Something Else Press
Courtesy the artist

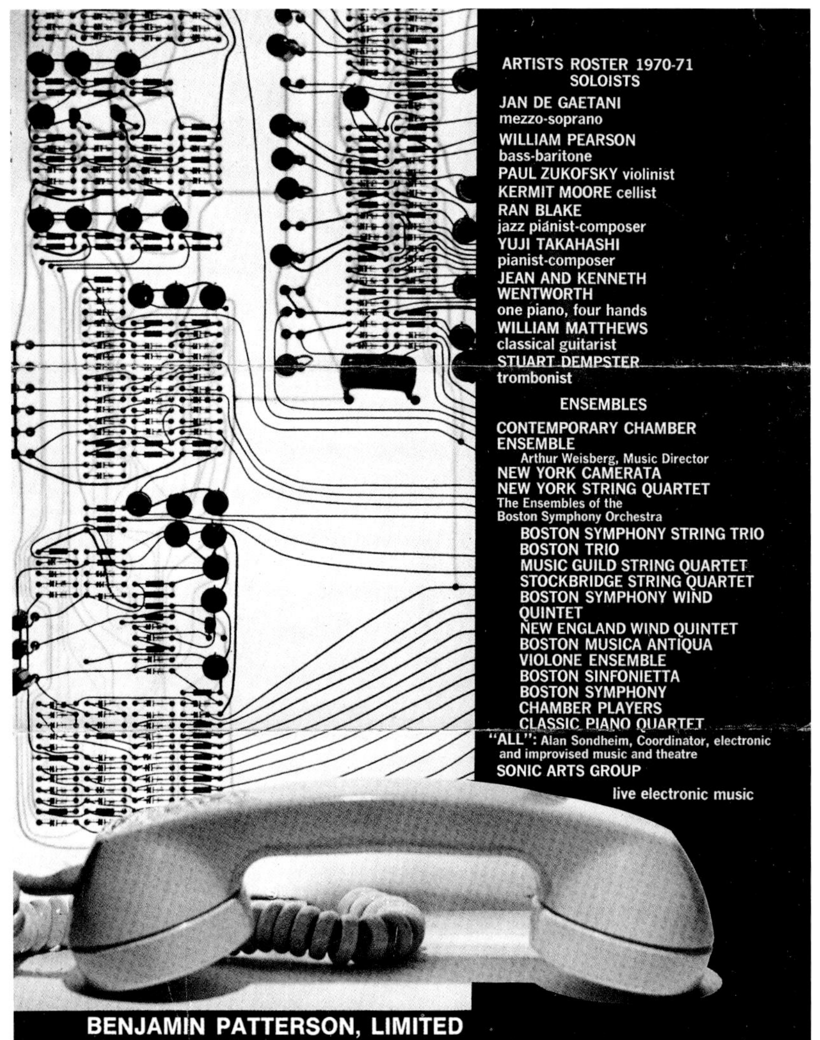

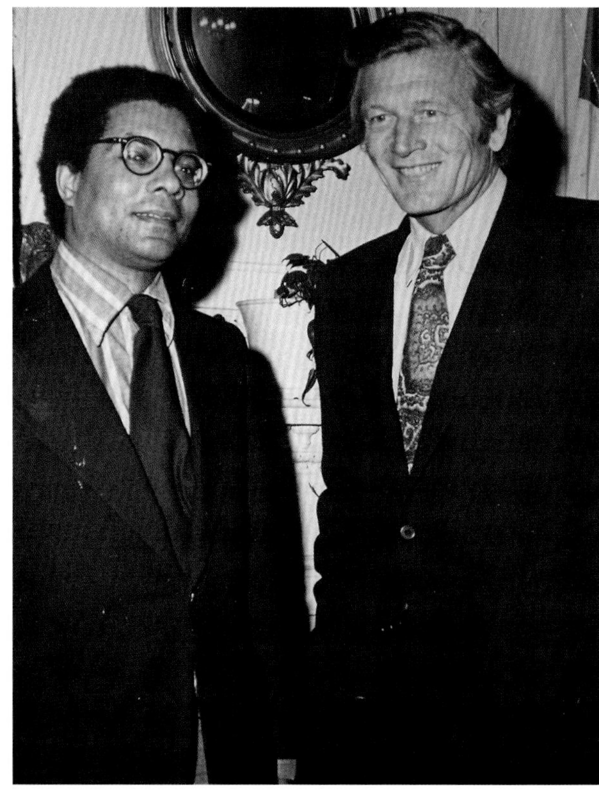

Brochure for Benjamin Patterson Limited
Music Management Company, c. 1970
Printing on paper
8 × 14 inches (folded)
Courtesy the artist

Photograph of Benjamin Patterson with Mayor
John Lindsay upon his appointment as assistant
director of the New York Department of Cultural
Affairs, c. 1972
Black-and-white photograph
8 × 10 inches
Courtesy the artist

FLUXUS - the most radical art movement of this century. *

[True ☐   False ☐   (check one)] **

In September 1962 a 14 day festival of the „newest of the new" manifestations in the arts of
music, poetry, film, dance and other related media was presented in Wiesbaden, Germany by
the ambitious and brilliant young Lithuanian/American George Maciunas. Wittingly or
unwittingly this notorious festival gave birth to, and was responsible for naming the „art
movement" entitled Fluxus. To note a curious footnote in contemporary art history: for a
surprisingly long time, in some cases even years, a number of artists responsible for the ideas
claimed by the „movement" were not even aware that the „movement" had been invented,
and/or, that they had been designated as members! This was indeed a bizarre situation.
Possibly, because it was <u>so</u> bizarre, a popular, but „wrong notion" developed that Fluxus was
an a-prior creation, aesthetically and ideologically unified through top-down directives and
manifestos from „great leaders/theoreticians".

However, judged from my involvement in the „birth of Fluxus", the „right notion" would see
Fluxus resulting from an empirical, broad-band, global scan --- which identified, networked
and presented a collegial (but, not necessarily stable), new constellation of young, radically
thinking artists. In other words, a bottom-up flow of ideas, propositions and theories. The
cohesiveness of this flow did not result from a well-defined, common aesthetic, but, rather from
a mutual commitment to a rigorous investigation of the fundamentals of art making. Thus,
Fluxus was not a style but an „attitude".

These early generic Fluxus artists considered themselves to be free-ranging experimentalists
with magic palettes of infinite range. Any observable phenomenon were fair game - from the
music of Beethoven to clouds in the sky. Although the general task was to explore new
territories, seek new solutions and refine the human spirit, each individual interpreted and
pursued this challenge in a uniquely personal way. Of course it was a utopian dream and
initially, no increments of change were visible. However, today --- some 35 years later --- new,
but established, art forms such as: performance art, mail art, body art, conceptual art, video
art, minimal art, food art, etc. trace their roots back to those classic early Fluxus experiments.

Yes, these directions all evolved from Fluxus, but, does that mean that these new forms have
superceded the „attitude" of Fluxus --- or, that Fluxus is „dead"? If Fluxus is seen as only a
1960's „agent-provocateur" then clearly it would be passé today. But, if the notion that the
primary goals of Fluxus were the exploration of new forms, techniques and media, then a
knowledge and understanding of its cornerstones are no less important than an understanding
of any of the other major art movements of the past 500 years.

The bad news is that documentation was haphazard in the 1960's and the information
generally available today is either recent exhibition catalogues (which emphasize the later
visual art works) or historical/critical texts (which cannot reproduce the flavor and experience
of a live performance).

The good news is that nearly all of the early Fluxus events/actions were designed to be
performed by anyone, anywhere and at anytime. Thus, written scores were prepared for future
realization by other interpreters.

Tonight's program is conceived to be both a demonstration of this important aspect of Fluxus
(differentiating it from „happenings" and much of performance art) and an abridged, but
important re-reading of the Fluxus legacy.

Ben Patterson, Zürich, 1997.

*   Harry Ruhe, (from his book of the same title),. Amsterdam 1972
** Ben Patterson, Zürich 1997

Excerpt from the 1972 book by Harry Ruhé,
*Fluxus: The Most Radical Experimental Art
Movement of the Sixties*, published by Galerie A
in Amsterdam
Ink on paper
8 × 11 inches
Courtesy the artist

<u>**Conference in Solidarity with the Liberation Struggles of the Peoples of Southern Africa**</u>
c/o United Methodist Office for the UN, 777 UN Plaza, New York, New York 10017   (212) 661-0176

September 24, 1981

Community Review Board
North Star
80 Fifth Ave., RM 1204
New York, N.Y. 10011

Dear Board Members;

This letter and attachments will update the previous materials in your
file related to the "Conference in Solidarity with the Liberation Struggles
of the Peoples of Southern Africa".

First, I am pleased to inform you that all in all - including the
expected and normal problems and complications- the preparations for the
conference are going well. The list of sponsors grows daily. Among the
latest additions are Arthur Ashe, the International Longshoremen's Association, AFL-CIO and Congresswoman Shirley Chisolm. (See attached press
release September 9 for others). The major conference speakers have been
confirmed and all papers and fact sheets will be ready for printing by
Monday. Based on the reports of the regional coordinators and pre-
registrations arriving in the office it appears that we will at least come
very close to our target of 1000 delegates. Even the press and electronic
media are beginning to show genuine interest in the conference.

On the fund raising front, progress is reasonable and improving. You
will note from the attached revised budget that we have been able to
reduce the overall estimated expense budget from $124,000 to $106,400.
On the income side to date we have received a little over $25,000 and
anticipate checks for another $25,00 from the Norman Foundation, The
National Council of Churches, and the UN Center Against Apartheid
within the next 5 days. Also antipated before the conference is $20,000
from the Council on Namibia and $5000 from the World Council of Churches.
The balance needed we hope will be made up between the results of appeal
letters from Harry Belefonte and Arthur Ashe, the benefit reception with
Peter Tosh, registration fees and outstanding requests to the Rubin
Foundation, The Boehm Foundation and North Star.

Our request to North Star for a emergency grant of $1000 focuses
specifically on the Saturday evening Solidarity Rally. Enclosed are the
draft of the program and budget for this event. In addition to "greetings"
from religious, political, labor and community leaders, the major addresses
will be given by representatives of ANC, SWAPO and Angola (probably the
Presidents) and a United States Congressperson (probably John Conyers).
A number of celebrities have been invited and there is a good possibility
that Dustin Hoffman, Rip Torn, Roscoe Lee Brown and Stevie Wonder will
make appearances. The probable presence of the two liberation movement
presidents presents very real security concerns- thus the major expense

Hon. Ronald V. Dellums, President of the Preparatory Committee
Lennox S. Hinds, Esq., Chair of the Preparatory Committee Secretariat ● Carl Bloice, Conference Coordinator
In co-sponsorship with the African National Congress of South Africa (ANC) and the South West Africa People's Organization (SWAPO)
In cooperation with the International Committee Against Apartheid, Racism and Colonialism in Southern Africa (ICSA).

Hosts: The Southern Africa Team/Outreach Ministry, Riverside Church; Dr. Carl Fields, Leader, and The Rev. George Thomas, Minister of
Outreach, Riverside Church.

Correspondence from Patterson to the Community
Review Board regarding the "Conference in
Solidarity with the Liberation Struggles of Peoples
in Southern Africa," September 1981
Ink on paper
8 × 10 inches
Courtesy the artist

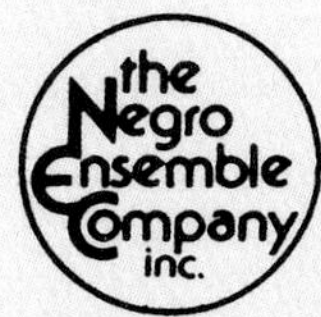

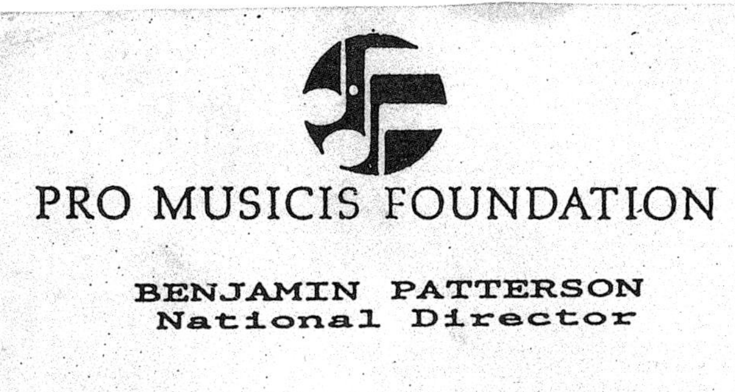

Announcement card for Negro Ensemble
Company in New York, c. 1982
Offset on card, envelope
Card: 5⁹⁄₁₆ × 4⁵⁄₁₆ inches
Envelope: 4⁷⁄₁₆ × 5¹¹⁄₁₆ inches
Getty Research Institute, Los Angeles

Patterson's business card for Pro Musicis,
c. 1984
Ink on paper
2 × 3 inches
Courtesy the artist

EMILY HARVEY GALLERY
537 Broadway, 2nd Floor (at Spring)
New York, N.Y. 10012

Tel. 212-925-7651   September 15, 1988

IMMEDIATE RELEASE

BEN PATTERSON: ORDINARY LIFE

Emily Harvey Gallery presents an exhibition of assemblages, constructions, texts, games and other new works dedicated to ordinary life by an original FLuxus artist **Ben Patterson** entitled **"Ordinary Life"**.   This show, a continuation of a life long project, focuses on domestic tranquility and national security.

Exhibition dates: Sept. 23 - Oct. 22, 1988

Gallery hours: Tues. - Sat. Noon - 6:00

For those who have known Ben Patterson primarily as a seminal creator of works in the areas of conceptual art, performance art and music theatre, this exhibition of his recent visual assemblages will be a great and exciting surprise.

Ben Patterson was born in 1934 in Pittsburg, Pa. He was in Wiesbaden with George Maciunas to organize the historic 1962 Fluxus International Festival and continued to be a major presence at Fluxus events until the early 1970's when he retired to pursue an ordinary life.   Although he has remained out of the art world in the past decade, he did surface with performances and new works for such events as the 20th anniversary Fluxus Festival in Wiesbaden in 1982 and the 1983 Bienal de São Paulo, Brazil.

His best known early works include "Paper Piece" (1960), "Methods & Processes" (1961-62) and "Seminar II" which were published in The Four Suits, Something Else Press, 1965.

Press release and postcard announcing
Patterson's solo exhibition *Ordinary Life*, at
Emily Harvey Gallery, New York, 1988
Printing on paper
Press release: 8 × 10 inches
Postcard: 4 × 6 inches
Courtesy the artist

Ordinary Life

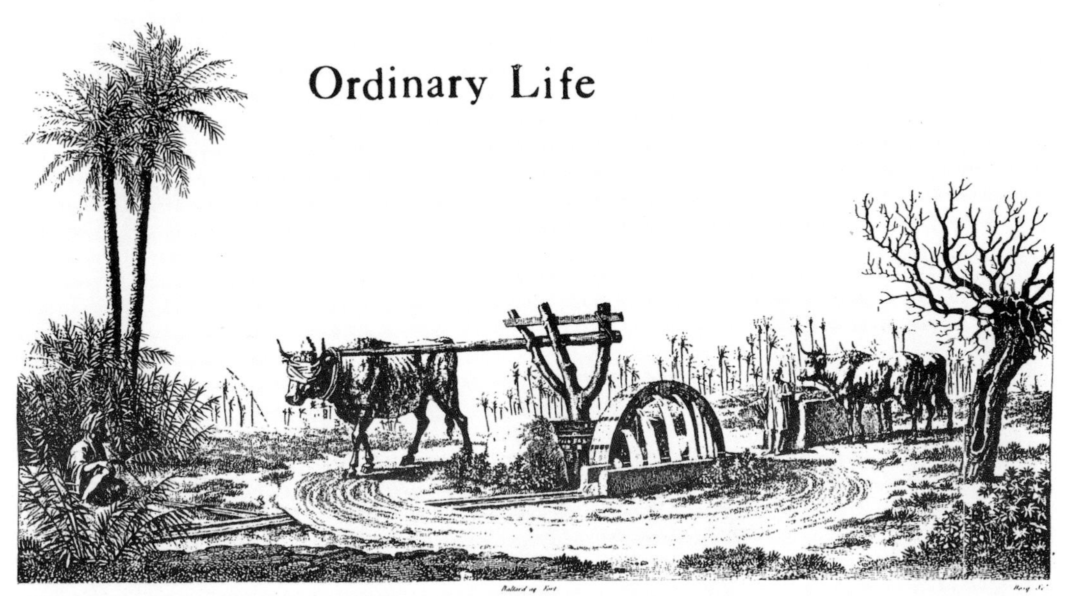

Ben Patterson

Manuals, Models, Games
and other Lessons

Sept. 23 - Oct. 23, 1988
Tues-Sat.   Noon - 6:00

Opening: Friday, Sept. 23rd
                6:00 - 8:00 p.m.

Emily Harvey Gallery
537 Broadway at Spring - 2nd Floor
New York, New York 10012
(212) 925-7651

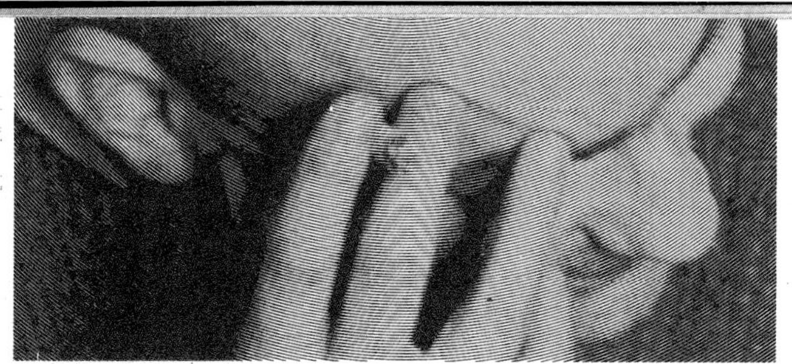

Announcements for Fluxus anniversary
exhibitions/events
Fluxus Festival, Chicago, 1993
Fluxus Da Capo, Wiesbaden, 1992 (opposite)
Offset on paper
22 × 33¾ in., 33 × 23⅝ in.
Courtesy the artist

F EINLADUNG F

WIESBADEN
6. SEPT. – 18. OKT.

Dokumente
Objekte
Environments
Filme
Konzerte

FLUXUS FLUXUS

John Cage
Henning Christiansen
Geoffrey Hendricks
Dick Higgins
Joe Jones
Milan Knížák
Alison Knowles
Nam June Paik
Benjamin Patterson
Emmett Williams

1 9 9 2

da capo

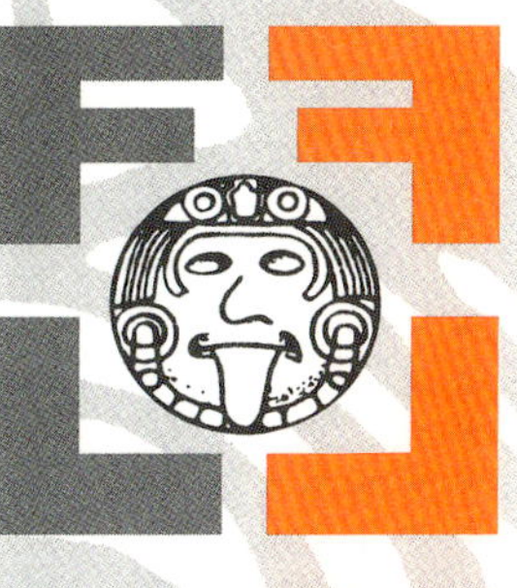

Veranstaltungsorte:
Archivkino Caligari
Bellevue Saal
Büchergilde Gutenberg
Galerie Ressel
Harlekin's Fluxeum
Kunsthaus
Muschel im Kurpark
Nassauischer Kunstverein
Pariser Hoftheater
Rathaus
Villa Clementine

Fluxustelefon:
06 11 / 30 11 36
Nassauischer Kunstverein
Wilhelmstraße 15
6200 Wiesbaden
Veranstalter:
Kulturamt der Landeshauptstadt Wiesbaden
Harlekin Art
Nassauischer Kunstverein

Fluxus-Virus
1962-1992
in Köln
Info: 02 21 / 23 77 36

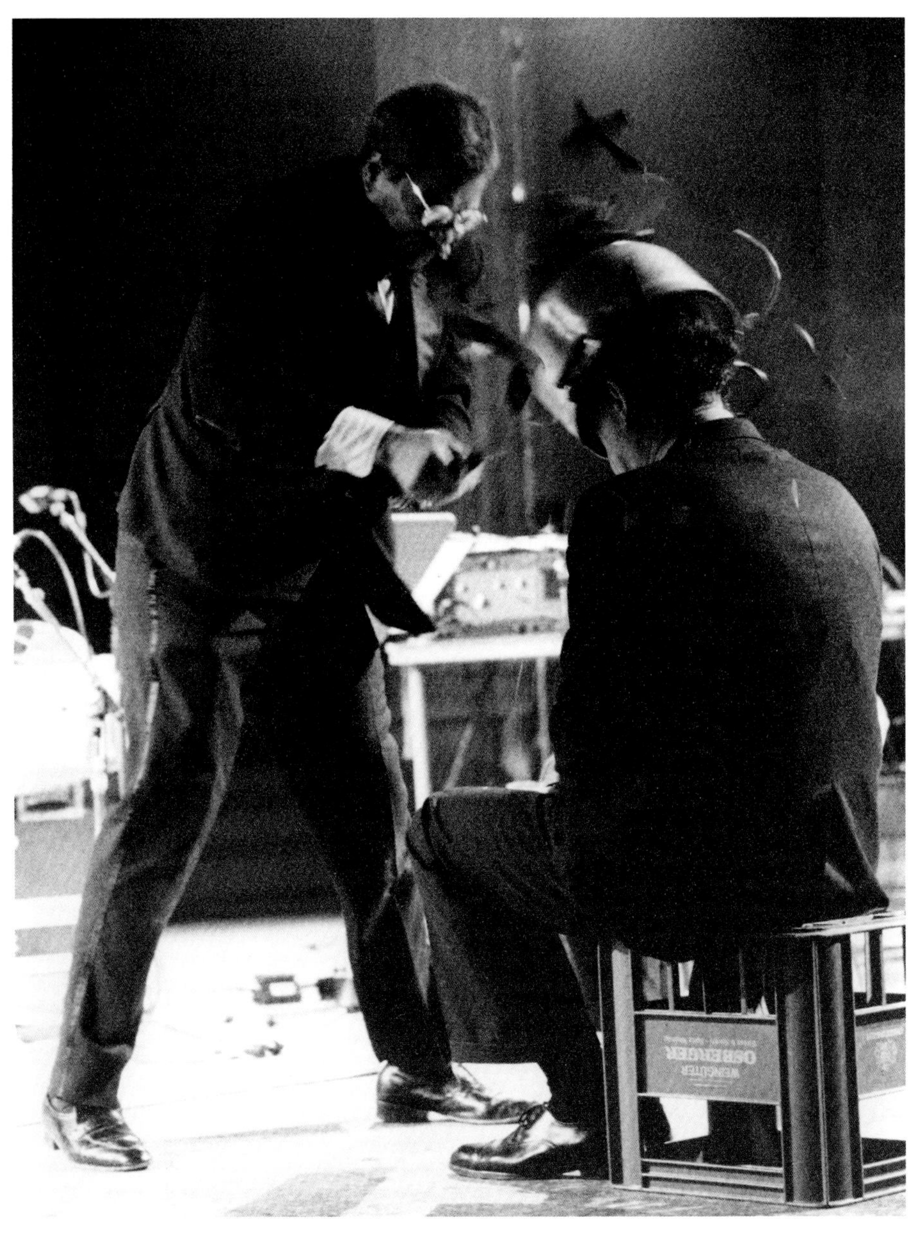

Patterson performing Nam June Paik's *One for Violin* (1962) with Peter Kotik of SEM Ensemble, New York, Akademie der bildenden Kunst, Vienna, June 1989
Black-and-white photograph (by Wolfgang Träger)
7 × 5 inches
Courtesy the artist

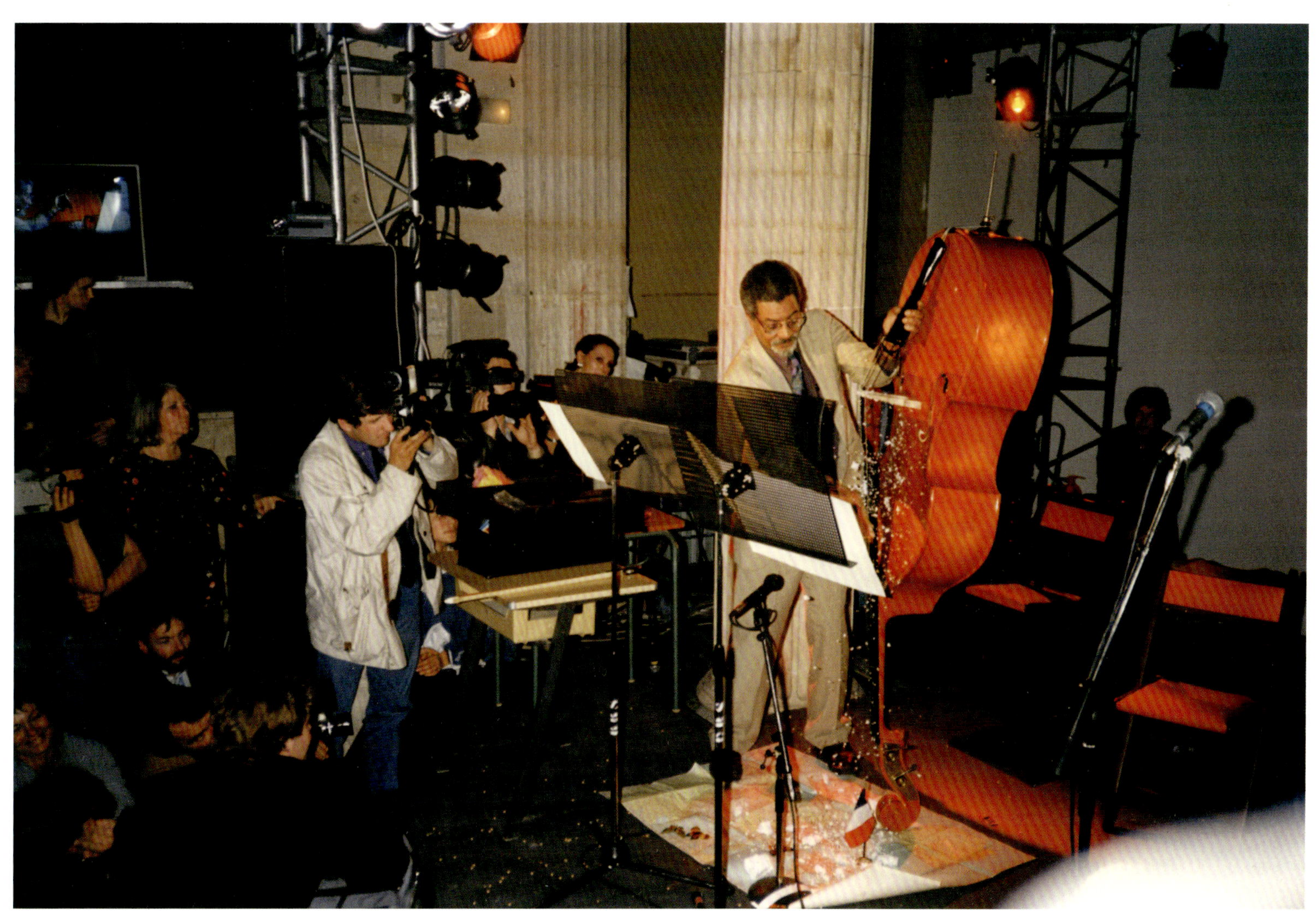

Patterson performing *Variations for Double Bass*
as part of the concert event Happenings and
Fluxus, Ecole Nationale des Beaux-Arts,
with an exhibition at Galerie 1900–2000, Paris,
August 8–29, 1989
Color photograph (by Francesco Conz)
8 × 10 inches
Courtesy the artist

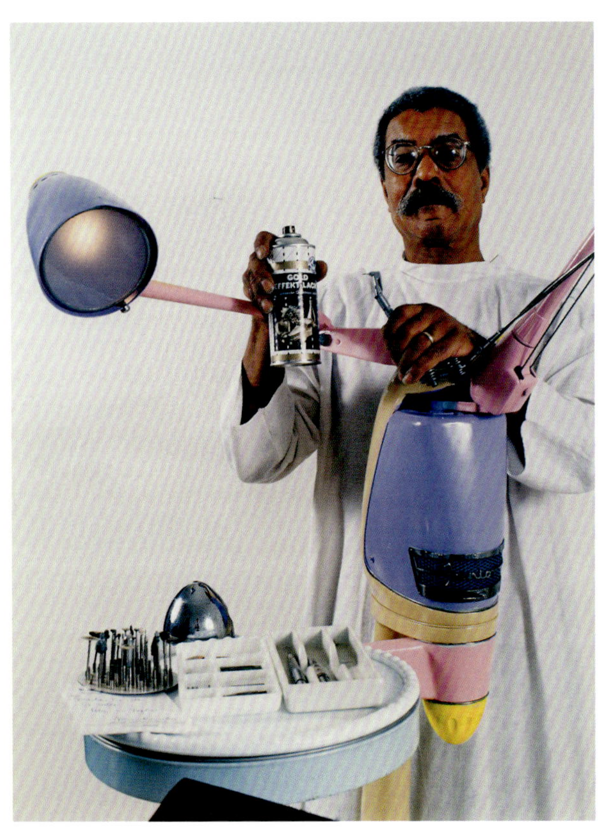

Patterson performing *The Clinic of Dr. Ben (BM, MS)* as part of the anniversary exhibition *Fluxus Da Capo* at Villa Clementine, Wiesbaden, Germany, 1992
Color photograph (photographer unknown)
16 × 12 inches
Courtesy the artist

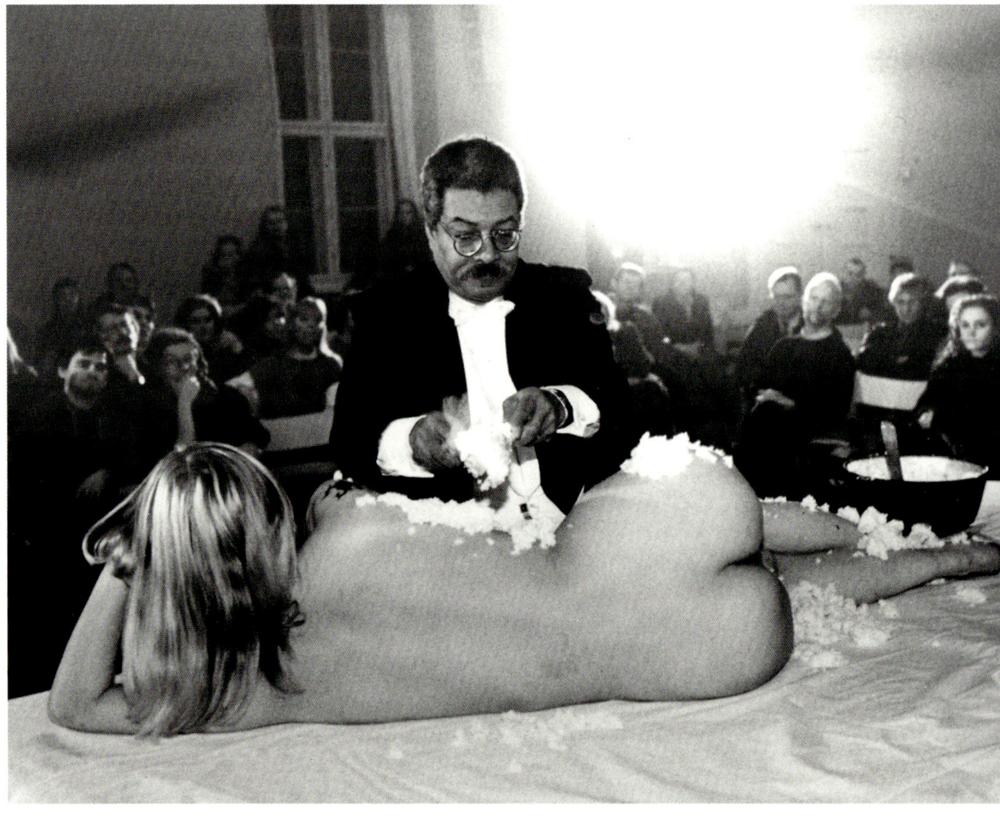

Patterson and unidentified performer in *Tristan and Isolde*, Royal Danish Academy of Fine Arts, November 17, 1993
Gelatin silver print (photograph by Morten Langkilde)
4¾ × 7 inches
Courtesy the artist

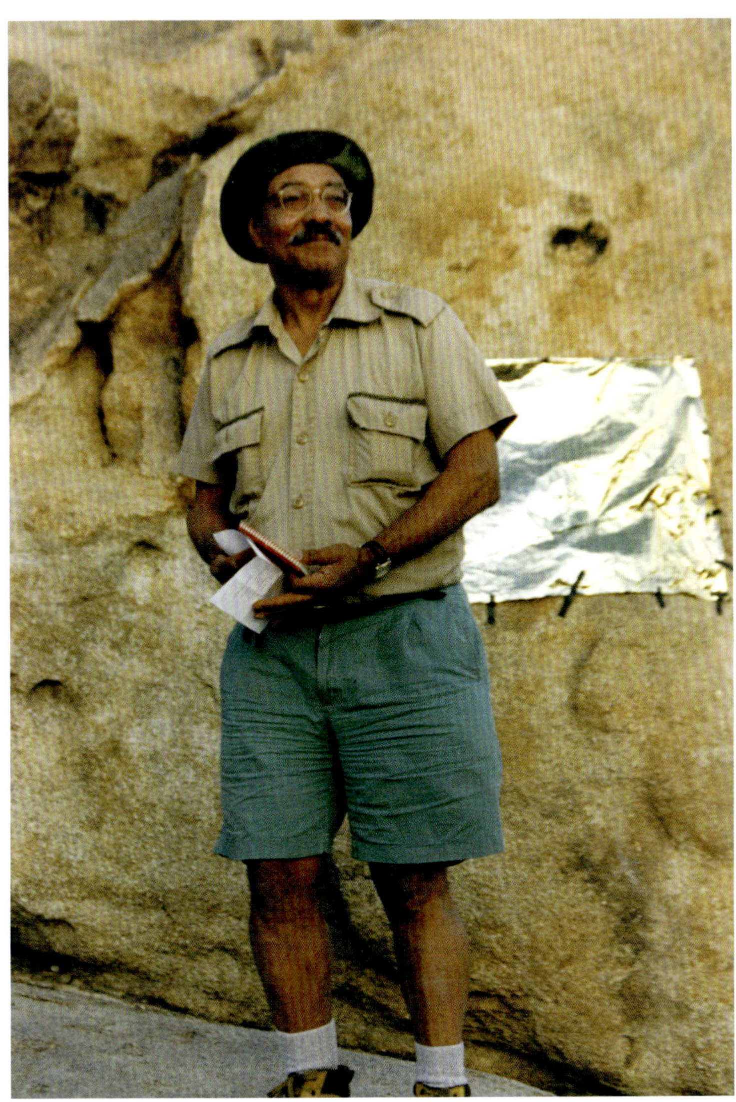

Patterson at dedication ceremony for the
Museum of the Subconscious in Namibia, 1996
Color photograph (by Francesco Conz)
12 × 8 inches
Courtesy the artist

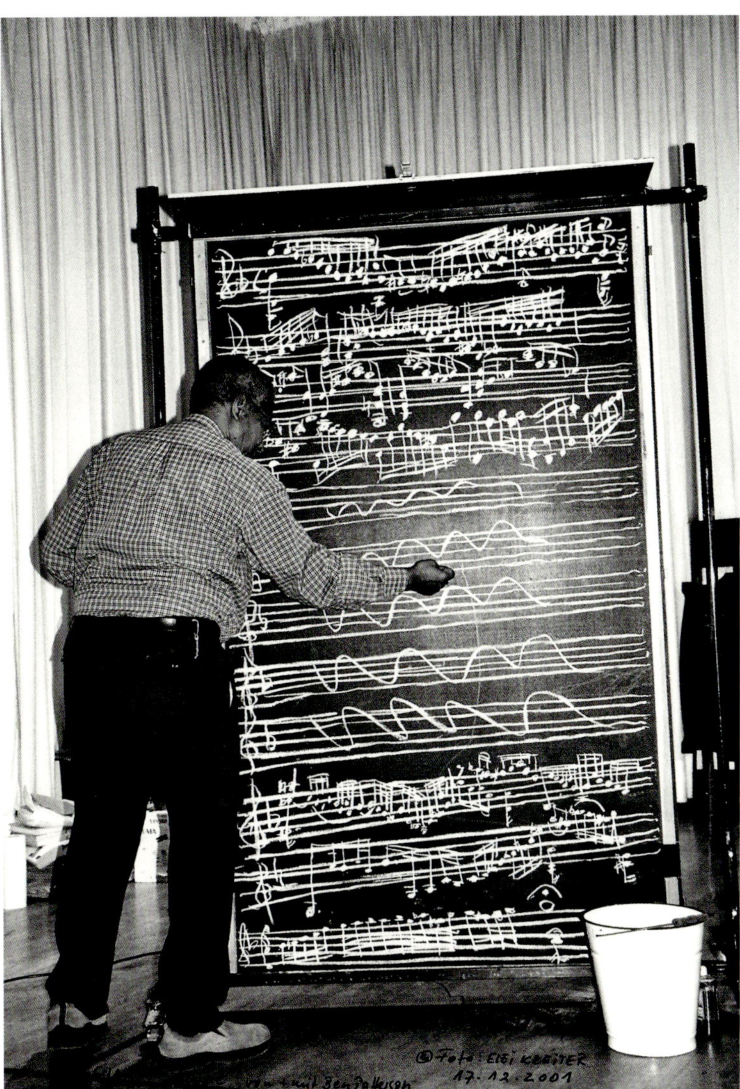

Patterson performing *A Clean Slate* at Haus
der Deutschen Ensemble Akademie, Frankfurt,
December 16, 2001
Gelatin silver print (photograph by Elfi Kreiter)
12 × 8 inches
Courtesy Elfi Kreiter, Wiesbaden, Germany

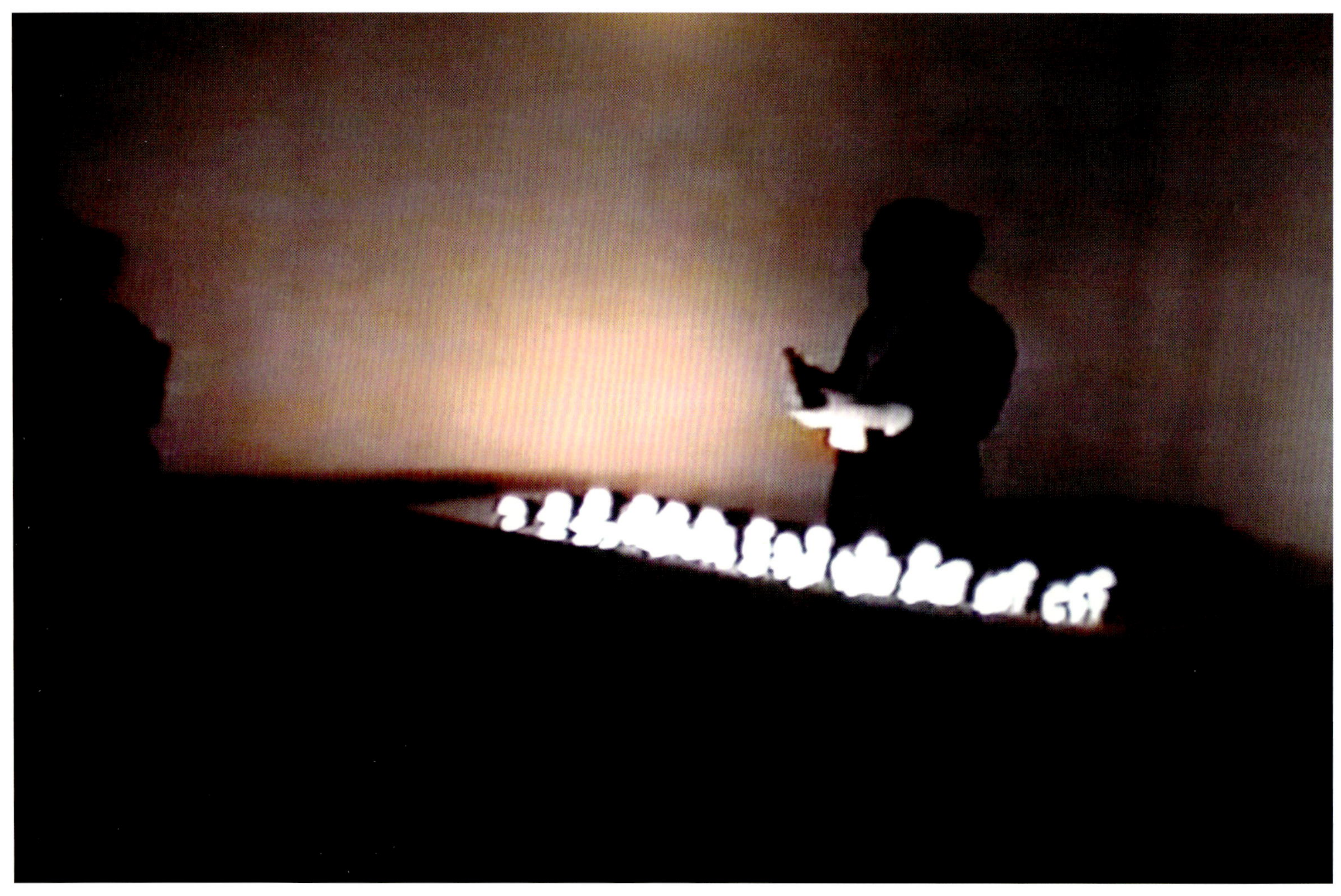

Bolero, 1995
Performed at Konzertsaal der Stadt Gera, Gera, Germany,
May 13, 1995
Digital video
22 minutes
Courtesy the artist

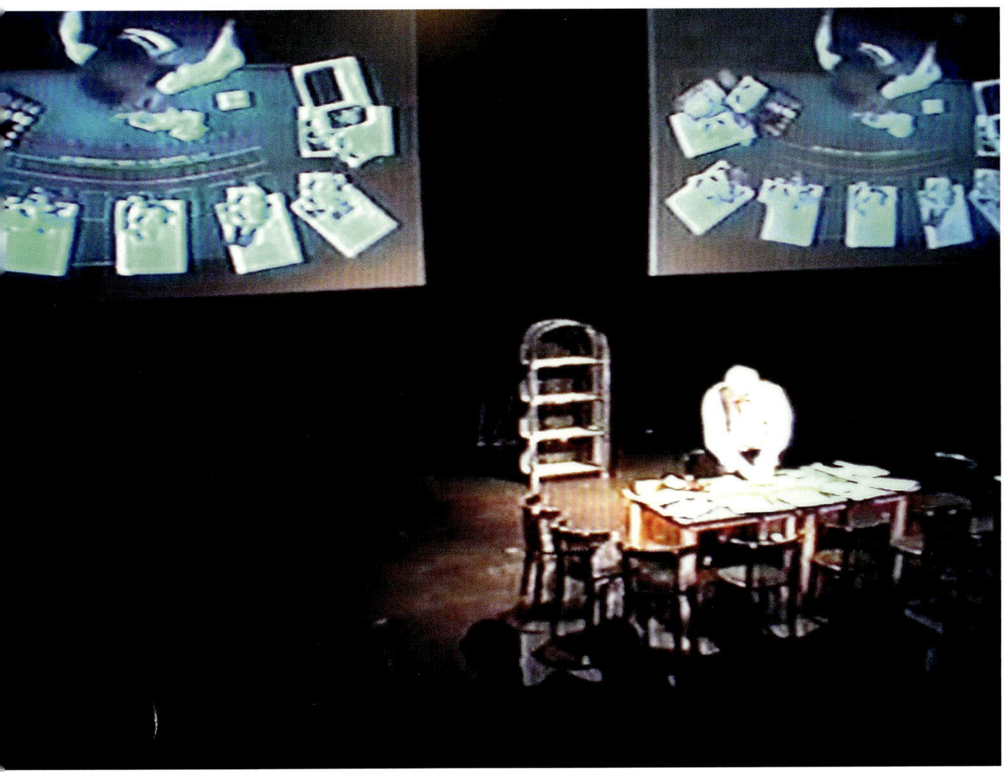

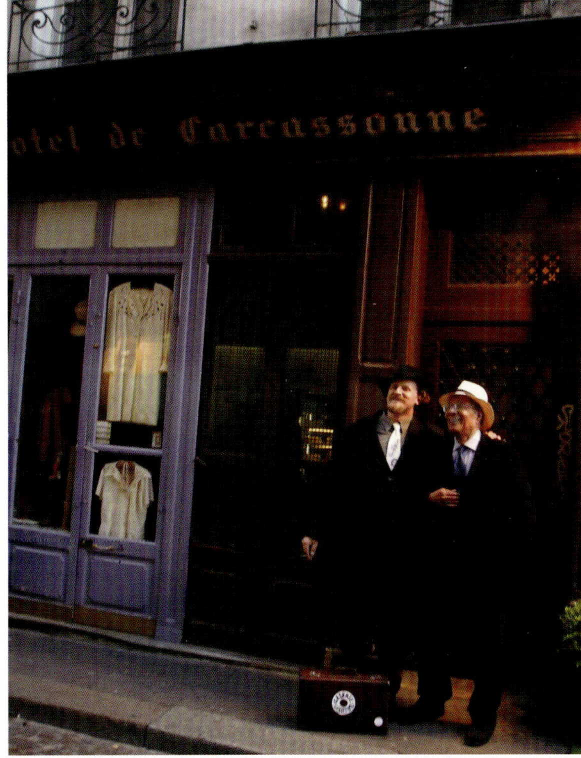

Creation of the World, 2003
Performed at the Goethe Institute, Madrid, February 6, 2003
Digital video
25 minutes
Courtesy the artist

Galerie Légitime: A Reenactment, 2009
Performed by Benjamin Patterson and Bertrand Clavez in the
streets of Paris, June 7, 2009
Digital video
15 minutes
Courtesy Bertrand Clavez, Paris

Patterson's Parisian Years: *A Seminal Moment on a Fertile Ground*

BERTRAND CLAVEZ

The presence of Benjamin Patterson in Paris in 1961 might be somewhat surprising. At the time Patterson was deeply involved in the Cologne experimental music and art scenes and freshly wed to a successful German fashion illustrator, Pyla Patterson, soon to be the mother of their first child, Ennis, so his departure for Paris would seem to be highly counterproductive. Moreover, with regard to the evolution of the art world, this choice seems to be a mistake: Paris was then losing its preeminent position as a cultural capital, whereas New York and the German scene at large were taking an increasingly prominent role.[1] Nevertheless, one has to minimize what might appear today as a strategic failure—first, because in 1961 the art scene in Paris was still very competitive with that in New York and, second, because this choice was highly beneficial for the artist and his art. In effect, it was during his sojourn in the French capital that Patterson expanded his work from the music sphere to encompass the broader poetic and visual ground that it still occupies today. From his book *Methods and Processes* (1962)[2] to his puzzle-poems (1962),[3] it was a whole new universe that he first envisioned in Paris, and even his actions were transformed and informed by his presence in the City of Light.

When, during the autumn of 1961, Ben and Pyla arrived in Paris, he was already quite active on the Cologne art scene: having met Karlheinz Stockhausen and John Cage on the same day,[4] he quickly got involved in the new music scene. He had played with David Tudor and Richard Maxfield, performed at Mary Bauermeister's studio, worked with Haro Lauhus at his gallery and premiered his own *Septet from Lemons* in Wolf Vostell's studio. He had met and worked with everyone: those gravitating around Stockhausen's studio in Cologne (François Bayle, Cornelius Cardew, Mauricio Kagel, György Ligeti, and Luigi Nono) and those brought together by the counterfestival dynamic and Bauermeister's studio (Bauermeister herself, Lauhus, Maxfield, Tudor, Vostell, Theodor W. Adorno, Merce Cunningham, Heinz-Klaus Metzger, and Nam June Paik), not to mention those involved in action art at large in Germany (Joseph Beuys, George Maciunas, Daniel Spoerri, and Emmett Williams).

However fully engaged Patterson might have seemed to be, he felt early enough that the possibilities provided by the art situation in Germany would remain fairly limited. As he once told me: "Germany was mainly Cologne and a little bit Düsseldorf, and once you got past this new music thing, there was not that much more going on. And Paris just appeared to be a larger situation and a more, quote, cosmopolitan situation, just . . . a richer environment to work in, and Paris itself is of course a bit more attractive than Cologne."[5] Beyond the romantic situation underlined by the "attraction" exerted by Paris on a young couple in love, what is also evident in this comment is an implied critique of the art situation in Germany: the experimental music scene, as interesting as it could be and despite its apparent diversity, was pretty uniform under the two axes of the new possibilities offered by electronic and electroacoustic technologies, on the one hand, and the heritage of serialism and dodecaphony, on the other. On such a basis, as sensible an observer as Patterson could easily conclude that the whole phenomenon of new music was not free of academicism or, even worse, formalism. Moreover, if his encounter with the music of John Cage was a mind-opener for Patterson, this music was only a small part—and in many ways still is—of the experimental music scene, and there was something unsatisfying to him about such a situation.

The scores that Patterson was producing then, in their diversity of structure as much as in their nature and inspiration, are quite revealing of this gap. Between *Ants,* still pretty much influenced by Cagean serendipitous processes of composition and dated 1960,[6] and *Variations for Double Bass* from 1961, something had definitely shifted away: the possibility of envisioning music as a satisfactory medium. Beyond its humorous and actionistic aspects, *Variations for Double Bass* is a genuine farewell to the instrument. Starting with the instruction to "produce a number of arco, quasi-webern sounds," it goes on with a sample of a score ("Andante mosso," a solo for double bass in act 2 of Verdi's *Rigoletto*), followed by a recipe for the realization of a "classic" prepared instrument in the manner of Cage's early prepared pianos: "place a number of wooden and plastic spring-type clothespins on strings just above bridge in such a manner that they rattle and/ or produce odd tones. Arco, tremolo, trills and/or long tones." Once again followed by an excerpt of the same Verdi score, to be played with the prepared double bass. On the fifth movement, in which "plastic butterflies" are fastened to the strings, one is supposed to perform "normal Bartok" and/or "fingernail pizzicati" in order to "catapult butterflies from strings."[7] From Verdi to Cage, passing through Webern and Bartok, Patterson presents a whole history of modern music since romanticism, even if in a very ironic mode. He proves his virtuosity through Verdi's solo for double bass, which is a well-known *morceau de bravoure* for the instrument, but he also dismisses this virtuosity by applying various experimental music recipes to the mix: preparation of the instrument, overuse of pizzicati or long tones—a kind of play extensively practiced by Charlotte Moorman, for example, in her numerous collaborations with Nam June Paik. In short, *Variations for Double Bass* shows the limits of instrumental music. Even pushed beyond its limits into pure action, even disguised under the mask of the burlesque, even empowered by the virtuosity of a talented young instrumentalist with superb academic training, still the result did not provide Patterson with what he really sought.

The enlightenment offered by Cage's compositional and musical devices, despite its lifelong influence on Patterson's scores and pieces, was nevertheless inadequate by itself to give shape to the artistic universe that the young artist was inventing, and one can see from the scores that Patterson's universe was widening—to encompass action art, of course, but also poetry and visual art. *Lemons* (1961) is an interesting example of such an evolution. Linked to a complex code of colors, not far from the synesthetic researches of the early twentieth century, the score is annotated by Wolf Vostell, with whom Patterson then often worked, and one can see the influence, not of Vostell himself, but of painting and the picturesque, on the conception of the composition: a singer (William Pearson), a musician (Patterson), a dancer (Gisela Olroth), and a painter (Vostell) are to work together under the spell of a series of colors that determine the actions, for example: "'17.5'—dancer (iron balls), painter (blow torch), musician (thunder-sheet): blue." One thinks of Wassily Kandinsky's *Klängen* as much as of Dick Higgins's 1959 *Stacked Deck Opera* or the decadelong collaboration between Cage, Robert Rauschenberg, and Merce Cunningham as fruitful sources for Patterson. In fact, going to Paris somehow completed the process: in a symbolic way, getting out of Germany was getting out of music, and entering France was entering the visual arts.

Interestingly enough, *Lemons,* performed in Vostell's studio on July 14, 1961, was followed by *Septet from Lemons,* briefly described in *Lemons* as "'90.5'—painter, singer, musician (whistle-kettle septet): 'white,'" which radically differs from *Lemons*. Isolated from its original composition, the *Septet* is a genuine event, in the Fluxus mode, in which performers are asked to throw darts at balloons inflated by boiling water in a tea kettle: every time one succeeded, a new whistle would enter the action. This emphasis on a meaningless device to produce a whimsical interpretation of the competition at the heart of musicianship is typical of the new manner that Patterson was developing at the time, the one that led him to produce some of the best pieces ever performed under the banner of Fluxus: *Paper Piece* (1960), *Solo for Dancer* (1961; also present in *Lemons*), *Tour* (1963), *Lick Piece* (1962; published in *Methods and Processes*), and a few others.

Ben's arrival in France was nothing but triumphant: the young couple first stayed in a hotel before finding a small apartment on rue Juge, near Montparnasse, an area well known for its artists' colony. If Pyla was successful in her work, Ben never succeeded in getting a work permit and ended up doing what a lot of young American expatriates were doing at the time: selling encyclopedias and Bibles to American soldiers based in France and Germany. Strangely enough, and clearly demonstrating how much his attitude toward musical performance had changed, he never played double bass while he lived in Paris, even though he could easily have earned his living in its numerous and very active jazz clubs.

Being in Paris during this period was not very easy: the Algerian War was in its final months, there had been a putsch against the French Fifth Republic[8] and assassination attempts against Charles de Gaulle, and terrorism was coming from both sides: independence fighters as well as colonialists were exploding bombs every day in Paris and executing people. The Parisian *bohème* was more active than ever, and aside from seeing American artists and friends,[9] Patterson was also meeting Daniel Spoerri and Robert Filliou on a daily basis. These two artists really introduced him to the Parisian bohemian life:

even though he was not directly involved in Situationism, which Filliou knew pretty well; in Nouveau Réalisme, which Spoerri was officially part of; or in the soon-to-be Domaine Poétique,[10] whose principal instigator, Jean-Clarence Lambert, had liked *Methods and Processes* enough to invite Patterson for dinner with his family, he was pretty well informed of what was going on in Paris by his friends involved in these circles.[11] Besides, if one looks at the Parisian *bohème* map of the 1950s and early 1960s, its epicenter is the Place de la Contrescarpe and more precisely its three cafés: the Mouffetard, the Cinq Billards, and La Chope, which served as the headquarters of the *bohème* and the departure point for every daily action, artistic or not. With the Lettrists at La Chope, the Situationists at the Café Moineau on rue du Four, and Spoerri and Erik Dietman living in the Hôtel Carcassone on rue Mouffetard, there was bound to be overlapping.

This played an influential role in Patterson's work, as we see him heading down new paths; toward poetry with *Methods and Processes*, toward visual arts with his puzzle-poems, which were so close to the processes of Nouveau Réalisme; and toward a conception of displacement as an art form, through the Galerie Légitime vernissage on July 3, 1962, and *A Very Lawful Dance for Ennis* (1962).

Displacement as an art form is one way to describe the Situationists' psychogeographic drift, yet there are substantial differences between Patterson's proposals and the Situationists', and one of the most obvious is their different backgrounds. The displacements proposed by Patterson, though apparently innocent, had a deeply political meaning, whereas those performed by the Situationists were, despite their political assertions, more closely related to the history of the French bohème. Since its very beginnings in the nineteenth century, the bohème was bound between two major concepts: the subversion of all aspects of life and *flânerie* as a mode of drifting in the modern city as a direct source of inspiration. As a movement through the city guided by spontaneous reactions to the atmosphere, chance encounters, and sudden desires—close to the desires aroused by merchandise on display, as theorized by Walter Benjamin[12]—it can be seen as a prototype for psychogeographic drift. Patterson's wanderings in Paris are recorded: he literally walked this town, but in a broader sense, he was himself drifting around the world, from Pittsburgh to Ottawa, from Ottawa to Cologne, from Cologne to Paris, and he was surrounded by professional drifters: Daniel Spoerri, born in Romania, bred in Switzerland, revealed in Darmstadt, then in Paris, soon to be in Düsseldorf; Robert Filliou, who had lived and worked in California, Korea, Egypt, and Denmark, and who was living in France before going to the next place; Emmett Williams, who had lived in England, Germany, and Paris; and Wolf Vostell, who, though living in Cologne, had spent a decade in Paris and was starting to live in Spain—not to mention George Maciunas and Nam June Paik!

These nomadic artists shall not, however, be compared with the art of displacement proposed by Ben Patterson. In effect, since 1955, Rosa Parks, and the Montgomery bus boycott, walking has also had the potential to be a political act. In the very simple score *A Very Lawful Dance for Ennis*, written in June 1962, the performers, while being perfectly respectful of the law as they cross the street on the green signal for pedestrians, end up completely blocking traffic with their unremitting crossing.[13] In a very similar manner, the participants in *Tour*,[14] created the following year, must fully entrust themselves to the "captured alive Negro"[15] about to lead their blindfolded odyssey as they wear brown paper bags on their heads: not only do they then resemble a Ku Klux Klan procession but, moreover, they can see only brown because of the paper bags.

Patterson minimizes this aspect of his work, however, recalling that he stopped making art in order to dedicate himself to the civil rights struggle. In *Postface*, Dick Higgins gives a highly sensitive account of *Methods and Processes*, linking Patterson's "way of using periodic repeats and the blues feeling that is produced" to his identity as a "negro."[16] Filliou also used similar techniques in his poems at the same moment, however, and considering their friendship, it is not surprising to find such similarities between the two artists.[17] In fact, the poems themselves, as much as their structure, reveal Patterson's early racial concerns, as in "think color of brown":

> Think color of brown
> (azure)
> think smell of roasting coffee beans
> think feel of brown suède leather
>
> think color of cognac
> think smell of coconut shelled crabs
> think feel of cognac brown indian silk
> (lavender)

The repeated references to the color brown, emphasized by the imagery employed by Patterson, is regularly contradicted by the interjection between brackets of pure bluish colors: whereas the interrupting blue is ideal and pure pigment, the brown is ingrained in reality and concreteness though powerfully poetic.

Methods and Processes brought Patterson early recognition from the French poets as much as from the American artists to whom he mailed it. This was the result of Spoerri's help: he advised Patterson to self-publish the book and to send it for free to a certain group of people on Spoerri's mailing list (who were at that time already very consequential given his international activities since the mid-1950s). This again recalls the Situationists' strategy regarding their own publication in the 1950s: *Potlatch*, an early review produced by Guy Debord and his friends, was sent to chosen persons not only because of their support of the blossoming movement but also because their opposition to it could help construct the situation.

The adherence to subversive values by this new *bohème* is evident, but this creates the need for a clarification: first, the Situationists stated that the revolution should come from the parties and not from the party, and all the members of that *bohème*, even the more politically conscious ones, had ceased their relationships with the Communist Party, which in the early 1960s was still an important leader in French culture as much as policy. The party, because of its involvement in the re-creation of a contemporary socially conscious realist art in the early 1950s, had failed to associate itself with new tendencies in art, and the contempt of the young poets for people like Louis Aragon was one consequence of this failure. The Surrealists, who were committed to Trotsky-ism in the 1930s, were also rejected as a gang controlling the art institutions and newspapers, and finally the notion of Sartrean engagement was also dismissed because of its obvious lack of effect on the social situation.

Second, the choice of subverting common social values does not mean the refusal of any kind of communion with the public, nor does it mean the dismissal of the quest for recognition. If the Situationists did choose to address themselves to only a tiny elite selected by them, whose members were sent copies of their publication, this is certainly not the case for people like Filliou, Patterson, or Spoerri, who did seek a communion with the public and, at least in the case of Spoerri, broad recognition. Spoerri's book *An Anecdoted Topography of Chance*, published in France in 1961, is a good example of what is meant here. Topography settles an open situation in which chance operations can turn into anecdotes, networks, and exchanges of utilities and ideas. Topography shows the situation as a ground and not as a field—that is, as a place to meet and not as a place to fight—whereas geography, undermined by the Situationists'

psychogeography, is of military origin. Filliou's *Galerie Légitime* might be the best example of this open situation. Located in his hat, the gallery aimed to create a direct encounter with the public through the display of small artworks by his friends to be sold on the street, just as the vendors near his home in the Jewish quarter of Paris would sell watches hidden in their coats.

Patterson's show was the first exhibition of the *Galerie Légitime*, and it was also the most famous, in part because of its invitation flyer printed by Maciunas with the mention of a "Fluxus Sneak Preview," which makes it the first manifestation under the rubric of Fluxus.[18] This anecdotal fame unfortunately overshadows the actual performance as well as the actual flyer, however, which clearly shows a symbolic map of the town drift to come: starting at 4 a.m., it ended at 10 p.m. in Ursula Girardon's gallery in the Montparnasse area, where a party was organized. The wandering artists alternated areas with a strong labor flavor, like Les Halles, where they went at 5 a.m., which was the time when the workers there were finishing their preparation of the market and eating in nearby restaurants and cafés, with entertainment districts such as Pigalle and cultural pilgrimages like the appointment at 9 a.m. in front of Gertrude Stein's grave at the Père Lachaise cemetery to perform a complete program of Fluxus pieces.

Actually, and surprisingly even to the artists themselves, the exhibition almost sold out. Pieces were sold for five francs each, and they managed to sell them to metro workers, to passersby going to or from work, and even to people who were leaving music bars and places of entertainment. And when they arrived at Ursula Girardon's gallery, almost nothing was left in the hat. Moreover, nothing is left from the performance but the flyer: no one took pictures; no one followed the artists. They were sometimes met by friends at the appointments marked on the map, which is significantly different from the later, highly publicized street actions under the leadership of George Maciunas or Ben Vautier after 1963, or even from Allan Kaprow's public space Happenings. Here two artists involve the public in their art in a very natural and traditional manner: they offer their production directly to the real, unfiltered population.

The year and a half spent by Benjamin Patterson in Paris was a crucial period in the development of his art: not only did he expand his work into areas with which he was not yet familiar, but he also fully absorbed the extraordinary creativity of the city at the beginning of the 1960s. To recall this sparkling experimental field is also to restitute part of the singularity of Patterson's work within the Fluxus movement: his later attraction to sociology and to the sociological framework as a way to create artworks—reflected in later works such as *Pets* and *Seminar II*, both from 1965—cannot be understood without considering their roots in the French situation.

In Germany, Patterson learned that he was a contemporary composer; in France, he learned to be an artist, before learning later in the United States that he was a "negro artist." He would soon choose to be "negro" fighting for his rights rather than an "artist" fighting for recognition.

NOTES

1. For a fuller account of the leadership shift, see Serge Guilbault, *How New York Stole the Idea of Modern Art: Abstract Expressionism, Freedom, and the Cold War* (Chicago: University of Chicago Press, 1983).

2. *Methods and Processes* was a self-published book produced in Paris in 1962 in an edition of one hundred copies. Pages are bound accordion fashion, giving the book its unusual form. Sent to various individuals whose addresses were given to Patterson by Daniel Spoerri, it was sold for five francs.

3. The "puzzle-poems" consisted of small puzzles made of found ads, articles, or pictures clipped from magazines, cut in parts and sold inside wooden boxes used for Camembert cheese.

4. Patterson met Stockhausen thanks to a letter from the German ambassador to Canada, who happened to be the composer's brother-in-law, and after this disappointing encounter, he met Cage, David Tudor, Merce Cunningham, and Carolyn Brown at an evening organized by Haro Lauhus and Mary Bauermeister on October 5, 1960. As soon as the following day, he was playing with Tudor and Cage one of the most famous of the latter's compositions, *Cartridge Music.* (For pictures of that first Cagean experience, see *Intermedial Kontrovers Experimentell: Das Atelier Mary Bauermeister in Köln, 1960–62* [Cologne: Emons, 1993], 51.)

5. Benjamin Patterson, interview with the author, October 14, 2004.

6. The score was made during an afternoon spent by Patterson in the comfortable villa of a wealthy German businessman whom the artist met while hitchhiking. Patterson had set a large sheet of white paper on the ground in the garden and then marked the displacements of the ants on the sheet, creating a random score visually close to Cage's scores.

7. Incidentally, Béla Bartók's lifelong enthusiasm for collecting led him to amass a collection of butterflies from all the countries he had traveled through. Patterson confirmed in an interview with the author on April 22, 2009, that he was aware of Bartók's hobby.

8. On April 21, 1961, four French army generals took power in Algeria and threatened the French government. Most of the five hundred thousand soldiers based in Algeria refused to follow them, however, and the putsch was aborted. The leaders of this operation then started an urban guerrilla movement through the secret army that they had created in 1960, the OAS, bombing numerous places where North Africans would meet and assassinating militant supporters of Algerian independence.

9. Patterson was, for example, having weekly meetings with Bob Thompson, an African American painter who was then living in Paris and eventually moved to Rome, where he died in 1966.

10. Founded by Jean-Clarence Lambert in December 1962, the Domaine Poétique was seen as the poetic equivalent of the Domaine Musical. Its founding was closely related to the Parisian Fluxus festival, insofar as the inaugural evening was scheduled on the last day of the festival. For more complete information about that organization, see Bertrand Clavez, ed., *Fluxus en*

France (Nanterre, France: Centre Pierre Francastel, 2005).

11. When asked whether he knew about the Situationists at that time, however, Patterson admitted that he recalled an exhibition of Situationist documents in Bauermeister's studio in 1961 but that he was not influenced by what sounded to him like an "overcomplicated, useless theoretical approach" (conversation with the author, October 14, 2004).

12. In a very prophetic way, if one considers the situation in Paris after World War II, in 1935 Benjamin wrote in "Paris, the Capital of the Nineteenth Century": "In the flâneur, the intelligentsia sets foot in the marketplace—ostensibly to look around, but in truth to find a buyer. In this intermediate stage, in which it still has patrons but is already beginning to familiarize itself with the market, it appears as the *bohème.* To the uncertainty of its economic position corresponds the uncertainty of its political function. The latter is manifest more clearly in the professional conspirators, who all belong to the *bohème.* Their initial field of activity is the army; later it becomes the petty bourgeoisie, occasionally the proletariat. Nevertheless, this group views the true leaders of the proletariat as its adversary." Walter Benjamin, *The Writer of Modern Life: Essays on Charles Baudelaire,* ed. Michael W. Jennings, trans. Howard Eiland (Cambridge, Mass.: Harvard University Press, 2006), 40.

13. "A traffic light, with or without special pedestrian signals is found or positioned on street corner or at stage center. Performer(s) waits at real or imaginary curb on red signal, alerts self on yellow signal, crosses street or stage on green signal. Achieving opposite side, performer(s) turns, repeats the sequence. A performance may consist of an infinite, undetermined or predetermined number of repetitions."

14. *Tour* is dated April 1963 and was written in New York, but it can be seen as the continuation of the pieces created earlier, together with *First Symphony* (May 1964), in which participants are asked by Patterson, "Do you trust me?" A similar path is followed by these pieces, insofar as they deeply engage the audience in the action. Besides, Ben and Pyla's departure from Paris happened in late January 1963, and the coffee used in *First Symphony* echoes the "smell of roasting coffee beans" of *Methods and Processes.*

15. Quotation from the poster for the Festival of Misfits at Gallery One in London (October 23– November 8, 1962), in which Robert Filliou is presented as "one eyed good-for-nothing Huguenot" and Daniel Spoerri as a "Rumanian adventurer."

16. Dick Higgins, *Postface* (New York: Something Else Press, 1964), 60.

17. As was also the case with some of the poems of Emmett Williams, though he was more interested in the structure of the meaning distorted by his permutations.

18. The previous Fluxus actions, which occurred in Wuppertal and Düsseldorf one month earlier and in which Patterson also performed, were still titled as neo-Dada evenings. Besides, the *Galerie Légitime* flyer was designed by Patterson and not Maciunas, as is often said.

Liner Notes for *Lick Piece*

FRED MOTEN

In *Eye/Body* Schneemann was not only image but image-maker, and it is this overt doubling across the explicit terrain of engenderment which marks *Eye/Body* as historically significant for feminist performance art. Though there are possible important correlatives that can be resurrected from history—such as, as some suggest, the proto-performance of nineteenth-century hysterics—in *Eye/Body* Schneemann manipulated both her own live female body and her artist's agency without finding herself institutionalized as mentally ill. Instead, she found herself excommunicated from the "Art Stud Club." George Maciunas, father of Fluxus, declared her work too "messy" for inclusion.

Rebecca Schneider[1]

I was jolted into a new appreciation of the work of Ben Patterson recently when I was made aware that a performance piece, *Lick*, which I had long attributed to Bob Watts, was really the work of Ben Patterson. Because the piece was performed nude, and was in the intimate yet publicly accessible surroundings of the Fluxus Canal Street loft, it was likely that Watts had to persuade me to do the performance. *Lick* was presented on a very hot summer (or spring) (May 9, 1964) day. My naked body was sprayed with whipped cream and the audience was invited to "lick" it off. The cream curdled or melted and ran in disgusting rivulets off my steamy body. My embarrassment and fear that some stranger might actually lick me probably also contributed to my overheated state. I don't think anyone in the audience volunteered to lick the cream off. . . . Ben and Bob demonstrated, but neither of them pursued the task with vigor. *Lick* may have been one of the culminating pieces in my history as an art world nude and in the Dada-Fluxus tradition of poking fun at the formal art convention of painting/sculpting the nude body and perhaps taking Duchamp's *Nude Descending a Staircase* a step further. This piece was only a "pubic hair" away from being a "blue performance," presenting as a public action a possible intimate portion of the sex act during a sexually conservative period.

Letty Eisenhauer[2]

I have this classic music background. I still love Beethoven, I still love Bach, I still love Brahms. You look at my record collection and there's very . . . . I hope I don't have any Stockhausen—but you know, everything else, Ravel and Avenaise. They're there because they were great musicians, they were good composers. The problem that I had with how they were perceived or how they were presented in a concert hall had nothing more to do with the music or what they were trying to do. It was much more about society—who's sitting in the first row, how wavy is the hair of the conductor, does he wiggle his rear end well, you know. And all of these marketing things . . . really have nothing to do with the music . . . . My three operas—*Madame Butterfly*, *Carmen*, *Tristan and Isolde*—all three in one hour! Some people think of it as persiflage but it's not really that. It's a tribute to them but reduced and pointed in a different direction so that "ah, that's what it was about. It's not about how much you paid for your ticket or if you are in the royal box."

Benjamin Patterson[3]

Music Discomposed

Nineteen sixty-four was a big year in the history of what Rebecca Schneider calls "the explicit body in performance."[4] Carolee Schneemann's *Site* and *Meat Joy* would follow her actions for camera of the previous year, *Eye/Body*. These performances are centered on a new mode of self-presentation in which the nude female body enacts a resistant reanimation of the aesthetic/sexual object. The sensed becomes an artist in her practice, in disruptive continuance of her trial. Is Benjamin Patterson allowed—or is he, in fact, required—to take up and adjudicate this cause? Is the double operation, which Schneider so aptly theorizes and describes, that renders Schneemann both eye and body, both subject and object, available for Patterson, particularly when he dons the worn mantle of the artist in appearing to make explicit another's body but not his own? After Schneemann, to be clothed is to be recognized as having staked a kind of claim, at the convergence of the explicit and the implicit. The claim is illegitimate not only because the brutal authority of its object—the power to expose—has been exposed but also because Patterson's assertion of it must remain unheard and invisible. The unrecognizability of the black male artist is part of the general constitution of the atmosphere—we'll call it the art world—within and out of which Patterson's work emerges. He stands, in that world, as a prefigurative variation on Adrian Piper's mythic being, whose accompanying Kantian cartoon bubbles set off a body whose inherence in an assumed bareness of life renders it explicit even when it is clothed. Anticipated by Schneemann, whom he anticipates, Patterson is subject to a double exposure. Overexposed, in the glare of the nothing that is not there and the nothing that is, he disappears.

Something remains, however: not just a photograph but also the ghost it captures (or the spirit that animates it). Patterson's *Lick Piece* was performed on May 9, 1964, at Fluxhall, George Maciunas's New York City loft. Peter Moore's photograph of the event becomes an event when accompanied by its inadvertent caption, Letty Eisenhauer's recollection of its precipitation, which is primarily composed of the performance of her explicit body, which Patterson arranges in obscurity, as imposition. Unseen, unrecognized, bare in its clothing, in performance, the hypervisible instrument is in position, has a plan, an open secret bearing more than eye/I can see, more than sound can bear, of other musics. (See the Fluxus ear in profile, naked in the disregard it suffers and enjoys, arranging the performance.) Schneider reminds us that in Schneemann and Robert Morris's live version of Manet's *Olympia*, the black maid is out of *Site*.[5] In something like the same place, at something like the same time, Eisenhauer mistakes Patterson for Bob Watts's assistant, such convergence requiring us to consider what the maid made as well as the relation, which will have been insubordinate to that between artist and object, between artist and servant. In Patterson's case, by way of an old-new musicopoetics of service that underwrites and undermines the attempt to rebehave an already behaved nakedness and thereby become an artist, an eye, an I emerging from an other, the explicit body prepares, offers protocols, knows the score:

> cover shapely female with whipped
> cream
> lick
>
> . . .
>
> topping of chopped nuts and cherries
> is optional[6]

As Philip Auslander argues with regard to all the foundational figures of the Fluxus movement, Patterson is a musician.[7] His best-known early works, *Variations for Double Bass* (1961) and *Paper Piece* (1960), as well as more recent works like *The River Mersey* (2002) and *Surveying*

Western Philosophy Using China Tools (2003), bear this out. There is an ethical and aesthetic obligation, then, to play back the photographic record. *Lick Piece* is one of those Fluxus works that seem always to have been more in the vein of performance art than music in what can be taken as its visual, tactile, gestural, and culinary displacements of sound. But it is precisely by way of the gestural and the culinary, which intimate that Patterson's concerns link with and echo some crucial formulations of Bertolt Brecht regarding the nature of opera, that the sound of Patterson's encrypted claim is revealed, as a kind of surprise.

Lick Piece's claim to a place in the history of opera is staked by its update, more than forty years later, in Patterson's discompositions of *Carmen* and *Tristan and Isolde* (p. 200), which render asymptotic the seemingly remote trajectories of Brecht and Schneemann. This proximate nonconvergence moves by way of intersection: consider the multiple positions that Patterson takes up on stage. He conducts. He composes. He cooks. He consumes. He is consumed. He serves. Focus is shifted—intermittently, glancingly—from the bodies (which is to say the questions) that he poses. One of those bodies is his, which remains explicit though it is not nude. The explicitness of the black body, the explicit body's blackness, is not only about the way a certain lived experience can be said to bear the traces of bareness; nor is it encompassed in what it is to bear the only black body on-site or onstage or in the room or in the frame. For what is also brought into relief is a kind of dynamic facticity, an "impossible purity," that the irreducible interplay of blackness and femininity bodies forth.[8] Does the black (who is, by illegitimate definition, never legitimately an) artist, in his composition of the female nude, also bear the bare sexuality that he exploits? Is the sheer corporeal fact of sex centered only on her figure? Is the artist transported outside of the sexuality that her exposure rearranges? Or does his

black body remain in a reductive hypersexualization held in the danger of his own arranging hands? One way to look at it is that Manet and his model and her maid and her cat occupy different worlds and different times. If, by contrast, in *Lick Piece* Patterson and Eisenhauer cohabitate, however temporarily, on the border between public and private, theirs is a criminal occupation, a dangerously black as well as blue preoccupation. The racial mark is emphatic but unremarked in Eisenhauer's recollection. Perhaps it's because she couldn't have known that Patterson was both composer and conductor when he was posed as a servant like Olympia's maid, helping her to prepare for visitors, within the tableau's narrative frame, which is broken again by another of its constitutive elements. In reality, it's Bob Watts who helps Patterson help Eisenhauer so that everybody but her can help himself. Who could have known? When Patterson takes the stage, music is discomposed and discomposes. Insofar as the servant was already there, helping to prepare the eye/body's active repose, discomposition is given, anoriginary, best understood as a kind of anticipatory refreshment.

Musical theater turned off Broadway at Canal Street so it could get something to eat. Letty Eisenhauer has a recipe in the Fluxus cookbook. Right down the street someone named Richard Eisenhauer designs and patents food warmers. Lick it up. I mean, look it up. Google is a kind of gumbo, a (web)site gag with endless permutations. It's easy to overindulge. Does too much whipped cream make you gag? It's messy. Did *Lick Piece* make Maciunas laugh, or is it too deformed by the kind of messiness he hated, the kind that got Schneemann kicked out of Fluxus, which she helped to start?[9] There's a relationship between messiness and gagging, between the gag and the gag reflex, between Fluxus and reflux, destructive recreativity and aesthetic indigestion. Fluxus traffics in acidity and corrosiveness. Messiness is its messianic, maniacal, Maciunac double gesture. The expression, through

Patterson, of "female creative will" against and therefore with Maciunas's will, disseminates overexposure, radiates overheating. *Lick Piece* must have made Maciunas laugh, a recurring event that Patterson describes as a hacking cackle that more often than not led to an asthma attack. *Lick Piece* must have made Maciunas gag. He couldn't have thought it was funny even though the gag became "George's litmus test for determining which works by whom would be included in a Fluxus performance or publication."[10] Why was it that Schneemann turned out to be insufficiently funny, too serious? Or was it that her seriousness was too funny, too piercing, too scary insofar as it was always already poking fun at the (wrong) man, which is another good way to start some mess? Schneemann certainly thinks it is fear that drove Maciunas unsuccessfully to try to gag her. He would have thrust something in her mouth, to keep it open and thereby silent just as he thrust absurdities down the throat of the art world, as Patterson implies. To prick, to wound, to make a thrust. To be a prick. To resist being pricked, though when one is pricked, one laughs to the point of gagging. Eisenhauer speaks of "George's need to control or to work with artists who were as constrained as he was [which] governed not only the art works produced for sale but also the performance of the scores. Ay-O's *Finger Boxes*, neatly engineered and executed to fit into a briefcase, are a good example of George's aesthetic and his personality: pristine on the outside but with a surprise—obviously sexual and potentially sadistic—when you poked a finger through the opening. . . . George did not like messes."[11] Did *Lick Piece* make Maciunas laugh? *Lick Piece*, too, is more than meat joy. The gag, as Patterson employs it, is more than "just a *persiflage*." It's a gag, a jest, a gig, on gest, some notes, on gesture, on Google, on YouTube.

Giorgio Agamben writes, by way of Gilles de la Tourette's descriptions of the syndrome that would bear his name (and by way of an unfinished text of Balzac's called "Theory of Bearing") about a European bourgeoisie that had, by the end of the nineteenth century, lost its gestures. The loss of gesture is all bound up with the loss of sense. Both, in turn, are bound to a double imposition: revolutionary agent of its own decay, the bourgeoisie loses itself (its sense, its gestures) in being itself. Itself insofar as it acquires itself, in loss of itself insofar as it constitutes itself by way of acquisition, the general catastrophe of the general equivalent sets what Peter Brooks calls "the melodramatic imagination" to work in an attempt to recover the sacredness that regulative understanding constantly endangers.[12] For Brecht, opera's particular interinanimation of *melos* and drama is the gestic/gestural medium in which this game of lost and found is serially played, replayed, long-played, if you will, like a record.

But what if the loss of gesture is more rigorously imagined as gesture's quickening, its internal differentiation, an enriched sounding and a continual initialization of the sacred? Agamben speaks of bearing, of carrying or carrying on, of gesture as enduring, as the emergence of pure means without end, of the human as pure mediality. Gesture, then, is the communication of communicability as, for Brecht, the theatrical activation of gest makes possible a movement from the realm of entertainment to that of mass communication. What characterizes gesture, Agamben adds, "is that in it nothing is being produced or acted, but rather something is being endured and supported. The gesture, in other words, opens the sphere of *ethos* as the more proper sphere of that which is human. But in what way is an action endured and supported? In what way does a *res* become a *res gesta*, that is, in what way does a simple fact become an event?"[13] This indexes a movement in the photograph of the explicit body in performance that goes against the grain of its having been posited, of her having been posed. Apposition is given in the form she bears, in bearing that moves and sounds, in stillness and silence. It steps across the distance between pose and gest, bridges the gap between gest and gesture, like a cinematic event, an operatic happening. But this is to say that what is at stake is not simply a reclamation of lost gesturality but something Brecht might recognize as that rich internal differentiation of gesturality that he speaks of as gest or, more precisely, as social gest. A certain fugitivity of the gest/ure will have already been remarked in apposition, as it awaits its music, in impure mediality, for an irruption of that seemingly held, seemingly stilled, irregularity (which Brecht associates with jazz and with what he calls "the freeing of the Negroes," but which is figured more precisely when blackness and escape combine to form the name of the general itinerant). This racialized irregularity moves now, not so much as what Brecht might have called gestic music or the music of social gest, but rather by way of a necessarily flavorful advance, something Miles Davis called social music, which is what Patterson discomposes, like a virus in Wagner's previously finite score.

Brecht avows his antipathy to the culinary by staging and inducing gluttony. Eating too much whipped cream, for instance, will have been always in bad taste, but it can be put to use insofar as it exemplifies and exposes the bourgeoisie's self-consumptive jones, which can be traced in opera's devolutionary arc.

The Magic Flute, Fidelio, Figaro all included elements that were philosophical, dynamic. And yet the element of philosophy, almost of daring, in these operas was so subordinated to the culinary principle that their *sense* was in effect tottering and was soon absorbed in sensual satisfaction. Once its official "sense" had died away the opera was by no means left bereft of sense, but had simply acquired another one—as sense *qua* opera. The content had been smothered in the opera. Our Wagnerites are now pleased to remember that the original Wagnerites posited a sense of which they were presumably aware. Those composers who stem from Wagner still insist on posing as philosophers. A philosophy which is of no use to man or beast, and can only be disposed of as a means of sensual satisfaction. We still maintain the whole highly-developed technique which made this pose possible: the vulgarian strikes a philosophical attitude from which to conduct his hackneyed ruminations. It is only from this point, from the death of the sense (and it is understood that the sense *could* die), that we can start to understand the further innovations which are now plaguing opera: to see them as desperate attempts to supply this art with a posthumous sense, a "new" sense, by which the sense comes ultimately to lie in the music itself, so that the sequence of musical forms acquires a sense simply *qua* sequence, and certain proportions, changes, etc. from being a means are promoted to become an end.[14]

Sense totters and is then absorbed in sensual satisfaction. The absorption of sense—of a philosophical, dynamic, daring element—leads to the acquisition of another one, a value that will have been, as it were, intrinsic to opera as opera. At stake is the relation between self-indulgent sensuality and fetishization, the illusion that art is or could ever be for its own sake. Sense has been absorbed by sensuality; content has been absorbed by form; operatic innovation produces a pale afterlife of sense in the form of a purely formal self-reference or, perhaps more precisely, self-regard. When opera acquires another sense and then posits that acquisition as always already its own, it asserts the acquisition of its form as an absolute value and the acquisition of a certain fetishized sense of itself, of a sense of itself as (its) sensuality, of that sensuality as the form that opera is, that opera has and that opera takes. This complex—wherein acquisition and element, sense and sensuality, blur—disturbs and therefore reveals a deeply regulatory and fundamentally Kantian impulse in Brecht, one whose roguish object is the nonsense that turns out to be irreducible in opera, the cantian irruptions or Kanted flights that constitute its form while deforming its content. But the deforma-tion of content need not be understood either as its absorption or its death if one can imagine that the one who is disposed of as a means of sensual satisfaction—the one who is posed, posited, but who troubles the already given content and the already assumed agency of composition—is a philosopher; or, perhaps more pre-cisely, that insofar as there is philosophy, it moves only in and by way of her impossible, impossibly sounded and sounding movement. Hers is an elemental philosophy of anacquisition, of that essential value of the outside that cuts and augments suffering and enjoyment. Her appo-sition of the pose from its interior, moving theatrically against a range of absorptions by way of the operatic gest/ure of the working girl, is social gest in social music, which Patterson's performative, compositional conduc-tion discomposes.

The convergence of content and pleasure is terrible. It is the cause and the cost of flight. Therefore Brecht must risk the scandal and the regression that attends plea-sure. Brecht will, as it were, allow himself to be absorbed by pleasure; he'll have whisky or you'll know why. Such absorption will have been both submission and release, a self-sending that is carried out in the interest of salva-tion, by way of being-consumed, within which the nec-essarily disagreeable, whose excessive flavor must be in bad taste, puts itself forward as a kind of pharmakonic

capsule meant to poison the glutton that consumes it. A more subtle realization of the structurally necessary rela-tion between enjoyment, flight, and resistance that the culinary brings to life is, for Brecht, nothing more than capitulation to the degraded and degrading hedonism of the bourgeoisie in the form of false innovation. Brecht is prepared to let us wallow in enjoyment in order to kill it; Patterson moves in and against his wake.

The opera's not over . . .

Phonic materialization is a visual, gestural, theatrical affair accomplished through a set of repeatable operations per-formed and interpreted severally, separately, every time. Music is an encoding and deferral of phonic material that is embedded and embodied in phonic materialization. The knowing enactment of this interplay of dematerial-ization and rematerialization is Patterson's métier, though more generally, Fluxus occupies, is preoccupied with, the precarious balance between bare materiality and unspar-ing dematerialization. Music's bare life, its mere material-ity, is, further, poised between gesture and the culinary, as if the rougher and more vulgar senses are the most likely locale of the likeliest and severest threat. More matter, less art? No. Because matter is only ever art's delivery system. Deployed in the interest of such delivery, opera is per-haps the most vulgar art form of all, born in and by the vernacular, delivered gesturally, by bodies more likely than not to be out of all compass, hyperbolic, hyperphysical, nonsensical. Opera always threatens, in the delivery of its material, to deliver nothing more. For the refined, who see art's ultimate refinement in dematerialization, opera is an embarrassment. The bourgeoisie, who may or may not adhere to this particular understanding of refinement, are willing to pay for it in any case.

In advance of such embarrassment, the most radi-cal movements toward dematerialization are the ones that are most bound to the material. Patterson not only enacts but also celebrates this paradox, reducing opera to its most base and basic elements. The materiality that insisted in and on such performance is in the air or, more precisely, in the airlessness of cyberspace, digitally recorded and disseminated but never by way of the transferable solidity of the compact disc or the DVD. You can see for yourself on YouTube.[15] The difference of this opera is in its being seen and seen again. Lip smacking, mouthwatering, the hyperbolic body made explicit, fully detached now from the sound (production) that would have justified such embodiment. There to be consumed, enjoyed, and nothing more. What led Conceptualists and Fluxists to dematerialize the work was, precisely, the intensity with which the work had been given over to and disappeared by the valuation of what was always immaterial in and to it. Aesthetic acculturation, as Adrian Piper discusses it, tends toward dematerialization, but so too does the resistance to it.[16] The critique of aesthetic value (or, more precisely, the critique of bourgeois aesthetic valuation) disappears but for a kind of *retrait* of the material. This insight—sense's oscillation between the lost and the found—is continually given and enacted in the work—the setting to work of the work, the working on or over of opera. The explicit invisibility of the servant is, too, a kind of dis/appearance. Within the strictures of an ethics of dematerialization, Patterson dis/appears. He reemerges in republication, in enactment, in repertory, by way of the recording and its digital and cybernetic reproduction—the paraontological remains of his performances take the form of a sifting of and through remains, a continual serving of leftovers, of fucked-up, funny, generatively unfunky licks and pieces of licks. Matter is art's embarrassment; enjoyment is its shame. This double illegitimacy betrays so much of what is valorized under the rubric of Fluxus, which moves within a disingenuous forgetting of this fact, which is, in turn, disingenuously and

sometimes profitably forgotten. There was a Fluxus show at the Hamburger Bahnhof, but Patterson's train never made it to the station. There is a structure of recognition in the retrospective—there was this man who did some things, made some things, or was involved in a particularly resonant and interesting mode of making whose methods and processes of fabrication never left us with anything ready or present-to-hand. There is, at the same time, a profound ethics of preparation—in the absence of something made, on the performative outskirts or against the phonographic backdrop of the readymade, Patterson works to make things ready. His is an aesthetics of preparation; his privileged genre is the recipe, in which the combination of stringency and extravagance sometimes achieves a kind of lyricism. At bottom, within and against a certain tradition of the inhabited and abandoned bottom, where bassists walk and walk away, Patterson cooks, prepares a table for us, a phrase resonant in its demand that we prepare ourselves and in the fearsome imposition of its constantly renewed offer to prepare us.

It is not so much that there is a thin line between licking and consumption but rather that there is a thin line between their interinanimation and a devouring that leaves nothing intact. But is anyone left intact? This is a question concerning the culinary-musical pleasures of the lick and what it prepares in and for us. The virtuoso bassist (fore)plays for us, the lick obstinately returns from variation, and we are prepared to make something out of nothing. But why extend this sacrificial economy just for the sake of a point you have to make? On the one hand, he prepares some food for us; on the other, he prepares it for himself, so he can eat in front of us. The careful preparation is onstage in Patterson's *Carmen*. The director as stagehand, performer, prop, asks us to consider the long, unbreakable connection between music, sex, and food. The musical material, ennobled by its dematerialization,

is rematerialized as dessert—there is no question of nour-
ishment or necessity. Patterson conducts from onstage,
after serving as stagehand. The characters present themselves in and by way of a gift of material that the players
bear to the conductor's hand. This transaction is staged
but detached from the music that constitutes that staging's background. The music is not played in the orchestra
pit but played back offstage, as if Patterson put a photograph on the phonograph. The music is the material trace
of a prior transaction. The players give themselves over to
be blended, discomposed.

When opera becomes emphatically, self-consciously
culinary, it also becomes more emphatically visual. Staging, and consequent revisions and invasions of the stage,
predominate. The music is reduced to backdrop, decor,
which is what Adorno would have the long-playing
record remedy. But Patterson deploys the LP and its compact variant to render visuality ever more insistently, not
in the interest of a nonvisual cum structural listening (in
which the visual experience to which the music is made
subordinate is eliminated so that the music itself can be
seen and not heard) but rather in the service of a total
subordination of the musical material so that it can be
given, now, as staging. Opera replaces the spectacle of
exertion in concert with staged gestures that are both
detached from and driven by the music that is produced
in the orchestra pit. Now the kinetics of musical production is rendered more remote by mechanical reproduction. Reproduced music brings unproductive gesture into
relief. In this counterproductive mise-en-scène the senses
become conceptual in their practice. The sensory appara-
tus is recalibrated. Or, rather, it's as if by way of Patterson
we can now go openly to the opera for what it is that we
always wanted: something to enjoy. The asceticism that
attempted to separate music from food and that, more
generally, wished to protect hearing from the contami-

nation of the other senses and which had to use a kind
of conceptual visuality to do so, thereby undermining its
own project, is hereby relinquished. The end of this open
enjoyment is the revaluation of means, which you can
almost taste when the bassist puts some flavor in your
ear, which you can feel when the hegemony of the end, of
the one who lives in the exclusive zone that ends inhabit,
which they have accumulated, where they accumulate,
where they exercise possession's brutal imperatives,
where they are exercised by owning, where they await
exorcism, having paid the highest possible price for their
ticket, cross-fades to black.

Because he is a DJ, Patterson is able to distinguish ownership and enjoyment. Because he is a bassist, for whom
the lick is, therefore, basic, Patterson plays on and in and
with the persistence, our repetitive consumption, of the
profane fragment, the culinary musical moment, the
stock pattern or phrase that always tempts and sometimes fills in the open possibility of social life that attends
the instrumentality to which such impure means con-
sent. Patterson's solo variations act out in that opening,
as if virtue and virtuosity—now that the bassist stages
himself in the feminized locus of a culinary transaction,
in the interest of a pleasure that is neither productive
nor reproductive—are breaking up just to let you know
that all along music was drama, a theatrical symposium
on the general antagonism. *Lick Piece* extends the discomposition of the lick—and the lick's discomposition
of the work—begun in *Variations for Solo Bass*, repeated
with differences in *Paper Piece*'s torn ostinato of tearing,
and revived in *Carmen*'s and *Tristan and Isolde*'s reflex-
ive, refluxive commensality. Patterson, Fluxus's practically
unacknowledged remainder, is given to festive, obstinate
rupture of the familiar. He reconstructs Schneemann's *Site*
specificity and regifts the puritanical indulgence Brecht
confers upon opera. Enabled and disabled by the thing

that he would correct, rearranging the submissive aggression to which he aggressively submits himself, having consented to become the more and less than singular instrument he abusively prepares, Patterson performs the messy, irregular, divine methods and processes by which violence overturns itself.

NOTES

1. Rebecca Schneider, *The Explicit Body in Performance* (New York: Routledge, 1996), 35.

2. Letty Eisenhauer, "A Version of Trace in 2008: An Interpretation of Scores," in *Fluxus Scores and Instructions: The Transformative Years,* ed. Jon Hendricks, with Marianne Bech and Media Farzin (Roskilde, Denmark: Museet for Samtidskunst, 2008), 35.

3. Benjamin Patterson, *Ben Patterson Tells Fluxus Stories (from 1962 to 2002),*? Records/Hundertmark Q 07, 2002, compact disc.

4. See Schneider, *Explicit Body.*

5. Ibid., 31.

6. Benjamin Patterson, *Methods and Processes,* 2nd ed. (Tokyo: Gallery 360°, 2004).

7. Philip Auslander, "Fluxus Art-Amusement: The Music of the Future," in *Contours of the Theatrical Avant-garde: Performance and Textuality,* ed. James M. Harding (Ann Arbor: University of Michigan Press, 2000), 110–29.

8. Certain iconic moments in nineteenth-century French art seem intent on playing this out in a range of inadequate modular calculations—*Olympia* is one instance, *Carmen*'s Afro-Cuban/ Afro-Romani thing is another. This is something Jennifer DeVere Brody illuminates with great precision. See "Black Cat Fever: Manifestations of Manet's *Olympia,*" *Theatre Journal* 53 (March 2001): 95–118.

9. See Schneider, *Explicit Body,* 189n24.

10. Benjamin Patterson, "What Makes George Laugh?," in *Mr. Fluxus: A Collective Portrait of George Maciunas, 1931–1978,* ed. Emmett Williams and Ann Noël (London: Thames & Hudson, 1997), 260–63.

11. Eisenhauer, "Version of Trace," 33–34.

12. See Peter Brooks, *The Melodramatic Imagination: Balzac, Henry James, Melodrama, and the Mode of Excess* (New Haven, Conn.: Yale University Press, 1976).

13. Giorgio Agamben, *Means without End: Notes on Politics,* trans. Vincenzo Binetti and Cesare Casarino (Minneapolis: University of Minnesota Press, 2000), 56.

14. Bertolt Brecht, "The Modern Theatre Is the Epic Theatre (Notes to the Opera *Aufstieg und Fall der Stadt Mahagonny*)," in *Brecht on Theatre: The Development of an Aesthetic,* ed. and trans. John Willett (New York: Hill & Wang, 1964), 39–40.

15. *Tristan and Isolde* and *Carmen* were performed at the Asolo Film Festival XXVI, November 22 and 23, 2007, respectively. Excerpts from *Carmen* last accessed August 18, 2010, at http://www. youtube.com/watch?v=4XStjkF2h Co&feature=related. *Tristan and Isolde* last accessed August 18, 2010, at http://www.youtube. com/watch?v=tKJhWR96MIc&fea ture=related.

16. Adrian Piper, "Critical Hegemony and Aesthetic Acculturation," *Nous* 19 (March 1985): 29–40.

The History of Gray Matter from the Avant-garde to the Postmodern

CHARLES GAINES

I have been thinking about the relationship between Benjamin Patterson's performance work and that of younger artists such as Dave McKenzie and Rodney McMillian. Central to my thinking is that each side holds both opposite and complementary views of performance. Trained as a musician, Patterson comes from the tradition of musical performance—that is, the performance (expression) of musical notation. This more than likely informed his idea of Fluxus, a contemporary art movement that he helped inaugurate. Because of his background in music and his involvement in avant-garde practices, Patterson investigated the idea of the autonomy of the performance event. In music performance there is a bilateral relationship between the composer and the performer. The composer writes the score, but it is the performer who interprets (performs) it. In this context the score can be understood as an autonomous element in relation to the performer, who responds to it, who transforms it from object to subject in the space of the performance. The avant-garde rethinks the role of the performer, however, taking away the power to transform according to his subjective interests.

The result is a concrete or pragmatic space of performance, which is, like a score, autonomous and independent of the performer. The importance of this is that rather than emphasizing the performance space as an opportunity for the self-expression of the performer,

there is in the Fluxus event a merging of avant-garde theater and concrete musical performance that gives little to no importance to the subjectivity of the performer. Performers follow a set of instructions that leave no room for subjectivity—no identity, no psychology, no theater (or if there is theater, it is the avant-garde theater of Jean Genet or F. T. Marinetti). This is generally the case with Benjamin Patterson's early Fluxus pieces. But as we will explore, there is in Patterson's work what I call "gray matter," the aura of the political and the social—that is, cultural references that imply but do not affirm the presence of subjectivity but possess a radical politics.[1]

Dave McKenzie, by contrast, thinks of the space of performance not only as a site of subjectivity but also as a rigorous interrogation of identity, culture, and politics. Performance becomes the opportunity to realize a particular understanding of self by positing it as the other. In an article about McKenzie, Glenn Ligon quotes Franz Kafka: "How pathetically scanty my self-knowledge is compared with, say, my knowledge of my room."[2] It is natural to want to reveal that which is obscured, and McKenzie intends to do precisely that. This "wanting to know" can be a forceful motivation coming from an artist who could be described as shy and unassuming. Performance for McKenzie is a type of psychological theater in which permission is given to behave in ways in which one would otherwise not, in which other identities can be assumed and used to interrogate the self, society, and cultural values. Glimpses of the self are realized at the limits of culture, and to these limits is where his work must take him. For to know the self one must know what is possible and what is not possible, experience the limits of the imagination in order to locate the limits of subjectivity. A mapping of these limits shows that they reveal where the self and the other meet. McKenzie uses performance to navigate this place in order to become the other. By employing performance as a type of ritualistic

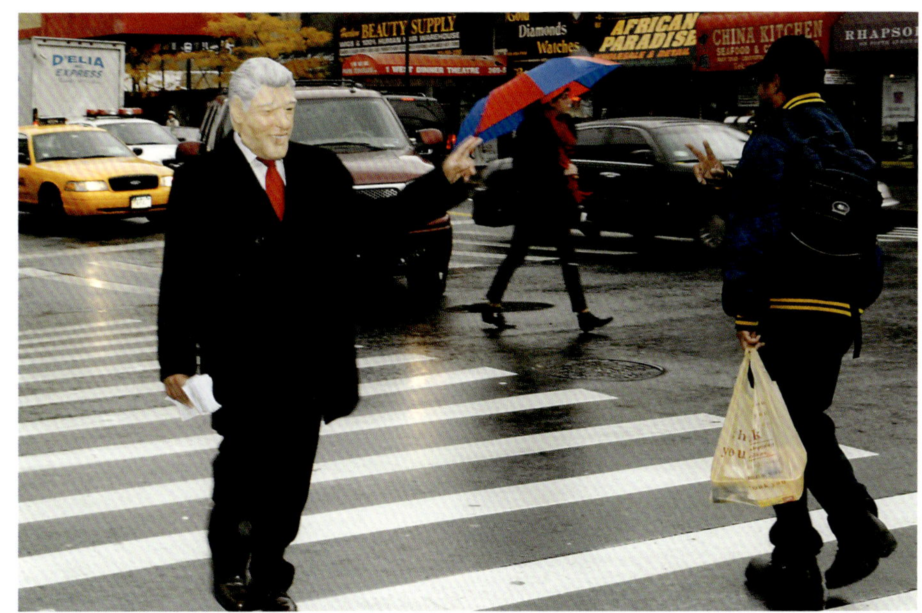

Dave McKenzie, *We Shall Overcome*, 2004

form—that is, by performing as an artist common acts or by appropriating common objects—he is able to merge art with ordinary life.

An interest in the commonplace is something that both Patterson and McKenzie share. For McKenzie, it is the site where ordinary experiences can be employed to push boundaries of the subject, and for Patterson, it is employed to push the boundaries of art. For both, it is the site where art and life merge. In this respect, Patterson fits David T. Doris's description of the Fluxus artists as a group who "surveyed the peripheral territories of their respective disciplines, or rather the margins *between* those disciplines. The new structures that resulted from these explorations tested received notions of the limits of the arts, as well as the limits of our ability to perceive those structures as art."[3] McKenzie inherits from Patterson (and from the avant-garde in general) the idea that art is about invention and change and that the strategy of displacement can be employed in order to invoke change. The primary purpose of this effort is not to question art practice but to realize displaced locations that the artist's subjectivity

can occupy. In doing this, McKenzie recursively extends the Patterson avant-garde. Patterson performed everyday actions in order to rethink accepted ideas of art practice, and McKenzie uses the everyday to interrogate the limits and nature of the self. The result is a rethinking of how representation works, a query into its limits. McKenzie is perhaps less interested in the limits of art than he is in the limits of social and cultural understanding.

We can now begin to understand the differences between Patterson's and McKenzie's ideas about performance, which the statement by Kafka that I quoted earlier underlines. In this quotation there is a dualism: one pole is the subjective realm of self-knowledge, and the other the objective world of things. McKenzie occupies the former, and Patterson the latter. To continue the Kafka metaphor, intriguingly it is the ability to describe the room and its objects empirically that interests Patterson, whereas it is the obscurity of the self that McKenzie finds fascinating. This subject-object relationship (McKenzie the subjective, Patterson the objective) forms the recursive structure that binds the two artists in the present day. A comparison of their performance works sheds light on this relationship. In Patterson's *A Very Lawful Dance for Ennis* (1962), the participants were asked to walk along a street in Manhattan, following the directions of the traffic lights at each intersection for a period of time until the piece was completed. In McKenzie's *We Shall Overcome* (2004), the artist wore a Bill Clinton mask and a suit and walked the streets of Harlem in a kind of homage to the fact that the former president had recently moved his offices into the neighborhood but that no one ever saw him.

The difference between the two works begins with what each "script" puts into place. Patterson's walk is an objectification of the situation in that he has no decision-making power but gives himself over completely to the minute-to-minute circumstances of the environment.

This makes his thoughts about past, future, and context irrelevant to the execution of the event or experience. In contrast, McKenzie's walk is designed to get the environment to respond to him. This begins with the fact that he assumes a character, Bill Clinton, and by wearing a mask of his likeness, undertakes in an alien fashion an ordinary activity of the Harlem street. Of course this draws the attention of people as they try to figure out what this means. Social tropes explode in this work as "a 30-year-old black artist assumes the role of the 'first black president'. Reactions [from passersby] ranged from jaded shrugs to shrieks of delight and even an appeal for government assistance: 'I'm homeless. Can you help me?' one woman asks."[4]

Patterson privileged the autonomy of the event over the subjectivity of the performer, whereas McKenzie's work seems to belie this idea. *We Shall Overcome*, like many of McKenzie's performances, is an allegorical narrative that invokes meditations on race, gender, and identity. In order to do this, it undertakes the trope of the ordinary even as it aims for extraordinary results. In this work concepts drawn from ordinary life find their representation as ordinary objects or subjects, and as such they actually constitute a looking back to Patterson and the idea of the primacy of the event. At the same time we are able to see in Patterson's early performance a looking forward to our contemporary moment. This is because Patterson's performance work is a bit more open-ended than the simple and direct instructions found in other Fluxus pieces of its time. Dick Higgins, in fact, said that his work "goes for the grey."[5] To help explain what Higgins meant by this, we might refer to a comment made by artist Paul McCarthy about one of Allan Kaprow's performances. According to McCarthy, the Happening, as Kaprow's events are called, is often "a type of absurd activity, but I think an activity to make you reflect on your life."[6]

This "gray area," or what I referred to at the beginning of this essay as "gray matter," is the moment of self-reflection that McCarthy talks about, a cognitive moment that is also at the core of McKenzie's performances, a faculty probably inherent in performance itself that perforce links the avant-garde to the postmodern. Hence we can hear echoes of McKenzie in Higgins's comment from 1964 that Patterson "seems to accept, even to encourage, the non-memorable, disappearing aspect of his work. In pieces such as 'A Lawful Dance,' . . . Patterson gets somewhere that nobody else is. Marvelous things happen to you while you cross the street. The last time I performed this piece at Times Square [which at that time was full of bars, porn shops and drugs], I . . . was, briefly, joined by Bea, Lindy, and Shirley, three overdeveloped young ladies with colossal hairdos. They saw me (and a group of others) crossing back and forth, and it occurred to them that it would be fun to join in, so they did, no questions asked."[7] The cultural interaction that compels McKenzie's work is also present in Patterson's. And in this way they come together. Patterson critiques culture through a radical removal of subjectivity, and McKenzie critiques culture by aggressively imposing subjectivity.

Fluxus grew out of several sources in the middle to late 1950s: the musical avant-garde, particularly the ideas of John Cage and Karlheinz Stockhausen; the radical theater of Claus Bremer,[8] Marinetti, and Genet; and Dada and Concrete Art. The common thread linking these various art forms was the radical critique of subjectivity and symbolic representation. Traditional theories that defined these disciplines—for example, theater, visual art, and music—stressed specialized techniques and executions that identified their specific genres. This specialization was necessary to produce a symbolic language of forms, one that was separate from the ordinary world but that gave art a metaphoric capacity to express and to represent on a level higher than what would be permitted by ordinary language. From the early to middle twentieth century a change took place, displacing these specialized techniques and strategies with ones that employed the objects and experiences of the everyday, hence challenging received ideas about art and resulting in a more radical approach to art. This had a defining effect on the development of Fluxus as it sought to continue this challenge by employing the antisymbolic language of the avant-garde through the use of either nonsymbolic abstraction or the pragmatic markers of ordinary objects or "lived experience." Fluxus performance particularly became identified with avant-garde practice because of its use of real time (duration) as "lived experience." (For example, in ordinary life when we hear the telephone ring, we do not interpret the event symbolically, nor do we identify it as an expression of someone's subjectivity. Instead we interpret it pragmatically: it is just the sound of the telephone existing in real time.) To a significant degree the appeal of performance was due to its ability to define itself as an inherently radical practice, to produce a nonsymbolic sense of "lived experience."

John Cage's theory of indeterminacy in musical composition was very important to the development of Fluxus artists such as Patterson since it was among the earliest attempts to critique the role of subjectivity. Cage called this idea "the autonomous behavior of simultaneous events."[9] The idea of indeterminacy in music developed out of Cage's interest in Zen Buddhism, with its critique of Western subjectivity, and from this George Maciunas developed his theory of the Fluxus event. Consequently, many works were performed from simple, concrete instructions that produced no "gray" area of interpretation, such as La Monte Young's *566 for Henry Flynt* (1960), in which a helmet was struck 566 times with a drumstick; Robert Watts's *Two Inches* (1963), in which the instruction was to stretch a two-inch ribbon across the stage or street and then cut it; or George Brecht's

Three Lamp Events (1961), in which a lamp was to be turned on, then off, then on, and so forth.

One of the more complex works performed at an early Fluxus-titled event, the Festvs Flvxorvm Fluxus, held in 1962 in Düsseldorf, was Patterson's *Paper Piece* (1960). In this work, "two performers entered the stage from the wings carrying a large 3' by 15' sheet of paper, which they then held over the heads of the front of the audience. At the same time, sounds of crumpling and tearing paper could be heard from behind the on-stage paper screen, in which a number of small holes began to appear. The piece of paper held over the audience's heads was then dropped as shreds and balls of paper were thrown over the screen and out into the audience."[10] At the time of the Düsseldorf event, Marxism was influencing Maciunas's Fluxus ideas, and he argued in a manifesto that Fluxus was an attack on bourgeois values. For him, Fluxus was about resisting the dominance of European social, political, and aesthetic values. By 1960 Theodor W. Adorno and Heinz-Klaus Metzger were denouncing the idea of autonomy in art in their lectures. And Maciunas was arguing that Cage's notion of the acceptance of the everyday was a critique of the social order.[11]

Before Patterson's performance in Düsseldorf began, the gallery director and art critic Jean-Pierre Wilhelm read a prepared script as an introduction to the event. *Paper Piece* followed this. Some of the paper that was tossed into the audience during the performance had Maciunas's manifesto written on it. The nature of Patterson's collaboration in this is unclear; the documentation is ambiguous. Patterson recalls, however, that the inclusion of the manifesto was an accident. It was neither his nor Maciunas's intention to include it as a political act: "It was only [a] 'practical act', to dump a lot of excess paper!"[12] The fact that the allusion to politics was accidental is exemplary of the "gray area" that Patterson's performances produce. Politics for him was not an entirely uninvited consequence of the performance. In other words, there was no intention for it to be directly political—that is, an activist participation in a very specific political agenda. But it is interesting to note that even though the inclusion of the manifesto text may not have been intentional, its (or any other "accidental" event's) link to the performance cannot be discounted. This sense of legitimate belonging sans intention might be understood through the metaphor of the "echo," in which a primary sound reverberates against surfaces as it passes through space and time. In repetition, the echo is linked to the primary sound even though each reverberation has its own unique qualities and is changed by circumstances of the echo that the primary sound cannot control.

The differing reactions to Maciunas's manifesto display the wide range of Fluxus positions regarding politics. According to Higgins, artists, mostly the Americans, would not sign on to Maciunas's Fluxus manifesto because Marxist ideology (or any specific agenda-driven ideology, for that matter) was for them antithetical to the ideas of Fluxus. But artists such as Nam June Paik and Wolf Vostell were becoming more political, and Joseph Beuys offered his own manifesto at a 1963 Fluxus performance.[13]

For many, politics was implicit in avant-garde radicalism even if that politics was not specifically Marxist. Patterson comments:

First, remember, doing anything as radical as Fluxus at that time, was by definition, POLITICAL! Perhaps, I did or did not agree with all of the points of that, or later manifestos, which George M. produced. But, we were all in the LEFT and "anti-establishment". (Actually, "Paper Piece" was a direct reaction to the "establishment-sponsored" elitism of the "official" new music scene at that time [which was] principally, the clique of Stockhausen, Boulez (company) based in the electronic music studio

at West German Radio (WDR) in Cologne. I was trying to find a way for "ordinary people"—people without years of technical training—to have a direct "musical" experience. Thus, "Paper Piece", in itself, was already a "political statement"!)[14]

So within this context, Patterson's *Paper Piece* and other works, such as *The Clinic of Dr. Ben (BM, MS)* (1992); his famous and provocative *Lick Piece* (1964), in which he covered a nude woman's body with whipped cream and asked the audience to come onto the stage and lick it off; and *A Very Lawful Dance for Ennis*, discussed earlier, all raise interesting questions about representation and the role of political and social critique in Fluxus.

Hence, in comparison to that of artists such as Brecht and Watts, Patterson's work passively administers a powerful and wider social effect; we think about gender issues when experiencing *Lick Piece*, and we think about the reaction of the environment in *A Very Lawful Dance*. In *The Clinic of Dr. Ben*, we think about the ineptitude of bureaucracies as he collects useless statistical information. In addition to the antiestablishment politics of the performance, the work opens pathways to provocative insinuations about subjectivity, even though Patterson himself does not become a subject in his work but, as has been stated, maintains a type of distance by being the composer-conductor in the tradition of the musical performance.

This is important when thinking about the relationship of Patterson's practice to that of another young artist, Rodney McMillian. Again we can speak about the similarities and dissimilarities between their practices in order to reveal Patterson's importance to younger artists and the way that their work is received. Like Dave McKenzie, McMillian often examines popular cultural production. He attempts to inhabit the space and time of this production through a process of reconstructing or

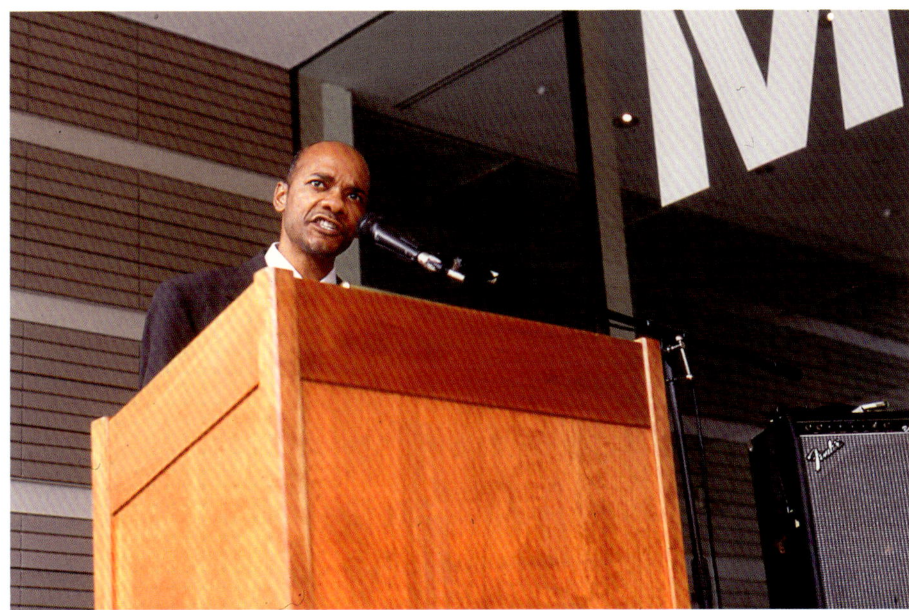

Rodney McMillian, *The Great Society*, 2006

recasting, using found objects and materials (in the case of his objects), or by "reliving" them (in the case of his performance work). Either way, his art transfers diachronic events into the synchronic present, thus allowing him to take possession of them within the space of his own subjectivity. In my view, McMillian believes that the cathartic experiences this produces double as a critique of these subjects, eliciting thoughts and feelings about them that are revelatory. Although this happens through the lens of his own subjectivity, the process can be extrapolated generally as an examination of the world at large rather than only an examination of his self.

One good example is McMillian's installation *Untitled (Unknown)* (2006). In this work he created an environment that loosely references classical architectural structures such as Greek or Roman temples, wrapping fifteen columns in fabric and placing them around a found bust of a man. McMillian uses the readymade to construct this mise-en-scène and by this action transfers a diachronic experience into a synchronic present. Found materials form the aesthetic and expressive language of this installation, thereby providing subjective markers that expand the subject of classical architecture to include the process by which it becomes subjectively experiential. For example, a reading of the column as an iconic object expands into one in which it becomes an agent of expressivity, particularly because of his use of materials, which contribute their own social references and visceral sensations to the reading of the object. Objects enter a space of existential struggle as the things and materials that form them are read as particular enunciative moments of the artist rather than simply material elements of the objects. This is classic expressionism, except that in McMillian's case it opens the door to social and political issues. The scene becomes psychological as all its parts form a synchronic pattern that is read as signs of expression in the same way that we read expression in faces.

This strategy of the readymade recalls Patterson's own interest in the idea of the event as a function of the present and in this manner locates the origin of this gesture in the avant-garde. But since synchronicity for McMillian produces subjectivity, this recasting of history into the present makes it possible for him to engage it as a subjective experience and, as Trinie Dalton correctly observes, creates the opportunity for his installations to "allude to his live performances."[15]

In a performance from 2006, for example, McMillian recited verbatim for more than two and a half hours Lyndon Johnson's 1968 "Great Society" speech. We can almost imagine him becoming the bust of the man from *Untitled (Unknown)*, now interpreted as a power icon. He performed it as an endurance work so that the exhaustion of his body would make the words from the past exist materially in the present. He did not anticipate that performing the work would result in an exhaustion that felt like, as he put it, "a little death." He recalled: "I finished the text as best I could and I exited the stage. . . . The next morning . . . I awoke [in] a state of shock, feeling like the biggest failure on earth . . . that I wasn't tough enough to actually see an idea through to fruition. I realized [later] that what I was citing as a failure was actually a learning experience."[16] McMillian realized that stopping the work was actually a good thing because the growing sense of "death" his exhaustion was producing was metaphorically attaching itself to the values of a speech that he actually admired. Stopping the performance halted that linkage. For McMillian, performing the speech, turning a historical artifact into a synchronic event, produced an experience that he could not have otherwise imagined. This conversion of time through performance led to a revelation. Because the performance was a work of art, his revelation became part of the subject of the work, to be experienced and interpreted by an audience.

The most obvious difference between McMillian and Patterson parallels the difference between McKenzie and Patterson: it lies in where they position themselves within the performance structure. Whereas Patterson's investment in the Fluxus event allows him to maintain a "distance" similar to that of a writer-director to a play or a composer-conductor to a musical score, McMillian, on the contrary, seeks to be completely invested psychologically and emotionally in the performance event, as his "Great Society" performance demonstrates. The domain of Patterson's investigation is the radical critique of bourgeois subjectivity, whereas the domain of McMillian's is his own subjectivity, something that for him seems to be a moving target rather than the fixed subjectivity that is the object of Patterson's challenge. Nevertheless, both artists share the idea of entering a domain of some sort through a radicalizing practice that leads to new or different understandings. And it is in this respect that Patterson is a very important figure for understanding the postmodern performance works of today.

Although McMillian's postmodern performance and Patterson's avant-garde performance operate within different domains, McMillian's use of performance as a means to engage ordinary experience, to reexamine his own subjectivity, to believe in the "performance event" as a radicalizing agent in this reexamination, are all possible because of the history of the avant-garde. Hence Patterson's commitment to rethinking the language of art becomes the formal means for both McMillian and McKenzie to rethink the language of culture, politics, and subjectivity. The gray area that Dick Higgins refers to in describing the effect of Patterson's performance work becomes a portal that allows postmodern artists to engage with their own subjectivity, found in ordinary events and used to widen the social, political, and poetic "gray matter" of representation.

NOTES

1. The term *gray matter* refers to neural tissue in the brain and spinal cord that controls and coordinates behavior, homeostasis, and mental functions such as cognition, memory, and learning.

2. Glenn Ligon, "Openings: Dave McKenzie," *Artforum* 44 (September 2005): 290.

3. David T. Doris, "Zen Vaudeville: A Medi(t)ation in the Margins of Fluxus," in *The Fluxus Reader*, ed. Ken Friedman (Chichester, England, and New York: Academy Editions, 1998), 95.

4. Brian Boucher, "Dave McKenzie, All Together Now," *Art in America* 96 (March 2008): 61.

5. Dick Higgins, *Postface* (New York: Something Else Press, 1964), 58. Higgins writes: "But Patterson, more than hardly any other composer, seems to understand that for a composer to divide activities into musical and non-musical, what-I-do and what-I-do-not-do is to accept the dualism of good and evil, of black and white, and, ultimately, to place one's work on a level of purely theoretical relevance. Patterson goes for the grey, and he seems to accept, even to encourage, the non-memorable, disappearing aspect of his work."

6. Sharon Mizota, "When Art and Life Converge, the Result Is Anything but Ordinary," *Los Angeles Times*, April 18, 2008.

7. Higgins, *Postface*, 59.

8. Ina Conzen, "From Manager of the Avant-garde to Fluxus Performer: George Maciunas in Germany," in *A Long Tale with Many Knots: Fluxus in Germany, 1962–1994*, ed. René Block and Gabriele Knapstein (Berlin: Institut für Auslandbeziehungen, 1995), 21.

9. Quoted in Higgins, *Postface*, 51.

10. Owen Smith, "Developing a Fluxable Forum: Early Performance and Publishing," in Friedman, *Fluxus Reader*, 3.

11. Conzen, "From Manager of the Avant-garde," 20.

12. Benjamin Patterson, e-mail correspondence with the author, January 29, 2009. He added, "The paper thrown into the audience was, basically, the 'left-overs' from the piles of paper that we (the performers on stage) had been using as 'musical instruments.' That some sheets of paper were imprinted with Maciunas's Fluxus manifesto was purely accidental!"

13. Conzen, "From Manager of the Avant-garde," 24.

14. Benjamin Patterson, e-mail correspondence with the author, January 29, 2009.

15. Trinie Dalton, "Rodney McMillian," in *Whitney Biennial 2008* (New York: Whitney Museum of American Art, 2008), 178.

16. Rodney McMillian, unpublished notes, 2008.

Works in the Exhibition

Methods and Processes: Action Poems, Instructions, and Books

ABC's, c. 1961
Children's coloring book, ink, crayon, collage
13 × 10¼ × ¹³⁄₁₆ inches
Getty Research Institute, Los Angeles

Prints and Comments (Prints, Lourdes Castro; Comments, Benjamin Patterson), 1962
Handmade paper, vellum, ink
10¹⁄₁₆ × 8⅞ × ⁹⁄₁₆ inches
10⅝ × 9 × ¹³⁄₁₆ inches
Getty Research Institute, Los Angeles

Puzzle-Poems, 1962
Collage on card, metal box
Box: ⁹⁄₁₆ × 3⁷⁄₁₆ × 3⁵⁄₁₆ inches
Puzzle-poem: 5⁹⁄₁₆ × 4¹⁵⁄₁₆ inches
The Museum of Modern Art, New York; The Gilbert and Lila Silverman Fluxus Collection Gift

Puzzle-Poems, 1962
Collage on card, wooden box (recto/verso)
Wooden box: 5¾ × 2¾ × 1½ inches
5-piece puzzle poem: 6 × 5 inches
Courtesy the artist

Puzzle-Poems, 1962
Collage on card, wooden box (recto/verso)
Wooden box: 8 × 2½ × 1¾ inches
3-piece puzzle poem: 5½ × 4 inches
Courtesy the artist

Untitled (A Case for Bombing Pause), c. 1962
Spiral-bound notebook, ink, crayon, collage
11½ × 8½ inches
Getty Research Institute, Los Angeles

A Volume of Collected Poems: Volume 1, Poem 2, 1962
Collage on card, yogurt cups, plastic bag
Plastic bag: 14⅝ × 9⅞ inches
Card: 3¾ × 8⅝ inches
Apricot: 3¹⁄₁₆ × 2⁷⁄₁₆ inches
Bananas: 3¹⁄₁₆ × 2⁷⁄₁₆ inches
Citron: 3¹⁄₁₆ × 2⁷⁄₁₆ inches
Framboise: 3¹⁄₁₆ × 2⁷⁄₁₆ inches
The Museum of Modern Art, New York; The Gilbert and Lila Silverman Fluxus Collection Gift

A Volume of Collected Poems: Volume 5, Poems 20, 21, 22, 23 and 24, 25, 1962
Collage on card, paper and linen boxes, plastic bag
Plastic bag: 14½ × 9⅞ inches
Card: 3¾ × 8⁹⁄₁₆ inches
Linen box: 2¹³⁄₁₆ × 11⅛ × 2⅞ inches
8-piece puzzle-poem: 17¹⁵⁄₁₆ × 8⁹⁄₁₆ inches
Matchbox: 16 × 2¹⁵⁄₁₆ × 4⁵⁄₁₆ inches
15-piece puzzle poem: 12⅜ × 6⁹⁄₁₆ inches
The Museum of Modern Art, New York; The Gilbert and Lila Silverman Fluxus Collection Gift

A Volume of Collected Poems: Volume 7, Poems 32, 33, 34, 44 and 36, 37, 1962
Collage on card, paper boxes, plastic bag
Plastic bag: 14¹¹⁄₁₆ × 9⅞ inches
Card: 3¾ × 8⁹⁄₁₆ inches
Tobler chocolate box: 1⅛ × 7½ × 3¹¹⁄₁₆ inches
9-piece puzzle-poem: 20¹³⁄₁₆ × 6⁹⁄₁₆ inches
Tuberculine Purifiée box: 1 × 6³⁄₁₆ × 4¾ inches
12-piece puzzle-poem: 21³⁄₁₆ × 7³⁄₁₆ inches
The Museum of Modern Art, New York; The Gilbert and Lila Silverman Fluxus Collection Gift

Regimental History: Fragments (for Jackson Mac Low), c. 1962–63
Ink on paper
11 × 8¹⁄₁₆ inches
Getty Research Institute, Los Angeles

Untitled (who taught you to think like that?), c. 1962–63
Printed ink on paper
11 × 8⁹⁄₁₆ inches
Getty Research Institute, Los Angeles

A Game: Three Capacities and One Inhibition, c. 1963
Index cards, collage, stamped ink, marker
4 index cards, 3 × 5 inches each
Envelope: 3⅝ × 6⁷⁄₁₆ inches
The Museum of Modern Art, New York; The Gilbert and Lila Silverman Fluxus Collection Gift

Notes: Instructions for the use of a new musical instrument, c. 1963
Typed ink on paper
2 pages, 10⁹⁄₁₆ × 8¼ inches each
Getty Research Institute, Los Angeles

A Study, 1963
Carbon copy on onionskin paper
2 pages, 11 × 8⁹⁄₁₆ inches each
Getty Research Institute, Los Angeles

Untitled (Dixie Beer), 1963
Typed ink and collage on index card
3 × 5 inches
Staatsgalerie Stuttgart, Hanns Sohm Archive

Untitled (Goldwater Can't Win), c. 1963
Typed ink and collage on card stock
7 × 7 inches
Staatsgalerie Stuttgart, Hanns Sohm Archive

Untitled (If You Think This Is a Dream), c. 1963
Typed ink and collage on paper
7½ × 6 inches
Staatsgalerie Stuttgart, Hanns Sohm Archive

Untitled (Sorry I Missed It), 1963
Paper collage, ink, envelope
2 pages, 11½ × 9 inches each
Envelope: 4½ × 9½ inches
Staatsgalerie Stuttgart, Hanns Sohm Archive

Watch Me, c. 1963
Stencil and marker on index card
3 cards, 2¹⁵⁄₁₆ × 4¹⁵⁄₁₆ inches each
Getty Research Institute, Los Angeles

What else is necessary?, 1963–64
Ink on index card, envelope
5 cards, 3 × 4¹⁵⁄₁₆ inches each
Envelope: 3⅝ × 6⁹⁄₁₆ inches
Getty Research Institute, Los Angeles

Instruction No. 1 (Now, Later), 1964
Ink and rubber stamp on construction paper
37⅝ × 26¾ inches (frame)
30¹¹⁄₁₆ × 20¼ inches (sheet)
The Museum of Modern Art, New York; The Gilbert and
Lila Silverman Fluxus Collection Gift

Instruction No. 1 (Steps 1–4), 1964
Ink and rubber stamp on construction paper
37⅝ × 26¾ inches (frame)
30¹¹⁄₁₆ × 20¹⁄₁₆ inches (sheet)
The Museum of Modern Art, New York; The Gilbert and
Lila Silverman Fluxus Collection Gift

Instruction No. 1 (Steps 1–12), 1964
Ink and rubber stamp on construction paper
37⅝ × 26¾ inches (frame)
30¹¹⁄₁₆ × 20¹⁄₁₆ inches (sheet)
The Museum of Modern Art, New York; The Gilbert and
Lila Silverman Fluxus Collection Gift

Instruction No. 2 (Please Wash Your Face), 1964
Fluxus Edition box
Plastic box, guest soap, paper hand towel with stamped
ink
Box: ½ × 3¹⁵⁄₁₆ × 4¹¹⁄₁₆ inches
Unfolded towel: 16¾ × 4⁷⁄₁₆ inches
Soap: ¼ × 1¹³⁄₁₆ inches
The Museum of Modern Art, New York; The Gilbert and
Lila Silverman Fluxus Collection Gift

Puzzle-Poem, 1964
Collage on board, plastic bag
Bag: 14¹¹⁄₁₆ × 9⅞ inches
Puzzle-poem: 14⁹⁄₁₆ × 10¹⁄₁₆ inches
Getty Research Institute, Los Angeles

Untitled (Scott Tissue), c. 1964
Photocopy paper collage
9½ × 14 inches
Staatsgalerie Stuttgart, Hanns Sohm Archive

It's Vital, 1965
Ink on index card, envelope
3 cards, 2¹⁵⁄₁₆ × 4⅞ inches each
Wrapper: 3⅛ × 2¾ inches
Envelope: 3¾ × 6½ inches
Getty Research Institute, Los Angeles

Speed of Light, 1965
Metal scale, marker, bulb, mixed media
12½ × 7½ × 3¼ inches
Collection Caterina Gualco, Genoa, Italy

*Untitled (Introductory Note . . . In Skinnerian Learning
Theory)*, 1965
Ink and colored pencil on index card, envelope
6 cards, 8 × 5 inches each
Envelope: 5¹¹⁄₁₆ × 8⁹⁄₁₆ × ¹¹⁄₁₆ inches
Getty Research Institute, Los Angeles

Untitled (Is Are What), 1966
Ink on paper
8 × 5 inches
Staatsgalerie Stuttgart, Hanns Sohm Archive

Valigetta, 1966
Box, antique glass bulbs, cut photo negatives, gloves, ink
6 × 8 × 3½ inches
Collection Caterina Gualco, Genoa, Italy

The Book of Genesis, 1969
Leather antique photo book, photographs, ink
6 × 4½ × 2½ inches
Collection Enzo Gazzerro, Genoa, Italy

Joyce and Eugene, 1973
Aluminum box, found autograph books, paper, ink
5½ × 12 × 2½ inches
Collection Marcel and David Fleiss, Galerie 1900–2000,
Paris

Aphrodisiacs, 1990
Cloth boxes, accordion book with text, bottles
Box 1: 13 × 3½ × 1 inches
Box 2: 8¾ × 3 × 2 inches
Collection Caterina Gualco, Genoa, Italy

How to Make Sushi, 2001
Wooden box, plastic sardine, knife, mixed media
8¼ × 25 × 4 inches
Collection Marc Schultz, Hanover, Germany

My Grand 70th Birthday Tour, 2003
Ink on paper, plastic, mixed media
5 × 14 inches
Courtesy the artist

Concrete Poem No. 6, 2005
Wooden box, concrete, marker, violin fragment, mixed
media
10 × 15½ × 4 inches
Courtesy the artist

Thank you, Luigi, 2005
Wooden box, vintage children's blocks, easel, mixed media
Book: 6 × 9½ × 2 inches
Easel: 17 × 5½ inches
Collection Bertrand Clavez, Paris

The Therapeutic: One Hundred Actions Poems, Volume A,
2009
Collage and ink on paper
28 pages, 11⅝ × 8¼ inches each
Courtesy the artist

Necessary Objects: Paintings, Sculptures, and Installations

Helmut, 1975
Buoy, bread board, handsaw, mixed media
32⅜ × 18 × 5⅞ inches
Courtesy Galerie Schüppenhauer, Cologne

Trout Bag, 1981
Canvas satchel, metal sinkers, fishing license, 10 altered
fishing lures in plastic boxes
Canvas satchel: 9¹¹⁄₁₆ × 7⅞ × 6½ inches
10 plastic boxes, 4³⁄₁₆ × 2¼ × 2¼ inches each
Watt's Pachyderm lure: 2⁹⁄₁₆ × 2¹⁵⁄₁₆ × 4⁵⁄₁₆ inches
Green Caddis lure: 3⅜ × 2⅝ × 3⅛ inches
Brown Stonefly lure: 1¼ × 1⁹⁄₁₆ × 2¹³⁄₁₆ inches
Yellow Paumgartner lure: 1¼ × 2½ × 2¾ inches
Deerfly lure: 2½ × 2⁷⁄₁₆ × 3⁹⁄₁₆ inches
June Nymph lure: 3¹⁵⁄₁₆ × 1⅞ × 5⅛ inches
Pink Ghost lure: 1¾ × 2⅝ × 3 inches
Royal Coachmen lure: 1⁷⁄₁₆ × 3¹⁄₁₆ × 2⁷⁄₁₆ inches
Wooly Bomber lure: 1⁵⁄₁₆ × 4⁷⁄₁₆ × 2¹¹⁄₁₆ inches
Rainbow Hopper lure: ⅜ × 3⁷⁄₁₆ × 4¹¹⁄₁₆ inches
The Museum of Modern Art, New York; The Gilbert and
Lila Silverman Fluxus Collection Gift

Candyland, 1988
Board games, toys, mixed media on wooden shelves,
brackets
40 × 36 × 14 inches
Courtesy the artist

Hell on Wheels, 1988
Wooden desk, plastic, cloth, steel
36 × 40 × 24 inches
Collection Heinrich Riskin, Bad Rothenfelde, Germany

It's a Nice Piece of Cake, 1988
Metal bakery display rack, traffic sign, decorative cake
toppers
55¼ × 24½ × 16¾ inches overall
Collection Marcel and David Fleiss, Galerie 1900–2000,
Paris

Old Chinese Proverb, 1988
Antique Chautauqua industrial art desk on stand, mixed
media
34 × 23 × 3 inches
Collection Klaus Fehlemann, Dortmund, Germany

Old Latin Proverb, 1988
Antique Chautauqua industrial art desk, mixed media
34 × 23 × 3 inches
Courtesy the artist and Galerie Schüppenhauer, Cologne

Smoker's Rights, 1988
Antique bottle rack, tape, cigarettes
27½ × 16 × 16 inches
Courtesy the artist

Double Your Pleasure, 1990
Poster mounted on plywood, mixed media
26 × 24 × 2 inches
Collection Enzo Cattelani, Modena, Italy

Pan Am, 1990
Poster mounted on plywood, mixed media
26 × 24½ × 3⅞ inches
Collection Enzo Cattelani, Modena, Italy

Pregnant?, 1990
Poster mounted on plywood, mixed media
25⅛ × 17¾ × 6 inches
Collection Enzo Cattelani, Modena, Italy

Say Your Prayers, 1990
Poster mounted on plywood, mixed media
38¼ × 25¼ × 3½ inches
Collection Enzo Cattelani, Modena, Italy

Show Off Your Skin, 1990
Collage paper and painted canvas mounted on wood,
mixed media
32 × 48 × 6 inches
Collection Heinrich Risken, Bad Rothenfelde, Germany

Small Beer, 1990
Poster mounted on plywood, mixed media
54 × 36 × 1¼ inches
Collection Enzo Cattelani, Modena, Italy

Un tipo suave, 1990
Poster mounted on plywood, mixed media
26 × 24 × 2 inches
Collection Enzo Cattelani, Modena, Italy

Untitled, 1990
Collage fabric and painted canvas mounted on wood
24¼ × 24⅜ × 1½ inches
Courtesy the artist and the Emily Harvey Foundation, New
York/Venice

Fluxus Protected, 1991
Wood and metal boxes, cloth, chain, mixed media
7⅞ × 10¾ × 5¼ inches
Collection Enzo Cattelani, Modena, Italy

Marble Hat, 1991
Cut Carrara marble
12 × 24 × 10 inches
Courtesy the artist

The Temptations, 1991
Wood, mixed media
66⅜ × 40 × 9¼ inches
Collection Carlo Cattelani, Modena, Italy

Two for Violin after Nam June Paik's One for Violin, 1991
Broken violin, wood cabinet door, music box
31 × 19 × 4 inches
Courtesy Galerie Schüppenhauer, Cologne

Early Chess, 1992
Wooden table, mixed media
29 × 25¼ × 24 inches
Collection Carlo Cattelani, Modena, Italy

Uncle Ben's Art Shoppe, 1992
Toy-dispensing machine, plastic containers, mixed media
19 × 10 × 9⅝ inches
Courtesy the artist

A Short History of Twentieth-Century Art, 1994
Mixed media on wood panels
5 parts, 11 × 14 × 3 inches each
Institut für Auslandsbeziehungen e.V., Stuttgart, Germany

Il primo segreto della grappa, 1994
Handblown glass bottle
11½ × 2⅞ inches
Collection Archivo Bonotto, Molvena, Italy

Museum of the Subconscious (Namibia, guidelines and ephemera), 1996
Metal plaque, wooden box, mixed media
Plaque: 11 × 14 inches
Box: 12⅝ × 12⅝ × 1⅜ inches
Courtesy the artist

Blame It on Pittsburgh; or, Why I Became an Artist, 1997
Silk screen on Plexiglas
18 panels, 59 × 39 × ¼ inches each
Courtesy the artist

Trains of Thought (Franz Liszt), 1997
Discarded train sign, wooden boxes, cassette tape player, audiocassette, mixed media
72 × 12 × 3½ inches
Courtesy the artist

Trains of Thought (Josef Hayden), 1997
Discarded train sign, wooden boxes, cassette tape player, audiocassette, mixed media
72 × 12 × 3½ inches
Courtesy the artist

Trains of Thought (Maurice Ravel), 1997
Discarded train sign, wooden boxes, cassette tape player, audiocassette, mixed media
72 × 12 × 3½ inches
Collection Elfi Kreiter, Wiesbaden, Germany

Trains of Thought (Verdi), 1997
Discarded train sign, wooden boxes, cassette tape player, audiocassette, mixed media
72 × 12 × 3½ inches
Collection Elfi Kreiter, Wiesbaden, Germany

Kohler Koffer, 1999
Leather briefcase, ink on paper, offset on paper, mixed media
14 × 11½ × 2 inches
Courtesy the artist

Cello (Blue), 2003
Wooden push broom, birdhouse, metal strings, wooden spoon
53⁵⁄₁₆ × 10 × 5 inches
Courtesy the artist

Cello (Red), 2003
Wooden push broom, birdhouse, metal strings, wooden spoon
53½ × 10 × 5 inches
Courtesy the artist

Fluxus Constellation, 2003
Silk screen on nylon, glass sconces, electrical system, tube lights
34 sconces, 23¾ × 8 × 2½ inches each
Dimensions variable
Museo d'arte contemporanea di Villa Croce, Genoa, Italy

It Was Roses All the Way (My Grand 70th Birthday Tour), 2004
Metal time-card machine, ink and marker on time cards, artificial flowers, Plexiglas
40 × 20 × 10 inches
Collection Archivo Bonotto, Molvena, Italy

Ski Poles (from Climbing Mt. Fuji), 2004
Broom handles, rubber plungers
60 × 6 × 1 inches
Courtesy the artist

Industrial Chic (a.p.), 2007
Cast silver toy tools, velvet jewelry boxes
6 parts, 3 × 2 × ½ inches each
Courtesy the artist

A Nose for Wine, 2008
Wine bottles with cast molding
12 bottles, 11½ × 2⅞ inches each
Collection Archivo Bonotto, Molvena, Italy

Galerie Légitime, 2009
Leather valise, paper, wooden cheese box, DVD
6 × 18 × 6 inches
Collection Jean-Louis Grobel, Paris

Effigy for Dick Higgins II, 2010
Effigy: paper jumpsuit, costume hat, mask, collage, mixed media
Base: collage on wood, dice, light, turntable
Effigy: 70 × 20 × 7 inches
Base: 21 × 20 × 1¾ inches
Courtesy the artist

Flying Bass II, 2010
Double bass, metallic ink, metal propane burners, mixed media
70 × 36 × 12 inches
Courtesy the artist

The Museum of the Subconscious—Houston Annex, 2010
Plastic, wood, paint, mixed media
Museum: 20 × 10 inches diameter
Hanging armature: 108 × 24 × 32 inches
Courtesy the artist

Sit Down, 2010
Pantone injection-molded plastic chair, metal rod with stuffed bear, recorder
Chair: 35¼ × 19¾ × 23½ inches
39½ × 39¾ × 23½ inches overall
Courtesy the artist

Swiss Symphony II, 2010
Wooden wall clock, collage on board, crossbow, mixed media
60 × 16½ × 5 inches
Courtesy the artist

Scores

Paper Piece, 1960
Ink on paper, envelope
8¾ × 6⅞ inches
The Museum of Modern Art, New York; The Gilbert and
Lila Silverman Fluxus Collection Gift

Papierstück für fünf Spieler, from *Ich bin schön*, 1960
Ink on paper
11 × 8⅛ inches
Getty Research Institute, Los Angeles

"Situations" for Three Pianos, 1960
Ink on composition paper
2 pages, 11 × 8¼ inches each
Getty Research Institute, Los Angeles

String Music, 1960
Ink on watercolor paper
Instructions: 10¹³⁄₁₅ × 16 inches
Graphic score, page 1: 10¹³⁄₁₆ × 16 inches
Graphic score, page 2: 11¹³⁄₁₄ × 15¹¹⁄₁₆ inches
Graphic score, page 3: 10¹³⁄₁₆ × 16 inches
Getty Research Institute, Los Angeles

From *String Music for Double Bass(es)*, 1960
Ink on paper
10¾ × 16¹⁄₁₆ inches
Getty Research Institute, Los Angeles

Ants, 1960–62
Ink on paper, black-and-white photographs
Photograph: 8⅛ × 11¾ inches
Photograph: 8¼ × 11¾ inches
Sheet: 10¹⁵⁄₁₆ × 7¾ inches
Getty Research Institute, Los Angeles

Composition for Any Situation, 1961
Ink on paper
8¼ × 8¼ inches
Getty Research Institute, Los Angeles

Décollage Piece for Wolf Vostell, 1961
Ink on paper and vellum
Title page: 11 × 8⅞ inches
Instructions: 10⁹⁄₁₆ × 8¼ inches
Score, page 1: 6⁷⁄₁₆ × 6¼ inches
Score, page 2: 6¼ × 6⅞ inches
Score, page 3: 6⅞ × 6⅜ inches
Score, page 4: 8¹¹⁄₁₆ × 8⁹⁄₁₆ inches
Getty Research Institute, Los Angeles

A Disturbing Composition, 1961
Typed ink on paper
10⅝ × 7¹³⁄₁₆ inches
Getty Research Institute, Los Angeles

Duo for Voice and a String Instrument, 1961
Black and colored ink on paper and transparency
Instructions: 2 pages, 11¹¹⁄₁₆ × 8¼ inches each
Transparency: 11⅝ × 4⅝ inches
Transparency: 11⅝ × 8¼ inches
Transparency: 11⅝ × 8¼ inches
Paper: 11⅝ × 8¼ inches
Getty Research Institute, Los Angeles

Lemons, 1961
Ink on paper
2 pages, 10⁹⁄₁₆ × 8¼ inches each
Getty Research Institute, Los Angeles

Overture, Overture (Versions II and III), 1961
Ink on paper
10⁹⁄₁₆ × 8¼ inches
Getty Research Institute, Los Angeles

Portrait of an Egg, 1961
Ink on paper
10⁹⁄₁₆ × 8³⁄₁₆ inches
Getty Research Institute, Los Angeles

Septet from Lemons, 1961
Ink on paper
11 × 8 inches
Getty Research Institute, Los Angeles

Décollage Piece for Wolf Vostell
(handwritten iteration), 1961
Typed and colored ink on paper (verso/recto)
10⅞ × 11 inches
Getty Research Institute, Los Angeles

Pavane for Flutes, 1961–62
Ink on paper
11 × 8⅛ inches
Getty Research Institute, Los Angeles

Variations for Double Bass, 1961–62
Ink on paper
5 pages, 11 × 8¼ inches each
Getty Research Institute, Los Angeles

Methods and Processes, 1962
Printed ink on paper
10¹¹⁄₁₆ × 7⅜ × ¹⁄₁₆ inches
Getty Research Institute, Los Angeles

Methods and Processes (with sender's note), 1962
Printed ink on paper
10¹¹⁄₁₆ × 7⅜ × ¹⁄₁₆ inches
Getty Research Institute, Los Angeles

Pond, 1962
Ink on paper
2 pages, 10⁹⁄₁₆ × 8³⁄₁₆ inches each
Getty Research Institute, Los Angeles

*Two Dances: "Solo for Dancer" and "A Very Lawful Dance
for Ennis,"* 1962
Ink on paper
3 pages, 11 × 8 inches each
Getty Research Institute, Los Angeles

Untitled (handwritten iteration of *Variations for Double
Bass*), c. 1962
Ink on poster for Fluxus internationale Festspiele neuester
Musik
16½ × 11¾ inches (unfolded); 5⅞ × 8¼ inches (folded)
Getty Research Institute, Los Angeles

A Biting Piece (for Pyla), 1963
Ink on paper
13 × 8½ inches
Getty Research Institute, Los Angeles

Tour, 1963
Ink on paper
11 × 7⅞ inches
Getty Research Institute, Los Angeles

Untitled (You are standing, perhaps drinking), c. 1963
Ink on paper
13¹⁄₁₆ × 8¼ inches
Getty Research Institute, Los Angeles

Symphony No. 1 & 7, 1963–89
Ink on paper
4 pages, 5⅛ × 11⅝ inches each
Envelope: 5⅞ × 12 inches
Courtesy the artist

First Symphony, 1964
Ink on paper
10½ × 16¹⁄₁₆ inches
Getty Research Institute, Los Angeles

Three Ways to a Tape, 1966
Ink on paper
14¹⁵⁄₁₆ × 10 inches
Getty Research Institute, Los Angeles

Das Bahnhof Requiem, 1995
Ink and collage on paper
Instructions: 2 pages, 11½ × 8⅛ inches each
Score: 4 pages, 10½ × 15½ inches each
Courtesy the artist

Learning by Doing, c. 1996
Ink on paper
11⅝ × 8¼ inches
Courtesy the artist

The Three Operas, 1997
Ink on paper
5 pages, 11⅝ × 8¼ inches each
Courtesy the artist

World Weather, 1997
Spiral-bound music composition notebook, ink and colored markers on paper, world map
11⅝ × 8¼ inches
Courtesy the artist

Benjamin Patterson: "The Black and White File": A Primary Collection of Scores and Instructions for His Music, Events, Operas, Performances and Other Projects: 1958–1998, 1999
Photostat paper in black binder
12½ × 11⁷⁄₁₆ × 1⅞ inches
Courtesy the artist

File includes the following scores and actions:
Paper Piece, 1960
Ants, 1960–62
Duo for Voice and a String Instrument, 1961
Lemons, 1961
Overture, Overture (Versions II and III), 1961
Septet from Lemons, 1961
Pavane for Flutes, 1961–62
Variations for Double Bass, 1961–62
Pond, 1962
Portrait of an Egg, 1962
Sneak Peek, 1962
Solo for Dancer, 1962
A Very Lawful Dance for Ennis, 1962
A Biting Piece for Pyla, 1963
Examination, 1963
First Symphony, 1964
How the Average Person Thinks about Art, 1983 (4 pages)
I Visited the U.S.A., 1987
Artists' Greeting, 1988 (5 pages)
Critical Encounters, 1988
Signature No. 1, 1990
Signature No. 2, 1991
Bolero, 1994
Das Bahnhof Requiem, 1995 (7 pages)

On the Road with Al . . . a Gedächtnisperformance für Al Hansen, 1996 (2 pages)
A Simple Opera, 1996 (7 pages)
The Future Makes Progress, 1997 (7 pages)
Some "Found Objects"—Quotations—Recently Discovered by Benjamin Patterson, 1997
The Three Operas, 1997 (*Carmen*, 1990; *Madame Butterfly*, 1993 [2 pages]; *Tristan und Isolde*, 1961–93)
World Weather, 1997
The Creation of the World, 1998 (3 pages)
How to Make Art: Benjamin Patterson's Foolproof Methods, 1998

Digging, 2000
Ink on paper
4 sheets, 10⅝ × 8⅛ inches each
Courtesy the artist

A Simple Opera, 2001
Ink and collage on paper
11⅝ × 8¼ inches
Courtesy the artist

My Tone, Your Tone, His Tone, Her Tone, 2005
Ink on white and colored paper
6 pages, 11⅝ × 8¼ inches each
Courtesy the artist

A Fluxus Elegy (Audiovisual Performance), c. 2006
Ink on paper
7⅞ × 11⅞ inches
Courtesy the artist

Ants Revisited, 2010
Ink on paper
3 pages, 11⅞ × 16½ inches each
Courtesy the artist

Duo for Voice and a String Instrument Arranged for Voice and String Quintet, 2010
Ink on paper
Instructions: 11¾ × 8¼ inches (folded), 11¾ × 24⅞ inches (unfolded)
Score (16 pages): 8¼ × 11¾ inches (folded), 8¾ × 23¼ inches (unfolded)
Courtesy the artist

Give Me a Break, 2010
Ink on paper
12 pages, 16⅜ × 11½ inches each
Envelope: 17½ × 12¾ inches
Courtesy the artist

Documentation of Performances, Actions, and Happenings

Performance documentation for *Paper Piece*, 1960
Performed by audience at Hypokriterion Theater, Amsterdam, June 23, 1963
Gelatin silver print (photograph by Oscar van Arpken)
7⅞ × 11 inches (unframed)
20 × 17 inches (framed)
Collection Archivo Bonotto, Molvena

Performance documentation for *Décollage Piece for Wolf Vostell*, 1961
Black-and-white photograph
8 × 11 inches
Photographer unknown
Getty Research Institute, Los Angeles

Performance documentation/brochure for *Lemons: Benjamin Patterson*, 1961
Offset on paper
8⁷⁄₁₆ × 27¼ inches (unfolded)
Getty Research Institute, Los Angeles

Performance documentation for *Variations for Double Bass*, 1961
Performed by the artist at Kleines Sommerfest/Après John Cage, Galerie Parnass, Wuppertal, Germany, June 9, 1962
Gelatin silver prints (photographs by Rolf Jährling)
2 prints, 9¹⁵⁄₁₆ × 7¹⁵⁄₁₆ inches each
2 prints, 13¾ × 10⅞ inches each
The Museum of Modern Art, New York; The Gilbert and Lila Silverman Fluxus Collection Gift

Performance documentation for *Variations for Double Bass*, 1961
Performed by artist at Happenings and Fluxus concert event, École Nationale des Beaux-Arts, Paris, June 8, 1989
Gelatin silver print (photograph by Francesco Conz)
8 × 10 inches
Courtesy the artist

Performance documentation for *Wolf Vostell: Decollages, Collages, Ausstellung 15.5–28.5.1961*, 1961
Offset on paper, mounted on paper
8¼ × 5¾ inches (sheet)
10⁹⁄₁₆ × 8¼ inches (mount)
Courtesy the artist

Performance documentation for *Duo for Voice and a String Instrument*, 1962
Performed by artist and William Pearson at Kleines Sommerfest/Après John Cage, Galerie Parnass, Wuppertal, Germany, June 9, 1962
Gelatin silver prints (photographs possibly by Rolf Jährling)
2 prints, 5 × 3½ inches each
1 print, 9¼ × 7 inches
The Museum of Modern Art, New York; The Gilbert and Lila Silverman Fluxus Collection Gift

Performance documentation for *Lick Piece*, 1962
Performed by Letty Eisenhauer and unidentified individual at Fully Guaranteed 12 Fluxus Concerts, Canal Street, New York, May 9, 1964
Gelatin silver prints (photographs by Peter Moore)
9³⁄₁₆ × 6⁵⁄₁₆ inches; 18¹¹⁄₁₆ × 14¹¹⁄₁₆ × 1½ inches (framed)
7⅝ × 9½ inches; 14¹¹⁄₁₆ × 18¹¹⁄₁₆ × 1½ inches (framed)
9½ × 6⁵⁄₁₆ inches; 18¹¹⁄₁₆ × 14¹¹⁄₁₆ × 1½ inches (framed)
The Museum of Modern Art, New York; The Gilbert and Lila Silverman Fluxus Collection Gift

Performance documentation/brochure for *Sneak Peek: Fluxus, Happenings, Environments, Poems, Dances, Compositions at Galerie Girardon*, 1962
Offset on paper with ink and postage stamp
7⅞ × 18⁷⁄₁₆ inches (unfolded)
The Museum of Modern Art, New York; The Gilbert and Lila Silverman Fluxus Collection Gift

Program for Kleines Sommerfest, June 9, 1962
Offset on paper
5½ × 8 inches (unfolded)
Courtesy the artist

Program for Neo-Dada in der Musik, June 16, 1962
Offset on paper
7 × 8 inches (folded)
7 × 16 inches (unfolded)
Collection Archivo Bonotto, Molvena, Italy

Patterson and unidentified person performing Yoko Ono's *String Music for Jesus*
Patterson performing Nam June Paik's *One for Violin* (1962) with Peter Kotik of SEM Ensemble, New York, Akademie der bildenden Kunst, Vienna, June 1989
Black-and-white photographs (by Wolfgang Träger)
7 × 5 inches each
Courtesy the artist

Patterson performing *Variations for Double Bass* as part of the concert event Happenings and Fluxus, Ecole Nationale des Beaux-Arts, with an exhibition at Galerie 1900–2000, Paris, August 8–29, 1989
Color photograph (by Francesco Conz)
8 × 10 inches
Courtesy the artist

Patterson performing *The Clinic of Dr. Ben (BM, MS)* as
part of the anniversary exhibition *Fluxus Da Capo* at Villa
Clementine, Wiesbaden, Germany, 1992
Color photograph and business card (photographer
unknown)
Photograph: 16 × 12 inches
Card: 2½ × 3 inches
Courtesy the artist

Patterson and unidentified performer in *Tristan and Isolde*,
Royal Danish Academy of Fine Arts, November 17, 1993
Gelatin silver print (photograph by Morten Langkilde)
4¾ × 7 inches
Courtesy the artist

Patterson at dedication ceremony for the *Museum of the
Subconscious* in Namibia, 1996
Color photograph (by Francesco Conz)
12 × 8 inches
Courtesy the artist

Patterson performing *The Creation of the World*,
OFKunstraum, Offenbach, Germany, May 29, 1998
Black-and-white photograph (photographer unknown)
9½ × 12 inches
Courtesy the artist

Patterson performing *A Clean Slate* at Haus der Deutschen
Ensemble Akademie, Frankfurt, December 16, 2001
Gelatin silver print (photograph by Elfi Kreiter)
12 × 8 inches
Courtesy Elfi Kreiter, Wiesbaden, Germany

Video Documentation

Performance documentation for *Variations for Double
Bass*, 1962
Performed at Fluxus Internationale Festspiele neuester
Musik
Video transferred to digital video
6 minutes (excerpt)
Courtesy the artist

Fluxus Films, 1992, with live music composed and
performed by Benjamin Patterson and Joe Jones at the
Caligari Theater, Wiesbaden, Germany, September 13, 1992
Digital video
100 minutes
Courtesy the artist

Bolero, 1995
Performed at Konzertsaal der Stadt Gera, Gera, Germany,
May 13, 1995
Digital video
22 minutes
Courtesy the artist

Performance documentation for Dedication Ceremony for
the Museum of the Subconscious (Tel Aviv Annex), 1999
Dedication of the museum annex on Jerusalem Beach, July
13, 1999
Digital video
23 minutes
Courtesy the artist

Performance documentation for *Clean Slate*, 2002
Performed at Kasseler Kunstverein, Kassel, Germany, on
October 5–6, 2002
Video transferred to digital video
7 minutes (loop)
Courtesy the artist

Creation of the World, 2003
Performed at the Goethe Institute, Madrid, February 6,
2003
Digital video
25 minutes
Courtesy the artist

Galerie Légitime: A Reenactment, 2009
Performed by Benjamin Patterson and Bertrand Clavez in
the streets of Paris, June 7, 2009
Digital video
15 minutes
Courtesy Bertrand Clavez, Paris

Ephemera: Notes from Fluxus/Notes from an Ordinary Life

Photograph from the Contre Music Festival, 1960, showing
the artist performing with John Cage, Nam June Paik,
Christian Wolff, Hans Helms, Sylvano Bussotti, David Tudor,
and Cornelius Cardew
Black-and-white photograph (by Klaus Barisch)
7⅞ × 10⅝ inches
Courtesy Galerie Schüppenhauer and Mary Bauermeister,
Cologne

For Ben: D-bass and piano, Madrid 1960, 1960
Score composed by Juan Hildago
Ink on paper, ink on printed staff paper
2 pages, 10¾ × 8⅜ inches each
8¹¹⁄₁₆ × 9¹¹⁄₁₆ inches (folded); 8¹¹⁄₁₆ × 19⁷⁄₁₆ inches (unfolded)
Getty Research Institute, Los Angeles

Ich bin schön, 1960
Offset on paper (artists' magazine)
12 × 8½ inches (folded); 23 × 33⅝ inches (unfolded)
overall
Courtesy the artist

Letter from Benjamin Patterson to Michael Porier, 1960
Ink on paper (verso, poster)
22⅝ × 16⅜ inches
Courtesy the artist

Poster designed by George Maciunas for Fluxus
Internationale Festspiele neuester Musik, Hörsaal
des Städtischen Museums, Wiesbaden, Germany,
September 1–23, 1962
Offset on paper
16¼ × 15⁹⁄₁₆ inches (unframed)
20⅞ × 16⅞ inches (framed)
The Museum of Modern Art, New York; The Gilbert and
Lila Silverman Fluxus Collection Gift

Program for Neo-Dada in der Musik, 1962
Offset on paper
7⅝ × 8¼ inches (folded)
7⅝ × 16½ inches (unfolded)
Courtesy the artist

Letter to Benjamin Patterson from George Maciunas, 1963
Ink on paper
10⅜ × 7⅞ inches
Getty Research Institute, Los Angeles

Letter to Emmett Williams from Benjamin Patterson, 1963
Ink on paper
11 × 8⁹⁄₁₆ inches
Getty Research Institute, Los Angeles

Mailer for Yam Day Festival, 1963
Offset on paper
22⅞ × 8⅜ inches
Courtesy the artist

The Four Suits, 1965
Book edited by Dick Higgins
Offset on paper
Brochure: 11 × 14 inches (folded)
Book: 9½ × 6⅜ × 1⅛ inches
Published by Something Else Press
Courtesy the artist

Photograph of Patterson portrait sketched by Alison
Knowles for brochure announcing *The Four Suits*, c. 1965
Gelatin silver print
6⅞ × 4½ inches
Getty Research Institute, Los Angeles

Jefferson's Birthday/Postface, 1965
Book edited and written by Dick Higgins
Offset on paper
8¼ × 5⅞ × 1⅛ inches
Published by Something Else Press
Courtesy the artist

Notations, 1969
Book edited by John Cage and Alison Knowles
Offset on paper
9 × 9 × 1⅛ inches
Published by Something Else Press
Courtesy the artist

Annual Report, New York State Council on the Arts,
1969–70
Offset on paper
7½ × 6½ × ¼ inches each
Courtesy the artist

Brochure for Benjamin Patterson Limited Music
Management Company, c. 1970
Printing on paper
8 × 14 inches (folded)
Courtesy the artist

Annual Report, New York State Council on the Arts,
1970–71
Offset on paper
7½ × 6½ × ¼ inches each
Courtesy the artist

Photograph of Benjamin Patterson with Mayor John
Lindsay upon his appointment as assistant director of the
New York Department of Cultural Affairs, c. 1972
Black-and-white photograph
8 × 10 inches
Courtesy the artist

Excerpt from the 1972 book by Harry Ruhé, *Fluxus: The
Most Radical Experimental Art Movement of the Sixties*,
published by Galerie A in Amsterdam
Ink on paper
8 × 11 inches
Courtesy the artist

Press release announcing Patterson's appointment at
Staten Island Community College, March 1974
Ink on paper
8 × 10 inches
Courtesy the artist

Correspondence from Patterson to the Community
Review Board regarding the "Conference in Solidarity with
the Liberation Struggles of Peoples in Southern Africa,"
September 1981
Ink on paper
8 × 10 inches
Courtesy the artist

Announcement card for Negro Ensemble Company in
New York, c. 1982
Offset on card, envelope
Card: 5⁹⁄₁₆ × 4⁵⁄₁₆ inches
Envelope: 4⁷⁄₁₆ × 5¹¹⁄₁₆ inches
Getty Research Institute, Los Angeles

Wiesbaden Fluxus, 1962–1982, 1982
Publication edited by René Block
Offset on paper
10¼ × 8¼ × 1 inches
Published by Harlekin Art Berliner Künstlerprogramm des
DAAD
Courtesy the artist

Patterson's business card for Pro Musicis, c. 1984
Ink on paper
2 × 3 inches
Courtesy the artist

Press release and postcard announcing Patterson's solo
exhibition *Ordinary Life*, at Emily Harvey Gallery, New
York, 1988
Printing on paper
Press release: 8 × 10 inches
Postcard: 4 × 6 inches
Courtesy the artist

Brochures announcing various Fluxus anniversary
exhibitions/events, 1989–92
Fluxus Festival, Chicago, 1993
Fluxus Da Capo, Wiesbaden, 1992
Offset on paper
22 × 33¾ inches, 33 × 23⅝ inches
Courtesy the artist

Vanity Fair, July 1993
Offset on paper (magazine)
10⅞ × 8⅛ inches
Courtesy the artist

Chronology

MEREDITH GOLDSMITH

1934–52   Benjamin Patterson is born on May 29, 1934, in Pittsburgh. He begins taking music lessons at age eight with Marie C. Hayes, then studies double bass with Herman Clemens beginning in 1949. His solo performance on the double bass is televised in 1951 on WQED-TV, Pittsburgh.

1952–60   Patterson studies music at the University of Michigan, Ann Arbor (BA, 1956). He becomes principal double bassist with the Halifax Symphony Orchestra in Canada. In 1958 he is conscripted into the United States Army, serving in the Seventh Army Symphony Orchestra in Stuttgart, Germany. Following his service, Patterson returns to Canada, where he is employed as principal double bassist and assistant conductor with the Ottawa Philharmonic Orchestra. In Ottawa, he meets Canadian composer Hugh Le Caine and begins experimenting with electronic music at a small studio in the National Research Center.

1960–62   Patterson's experimentation with electronic music leads him into a phase of creative exploration. During this period he publishes *An Experiment in Extended Rhythms* and *Paper Piece for Five Performers* (the first of his Paper Pieces) in the periodical *Ich bin schön*.

On June 14, 1960, Patterson arrives in Cologne to attend the International Society for Contemporary Music festival, intending to meet and possibly study with Karlheinz Stockhausen. Less than a day after his disappointing first meeting with Stockhausen, Patterson meets John Cage, who invites him to perform with him at the Contre Festival at Mary Bauermeister's studio. Along with other musicians, he performs works by La Monte Young, George Brecht, Toshi Ichiyanagi, and John Cage. Overnight Patterson converts from the "school of serial music" (Stockhausen, Boulez et al.) to the "school of indeterminate music" (Cage, Tudor et al.) His planned seven-day visit to Cologne is extended to one and a half years.

On May 14, 1961, Patterson performs *Paper Piece, Solo for Vostell, Situations for Three Pianos,* and *Duo for Voice and String Instrument* at the opening of an exhibition by Wolf Vostell at Galerie Haro Lauhus in Cologne.

In the following months Patterson performs *Variations for Double Bass* at the opening of an exhibition by Mimmo Rotella and *Improvisation* at the opening of an exhibition by Daniel Spoerri at Galerie Haro Lauhus. In July Patterson presents his first opera, *Lemons,* at Studio Vostell.

Kleines Sommerfest: Après John Cage is presented by Patterson, George Maciunas, and others at Galerie Parnass, Wuppertal, Germany. It marks the first "Fluxus" performance in Europe.

Continuing their collaboration, Patterson works with Maciunas to organize the historic Internationale Festspiele neuester Musik (later known as first Fluxus Festival), held at the Städtisches Museum in Wiesbaden in 1962. Emmett Williams interviews Patterson as publicity for the festival in *Stars and Stripes*, a military newspaper (Thursday, August 30, 1962). This interview is the first article ever written about Fluxus. Similarly, the first film documentation of Fluxus—news coverage by German television—features Patterson performing *Solo for Double Bass.*

In 1962 Patterson moves to Paris, where he self-publishes his book *Method and Processes*, followed by the works *Stand Erect*, *Draw Circle*, and *tournoi*. His published works lead to a collaboration with artist Lourdes Castro, who produces the magazine *KWY*.

Patterson also collaborates with French artist and poet Robert Filliou, exhibiting his puzzle poems in Filliou's *Galerie Légitime*. The two artists embark upon a twenty-four-hour vernissage, touring Paris by foot, bus, and metro, exhibiting Patterson's works out of a bowler hat. It is Patterson's first solo exhibition in Paris.

Patterson spends the second half of 1962 performing at Fluxus events held throughout Europe, including the Kleines Sommerfest at Galerie Parnass, Wuppertal, Germany; Neo-Dada in der Musik at the Kammerspiele in Düsseldorf, Germany; Fluxus Sneak Preview at Galerie Girardon, Paris; and the Fluxus Festival performances at the Städtisches Museum, Wiesbaden, Germany, and Nikolaj Kirke, Copenhagen. In absentia, his works are also performed at Gallery Monet, Amsterdam, and the Festival of Misfits, Gallery One, London.

At the close of the year, Patterson moves back to the United States. He resides in New York City.

1963–65 Patterson secures employment at the New York Public Library as a reference librarian in the library's music division.

During 1963, in absentia, Patterson's works are performed in three Fluxus concert events at the Staatliche Kunstakademie, Düsseldorf; Alleteatern, Stockholm; and Studentekroa, Oslo, as well as Festum Fluxorum at the Kunstakademie Düsseldorf. Later that year, also in absentia, his works are performed in group events at Biennale de Paris Arts du Langage and *Fluxus poésie et cetera* at the Musée d'Art Moderne, both in Paris.

Patterson participates in a series of lunch meetings with George Brecht, Robert Watts, and Geoffrey Hen-dricks. Their meetings take place at the Howard Johnson's hotel café in New Brunswick, New Jersey, and on occasion behind the New York Public Library, where Patterson works. The artists plan the launch of Yam Festival, a year-long festival of events and happenings. Events presented in conjunction with Yam (May spelled backward) include Yam Lecture, Yam Hat Sale, Water Day, Clock Day, Box Day, and Yam Day. The Yam Festival Delivery Event was an early mail art piece.

For his contribution, Patterson performs several pieces in conjunction with Yam Day and the Yam Festival in New York, including *Yam Day (Rush Hour)* at Penn Station. He is also featured in events with other Happenings artists, including *Yam Day Hat Sale* at Smolin Gallery; *Yam Day* at Hardware Poet's Playhouse; and two solo performances at Smolin Gallery, *Yam Day (Tour)* and *Yam Day (Final Examination)*.

Other solo performances in 1963 include *New York Audiovisual Group* at Douglass College in New Brunswick, New Jersey. In addition, the Fluxus Festival of Total Art performed his *Tour* in the streets of Nice, France, in absentia.

In 1964 Patterson performs a series of solo concerts at Fluxhall (the loft of George Maciunas at 359 Canal Street). Fluxus Concert No. 1 features *Lick Piece*, No. 3 and No. 7 feature *Slap*, and No. 9 features *Variations for Double Bass*. For his work *No. 11*, he is joined by other artists. He later performs with the Fluxus Symphony Orchestra at the Carnegie Recital Hall.

In absentia Patterson's works are represented in two Fluxus festivals in The Hague, Netherlands, the first in 1963 at the Hypokriterion Theater and the second in 1965 at various locations.

In January 1965 Patterson, Alison Knowles, Ay-O, and Emmett Williams perform Williams's *Opera* at Café au Go-Go in New York. Other group performances that year include the Third Festival of the Avant-garde at Judson

Hall and the Perpetual Fluxfest at New Cinematheque, both in New York, and the First World Congress: Happenings event at Saint Mary of the Harbor, Provincetown, Massachusetts. Patterson's work is presented in absentia at the Something Else concert at the Institute for Contemporary Art, London.

In September 1965 Patterson enrolls in Columbia University's graduate program in library science.

In November 1965 Patterson presents "A Lecture on Death" to Robert Watts's class of art students at Douglass College, Rutgers University. Twenty years later Patterson will use this text as the basis for a large triptych of the same title.

In 1965 Patterson also contributes two significant texts—"American Studies Seminar II" and "Notes on Pets"—to the book *The Four Suits*, edited by Dick Higgins for Something Else Press.

1966–69

In 1966 Patterson performs and/or has his compositions performed in the Other Benefit at the Village Gate, the Fourth Annual Avant-garde Festival in New York, the Festival de la Libre Expression at the Théâtre de la Chimère in Paris, Concert Fluxus in Prague, and in *Fluxus Exhibition* at the Avenue C Fluxus Room in New York. At the close of the year, Patterson works are presented at the Cédille Qui Sourit in Villefranche-sur-Mer and at Galerie Ranson in Paris.

In 1967 Patterson's works are performed in absentia for a variety of events in Europe: in France, in *Total Art* at the Cédille Qui Sourit in Villefranche-sur-Mer and Flux Concert in Nice; in Italy, in Concert Fluxus at Galleria la Bertescain in Genoa, Villa Cuccirelli in Milan, and Libreria Rinascita in Modena. His *12 Evenings of Manipulations* is also presented at Judson Gallery in New York. Patterson

himself performs *A Paper Event* at the Time-Life Building in New York.

Patterson receives a master's degree in library science from Columbia University in 1967.

In the spring of 1969 an evening of Patterson compositions is performed in absentia at La Cappelle in Trieste, Italy.

1970–73

From 1970 to 1972 Patterson is general manager of the Symphony of the New World in New York. He is charged with organizing programs and contracting artists.

From 1970 to 1971 Patterson's works are performed in Germany in *Happenings and Fluxus*, held at the Kölnischer Kunstverein and the Württembergischer Kunstverein in Stuttgart. Also, in 1972–73 Patterson's artwork is included in *Fluxshoe Exhibition*, which travels to Falmouth, Exeter, Croydon, Oxford, Nottingham, Cardiff, Blackburn, and Hastings in the United Kingdom.

1972–74

Patterson is appointed assistant director of the New York Department of Cultural Affairs by Mayor John Lindsay.

1974–76

Patterson is associate professor and chair of the Department of Performing and Creative Arts at Staten Island Community College (now the College of Staten Island, City University of New York).

1976

Patterson performs in *Evening on a Revolving Stage* at Judson Theater and *Concepta Omnibus Fluxi* at 134–36 Spring Street in New York, as well as *Fluxexhibit* at Galerie A in Amsterdam.

Patterson begins working as a freelance consultant, specializing in organizational development and fundraising. His clients include Harlem School of the Arts, Rod Rodgers Dance Company, Hudson Valley Philharmonic, Creative Music Foundation, Harlem Urban Development Corporation, Woodstock Guild of Craftsmen, and the Conference in Solidarity with the Liberation Struggles of the Peoples of Southern Africa. He continues his consulting work until 1981.

1977–79

Patterson's compositions are performed in the program *Fluxus & Co.* at Cannaviello Studio d'Arte in Rome. Patterson performs in *Flux Feast of Erotic Food and Cabaret* at New York's Grommet Art Theater. Later in 1977 he performs at the Flux funeral for George Maciunas held in the Flux Performance Hall in New York City. Shortly after Maciunas's death, Patterson's works are included in the major book *Fluxus, the Most Radical and Experimental Art Movement of the Sixties*, written by Harry Ruhé and published by his Galerie A in Amsterdam.

1980–82

For the Fifteenth Annual Avant-garde Festival in New York, Patterson holds an event at the Passenger Ship Terminal. He fishes in the Hudson River for whatever might be attracted by his specially designed Fluxus fishing lures. His work is also shown in the exhibitions *Fluxus: Aspekte eines Phänomens* at Kunst und Museumsverein, Wuppertal, Germany, and *Fluxus etc.*, organized by Jon Hendricks, curator of the Gilbert and Lila Silverman Fluxus Collection. *Fluxus etc.* opens at the Cranbrook Academy of Art Museum, Bloomfield Hills, Michigan, in 1981 and tours to the Baxter Art Museum, Pasadena, California; Neuberger Museum, Purchase, New York; the Contemporary Arts

Museum Houston; and the Walter Philips Gallery in Banff, Canada.

From 1982 to 1984 Patterson is director of development for the Negro Ensemble Company in New York.

1983–85

Works by Patterson from *Methods and Processes* and *Lemons* are performed in absentia at the Amerikahaus, Berlin. In October 1983 Patterson performs at the seventeenth Bienal Internacional de São Paulo.

In 1984 Patterson is included in Fluxus publications put together by Franklin Furnace, New York. The following year his work is shown in an exhibition at Staatsgalerie Stuttgart in Germany and in *Collaborations: Pioneer Performance* at the Alternative Museum, New York.

From 1984 to 1988 Patterson is the national director of Pro Musicis Foundation, Inc. In this capacity, he sponsors emerging classical artists in major recitals throughout the United States.

In the fall of 1985 Patterson presents a solo performance incorporating his work *Questionnaire* at the Third Avenue Cinema in New York.

1986–88

Between 1986 and 1988 Patterson does not perform, but his works are featured in many exhibitions at such venues as Muzej Savremene Umetnosti, Belgrade, Yugoslavia; the University of Iowa Museum of Art, Iowa City; Emily Harvey Gallery, Pierrefeu, France, and New York; and the Museum für Moderne Kunst, Berlin. In 1986 Patterson participates in *A Tribute to John Cage* at Carl Solway Gallery. In 1988 he helps to realize *FluxLux: The Last Event* at Robert Watts's farm in Martins Creek, Pennsylvania. Also in 1988 his work is included in *Fluxus: Selections from the Gilbert and Lila Silverman Collection*, organized by the Museum of Modern Art, New York, which tours for two years to such venues as Cranbrook Academy of Art, Bloomfield Hills, Michigan, and Baxter Gallery, Portland School of Art, Portland, Maine.

In 1988 Patterson emerges from semiretirement as an artist with his solo exhibition *Ordinary Life* at Emily Harvey Gallery, New York.

1989

Beginning in 1989, several exhibitions are organized with the intent to contextualize and historicize Fluxus. Patterson's works and performances are included in the exhibitions *Fluxus: Moment and Continuum* at Stux Gallery, New York; *The Theatre of the Object, 1958–1972* at the Alternative Museum, New York; and *Happenings and Fluxus*, which was held at four Paris venues simultaneously: the École Nationale des Beaux-Arts, Galerie 1900–2000, Galerie du Genie, and Galerie de Poche. He also performs at *Milano poesia* at Ansaldo, Milan.

Patterson presents a solo performance as part of the program *Taking Fluxus Around* at the Bonner Kunstverein, Bonn, Germany. He also has his second solo exhibition at Emily Harvey Gallery, New York, *What Makes People Laugh?*

At the close of the year, Patterson leaves New York and relocates to Mainz, Germany. He retires from his "ordinary life" to become a full-time artist.

1990

Patterson exhibits and performs in *Pianofortissimo* at Mudima Gallery, Milan, and the Carlo Felice Theater, Genoa, Italy, and he has a solo exhibition, *Proverbs Slogans and Quotations*, at Galerie Schüppenhauer, Cologne. Additionally, Patterson presents a solo performance as part of *Edge 90: Art in the Nineties* at the International Biennial of Innovative Arts, Newcastle, England, and his

series of Fluxus heraldic banners is presented at the Venice Biennale.

The artist participates in the eating event Cena Rossa, held at La Mangiatoia, San Gimignano, Italy.

Patterson's work is presented in a number of group exhibitions celebrating Fluxus at such venues as the Hovikkoden Art Center, Oslo; Galerie Krinzinger, Vienna; and Salvatore Ala Gallery, New York. He also participates in a number of exhibitions in Italy—at Galerie Fontanella Borghese, Rome; Salla delle Colonne ex Stalloni, Reggio Emilio; Studio Noacco, Chieri—and in Australia, at the Institute of Modern Art, Brisbane; Experimental Art Centre, Adelaide; and Perth Institute of Contemporary Art.

1991

On January 15, Patterson places a large advertisement in the *International Herald Tribune*, titled *World Event*, to protest the looming Gulf War. In February he opens his solo exhibition *How Man Makes Sense* at Galerie J & J Donguy in Paris.

In April, he performs for the exhibition *Creative Misunderstanding* at Galerie Schüppenhauer, Cologne.

The year culminates with an important homecoming to Pittsburgh, where Patterson is artist-in-residence at the Pittsburgh Center for the Arts and Carnegie Mellon University. Working with a psychotherapist six days a week for six weeks, Patterson researches his formative years to produce a large silk-screen-on-Plexiglas installation titled *Blame It on Pittsburgh; or, How I Became an Artist*, which is exhibited in *Fluxus Deluxe* at Pittsburgh Center of the Arts. He also performs *Pond, Paper Piece*, and *Symphony No. II* in the program *Iron City Flux*, held at Rosebud Center, and lectures at Carnegie Mellon University.

Patterson performs in a suite of Flux concerts with S.E.M. Ensemble at 25 Columbia Place, Brooklyn, and at the Kunstverein Düsseldorf, Germany.

Other group exhibitions this year include Hallways Contemporary Arts Center, Buffalo, New York; Galerie Vaclav Spala, Prague; Unimedia, Genoa, Italy; the Von der Heydt Museum, Wuppertal, Germany; Humor Kirche, Wiesbaden, Germany; 200 Gertrude Street, Melbourne, Australia; the Royal Academy, London; and Emily Harvey Gallery, New York. The Plug In Gallery in Winnipeg, Canada, exhibits Patterson's work in *Under the Influence of Fluxus*, which tours to North Dakota Museum of Art in Grand Forks and Istituto Italiano in Toronto, and the artist's work is also exhibited in *The Miracle of Fluxus: How It Saved the World* at Oldenburg Kunstverein, Germany, and in *Something Else Press* at Granary Books, New York.

1992

Patterson exhibits his work in *Getting Ready for 2000 A.D.* in Milan at Fondazione Mudima; at 25 Columbia Place, Brooklyn, he creates the installation *Rabbit Concert* and performs *A Dozen for Carmen* and *Paper Piece*, and later in the year at Galerie Schüppenhauer in Cologne, he presents his solo exhibition *What Is on My Mind?*

Patterson's work is included in Fluxus exhibitions at various museums, including Wilhelm Hack Museum, Ludwigshafen, Germany; the Bielefelder Kunstverein, Bielefeld, Germany; Nykytaiteen Museo, Helsinki; Whitney Museum of American Art, New York; and Museo d'Arte Moderna, Bolzano, Italy, where he installs the work *Jump into Fluxus*, a mini ski jump accompanied by instructions for use at the entrance to the museum. For his presentation in *Fluxus Virus, 1962–92*, Patterson presents the performance work *Roast Duck*. In *Roast Duck*, Patterson mounted a Citroen 2CV car (nicknamed *Ente*, "duck" in German) on a giant roasting spit over a glowing bed of charcoal. The exhibition opens at the Temporary Museum / Kaufhof Parkhaus, Cologne, and tours to Aktionsforum Praterinsel, Munich. Patterson also

shows in a Fluxus exhibition at the Museum of Contemporary Art, Chicago (with a coordinating performance at Art Club Chicago), and at Smolin Cathedral, Saint Petersburg, Russia, with a coordinating performance and workshop.

In 1992 Patterson's work is included in exhibitions at Galerie M, Montreal; BWA Gallery, Warsaw; Emily Harvey Gallery, New York; Gallerie Stenström, Stockholm; and Arsenat Gallery, Bialystok, Poland. For his contribution to *Fluxus Da Capo*, Patterson creates a five-room installation, *The Clinic of Dr. Ben*, in Villa Clementine, Wiesbaden, Germany.

With Joe Jones, Patterson performs live music to silent films for *Fluxus Films/100 Minute Version* at the Caligari Theatre in Wiesbaden, the Frankfurt Film Museum, and Galerie Leerer Beutel, Regensburg, all in Germany.

1993

Patterson presents the solo performance *Beethoven's Fifth* at HH-Bonn in Bonn, Germany.

For the exhibition *The Seoul of Fluxus*, organized by the Seoul Art Center in Korea, Patterson debuts the work *Three Operas: Carmen, Madame Butterfly, and Tristan and Isolde*. The artist's work is also featured in four traveling exhibitions: *In the Spirit of Fluxus*, organized by the Walker Art Center, Minneapolis, which traveled to the Whitney Museum of American Art, New York; the Wexner Center for the Arts, Columbus, Ohio; the San Francisco Museum of Modern Art; and Fundació Antoni Tàpies, Barcelona, Spain. *Fluxus: A Conceptual Country*, organized by the Institute for Cinema and Culture in Iowa City, tours to Montgomery Museum of Fine Arts, Montgomery, Alabama, and the Block Gallery, Northwestern University, Evanston, Illinois. *Theatre of Refusal* is organized by the galleries of the University of California at Irvine, Davis, and Riverside. *Block Collection* is exhibited at the Reykjavik

Art Museum and at Kunsthalle Nürnburg, Nuremburg, Germany.

Other exhibitions this year include Il Campo delle Fragole, Bologna, and Restructura, Turin, both in Italy.

1994

Patterson performs *The Diaries of Orpheo and Euridice* at the Landesmuseum, Mainz, Germany, and has a solo exhibition, *Symphonic Fragments, Sonatinas, and Other Bagatelles*, at Galerie am Kleinen Markt, Mannheim, Germany.

At PrivArt in Wiesbaden, Germany, Patterson presents *Reisebüro Fluxus*, an interactive installation in which the artist simulates a travel agency that specializes in tours to historic Fluxus sites. Later in 1995 Patterson does conduct a series of tours to historic Fluxus sites in Paris, Nice, Stuttgart, and areas in Northern Italy. Another solo exhibition, *Sofa Bilder*, is held at Galerie Cornelissen, Schlangenbad, Germany.

Additional performances this year include one in conjunction with the exhibition *Isole del disordine* at various sites around Cortona, Italy; *Fluxus Reunion Program #1*, Courthouse Theater, New York; and *Wedding in Denmark*, in the streets of Copenhagen.

Group exhibitions featuring Patterson's work include *Fluxus and Happenings*, Museo Vostell, Malpartida, Spain; *Fluxus* at Queensland Art Gallery, Brisbane, Australia; Villa Pacchiani, Santa Croce sull'Arno, Italy; Kunsthalle, Basel, Switzerland; and Salvatore Ala Gallery, New York.

1995

Galerie am Kleinen Markt features the Patterson performance *Bolero*, which he also performs during the next few years in Germany at Alte Kirche, Volxheim; in Rosenheim; and at F.A.W. Ulm. Patterson's composition for an a cappella chorus, *Das Bahnhof Requiem*, is performed at Sankt Ignaz Kirche in Mainz, Germany. His action piece *Tour* is performed by six hundred people during *Schritt für Schritt: Kunstprozession* at Evangelischen Kirchentages, Hamburg, Germany. Other performances presented throughout the year include *Flashbacks* and *I Am Looking at You, Beethoven* for an Al Hansen exhibition at Kunstverein, Rosenheim, Germany; *Carmen für Armin*, Stadtsmuseum, Cologne; *Classic and Contemporary Fluxus*, Mimar Sinan University, Istanbul, and Bilkan University, Ankara, Turkey; and *A Simple Opera* at his exhibition of new work at Galerie Cattalini, Modena, Italy.

Patterson has a solo exhibition at Galerie Vostell, Berlin, and at Fachhochschule, Mainz, where he delivers the lecture "Fluxus and Experimental Music." The lecture is also presented at the International Artists' Museum, Lodz, Poland, where the artist conducts a workshop on Fluxus events.

The artist participates in several major group exhibitions, including *Fluxtuat nec mergitur: L'esprit de Fluxus* at MAC Galeries Contemporaines de Musée de Marseille, France; *Revolution: Art of the Sixties*, Museum of Contemporary Art, Tokyo; and *Fluxus in Germany, 1962–1994*, organized by the Institut für Auslandsbeziehungen, Stuttgart, which opens at Kunstsammlung, Gera, Germany. The exhibition toured for fourteen years, traveling around the world to such venues as Ataturk Cultural Center, Istanbul; Zacheta National Gallery of Art, Warsaw; Mücsarnok, Budapest; Moderna Galerija, Ljubljana, Slovenia; Dum Umeni Haus der Kunst, Brno, Czech Republic; Skopje Museum of Contemporary Art, Macedonia; Museum of Foreign Art, Sofia, Bulgaria; Ergostasion at the Academy of Art, Athens, Greece; Arken Museum of Modern Art, Ishoj, Denmark; and the Tel Aviv Museum of Art, Tel Aviv, Israel.

1996

Patterson's solo engagements continue to increase. His individual performances include *Three Operas* at Galerie

KK im Fisch in Brunswick, Germany; *Remembering Al Hansen*, Interims Kunsthalle, Berlin; *A la Carte and Live an Ihrem Tisch*, Hotelschiff, Cologne. His solo exhibitions include *Beauty Lurks in the Chaos of the Beholder* at Gallery Caterina Gualco, Genoa; *Nasen Flaschen*, Galerie Cornelissen, Schlangenbad, Germany; *Extreme Measures: The Great American Game Exhibit*, Carl Solway Gallery, Cincinnati; and the installation and dedication of his *Museum of the Subconscious* in Okandukaseibe, Namibia.

The artist also participates in events at exhibitions at Zentral Haus der Künstler, Moscow; Galerie Schüppenhauer, Cologne; and Espace Electra, Paris.

1997

Benjamin Patterson begins the year with a solo exhibition, *Blame It on Pittsburgh; or, Why I Became an Artist* at Emily Harvey Gallery, New York. Other solo exhibitions follow: *Rimedi, ricette e procedure* with the performance piece *Grandi momenti nella storia della medicina*, Galleria Fioretto, Padua, Italy; and *Trains of Thought* and *Just in Time*, an exhibition and performance held at Galerie Fruchtig, Frankfurt, Germany. As one of several artists from Germany selected for a residency in Thailand, he organizes an exhibition with local rickshaw drivers, exhibiting their photographs of the city and their families in an installation work called *My Chiang Mai* at Thapae Gate.

Performances by the artist also increase, and he is invited to perform *Fluxus Classics* and *The Three Operas* at Helmhaus, Zurich; *The Three Operas* at Schloss Solitude, Stuttgart, Germany; *The Future Makes Progress* at a performance festival in Odense, Denmark; and *World Weather* at the Princess Palace Gardens, Bangkok, Thailand, and the Queensland Art Gallery, Brisbane, Australia.

His work is included in several group exhibitions, including *Francesco Conz and the Avant-garde* at the Queensland Art Gallery, Brisbane, Australia; *Portraits? Yes, Portraits* at Galleria Caterina Gualco, Genoa, Italy; and

Dadismo, Dadismi, da Duchamp a Warhol, Galleria d'Arte Moderna e Contemporanea, Verona, Italy.

Patterson lectures and leads workshops on Fluxus at the University of Padua, Italy, and later in Zurich.

1998

In conjunction with *Fluxus in Germany, 1962–1994* at the National Gallery for Foreign Art in Sofia, Bulgaria, Patterson conducts a Fluxus workshop and performs *The Three Operas*. He continues to perform and lecture in the region at Divaldo Stoka in Bratislava, Slovakia, and Mucsarnok Palace of Art and C3 Auditorium in Budapest, Hungary.

He returns to Germany and performs *The Meisterspargel* and *The Creation of the World* at Schloss Solitude in Stuttgart. A new work, *The Creation of the World*, is also performed at Galerie Schüppenhauer, Cologne. In addition, Patterson tours a performance of *Bolero* to the Divadle Na Zabradli in Prague; to Skleněná Louka, Brno, Czech Republic; and to Sound Off Studio Erte in Nové Zámky, Slovakia.

Other solo performances and exhibitions occurring throughout the year include *The 15th of May* and *Smokers Rights*, Art Base, Cologne; *Lemons Revisited*, Museo Vostell, Malpartida, Spain; *The Three Operas*, OFKunstraum, Offenbach, Germany; *Topology of Thought* at Nassauische Sparkasse, Wiesbaden, Germany; and *Topologies des Denkens: No Poetry, No Concept*, Galerie Vostell, Berlin.

Toward the end of the year Patterson participates in a performance with the S.E.M. Ensemble in memory of Dick Higgins at the Paula Cooper Gallery, New York.

1999

Patterson performs *Solo for Dancer* in conjunction with his solo exhibition *No Poetry, No Concept* at the Kunstverein, Rosenheim, Germany. Other solo exhibitions and performances include *Word Volume* at Galerie

Schüppenhauer, Cologne; *The Evolution of Wisdom* at OFKunstraum, Offenbach, Germany; *Bolero* at Muzeum Narodowe, Szczecin, Poland; *Tristan and Isolde* at Jazz Café, Prague, and *The Hunt* at the StadtRaumBegegnung, Wiesbaden, Germany.

The artist conducts workshops and delivers a lecture at the Kunstverein, Rosenheim, Germany. He is later invited to the Helena Rubenstein Museum and Forum Shelter 209, Tel Aviv, Israel, where he directs the installation and dedication of *The Museum of the Subconscious Annex* at Jerusalem Beach.

Patterson also participates in several group exhibitions throughout the year at such venues as Galerie Vostell, Berlin; Il Gabbiano, La Spezia, Italy; Forum Rathaus, Knittelfeld, Germany; Zamecka Galerie, Opocno, Czech Republic; the V2 Organisation, Rotterdam, the Netherlands; Galerie Stadt Kornwestheim, Germany; Whitney Museum of American Art, New York; Galerie im Ganserhaus, Wasserburg, Germany; Galleria Caterina Gualco, Genoa, Italy; and Galerie Gambit, Prague.

He contributes work to and performs as an extension of the exhibition *Homage to Dick Higgins*, Ernst Museum, Budapest, Hungary. He also performs in a public program celebrating the donation of works by collector Francesco Conz to the Museum of Contemporary Art, Zagreb, Croatia.

Patterson records *Ben Patterson: Early Works* on the Alga Marghen label in Milan.

2000

Patterson opens his solo exhibition *The Evolution of Wisdom, Chapter 3* at Galleria Caterina Gualco in Genoa, Italy. In conjunction with this exhibition, he dedicates his permanent installation *The Evolution of Wisdom, Chapter 4* at Villa Solaria in Chiavari, Italy. Later in the year, Patterson's solo exhibition *Landscape, Still-Life, and Allegorical Paintings in the Grand Tradition of Everyday Racism* opens

at Gallerie Pari & Dispari in Reggio Emilio, Italy. His work is featured in a multisite installation, *Shoes or No Shoes: Collection of Pierre B-V Swenters*, presented in four locations in the United Kingdom: Kent Institute of Art and Design, Kent; George Rogers Gallery, Maidstone; Herbert Read Gallery, Canterbury; and Zandra Rhodes Gallery, Rochester.

Patterson performs extensively in such events as *Serata Fluxus per Wolf Vostell* at the Auditorium Istituto "A Peri" in Reggio Emilio, Italy, and a guided tour through Germany titled *Reisebüro Fluxus—Kurt Schwitters and J. S. Bach* in Leipzig, Germany. He also restages *Bolero* at Galerie Herbert Mayer in Kitzbühl, Austria, and contributes the performance of Symphony No. 6 to the festival Sentieri Interrotti per la Città in the Piazza della Libertà, Bassano del Grappa, Italy.

Patterson is invited to Poland, where he composes and performs the work *Digging* in Bydgoszcz. He also orchestrates a "walk-about" operatic adaptation of *Summer Nachts Träume* at Neroberg, a public park in Wiesbaden, Germany. He collaborates with his longtime friend and fellow Fluxus artist Emmett Williams in the presentation of *Alphabet* at the Gutenberg Pavilion in Mainz, Germany.

Patterson travels to Quebec City, Canada, to perform *The Creation of the World* at Le Lieu Centre en Art Actuel.

His visual work is also featured in a number of group exhibitions, including *La chiave del duemila* at Il Gabbiano, La Spezia, and *Cravatte d'artista: Collezione A & F Boggiano* at Complesso Monumentale del Priamar, Savona, both in Italy. His work is also featured in the exhibition *Die Bücher der Künstler* at Galerie der Stadt Mainz-Brückenturm, Mainz, Germany.

In conjunction with the traveling exhibition *Fluxus in Germany, 1962–1994*, Patterson travels to New Zealand to perform *The Three Operas* at the Govett-Brewster Art Gallery in New Plymouth.

Patterson serves as artistic adviser for the yearlong event Gutenberg 2000 in Mainz, Germany, which celebrates the inventor's six hundredth birthday and the history of printing. In conjunction with the festival, Patterson performs *Happy Birthday Johannes (Gutenberg)* at the Gutenberg Pavilion in Mainz and *Rhein Post* at Gutenberg 2000 in Basel, Switzerland.

Patterson records *Ben Patterson: Drip Music/370 Flies* on the Alga Marghen label in Milan.

2001

Patterson travels to the Czech Republic, where he performs and exhibits *Film Music No. 2* at Café Indigo, Prague, and participates in the exhibition and performances *P.S.:H.N.* at Slovácké Muzeum in Uherské Hradiště.

Closer to home, Patterson performs *Symphony #6* at OFKunstraum, Offenbach, Germany, before traveling to Kraków, Poland, where he performs *Fluxus Classics* and *Three Operas* at Bunkier Sztuki. In addition to these performances, his paintings and sculptures are presented in a solo exhibition at the Galerie Potocka, also in Kraków. The artist continues a major weekend of solo work in Kraków with the performance *Explaining Fluxus in Polish*.

Patterson is invited to participate in the Third Odense Performance Festival in Odense, Denmark, where he performs *The Creation of the World* and *Madame Butterfly*. He later performs in a festival of Fluxus events at the Scène Nationale de Bonlieu, Annecy, France. Back in Germany, Patterson performs *A Clean Slate*, *Pond*, and *Paper Piece* at Haus der Deutschen Ensemble Akademie, Frankfurt am Main, Germany.

Patterson participates in several solo exhibitions, including *Esercizi di Stile* at Museo d'Arte Moderna, Senigallia, Italy, and his exhibition *Now* is shown at Gallery 2211, Los Angeles. While in Los Angeles, Patterson delivers a lecture and performs at the University of California, Los Angeles. Later in the year, he performs and conducts a workshop at *Sympozium Act in Art*, Kinosala SNG, Bratislava, Slovakia.

Throughout the year Patterson's work is featured in several group exhibitions, including *Leonardo in Action and Poetry*, at Museo Ideale Leonardo da Vinci in Vinci, Italy; *537 Broadway Comes to Venice*, organized by Emily Harvey Gallery in Venice, Italy; *Markers: An Outdoor Banner Event* for the Peggy Guggenheim Collection Museum during the Venice Biennale; *Minimalismos, un signo de los tiempos* at Museo Nacional Centro de Arte Reina Sofía, Madrid; and the exhibition *Shoes or No Shoes?* at Provinciaal Centrum voor Kunst en Cultuur in Ghent, Belgium.

The artist contributes work to *Zusammenflüsse und Quellen* at Kunst Keller Klingelpütz and participates in a concurrent workshop at Stadtgarten in Cologne. He also participates in *Art and Music*, shown simultaneously at Anton Meier Galerie in Geneva and Galerie Marlene Frei in Zurich.

2002

Patterson performs extensively in and around Europe. His work is also featured in group and solo exhibitions.

A selection of performances include *Music at the Edge* at Museo Nacional Centro de Arte Reina Sofía, Madrid; *Fluxus Classics* at Menagerie de Verne, Paris; *Polyphonics 40*, first at the Swiss Center in Paris, then at Le Fresnoy in Tourcoing, France; *Tell Me for Arditti String Quartet by Ben Patterson* at Museum Wiesbaden in Germany; *Rheingold* at the Landesmuseum in Mainz, Germany; and the event *Fluxus and Friends*, organized by the Musée d'Art Contemporain, Marseille, France.

Patterson conceives and performs *Lazy Anarchist*, first at Humor-Kirche, Wiesbaden, Germany, then in Nové Zámky, Slovakia, and in Brno, Czech Republic. He also participates in the project *Walking from Here to There* at Galerie Behemot, Prague.

He also stages the performance work *Hello! Benjamin Patterson Welcomes You to His Life in Real Time*, a series of twelve solo performances at Kasseler Kunstverein in Kassel, Germany.

Patterson's work is featured in several exhibitions during the year, including *Courdes de Saint Ouen* at Théâtre des Mains d'Oeuvres in Paris; *The Fluxus Constellation* at Museo d'Arte Contemporanea di Villa Croce in Genoa, Italy, where he creates and installs the work *Fluxus Constellations*; and *40 Jahre: Fluxus und die Folgen*, held in locations around Wiesbaden. Patterson's work is also featured in *Fantasy Gardens* at the Werkstättengalerie Dresden-Hellerau in Dresden, Germany.

Patterson participates in two events in Paris: the performance *Nano Fluxus* at the École Normale Supérieure and the symposium "Colloque Fluxus" at École Nationale Supérieure des Télécommunications. In the United Kingdom, he delivers his lecture "Fluxus and Performance" at John Moores University, Liverpool; the University of Central Lancashire, Preston; and Liverpool Community College. He also presents an evening of music with the Fracture Band, playing *The River Mersey* and other works at the Bluecoat Arts Centre in Liverpool.

Patterson simulates a television cooking show, titling the performance *Ben's Bar, the Exhibit That Talks Hard and Cooks Good* for the Künstlerhaus Schloss Balmoral in Bad Ems, Germany. He also installs the work *Ben's Bar (Social Headquarters 40 Jahre)* in Spiegelgasse, Wiesbaden. The installation is later moved to the Nassauischer Kunstverein, Wiesbaden, Germany, in 2008.

Patterson records *Ben Patterson Tells Fluxus Stories (from 1962 to 2002)* for the Hundertmark label in Cologne.

2003

Patterson's work is featured in two solo exhibitions: *Happenings and Fluxus* at Galerie Vostell, Madrid, and *Sweet Nothings* at Galleria Caterina Gualco, Genoa, Italy.

Patterson performs *The Creation of the World* at the Goethe Institute in Madrid, and serves Fluxus cocktails at Hotel Riess in conjunction with the traveling exhibition *Fluxus in Germany, 1962–1994* at its presentation in Kassel, Germany.

Patterson speaks at the symposium for the exhibition *Fluxus et la France* at Convent de la Tourette, L'Arbresle, France.

Patterson contributes works and performance to the group exhibitions *Walking from Here to There* at Dum Umeni, Opava, Czech Republic; *Concert Fluxus Border Line* at Rencontres d'Ensembles de Violoncelles, Beauvais, France; *Homage Emily Harvey*, Emily Harvey Gallery, Venice, Italy; and *Centraal Fluxus Festival* at the Centraal Museum, Utrecht, Netherlands. While in the Netherlands, Patterson performs *12 Ave Marias*, singing twelve versions of "Ave Maria"—arranged by such composers as Liszt, Verdi, Mozart, and Mendelssohn—in front of twelve churches across the country.

Patterson releases the albums *Liverpool Soundworks*, volumes 1 and 2, recorded on the Audio Research Editions label in London.

2004

Beginning in April, Patterson embarks upon his *Grand 70th Birthday Tour*. He travels by railroad and boat for a two-month tour of solo performances across Russia, Mongolia, China, and Japan. Venues include DOM Culture Center and Club Brestaskaj, Moscow; House of Science, Yekaterinburg, Russia; Non-Profit Project, Novasibirsk, Russia; Igor's Datscha, Baikal Lake, Russia; Rail Station, Ulan Batoor, Mongolia; Club Central, Beijing; Bund, Shanghai; Xebec, Kobe, Japan; Club Canol Fan, Nagoya, Japan; and Gallery 360°, Tokyo. The tour ends with a birthday party on Mount Fuji in June.

Upon completion of this journey, Patterson exhibits a series of photographic works titled *Grand 70th Birthday*

Tour Homecoming at Galerie Schüppenhauer in Cologne and Galleria Caterina Gualco in Genoa, Italy. In July, he returns to Galerie Schüppenhauer to perform *My Fuji* along with *Paper Piece*. In September Patterson performs another Fuji-inspired work, *Finishing Fuji*, at the International Artists' Museum in Lodz, Poland.

Patterson returns to Japan for a solo exhibition at Gallery 360°, Tokyo, titled *Interrupted Fairy Tales* and also contributes to the exhibition *Fluxus: Art into Life* at the Urawa Art Museum, Saitama City.

Patterson's work is also included in the group exhibition *Sounds and Lights*, at Centre Pompidou, Paris; *Moments d'arts contemporaines*, Université de Paris; and *Voolare*, at the Palazzina delle Arti, La Spezia, Italy.

2005

Patterson's work is featured in the solo exhibitions *Rimedi, ricette e procedure Part II* at Galleria Fioretto Arte, Padua, Italy, and *He Is Nouveau Réalisme* at MUMOK (Museum Moderner Kunst) in Vienna.

Patterson performs *A Simple Opera* at Künstlerhaus, Dortmund, Germany, and *370 Flies* at Cuba Culture, Münster, Germany, and Espace Multimédia Gantner, Bourogne, France.

In Hannover, Germany, the artist presents a radio broadcast of the work *There Is a Problem on the Line*. His work is also included in the exhibition *Joe Jones Music Machines* at the Ateliergemeinschaft Grammophon, Hannover.

Patterson participates in the group exhibition *Words and Games for George*, Galerie Schüppenhauer, Cologne.

2006

Patterson has two solo exhibitions: *A Famous Pittsburgh Product* at Galerie Harry Ruhé, Amsterdam, and *Dividing/Bridging*, Solway Jones Gallery, Los Angeles.

While in California, Patterson performs *Draw a Line and Follow It* at Los Angeles Contemporary Exhibitions and *Fluxus Hot and West* at Joshua Tree National Park.

Back in Europe, Patterson participates in numerous performance events, including *12 Piano Compositions for Nam Jun Paik* at Caligari Film-Bühne, Wiesbaden, Germany; *Fluxus Ton-Aktion*, Bel Etage, Berlin; *My Tone, Your Tone, His Tone, Her Tone*, KNHO, Hannover, Germany; and Over Sixty—Festival de Performance, organized by Le Théâtre de l'Usine, Geneva, and Schlachthaus Theatre, Bern, Switzerland, where he performs *A Simple Opera* and *The Creation of the World*.

The artist is also featured in the group exhibition *FAMA Fluxus Mythos Beuys* at Kunst + Projekte, Sindelfingen, Germany.

Patterson records *A Fluxus Elegy* on the Alga Marghen label in Milan.

2007

Patterson is featured in the solo exhibitions *Ben Patterson: Conversations along the Wall*, Studio d'Arte Fioretti, Bergamo, Italy; *A Fluxus Elegy*, Kleiner Raum Clasing and Galerie Etage, Münster, Germany, and *Feinbilder* at Emerson Gallery in Berlin, where he also writes and performs the work *My Favorite Sin*.

Patterson's work is also featured in several group exhibitions, including *Black Light/White Noise: Sound and Light in Contemporary Art* at the Contemporary Arts Museum Houston; *Fluxus, c'est gratuit*, Benaki Museum, Athens, Greece, where he also performs *Fluxus Musique* at the Institut Français d'Athènes; *Fluxus: Una larga historia con muchos*, Centro Anduluz de Arte Contemporaneo, Seville, Spain, where he performs *Concierto multidisciplinary, 1a parte & 2a parte*; and *Fluxus East* at Bunkier Sztuki, Kraków, Poland, where he also performs *A Simple Opera* and *370 Flies*.

Patterson presents a number of solo performances throughout the year, including *Fluxus wird 40*, Fluxus Freunde Social Headquarters, Wiesbaden, Germany; *Why Do People Attend Bars?* Nassauischer Kunstverein, Wiesbaden; *The Three Operas*, Asolo Art Film Festival, Asolo, Italy; and his own adaptation of *King Lear* at Maschinenhaus Essen, Essen, Germany.

Patterson installs a large-scale installation at Lichtsicht, 1. Projektions Biennale, Bad Rothenfelde, Germany.

2008

Solo exhibitions include *Urbanity: Solutions to Survive Urban Living* at UnimediaModern Contemporary Art, Genoa, Italy; *Requiem für einen Flügel: Finale Klaviermusik für 8 Hände und Werkzeuge* at Deutzer Brücke, Cologne; *Do We Still Have Time?* at Galerie Wildwechsel, Frankfurt, Germany.

Performances include *My Favorite Sin*, presented at Emerson Gallery, Berlin (where Patterson's work is featured in a solo exhibition), and later at Encuentro Internacional Performance, Institut Valencià d'Art Modern, Valencia, Spain; *A Ssssuuuurrrrppppprrrriiiiissssseeee Performance*, Kurpark, Wiesbaden, Germany; *A Simple Opera* at Freistaat Burgstein Aktion, Villa Tivoli, Merano, Italy; *Wundergrund/US election night*, Centre for New Music (SNYK)/Literaturhaus, Copenhagen; *Acción!o8MAD*, Off-limits, Madrid; *Flux Us (Dada & Fluxus)*, Cabaret Voltaire, Zurich.

Patterson's work is featured in several group exhibitions, including *Fluxus East* at Bunkier Sztuki, Kraków, Poland, which travels. In conjunction with this exhibition, he performs *A Simple Opera* and *370 Flies*. Additionally, his work is featured in group exhibitions such as *Martian Museum of Terrestrial Art* at the Barbican, London; *Fluxus in Germany, 1962–1994* at the National Gallery of Modern Art, Mumbai, India; and *BAU contenitore di cultura contemporanea 4+5* at Galerie Claus Semerak, Munich.

During the year Patterson also performs with Keith Rowe in conjunction with the exhibition *Hauptsache Musik: Collages, Objects, Manuscripts, Sounds, and Instruments*, Galerie Schüppenhauer, Cologne. He also took part in the inaugural performance series (performing *Flux-Folk*) presented for the opening of the Fluxus + Museum in Potsdam, Germany.

In Madrid, Patterson conducts the workshop Learning by Doing at the Facultad de Bellas Artes, Universidad Complutense de Madrid.

2009

Patterson begins the year with a performance as part of the exhibition *Creative Revolution: Fifty Years of Fluxus from Archivio Bonotto* at the Source, Barcelona, Spain. His work is featured in many other group exhibitions, including *Fluxus: Eine Ausstellung als Videobibliothek* at Cabaret Voltaire, Zurich; *Editions*, Solway Jones Gallery, Los Angeles; *1 Turm–4 Türmer*, Museum Zündorfer Wehrturm, Cologne; *Ceci n'est pas une Barbie*, DAC—De Simoni Arte Contemporanea, Genoa, Italy.

Solo exhibitions include *Amazing Discovery—Astrophysics Finds the Mother of God*, Galerie Wildwechsel, Frankfurt; *A Carnival of Clowns, Animals, and Religions*, Galleria Michela Rizzo, Treviso, Italy; *Passing Through*, Galerie Kunstpunkt Berlin.

Patterson unveils several commissioned works, including *Vecchio Salami Fluxus* at the Luigi Bonotto Collection in Bassano del Grappa, Italy; *Shoes or No Shoes*, a permanent installation in Kruishouten, Belgium; *Dolphine Statue*, at the Museo del Parco, Portofino, Italy; and *Pacioli Luka*, a mural commissioned by Studio Michele Furlanetto, Treviso, Italy.

He presents several performances over the year, including *Nano Fluxus; or, Fluxus through the wrong end of a telescope* (a "standard, classic Fluxus repertoire, in miniature"), Iglesia de la Magdalena, Zamora, Spain; *Shaggy*

Dog Stories, Galeria Michela Rizzo, Venice, Italy; *A Bunch of Older Bad Boys*, Nassauischer Kunstverein, Wiesbaden, Germany; *A Fluxus Aranykara*, Artus, Budapest, Hungary; *Spaghetti Pop Festival 2009*, Studio d'Arte Fioretti, Bergamo, Italy; *World Weather*, Tiroler Landesmuseen, Innsbruck, Austria; *The Golden Age of Fluxus: A Lecture / Demonstration* for *Soudain l'été Fluxus*, Passage de Retz, Paris; *The Golden Age of Fluxus*, Ludwig Museum, Koblenz, Germany.

In the summer Patterson collaborates with Bertrand Clavez to restage the 1962 performance work with Robert Filliou, *Galerie Légitime*, in Paris. The restaging, simply titled *Galerie Légitime: A Reenactment*, proceeds as in the 1962 performance, with Patterson and Clavez traveling throughout the city by bus, train, and foot, exhibiting the work *Three Hundred Therapeutic Poems*.

Two compositions are staged during the year in absentia: *A Simple Opera*, performed by Ensemble l'Art pour l'Art Mouvement, Festival für Neue Musik, Saarbrücken, and *Variations for Double Bass*, performed by Christopher Williams at the Institute for Intermediate Studies/Gelegenheiten, Berlin.

2010

Patterson holds the opening dedication of his *Museum of the Subconscious Annex* in El Milagro, La Candelaria, Argentina.

In Paris, he is invited to perform at La Maison Rouge and presents *A Simple Opera*, *370 Flies*, George Brecht's *Drip Music*, and the composition *It Is Me*.

At a YAM Day Memorial Concert at the Auditorium Parco della Musica in Rome, Patterson performs *A Simple Opera*, *370 Flies*, *Paper Piece*, and Brecht's *Piano Works* and *Drip Music*. He is invited to Seoul, where he performs *Greetings to Nam June Paik* at the Nam June Paik Art Center. He also composes a new work, *A Message To . . .* which is performed in Verona, Italy, at a memorial service celebrating the life of collector Francesco Conz. Other performances take place at the Rhein-Main Designers Club at the Schlachthof in Wiesbaden.

Patterson is commissioned to compose a new work, *Give Me a Break*, which debuts at the Huddersfield Contemporary Music Festival in Yorkshire, England.

Patterson's work is featured in a solo exhibition, *Disasters and Catastrophes*, at Galerie Wildwechsel in Frankfurt. The exhibition *1 Turm–4 Türmer* travels to Prague, where it is presented at the Clock Tower.

The major retrospective *Benjamin Patterson: Born in the State of FLUX/us* opens at the Contemporary Arts Museum Houston.

Selected Bibliography

COMPILED BY MEREDITH GOLDSMITH

General Reading

Baerwaldt, Wayne, ed. *Under the Influence of Fluxus.* Verona, Italy: Conz, 1991.

Banes, Sally. *Greenwich Village, 1963: Avant-garde Performance and the Effervescent Body.* Durham, N.C.: Duke University Press, 1993.

Battcock, Gregory, ed. *Breaking the Sound Barrier: A Critical Anthology of the New Music.* New York: Dutton, 1981.

Battcock, Gregory, and Robert Nickas, eds. *The Art of Performance: A Critical Anthology.* New York: Dutton, 1984.

Beauvais, Yann, ed. *Mot: Dites, image.* Paris: Scratch and Musée National d'Art Moderne, Centre George Pompidou, 1988.

Becker, Jürgen, and Wolf Vostell. *Happenings: Fluxus, Pop Art, Nouveau Réalisme: Eine Dokumentation.* Hamburg: Rowohlt, 1965.

Benaumou, Michael, and Charles Carmello, eds. *Performance in Postmodern Culture.* Milwaukee: Center for Twentieth-Century Studies, University of Wisconsin, 1977.

Berner, Jeff, ed. *Aktual Art International: Posters, Manifestos, Objects, Drawings, Collages, Lithographs, Books, Photographs, Happenings Kits, Periodicals, Memorabilia and Ephemera; Neo-Dada, Concretisme, Letterism, Spatialism, the Mediocres, Fluxus, De-coll/age, etc.* Stanford, Calif.: Department of Art and Architecture, Stanford University, 1967.

Cage, John. *Notations.* New York: Something Else Press, 1969.

Clavez, Bertrand, ed. *Fluxus in France.* Nanterre, France: Centre Pierre Francastel, Université Paris X–Nanterre, 2005.

Conzen-Meairs, Ina, ed. *Liber Maister S: Hanns Sohm zum siebzigsten Geburtstag.* Stuttgart: Staatsgalerie Stuttgart, 1991.

Dehò, Valerio. *Vostell: The Disasters of Peace.* Milan: Charta, 1999.

Dreyfus, Charles. "From History of Fluxus." In *Flash Art: Two Decades of History: XXI Years,* edited by Giancarlo Politi and Helena Kontova, 49–51. Cambridge, Mass.: MIT Press, 1990.

Ferro, Antonio. *La Post/Avanguardia: Marginal Art and Marginality of Art.* Benevento, Italy: Museo del Sannio, 1978.

Friedman, Ken, ed. *The Fluxus Reader.* Chichester, West Sussex, UK: Academy, 1998.

———. *Rethinking Fluxus.* Hovikodden, Norway: Henie Onstad Foundations, 1989.

Gray, John. *Action Art: A Bibliography of Artists' Performance from Futurism to Fluxus and Beyond.* Westport, Conn.: Greenwood, 1993.

Harding, James M., and Rouse, John. *Not the Other Avant-garde: The Transnational Foundations of Avant-garde Performance.* Ann Arbor: University of Michigan Press, 2006.

Hendricks, Jon. *Fluxus Codex.* Detroit: Gilbert and Lila Silverman Fluxus Collection; New York: Harry N. Abrams, 1988.

Higgins, Dick. *Jefferson's Birthday/Postface.* New York: Something Else Press, 1964.

Higgins, Hannah. *Fluxus Experience.* Berkeley and Los Angeles: University of California Press, 2002.

Kellein, Thomas, and Jon Hendricks. *Fluxus.* London: Thames & Hudson, 1995.

Lewis, George. *A Power Stronger than Itself: The AACM and American Experimental Music.* Chicago: University of Chicago Press, 2008.

Lippard, Lucy R., ed. *Six Years: The Dematerialization of the Art Object from 1966 to 1972.* New York: Praeger, 1973.

Moore, Barbara. *What Ism Fluxism?* New York: Bound & Unbound, 1991.

Moren, Lisa. *Intermedia.* Baltimore: University of Maryland, Baltimore County, 2003.

Patterson, Benjamin, and Robert Filliou. "Ein Gespräch / Conversation." In *Lehren und Lernen als Auffuehrungskuenste / Teaching and Learning as Performing Arts.* Cologne: Gebr. König, 1970.

Pijnappel, Johan, ed. *Fluxus: Today and Yesterday.* London: Academy, 1993.

Ruhé, Harry. *Fluxus, the Most Radical and Experimental Art Movement of the Sixties.* Amsterdam: "A," 1979.

Sayre, Henry M. *The Object of Performance: The American Avant-garde since 1970.* Chicago: University of Chicago Press, 1989.

Schmidt-Burkhardt, Astrit. *Maciunas' Learning Machines: From Art History to a Chronology of Fluxus.* Detroit: Gilbert and Lila Silverman Fluxus Collection; Berlin: Vice Versa, 2003.

Sell, Mike. *Avant-garde Performance and the Limits of Criticism: Approaching Living Theatre, Happenings/Fluxus, and the Black Arts Movement.* Ann Arbor: University of Michigan Press, 2005.

Smith, Owen. *Fluxus: The History of an Attitude.* San Diego: San Diego State University Press, 1998.

Sohm, Hanns, and Harald Szeemann, eds. *Happening und Fluxus: Materialen.* Cologne: Kölnischer Kunstverein, 1970.

Stiles, Kristine, and Peter Selz, eds. *Theories and Documents of Contemporary Art: A Sourcebook of Artists' Writings.* Berkeley and Los Angeles: University of California Press, 1996.

Vostell, Wolf. *Dé-coll/age.* Translated by Laura P. Williams. New York: Something Else Press, 1966.

Warr, Tracey, and Amelia Jones. *The Artist's Body.* London: Phaidon, 2000.

Williams, Emmett. *My Life in Flux—and Vice Versa.* London: Thames & Hudson, 1992.

Exhibition Catalogues

Armstrong, Elizabeth, and Joan Rothfuss. *In the Spirit of Fluxus.* Minneapolis: Walker Art Center, 1993.

Block, René. "Fluxus and Fluxism in Berlin, 1964–1976." In *Berlinart,* edited by Kynaston McShine, 65–79. New York: Museum of Modern Art; Munich: Prestel, 1987.

———, ed. *Fluxus in Wiesbaden 1992.* Wiesbaden, Germany: Nassauischer Kunstverein, 1983.

Block, René, and Gabriele Knapstein. *A Long Tale with Many Knots: Fluxus in Germany, 1962–1994.* Stuttgart, Germany: Institut für Auslandsbeziehungen, 1997.

Bonito Oliva, Achille, ed. *Ubi fluxus ibi motus, 1990–1962.* Milan: Mazzotta, 1990.

Borja-Villel, Manuel J., Bernard Blistène, and Yann Chateigné. *A Theater without Theater.* Barcelona, Spain: Museu d'Art Contemporani de Barcelona; Lisbon: Museu Colecção Berardo, 2007.

Daniels, Dieter. "Fluxus Is Only a Word." In *Wortlaut,* 84–92. Cologne: Galerie Schüppenhauer, 1989.

Donguy, Jacques. *1960–1985: Une génération.* Paris: Artefact, 1985.

Dreyfus, Charles. *Happenings et Fluxus.* Paris: Galerie 1900–2000, 1989.

Frieling, Rudolf, ed. *The Art of Participation, 1950 to Now.* San Francisco: San Francisco Museum of Modern Art; New York: Thames & Hudson, 2008.

Gaines, Charles, and Catherine Lord. *The Theater of Refusal: Black Art and Mainstream Criticism.* Irvine: Fine Arts Gallery, University of California, 1993.

George, Adrian, ed. *Art, Lies, and Videotape: Exposing Performance.* London: Tate, 2003.

Haskell, Barbara. *Blam! The Explosion of Pop, Minimalism, and Performance, 1958–1964.* New York: Whitney Museum of American Art in association with W. W. Norton, 1984.

Hendricks, Geoffrey, ed. *Critical Mass: Happenings, Fluxus, Performance, Intermedia, and Rutgers University, 1958–1972.* New Brunswick, N.J.: Rutgers University Press, 2003.

Hendricks, Jon, ed. *Fluxus, etc.* Bloomfield Hills, Mich.: Cranbrook Academy of Art, 1981.

———, ed. *Fluxus, etc.: Addenda I; The Gilbert and Lila Silverman Collection.* New York: Ink &, 1983.

———, ed. *Fluxus, etc.: Addenda II; The Gilbert and Lila Silverman Collection.* Pasadena, Calif.: Baxter Art Gallery, California Institute of Technology, 1983.

———, ed. *O que é Fluxus? O que não é! O porquê / What's Fluxus? What's Not! Why.* Rio de Janeiro: Centro Cultural Banco do Brasil; Detroit: Gilbert and Lila Silverman Fluxus Collection Foundation; 2000.

———, ed., with Marianne Bech and Media Farzin. *Fluxus Scores and Instructions: The Transformative Years; "Make a Salad"; Selections from the Gilbert and Lila Silverman Fluxus Collection, Detroit.* Roskilde, Denmark: Museum of Contemporary Art, 2008.

Levanto, Marjatta. *Pää läpi seinän Nykytaiteen museossa / Fluxus.* Helsinki: Nyktaiteen Museossa, 1993.

Liesbrock, Heinz. *Reiner Ruthenbeck: Fotografie, 1956–1976.* Düsseldorf: Kustverein für die Rheinlande und Westfalen; Stuttgart: Cantz, 1991.

Martin, Henry. *Fluxers.* Bolzano, Italy: Musieon, 1992.

Milman, Estera, ed. "Fluxus: A Conceptual Country." Special issue, *Visible Language* (Rhode Island School of Design) 26, nos. 1–2 (1992).

———. *Fluxus and Friends: Selections from the Alternative Traditions in the Contemporary Arts Collection.* Iowa City: Museum of Art, University of Iowa, 1988.

Phillpot, Clive, and Jon Hendricks. *Fluxus: Selections from the Gilbert and Lila Silverman Collection.* New York: Museum of Modern Art, 1988.

Quaroni, Ivan. *Ben Patterson: Conversations along the Wall.* Bergamo, Italy: Studio d'Arte Fioretti, 2006.

The Readymade Boomerang. Sydney: Biennale of Sydney, 1990.

Ritratti?! Sì, ritratti!!! Philip Corner, Ben Patterson, Ben Vautier. Genoa, Italy: Galleria Caterina Gualco, 1997.

Schimmel, Paul. *Out of Actions: Between Performance and the Object, 1949–1979.* Los Angeles: Museum of Contemporary Art, 1998.

Schüppenhauer, Christel. *Fluxus Virus, 1962–1992.* Cologne: Galerie Schüppenhauer, 1992.

Smith, Owen. *Fluxus: The History of an Attitude.* San Diego: San Diego State University Press, 1990.

Solimano, Sandra. *The Fluxus Constellation.* Genoa, Italy: Villa Croce, Museo d'arte Contemporanea, 2002.

Stegmann, Petra. *Fluxus East: Fluxus Networks in Central Eastern Europe.* Berlin: Künstlerhaus Bethanien, 2007.

Articles and Journals

Décollage: Bulletin aktueller Ideen, nos. 1–7 (1962–69).

Drott, Eric. "Ligeti in Fluxus." *Journal of Musicology* 21, no. 2 (2004): 201–40.

Friedman, Ken, ed. "Fluxus." Special issue, *White Walls: A Magazine of Writings by Artists*, no. 16 (Spring 1987).

Friedman, Ken, and Peter Frank. "Fluxus: A Post-Definitive History: Art Where Response Is the Heart of the Matter." *High Performance* 7, no. 3 (1984): 56–61, 83.

Johnston, Jill. "Dance Journal: Fluxus Fuxus." *Village Voice,* July 2, 1964, 7.

———. "Flux Acts." *Art in America* 82 (June 1994): 70–79.

Kostelanetz, Richard, "The Discovery of Alternative Theater: Notes on Art Performances in New York City in the 1960s and 1970s." *Perspectives of New Music* 27 (Winter 1989): 128–72.

Lewis, George E. "Benjamin Patterson: Paper Piece." *Chamber Music,* September–October 2009, 107.

Moore, Barbara. "Hocus Fluxus." *Ear Magazine of New Music* 15, no. 3 (1990): 20–24.

Moore, Peter. "Fluxus Focus." *Artforum* 21 (October 1982): 33–37.

Writings by the Artist

"An Experiment in Extended Rhythms." In *Die Villa ist verstaubt.* Hamburg: Ivar Radowitz, 1960.

"Papierstuck." *Ich bin schön,* February 4, 1961, 3.

"Prints and Comments" With Lourdes Castro. Special issue, *KWY* (1961).

"Stand Erect," "Draw a Circle," and "Tournoi." *KWY,* no. 9 (1961).

Methods and Processes. Paris: Privately printed, 1962.

The Four Suits. With Phillip Corner, Alison Knowles, and Tomas Schmit. New York: Something Else Press, 1965.

"A Fluxus Horse Race in Europe 1972." *VTRE Extra,* no. 11 (1979): 13.

"Ich bin froh, daß Sie mir diese Frage gestellt haben." In "Fluxus, ein Nachruf zu Lebzeiten: Fünf Epitaphe." Special issue, *Kunstforum International*, no. 115 (September–October 1991): 166–77.

"Getting Ready for 2000 A.D." and "I'm Glad You Asked Me That Question." *Bull shit,* no. 2 (1992): 3–6.

"Ist bis heute ein echter Fluxianer." *Art Kaleidoscope* (Frankfurt), April 2009.

Discography/ Filmography

Dust Out of My Brain / Staub aus dem Gehirn. With Henning Christiansen and David Moss. Museum für Moderne Kunst, Weddel, Germany, 1993. Compact disc.

Benjamin Patterson: Early Works. Alga Marghen, Milan, 1999. Compact disc.

Benjamin Patterson: Swan Lake. Hundertmark Records, Cologne, 2001. VHS video.

Ben Patterson: Drip Music/370 Flies. Alga Marghen, Milan, 2002. Compact disc.

Ben Patterson Tells Fluxus Stories (from 1962 to 2002). Hundertmark Records, Cologne, 2002. Compact disc.

Liverpool Soundworks, Volume One. Audio Research Editions, London, 2002. Compact disc.

Experimentelles Musiktheater: Fluxus Happening—Performance. RCA Red Seal, Germany, 2004. Digital video.

Liverpool Soundworks, Volume Two. Audio Research Editions, London, 2004. Compact disc.

Ben Patterson: Fluxus Hot and West. SolwayJones Gallery, Los Angeles, 2008. Digital video.

A Fluxus Elegy. Alga Marghen, Milan, 2008. 33 1/3 rpm.

Contributors

Valerie Cassel Oliver is senior curator at the Contemporary Arts Museum Houston, where she has organized numerous solo and group exhibitions, including the acclaimed *Double Consciousness: Black Conceptual Art since 1970* (2005); *Black Light/White Noise: Sound and Light in Contemporary Art* (2007); and, with Dr. Andrea Barnwell Brownlee, *Cinema Remixed and Reloaded: Black Women Artists and the Moving Image* (2008–9). Most recently, she organized the group exhibition *Hand+Made: The Performative Impulse in Art and Craft* (2010), and in 2011 she presented the first survey exhibition devoted to the painter Donald Moffett.

Bertrand Clavez is a professor of contemporary art history at the University of Lyon, France. He is the president of 4T FluXuS, an association that celebrates the work and practice of Fluxus, and has organized many Fluxus-related events in France. He is the author of the books *Fluxus en France* (2005) and *George Maciunas, une révolution furtive* (2009) as well as numerous articles on Fluxus and related topics.

Charles Gaines is a conceptual artist, curator, and theorist. He is also a professor of art at the California Institute of the Arts, Valencia, and a talented and engaged theorist who has written extensively. He has published several articles, including "Art and Culture: Metonymy and the Postmodern Sublime" in the exhibition catalogue *Snake River: Charles Gaines and Edgar Arceneaux* (2006); "Art, Post History, and the Paradox of Black Pluralism" in the journal *Merge* (2003); and "Theater of Refusal: Black Art and Mainstream Criticism" in the catalogue for the exhibition of the same name at the University of California, Irvine (1993).

Jon Hendricks is an artist and curator. He is currently Fluxus consulting curator for the Gilbert and Lila Silverman Fluxus Collection at the Museum of Modern Art, New York, and curator of Yoko Ono Exhibitions. He has organized many exhibitions involving the work of Fluxus artists, including *Fluxus etc./Addenda II* (Baxter Art Gallery, California Institute of Technology, 1982); *Yes Yoko Ono* (with Alexandra Munroe, Japan Society, New York, 2000); *What's Fluxus? What's Not! Why* (Instituto Takano, Brazil, 2002); and *Fluxus Scores and Instructions: The Transformative Years* (Gilbert and Lila Silverman Fluxus Collection, Detroit, and Museum of Contemporary Art, Roskilde, Denmark, 2008).

George E. Lewis is a trombone player, composer, and scholar of jazz and experimental music. He is also a professor of music at Columbia University in New York. He specializes in computer exploration for music and has composed for multimedia installations, often integrating text and sound, as well as computerized notation frames. Lewis has published articles in such journals as *Contemporary Music Review*, *Black Music Research Journal*, and *Leonardo Music Journal*. He has recorded and performed with Anthony Braxton, John Zorn, Roscoe Mitchell, Douglas Ewart, Laurie Anderson, Muhal Richard Abrams, Count Basie, Gil Evans, Karl E. H. Seigfried, Fred Anderson, Evan Parker, and many other musicians.

Fred Moten works at the intersection of black studies, performance studies, poetry, and critical theory. He is author of *Arkansas* (Pressed Wafer Press, 2000); *In the Break: The Aesthetics of the Black Radical Tradition* (University of Minnesota Press, 2003); *I ran from it but was still in it* (Cusp Press, 2007); and *Hughson's Tavern* (Leon Works, 2008). Moten is an associate professor at Duke University, where he teaches English, African studies, and African American studies.

Benjamin Patterson is a classically trained contrabassist, visual artist, librarian, and arts administrator who lives in Wiesbaden, Germany.

Marcia Reed has been head of collection development at the Research Library of the Getty Research Institute since 1983. In this capacity, she has developed general library collections and archives and, as the institute's first curator of rare books, has acquired many rare books and prints. She has organized numerous exhibitions at the Getty, including *The Edible Monument*, *Naples and Vesuvius on the Grand Tour*, *China on Paper: European and Chinese Works from the Late Sixteenth to the Early Nineteenth Centuries*, and *The Magnificent Piranesi*. Current projects include a forthcoming exhibition and catalogue of the Jean Brown collection, now at the Getty.

Index

Reproduction Credits

Unless otherwise noted, photographs are reproduced courtesy of the artist or the lenders of the material depicted. Numbers refer to the page on which an image appears.

Courtesy Archivo Bonotto: 93, 101, 103 (bottom), 131, 175
Courtesy Mary Bauermeister and Galerie Schüppenhauer; photo Klaus Barisch: 19
Photo Valerie Cassel Oliver: 29, 71
Courtesy Enzo Cattelani: 80 (left and right), 81 (left and right), 85 (top)
Courtesy Bertrand Clavez: 69, 203
Courtesy Contemporary Arts Museum Houston: 106 (left)
Photo Francesco Conz: 199, 201 (left)
Courtesy Emily Harvey Foundation, New York/Venice: 82–84, 95 (left and right)
Courtesy Galerie 1900–2000: 66 (right), 77
Courtesy Galerie Schüppenhauer: 73, 78 (left)
Photo Rick Gardner: 82, 83, 86, 87, 88 (bottom), 99, 104, 107, 178
Courtesy Enzo Gazzerro: 64 (center)
Courtesy Getty Research Institute: endsheets, back cover, 20, 27 (left), 36, 37, 43, 44 (left and right), 51, 52, 54 (left and right), 57 (top and bottom), 61, 63, 65, 136–61, 165, 176, 177, 179 (left), 180 (right), 185, 186, 188, 193 (left)
Courtesy Caterina Gualco: 64 (left and right), 67
Photo Fabian Hild: 106 (right)
Courtesy Institut für Auslandsbeziehungen; photo Frank Kleinbach: 90–93
Photo Rolf Jährling: 39, 122, 180 (left and right)
Photo Elfi Kreiter: 201 (right)
Photo Paula Lahad/Studio Bozzetto: 93, 101, 103 (bottom)
Photo Morten Langkilde: 200 (right)
© Estate of Peter Moore/VAGA, New York: 132, 182
Courtesy Museo d'arte contemporanea di Villa Croce, Genoa; photo Mario Parodi: 100
Courtesy The Museum of Modern Art, New York: 28, 39, 45, 48, 49, 53, 58 (left and right), 59, 60, 74, 122, 135, 183, 180 (left), 181, 182
Photo Christel Schüppenhauer: front cover
Photo Reinhard Spiegel: 76 (bottom), 79, 97
Courtesy The Studio Museum in Harlem: Dave McKenzie, *We Shall Overcome,* 2004. DVD single-channel video projection, color, sound; 5:46 minutes. The Studio Museum in Harlem; Museum Purchase with funds provided by the Acquisition Committee, 04.13.10: 223
Courtesy Susanne Vielmetter Los Angeles Projects: 227
Photo Wolfgang Traeger: 46, 47, 70, 94, 98, 102, 103 (top), 105, 164, 198

CD-ROM (Music) Liner Notes

EMANUELE CARCANO

Ants, Revisited, 1960/2010
For a group of performers,
Yamaha DJX-II keyboard/
workstation, clickers, combs, and
cutlery
Clickers, combs, cutlery: Fatima
Bianchi, Gabriele Bonomo,
Emanuele Carcano, Paolo
Ferraguti, Francesco Lelli Mammi,
Valeria Lenchi, Georges Macarez,
and Nicola Ratti
Narration, Yamaha DJX-II, and
conducting: Ben Patterson
Recorded at via Telesio 19, Milan,
Italy, May 5, 2010
Duration: 15:36 minutes

The story of this composition
begins in July 1960. Discovering
an "ant hill" in a garden in
Düsseldorf, I believed that I
had found a new approach to
aleatoric music. I scooped up a
bunch of these ants, dumped
them into the center of a sheet
of paper, and then made six
photographs over a period of
ten minutes, recording the new
positions of the ants at each of
these six moments. I transferred
these "random" dots (ants)
to pages of blank music staffs,
expecting interesting "music." A
tryout on my double bass was
quite disappointing. (Only much
later did I realize that what I had
discovered was a "method," . . .
and of course, a "method" is not
"music.") Thus, this first attempt
was abandoned and placed in
the "future projects" file.

Four years later . . . 1964 in New
York, I opened this file again and
published *Ants II*, a composition
to be used in conjunction with
any 1962 composition of George
Maciunas. To date, I know of
no public performance of this
version.

Now, fifty years later, we have
Ants, Revisited, based on recent
scientific behavioral studies of
the methods of communication
among ants. In this version I
have assumed that the original
ants organized their escape from
that sheet of paper, primarily
through communication with
pheromones (in this score
represented by an accumulating
cloud of long tones) and
secondarily with stridulations
(intermittent rasping or
clicking sounds). One original
photograph has served as a
reference for determining time
and pitch relationships. The
resulting "composition" is not a
true transcription of the original
traffic of pheromones and
stridulation signals among those
ants but rather a presumptive
acoustic model based on the
remaining evidence.

*Duo for Voice and a String
Instrument*, 1961
Voice: William Pearson
Double bass: Ben Patterson
Recorded at Galerie Parnass,
Wuppertal, Germany, June 9,1962
Duration: 11:01 minutes

This duo was my most ambitious
and last attempt to combine
graphic notation and chance
operations for the realization
of a performance score. The
complete set of materials
necessary to realize a version of
this work consisted of two pages
of instructions, three pages of
a general universe of symbols,
and two transparencies (on
which circular and rectangular
contours were drawn) used to
abstract sets of symbols (graphic
notations) from the general
universe in the preparation of
a performance score (see pages
reproduced in these notes). This
work was first performed at
Galerie Haro Lauhus in Cologne,
Germany, on May 14, 1961.

Variations for Double Bass, 1961
Double bass: Ben Patterson
Recorded at Galerie Parnass,
Wuppertal, Germany, June 9,1962
Duration: 11:22 minutes

Within days after the first
performance of *Duo*, I realized
that what interested me most
about the work was my tentative
experiments with "prepared
double-bass." I immediately
began working on a set of
variations for double bass. And
then, unexpectedly, out of some
unknown place, something new
entered the process—humor!
I still remember the joy and
excitement of those next days,
as ideas fell into place. The piece
was finished within a week, and
the first performance took place
shortly thereafter, on June 8, 1961,
again at Galerie Haro Lauhus.

Paper Piece, 1960
Performers: Gabriele Bonomo,
Philip Corner, Walter Marchetti,
Davide Mosconi, Phoebe Neville
Direction: Ben Patterson
Recorded at Massive Arts, Milan,
Italy, April 15, 1999
Duration: 17:05 minutes

This work cut the umbilical cord
to all of my previous classical
and contemporary musical
training and experience. The
process had begun during my
first encounter with John Cage
at Mary Bauermeister's Contre
Festival (May 1960 in Cologne).
Three months later, my reaction
to the first performance of
Stockhausen's *Kontakte* made
the completion of this process an
urgent necessity. *Paper Piece* was
completed in September 1960
and received its first performance
at Galerie Haro Lauhus, Cologne,
on May 14, 1961. However,
despite my reasonably precise
instructions (see reproduced
score), beginning with the first

Fluxus Festival concerts in 1962,
Paper Piece grew a life of its own.
It literally began enveloping and
involving entire audiences in a
wonderfully messy happening.
Now, nearly forty years later, this
studio recording returns to the
acoustic origins of this work.

Pond, 1962
Performers: Gabriele Bonomo,
Emanuele Carcano, Philip
Corner, Fabio Constanino, Walter
Marchetti, Davide Mosconi,
Phoebe Neville, and Elisabetta
Roncucci
Direction: Ben Patterson
Recorded at Massive Arts, Milan,
Italy, April 15, 1999
Duration: 5:24 minutes

Critics or historians searching
for autobiographical references
in my work should consider
the following: (1) As a "country
boy" in a rural area outside
Pittsburgh, listening to the
crickets, "caddiies," and frogs
at a nearby pond was what I
considered "night life," and (2) I
did not decide whether to study
music or herpetology until the
last month before entering the
University of Michigan. *Pond* was
first performed at Nikolai Kirke,
Copenhagen, on November 26,
1962.

*A Simple Opera (Lago di Como
version)*, 1995
Performers: Gabriele Bonomo,
Emanuele Carcano, Philip Corner,
Fabio Constantino, Walter
Marchetti, Davide Mosconi,
Phoebe Neville, and Elisabetta
Roncucci
Narrator: Ben Patterson
Recorded at Massive Arts, Milan,
Italy, April 15, 1999
Duration: 15:15 minutes

I have included this new work
for reasons that can be deduced
from the subtitle and the libretto.

Fluxus historians may recognize
similarities between this work
and a 1960s opera by Emmett
Williams. These similarities are
intended, as my first version
of this opera was an homage
to Emmett Williams on his
seventieth birthday.

370 Flies, 2003
For voice and electronics
Narrator: Ben Patterson
Produced by Emanuele Carcano
for Alga Marghen in September
2003
Recording engineer: Sacha
Gattino
Recorded in Paris on May
4, 5, and 7, 2003, with period
instruments and electronics
Duration: 15:17 minutes

The double bassist Ben Patterson
(b. 1934) thanks the double
bassist Sylvester Paumgartner
(1763–1841) for inspiring this
work.

Chamber music lovers and
double bass players will recognize
that the "loops" are derived from
the fourth movement of Franz
Schubert's string quintet D. 667,
the "Trout Quintet." The list of
flies was compiled from several
lexicons and my own memory.

Confession: Although I have
successfully fished for trout
and salmon in waters from
Newfoundland to Patagonia, I
have always used "spinning"
equipment and lures—never
artificial flies. For too many
years I was duly inhibited and
intimidated by the mystique and
costs of this sport, which in my
youth was the exclusive preserve
of "Rich White Men Only." Thus,
maybe this is my paean to "get
even."

A Fluxus Elegy, 2006
For voice and electronics
Narrator: Ben Patterson
Recorded in Wiesbaden,
Germany, 2006.
Duration: 24:23 minutes

To introduce this work, I must tell you a story told to me in 1975 by Robert Mann, then the first violinist for the Julliard String Quartet. The story took place around 1967–68, when the USA and the USSR were conducting a "cultural" Cold War to win the "hearts and minds" of "third world countries." In this context the U.S. Department of State sent performing arts ensembles on tour throughout the world. Thus, the Julliard String Quartet was sent on a two-week tour to Africa.

After concerts in major cities of Ghana, Nigeria, Congo, etc., the quartet discovered that the final concert would be in a Bantu tribal village . . . deep in the "bush." Arriving at the village, they found their suspicions confirmed: the setting was worthy of a 1930s ethnological documentary film. Of course, the first question the quartet asked themselves was "What do we have to play for this audience?" Finally they decided to perform those works for which they enjoyed worldwide acclaim. So, sitting in the open in front of the chieftain's hut, under an African moon and encircled by several hundred villagers, the Julliard String Quartet performed Beethoven's three "Rasumovsky Quartets," opus 59.

According to Robert Mann, this extraordinary circumstance inspired the quartet to present its "best-ever" performance. Each member of the quartet felt that they had achieved truly transcendental interpretations of

these works. Greatly disturbing for the quartet members, however, was the complete lack of audience reaction—no applause, no tapping of feet, no presentation of flowers or anything to suggest that they appreciated this extraordinary concert! The villagers simply stood up with saddened faces, milled around silently, and finally sat down to begin the festive meal ending this event.

Seated next to the chieftain, and after some polite conversation and having consumed an appropriate amount of food and drink, Robert Mann dared to ask the chieftain about this public relations disaster. He explained that the quartet members thought that they had just presented their "best-ever" performance and that they were surprised that the villagers apparently did not appreciate their effort. The chieftain— gazing into the distance, not wishing to present bad news eye to eye—replied: "My people feel great sympathy for you. They see that you are already so old, and they feel sad that you have not yet found your tone."

Postscript
To understand this reply by the chieftain, it is necessary to understand a few basic principles of the polyphonic music of the Bantu tribes of West and Central Africa:

First principle: the practice of interlocking individual pitches or tones performed by one person into spaces between other pitches and tones performed by another person, thus alternating pitches or tones of one part with those of another part to create a whole.

Second principle: the use of cyclical and open-ended forms involving one or more ostinato melodic/rhythmic patterns as a foundation.

Third principle: community participation—nonspecialists are encouraged to join in long performances with much repetition.

Fourth principle: rhythmic complexity with juxtaposition of double and triple patterns, multiple layers of different patterns, and interruption between a core foundation and improvised parts.

However, the most important principle of the music of these Bantu tribes is the family "ownership" of a specific "tone." In the musical culture of these tribes, each ancestral family "owns" and is responsible for one or more specific "tones," which must be sounded at specific points, sequencing with many other specific "tones," owned by other families, to create a seamless melody. Traditionally, these "family tones" and their specific places in a melodic line are passed down orally from father to son and mother to daughter. Thus, it is of primal importance to the survival of musical culture of the tribe that each member of the tribe masters his family's unique "tone" . . . and knows exactly when and where to perform it. In short, it is this "musical glue" that regulates the relationships, sustaining the social life of the tribe.

Now we understand the "sadness" of this village audience. The fingers of these distinguished American musicians are running up and down the fingerboards of their instruments, grasping at hundreds of "tones" . . . still trying to find "their tone."

So how did I make this music based on this information? Actually it was quite simple . . . as simple as Ravel's *Bolero*. The initials (family and given names) of artists listed in *Fluxus, the Most Radical and Experimental Art Movement of the Sixties* (Harry Ruhé, 1976) were encoded in basic international Morse code ("dots and dashes"). The "dots and dashes" were then "performed" on a Yamaha DJX keyboard (voice pattern setting), connected to a Digitech JamMan Looper (overdub setting), connected to a Euroack MX 602A mixer. Finally, the output was recorded with a Sony stereo cassette recorder TCS-430 on Sony magnetic tape Type I, normal bias, 120 qs EQ.

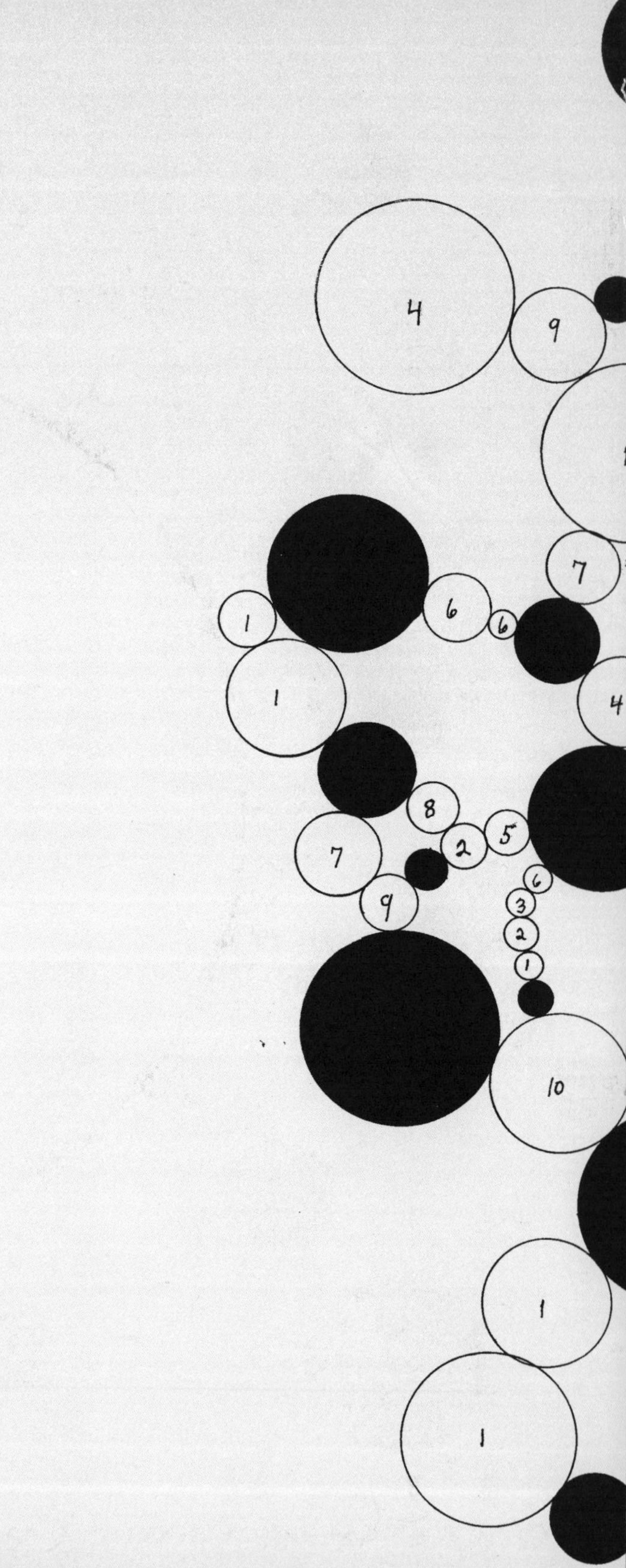